Management of Port Maintenance

A Review of Current Problems and Practices

Dr B J Thomas
Senior Lecturer, Department of Maritime Studies
University of Wales College of Cardiff

Dr D K Roach
Managing Director, Interface4 Ltd, Cardiff

with contributions from

J H Northfield
Port of Felixstowe International

E E Pollock
Associated British Ports Research & Consultancy Ltd

This study has been prepared for the Transport Development Division of the World Bank
and the Shipping Division of the United Nations Conference on Trade and Development,
and has been supported and funded by the Projects and Export Policy Division of the UK
Department of Trade and Industry.

LONDON: HER MAJESTY'S STATIONERY OFFICE

Contents

Chapter 2 The Institutional Framework

Chapter 3 Planning the Port Inventory

Chapter 5 Operations and Maintenance

Chapter 6 Maintenance Strategies and Practices

Chapter 8 Management and Manpower Development

Chapter 9 Engineering Management Information Systems

CHAPTER 1

Introduction to the Study

1.1 Background to the Project

1.1.1 Project Origins

The World Bank and other international agencies have been concerned for some time about deficiencies in port maintenance in developing countries. Indeed, maintenance is seen by the World Bank's Transport Development Division as possibly the biggest difficulty facing port management. Because of the technological developments in shipping in the past two decades, and the consequential changes to cargo-handling methods, there has been a vast investment in port mechanical equipment and an even bigger investment in infrastructure, all of it needing continuous and effective maintenance. In particular, ports have had to purchase large quantities of specialized, high-capacity and complex cargo-handling equipment; a very high proportion of the capital and operating budgets of port authorities and cargo-handling companies is now devoted to the purchase, operation and maintenance of mechanical handling equipment. In a typical, medium-sized seaport in a developing country, handling about 5 million tonnes of break-bulk cargo in a year, the total investment in mobile cargo-handling equipment (measured on a replacement cost basis) may be more than US$30 million. A large port could have $200 million invested. The buildings, quays and other infrastructure facilities represent many more hundreds of millions of dollars of capital investment.

The benefits that all this investment in mechanization can bring to seaports will not be realized if the equipment and infrastructure are not properly maintained. While much of the port's infrastructure can continue to function for some time in the absence of regular maintenance (albeit at lesser efficiency and with increasingly serious signs of decay), neglect of mechanical equipment causes very rapid and very obvious deterioration. If current problems with equipment procurement, operation and maintenance are not resolved, the efficiency of cargo-handling operations will be threatened and the financial and other benefits of technological change will be lost to the economies of those countries. Despite considerable assistance from international agencies in the past two decades, experience shows that the port maintenance problems in many developing countries – far from being solved – are actually becoming more serious. In some regions, maintenance deficiencies threaten the ability of the ports to perform their primary task of providing the facilities and services required to meet maritime trading requirements.

It is because the situation is so serious, and because the scope for improvement and the scale of the potential benefits from improving port maintenance are so great, that the Transport Development Division of the World Bank initiated a major research project on the problems and issues in port maintenance in less developed countries. The present study forms part of that project, and is being supported and funded by the UK Department of Trade and Industry, while the Shipping Division of the United Nations Conference on Trade and Development (UNCTAD) is adding its support and is financing two related studies, carried out by consultants from the ports of Antwerp and Bremerhaven.

1.1.2 The Port Maintenance Problem

Although many factors contribute to the present unsatisfactory state of port maintenance in the ports of developing countries, a root cause is the failure by senior management to develop a comprehensive set of policies, strategies and procedures for maintaining its assets – particularly its equipment – and for procuring and operating its cargo-handling and other machinery. The symptoms of the problem are familiar to informed visitors to the ports:

— The port's stock of equipment and attachments does not meet the needs of the cargo-handling operators, in terms of numbers and types;

— There is an unsatisfactory mix of equipment (often incompatible with the port's trades and causing operating and maintenance problems) because of failure to adopt a sensible procurement strategy;

— Availability of equipment is poor and downtime is high, because of poorly designed and executed preventive maintenance schemes;

1

— Spare parts and consumable supplies are unavailable to workshop staff, because inadequate budgetary provision was made for their purchase, and because management fails to apply strict spare parts control;

— Workshop premises and facilities are unsuitable or inadequate, and good engineering practices are not followed;

— There is inefficient maintenance, excessive damage repair and premature scrapping of equipment because maintenance staff and equipment operatives are poorly trained and supervised;

— Equipment control is ineffective, because management does not collect data regularly and there is no management information system to monitor the performance of equipment;

— Port buildings, quays and working surfaces are allowed to deteriorate, to the extent that they interfere with and threaten cargo-handling operations, again because of a lack of good engineering management;

— There is poor communication between operational and engineering units, because the communications systems have been neglected and because of a lack of collaboration between departmental managements.

Many more signs and symptoms could be quoted – and, indeed, will be discussed later in this and subsequent chapters – to demonstrate the seriousness of the present situation in very many ports.

The present survey, as part of the overall World Bank Project, sets out to investigate the principal causes of poor port maintenance (with particular reference to the all-important equipment management function) and to identify the steps needed to improve the situation.

1.2 Project Execution

1.2.1 Project Aims
The broad aims of the project were to collect and analyse sufficient and appropriate data to permit the nature, extent and causes of the maintenance problems experienced in the ports of developing countries to be identified, and to suggest ways in which those problems may be overcome. The project aimed to investigate equipment planning and procurement policies, the effect of government controls (particularly foreign exchange controls) on equipment management, and operating and other factors which impinge on maintenance, as well as maintenance strategies and techniques themselves.

The resulting Project Report (the present document) was intended to describe the findings of the investigation, to review the advantages and disadvantages of alternative policies, strategies and techniques and to make recommendations on the essential elements of comprehensive and effective procurement policies, capital budgeting, replacement strategies, operating and manpower needs, and maintenance strategies (including spare parts management). These recommendations would be used in the wider World Bank project, as bases for a set of guidelines for use by World Bank staff when appraising schemes involving investment in cargo-handling equipment and when advising ports on maintenance and equipment management policies. The Report itself was also intended to increase senior managers' awareness of the importance of the port maintenance (and especially the equipment maintenance) function in achieving cargo-handling efficiency.

The specific objectives of the project were:

— to examine the nature, extent and causes of the major maintenance problems in the ports of developing countries;

— to review the policies, strategies and management techniques used in port maintenance, and to identify weaknesses;

— to provide advice on the essential components of a port maintenance policy and to recommend good management practices;

— to provide detailed guidance to senior port managers on maintenance strategies and spare parts management, including relevant manpower development and training needs.

1.2.2 Project Methodology
The central activity of the investigation was a series of fact-finding missions by a group of specialists to selected ports, in developing and developed countries, to study their port maintenance techniques and problems. Between two and four days were spent in each country, meeting senior port managers and government officials to discuss policies and strategies, and visiting workshops, operational areas, training schools and other relevant units, to inspect the facilities and to review management and maintenance practices. Where appropriate, meetings were also held with representatives of central banks and with such port users as ships' agents and clearing and forwarding agents.

To improve the planning and co-ordination of the visits, and to ensure that the maximum amount of information was collected during the meetings, a project document was distributed in advance to each port, containing a clear statement of the objectives of the mission and a detailed list of the information topics to be covered. Several ports put these advance documents to excellent use, preparing a great deal of data and documentation in readiness for presenting to the team. During the meetings, the project team used semi-structured interviewing techniques; a series of pivotal questions was prepared in advance to act as cues and stimuli for the discussions, but each conversation was allowed to follow its natural course within that framework.

The information gathered during the fact-finding missions was supplemented by background research on published reports, papers and texts, and by discussions with equipment manufacturers, research organizations and representatives of international agencies involved in financing the purchase of equipment. To broaden the database, a comprehensive questionnaire, covering all the topics to be raised during the visits, was distributed at the outset of the project to 23 selected port authorities and organizations throughout the world; ten questionnaires were satisfactorily completed and returned – a response rate of 40% (slightly above average for such studies). The questionnaire is reproduced in Appendix 1; it will provide a clear impression of the ground covered in the discussions.

1.2.3 Project Management and Personnel

The project was funded by the Projects and Export Policy Division of the United Kingdom Department of Trade and Industry. Responsibility for the planning and management of the study and for the preparation of the project report was contracted to the Department of Maritime Studies, University of Wales Institute of Science and Technology (UWIST; from September, 1988, incorporated within the new University of Wales College of Cardiff). Dr B. J. Thomas was appointed Team Leader and chief point of liaison between the various organizations involved: the Transport Development Division of the World Bank, the Shipping Division of UNCTAD and the Department of Trade and Industry. It was by agreement among representatives of those bodies that the form of the survey was established, the team of consultants chosen, and the list of countries and ports to be visited assembled.

The project team consisted of:

— Dr B. J. Thomas, Senior Lecturer, Department of Maritime Studies, UWIST; with nearly 20 years of consultancy experience with international agencies, covering all aspects of port management and the preparation of training courses and materials for senior managers; as well as being Team Leader, responsible for

planning, organizing and co-ordinating the study, Dr Thomas' primary concern was operational aspects of the investigation, inventory planning, management information systems and institutional and commercial factors.

— Mr J. H. Northfield, Engineering and Technical Services Director, Port of Felixstowe International; formerly the Chief Engineer at Felixstowe (with responsibility for procurement and stores management), Mr Northfield has a lifetime's experience in engineering line management, and his primary responsibility within the survey was for engineering, supplies and workshop issues.

— Mr E. E. Pollock, Managing Director, Associated British Ports Research and Consultancy Ltd.; with 30 years of consultancy experience, Mr Pollock was formerly the Economist and Marketing Manager for the British Transport Docks Board before it became Associated British Ports; his special interests during the study were institutional, financial and commercial factors.

— Dr D. K. Roach, Managing Director, Interface 4 Ltd, Cardiff; has spent over 25 years in tertiary education and training, the last ten years working extensively within the maritime industry, developing training materials for UNCTAD and other international agencies; special interests during the study were management development, training and management information systems.

The members of the team had, within the months preceding the port study missions, individually visited many ports in developing countries – in Africa, the Indian subcontinent, the Far East, the Caribbean and Latin America – while on other international consultancies, and these experiences were invaluable in spreading the information-gathering net even wider than the directly scheduled visits. The fact-finding was also supplemented valuably by port visits specially undertaken by Mr J. R. Lethbridge, Ports and Aviation Adviser, Transport Development Division, Infrastructure Department of the World Bank and Project Manager of the overall World Bank *Guidelines* Project. Mr Lethbridge followed the same semi-structured interview approach, based on the same discussion outline, as the UK team.

1.2.4 Project Visits

The ports to be visited were selected deliberately from a variety of geographical regions, were of varying sizes and activities, and illustrated a wide range of institutional and management conditions. Between 1st February and 16th March, 1988, Dr Thomas and Dr Roach visited a series of European ports: the Felixstowe Dock and Railway Company, Associated British Ports (Grimsby, Immingham, Southampton and Port Talbot), BLG Bremerhaven, and the Port of Antwerp (the Port Authority, Antwerp Port Engineering and Consulting v.z.w., Stevedoring Company Gylsen N.V. and Hessenatie C.V.). Visits were also made to the Production Engineering Research Association (PERA) at Melton Mowbray, to Lansing Ltd. at Basingstoke and to Lansing Henley Ltd. at Redditch.

The visits to the ports of developing countries were made between 19th March and 17th April, 1988. The four-member team visited, in sequence, the ports of Alexandria and Dar Es Salaam in Africa and those of Madras, Colombo, Singapore and Penang in Asia. Mr Pollock also visited relevant government ministries in Delhi and Kuala Lumpur, and Mr Lethbridge visited the ports of Buenaventura, Santa Morta and Cartagena in Colombia and had discussions with representatives of COLPUERTAS, the national port authority, in Bogota.

The team members were everywhere received with the utmost courtesy, openness and co-operation. Their gratitude to all the port Chairmen, General Managers, Senior Managers and staff must be recorded. Without the full and enthusiastic assistance, time and efforts of those busy port employees, as well as the contributions of government and other officials, representatives of international agencies, manufacturers and other organizations, the data-gathering exercise would have been fruitless. In the event, the team returned with a wealth of data, experience and valuable opinion, upon which the bulk of this report rests.

1.2.5 Other Sources of Information

The port maintenance problems identified during the study and the recommendations presented in this report are based on a thorough analysis of the information collected during the port visits and by the advice, opinion and comment freely given by those interviewed, as well as on the collective previous experience of the project team. Specifically, the major difficulties confronting port management in developing countries with respect to maintenance (particularly of cargo-handling equipment) were identified from:

— observations by the team during the visits to the ports of developing countries;

— analysis of documentation supplied by managers of the ports visited;

— information, opinions and advice provided by government and port officials during formal and informal discussions. Much of this information, as reported in face-to-face meetings, was not at the time verifiable from published or audited figures, but wherever possible the data were checked subsequently by reading Annual Reports and other port publications, and by asking the same questions (from slightly different viewpoints) of different officials;

— analysis of the completed questionnaires, which were returned by port authorities and individuals in Cyprus, Gabon, India, Kenya, Malta, Morocco, Papua New Guinea, the Philippines, South Korea and Trinidad;

— the collective experience of the project team, obtained in previous consultancy projects in developing countries.

The evaluation of alternative policies and strategies, the identification of appropriate maintenance practices and the preparation of the recommendations made in the report have been based on:

— observations made at, and advice received from, ports that have developed successful maintenance policies and practices;

— discussions with leading consultants in the port transport industry, particularly in the engineering and technical services fields, and with experienced port managers, representatives of equipment manufacturers and research organizations;

— a comprehensive literature search, of textbooks, published reports, academic journals and the technical press (a bibliography of relevant work is presented in Appendix 2);

— discussions held with representatives of the World Bank and UNCTAD, and regular 'brainstorming' sessions among the team members, both before, during and after the main overseas mission.

1.2.6 Project Outputs

This report, published by the UK Department of Trade and Industry, forms only one of the outputs of the World Bank project. Two further contributions, financed by UNCTAD, are a report on *Manning Levels in Port Maintenance* (Thuis, 1988) and *Principles and Practices of Preventive Maintenance in Ports* (Jerusel, 1988). All these reports will be incorporated with further research undertaken at the World Bank and by contracted consultants in a major World Bank Technical Paper, to be completed by the end of March, 1989, on *Problems and Issues in Port Maintenance in Less Developed Countries*. This technical paper will set out guidelines and conditions for the establishment of an effective port maintenance function, and is intended for senior port managers, consultancy companies, and officials of the major international agencies in the ports field. The paper will be useful when evaluating port projects, particularly requests for loans for equipment purchase, when examining existing port maintenance systems and when making recommendations for improvement of maintenance management.

The present report, together with the two UNCTAD papers, is currently also being used in the preparation of materials for courses and seminars in UNCTAD's *Improving Port Performance* series, dealing with equipment management policy, procurement practices and maintenance strategies. These courses will be available in early 1989.

1.2.7 Terminology and Definitions

One of the conditions offered by the investigating team to all the ports participating in the study was complete confidentiality of sourcing; none of the data appearing in this report is attributed, except in such terms as 'a major port', 'a container terminal'. It was on this basis that commercially sensitive information was provided and critical comment made possible without unnecessary embarrassment. However, where appropriate, clear distinction has been made between data from developed and developing countries. Information taken from published sources has, of course, been acknowledged and referenced. While acknowledging with gratitude the generosity with which all this information was provided, the authors must take complete responsibility for any errors of fact or interpretation unintentionally introduced when analysing the enormous quantity of data collected during the study.

It has been decided to adopt the term 'Less Developed Country' (abbreviated to LDC) as the most acceptable currently in use to denote 'developing countries' or 'underdeveloped countries' of the 'Third World'. Another convenient shorthand adopted is the use of the word 'port ' to encompass all the many types of organizations responsible, in their different ways, for the ownership and operation of the plant and equipment used in cargo-handling operations and for the infrastructure within which cargo handling is carried out. The term thus does service for port authorities of all types, terminal operators, stevedoring companies and related organizations, on the basis that, as far as the management and practices of port maintenance are concerned, the exact nature of the responsible organization is rarely significant. Chapter 2 considers the enormous diversity of such organizational responsibility and the effect that has on maintenance, but in the bulk of this report the distinctions are hardly relevant, and the generic term 'port' saves a great deal of verbal redundancy.

Finally, it should be pointed out that, to make comparisons possible, all cost information is presented in US dollar equivalents (at the exchange rates prevailing in April 1988). To save unnecessary repetitious explanation, the costs are denoted simply as '$.....'.

1.3 The Scope of Port Maintenance

1.3.1 The Range of Maintenance Functions

The functions of the port's engineering department are to provide and maintain, to a high standard, the port's civil works and infrastructure, its marine craft and navigational aids, its cargo-handling equipment and its technical services. It performs these duties with the sole purpose of allowing ships safely and quickly to enter and leave port, and to lie securely at berth while their cargoes are loaded and discharged, stored, received and dispatched as quickly and efficiently as possible. The engineering services are not, therefore, ends in themselves, but merely means to the end of providing full support for the operating units of the port as they strive to serve the needs of port users. To that end, the engineers must ensure that the port's infrastructure is in good condition to receive vessels and their cargoes and to allow the rapid, unimpeded movement of inland transport, and that enough equipment of the right type is available to operators to allow them to achieve high levels of output.

So, while the engineers are not *directly* involved in serving the port's customers, they have a vital role to play in achieving the port's corporate objectives and the performance objectives of the operational units, and in promoting the commercial success of the port. That role includes the design, planning, development and acquisition of civil works, fixed plant and mobile equipment, but the engineers' primary task is the maintenace of those assets in such a condition that the port can handle its traffic efficiently and profitably.

The demand for maintenance in a large, modern

5

seaport is very diverse in nature. It ranges from the upkeep of civil works and marine structures, the dredging of entrance channels and the maintenance of navigational aids, to the servicing and repair of marine craft and the latest cargo-handling equipment, with their complex mechanical, hydraulic and electrical/electronic systems. Those maintenance demands are constantly expanding in extent, diversity and complexity with the wider application of mechanization and the increasing use of automation. Pressure is also mounting on engineers to increase the speed with which maintenance is carried out, to improve the utilization of facilities, and at the same time to upgrade the quality of their work, so that the port can become more profitable and competitive. Consequently, ports need engineers with an ever greater range of managerial and technical skills, and the engineering departments have to provide an increasingly wide variety of maintenance facilities and services.

Port maintenance is also assuming increasing importance financially. A high proportion of the capital invested in ports is represented in such fixed assets as civil works and equipment – some hundreds of millions of dollars – and the cost of maintaining these assets forms a major item of port operating expenditure. In a modern seaport, the combined expenditure on civil, mechanical and electrical maintenance – including the costs of staff salaries, spare parts and materials, and departmental overheads – accounts for between 25% and 40% of total operating expenditure; there is some evidence that this proportion is rising steadily. The direct and indirect economic consequences of failure to maintain assets are extremely serious; many instances will be discussed in the pages that follow, but a few examples will illustrate the problems:

— If navigational aids are not properly maintained, night-time shipping movements, especially in complex channel approaches, will be difficult or dangerous, and ships may have to wait for daylight; this puts up the cost of their time in port.

— Non-maintenance of dredged channels to their scheduled depth will reduce the maximum possible vessel draught and loadings, forcing ship operators to use smaller, less economical ships and again putting up cargo transport costs.

— If tugboats are out of service and not available to assist ships entering and leaving port, the risk of marine accidents will increase; the port may be involved in substantial expenditure in repairing damage to marine structures and to shore-based facilities, such as quayside gantry cranes.

— If such civil works as lock entrances and swing bridges are not maintained, they will eventually fail, with catastrophic consequences on the port's ability to handle vessels; remedial work will be extremely expensive.

— Poor maintenance of roads, quay aprons and backup areas can damage road vehicles and mobile cargo-handling equipment – as well as the cargoes they are carrying; costs of repair and reparation can be substantial.

— Cargo deterioration can arise through failure to maintain transit sheds and warehouses to keep them waterproof.

— Poor maintenance of barges and lighters can also give rise to water damage to cargo.

— If equipment is in short supply, because of poor maintenance, cargo-handling rates will suffer and ships will stay longer in port, again putting up maritime transport costs; freight rates may have to be raised, and traffic may be lost to competing, more efficient ports.

— Equipment breakdowns, production losses and failure to meet vessels' schedules also raise direct cargo-handling costs.

— Premature scrapping of equipment, through poor maintenance, increases the need for capital investment – again, up go port costs.

The scope of the maintenance requirements depends on the nature of the port, on the type of traffic handled, the range of facilities provided to port users and the methods used in handling the cargoes. Exactly who provides the maintenance will also depend on institutional factors. In some ports, the port authority provides a comprehensive range of marine and shore facilities, equipment and services, and so has to maintain all those resources. Elsewhere, the port authorities are merely landlords, providing little more than the basic infrastructure within which private or public organizations carry out most of the services and maintain their own facilities. In between those two extremes, there are many variations in responsibility. However, in the context of this study, it is of little concern whether the port authority or some other organization provides the services; whoever is responsible, the facilities have to be provided and someone has to maintain them. It is the maintenance itself, and how it is performed, that is the present concern, and 'the port' somehow has to carry out that maintenance, in its great variety and complexity.

Because of that variety, it is convenient – if not essential – to consider the full range of maintenance work under four separate headings: civil, marine, technical services and equipment. In practice, of course, the functions are interdependent and must be fully co-ordinated. In the next few sections, the extent and scope of maintenance work encompassed within those broad divisions will be briefly described.

1.3.2 Civil Maintenance

The civil maintenance function has both marine and shore components. The marine element includes the maintenance of breakwaters and retaining works, lock entrances, quay structures and jetties (including fendering) and (in some ports, at least) navigation channels. The shore infrastructure consists of quay surfaces, roads and vehicle parking areas, railway tracks, warehouses and transit storage facilities, buildings, workshops and offices. In some countries, the port also provides and maintains large housing estates for employees (requiring carpentry and joinery shops), medical centres and hospitals.

The scale of all these civil maintenance activities varies with the size, type and location of the port. Ports located on the banks of rivers well inland, and those situated on estuaries where siltation is severe, may have to maintain long lengths of navigable channel, while those sited in natural deep-water harbours may require no dredging. Some ports, established many years ago when required water depths in entrance channels were considerably less than today, often have to dredge continuously to accommodate modern deep-draughted vessels; this may represent a major item of port expenditure. Ports with enclosed or impounded dock basins, constructed where there is a large tidal range, must maintain lock entrances, bridges and culverts, while other ports located on exposed coastlines have to do major maintenance work on breakwaters and other protective civil works. Some ports have to maintain piled quays, while others have stone-clad solid structures. In some ports, extensive land reclamation and coastal protection are necessary. Many ports have huge dock estates to maintain, covering thousands of square hectares and with many kilometres of roads and railways, while others have quite limited dock estates and infrastructure. The variation is, then, considerable.

A distinctive feature of port civil works, particularly of quay structures and breakwaters, is that they are long-lived assets; civil works built in the 18th and 19th Centuries are still in use in many ports. This long life often disguises the need for maintenance. Indeed, civil items may need very little attention for many years, and there is an undoubted temptation for engineers to overlook essential maintenance work. In the short term, such neglect may not appear too detrimental, but the long-term effects of not regularly inspecting these assets and putting right any defects can be extremely serious. For example, poor maintenance of quay surfaces is a frequent cause of damage to cargo-handling equipment. If the roofs of transit sheds and warehouses are not maintained, stored cargoes can be water-damaged. Poor maintenance of workshops can lead to damage to equipment and machine tools. The poor state of roadways and parking areas contributes to traffic delays, damage to vehicles and excessive wear and tear on cargo-handling equipment. Piles can corrode and quay walls can collapse, the strength of quay surfaces can be de-rated so that cargo stacking height has to be reduced – all because of failure to maintain these structures.

Another feature of civil maintenance work, particularly its shore-based component, is that many ports (especially in developed countries) now contract it out and have abandoned direct labour. They find that it is cheaper to do it this way, as demand is very intermittent and the skills required are extremely diverse. It is likely that this trend will continue and will spread within LDC ports.

1.3.3 Marine Maintenance

Among the wide range of marine engineering functions in which ports may be involved are the provision and maintenance of navigational aids within the port approaches. Buoys, navigation lights, lighthouses and light vessels may extend many kilometres out to sea or cover long river channels; the jurisdiction of the port, and the responsibilities of its marine engineers, may extend over a very wide area. Other navigational aids, such as radar, radio and position-fixing systems, are now a common requirement in ports; these, too, have to be maintained (although many of these very specialized tasks are now contracted out).

Most ports also maintain a large fleet of floating craft and plant. Pilotage and towage services need the support of pilot cutters, mooring craft and tugboats. Most ports have at least a few tugs – one or two, up to five or six – and some have large fleets, of 25 or more; these represent a significant maintenance requirement. Many ports have heavy-lifting floating cranes and floating bulk-handling plant, for working ships at anchor in the stream. They may also have barges or pontoons, either for purely localized overside lighterage, for cargo-handling between shallow jetties and ships working in the stream, or as part of a through-transport system to and from inland waterways. The barge or pontoon fleet may be very large indeed – many hundreds in some ports – and they are prone to damage by the very nature of their work, so they may impose a major maintenance commitment on the port. Marine craft are also needed for maintaining underwater structures and navigational aids, and many ports own and operate their own hydrographic survey vessels. Some ports even have a statutory obligation to provide passenger/freight ferry services between the mainland and adjacent islands, or across an estuary. Launches for carrying port workers, craft used for removal of wrecks, and various other boats may also be owned by the port; all need maintenance.

A feature of marine maintenance is the wide range of very specialized facilities it needs. They include:

— dry-docks and slipways, at which statutory surveys are carried out and where the hull and machinery of vessels are maintained to classification society standards;

— special machine tools and rigs for the repair of propulsion systems, including complex, state-of-the-art propellers;

— heavy lifting equipment for removing deck structures, rigging, motors and other machinery for repair and servicing;

— special facilities for the maintenance of dredgers, mooring cables and bouys, anchors and other gear.

Marine maintenance is almost always a divided responsibility within the port. The Harbour Master's Department, and the civil, marine and mechanical engineering sections can all be involved in the operation and maintenance of the floating equipment. For example, preventive maintenance and routine minor repairs to vessels are normally carried out by the crew (who are usually directly responsible to the Harbour Master) while major work, such as the overhaul of the hull and machinery, is undertaken in the workshops under the control of the marine engineering section. Staff from the mechanical and electrical workshops may also be involved in the maintenance of engines and generators. In one port visited, the Marine Section provides crews and maintains the floating craft, but their operation is controlled by the Harbour Master; the Harbour Master administers the craft and crew while they are operational, while the Marine Engineer schedules and maintains the vessels. Lighters, on the other hand, are 'owned' and operated by the Operations Department, with the Marine Engineer responsible solely for their maintenance. A fire float is crewed by the Fire Service, operated by the Harbour Master and maintained by the Marine Section. In spite of these administrative complications (not uncommon with respect to marine matters), no major functional problems seem to arise at that port.

1.3.4 Technical Services

A variety of technical services and utilities are required within a port, from electricity supply and distribution, lighting of cargo-handling and other operational areas, water for washing and firefighting purposes, and disposal of sewage, to telephones and radio communication systems. Ports operating very old equipment may have to maintain a high-pressure hydraulic ring main and possibly a compressed air system. Responsibility for the provision and maintenance of such services varies from port to port, but at least some of them, and in many ports most of them, come under one or other of the engineering sections.

Few ports generate their own electricity, but most have standby generating equipment to ensure that essential services can be sustained in the event of supply failure. Usually, the national electricity supply authority provides a high-voltage supply at one or more points within the port estate, and the port engineers distribute it from there, after reducing the voltage to suit port equipment. At one Asian port, for example, the electricity is brought into the port at 11 kV and is stepped down to 3.3 kV for the newer cranes, 400 V for the older cranes, and 220 V for distribution to workshops and offices. A large port (such as that Asian one) may have an electrical distribution system as extensive as that of a small town, particularly if it also owns large housing estates for its workers. The high-voltage sections of such a system, particularly the switching and transforming units, place particular demands on maintenance and safety staff.

Fresh water for ship supply, firefighting, washing and domestic purposes (workshops, offices, canteens, toilets and housing) is invariably supplied by the public water utility or authority, but the port is again usually responsible for distributing it within the port boundaries. In many countries, the mains supply pressure is insufficient to meet peak demand, and the port engineers have to construct water towers or reservoirs, with associated filtration plant, to ensure a supply at constant head. The port is usually also responsible for drainage and sewerage services, and for general exterior and interior cleaning of the quays, roadways, sheds, offices and other buildings (though cleaning is among the easiest of services to contract out).

Telephone systems are usually installed and maintained by telecommunications authorities or companies, on a contract basis, but internal systems may be independently maintained by the port. Short-range VHF radio links are now commonly used to pass information and instructions within the port areas, as well as to assist in ship navigation and cargo-handling. Telex and facsimile transmission ('fax') systems are also becoming more common as means of transmitting and receiving information; these are commonly contracted or leased facilities. Computer links and sophisticated communication and automated control systems are increasingly widely used in relation to cargo-handling equipment (some with optical fibre links), introducing new and more complex maintenance responsibilities.

1.3.5 Port Equipment

Ports operate and maintain a vast range of cargo-handling and other mobile equipment and fixed plant. Which types of equipment are in use at a particular port or terminal will, clearly, depend on the traffics handled and on the methods of cargo-handling adopted, particularly the degree of mechanization achieved. Trade in raw and refined bulk commodities, both liquid and dry-bulk, forms a significant role in the economies of many countries, and ports frequently undertake the handling, storage and transfer of those materials on behalf of importers and exporters. Containerized, roll-on-roll-off and break-bulk general cargoes each demand their own types of handling equipment, the operation and maintenance of which pose their own particular problems. The major ranges of equipment used, and their significance in terms of maintenance, will be considered briefly under the headings of dry-bulk trades, liquid-bulk trades, containerized and other unitized traffic, and break-bulk cargoes.

1. **Dry-bulk** installations have specialized grabbing cranes or continuous unloaders linked by conveyor belts to silos, sheds or open storage areas. At the storage points, equipment is needed for receiving and stacking cargo, retrieving and loading it to ship, rail or road transport, and possibly for bagging it before dispatch. The capital invested in equipment at a typical dry-bulk handling facility (e.g. an iron-ore terminal) may be more than $50 million, and annual maintenance costs between $5 million and $7 million. Such systems are often required to work continuously in a harsh environment for long periods with the minimum of maintenance. Highly automated, integrated berth handling systems, linking ship loading/discharging directly to storage areas, feeder vessels and inland transport, handle many thousands of tonnes per working hour, and are designed to keep ship's turnround time to a minimum. Failure of one of these interlinked systems can have disastrous effects on operations, and there are penalties (in the form of demurrage and other costs) in the event of breakdown. Such increasingly complex plant, in which material can be received, weighed, conveyed to the quay and loaded into the vessel as a continuous process, involves the incorporation of sophisticated, solid-state electronic control, safety and condition monitoring systems. Terminals of this sort regularly and successfully cope with berth occupancies of over 90%, and plant utilization is extremely high, so that it is rarely possible to take the plant out of service at regularly prescribed times for maintenance. A very different maintenance strategy has to be adopted for these terminals to that for, say, a general cargo berth and its equipment.

2. Installations for the handling of **liquid-bulk** commodities pose similar maintenance problems. Like dry-bulk terminals, the pipeline systems and pumping stations linking the tankers to the extensive tank farms are in almost constant use for very long periods, and access for maintenance is difficult. The commodities handled vary from the relatively innocuous palm oils and molasses to the highly corrosive liquid fertilizers and the very inflammable petrochemicals and other liquid chemicals. Segregation of cargoes is a particular operational problem, and special maintenance problems are posed by such relatively new practices as single-buoy moorings for very large tankers, involving offshore pumping and long pipelines to bring the liquids ashore. There are often very special safety and emergency measures that have to be taken with liquid-bulk handling, involving many departments and even such civil authorities as the police and fire services.

3. The introduction of the **container** has resulted in the weight of unit lifts increasing from about one tonne to up to 30 tonnes. Obviously, this has had a major impact on the type of equipment needed in ports. Instead of level-luffing or slewing dockside cranes, there are enormous container gantry cranes, fitted with complex spreader attachments, while quay transfer is performed by high-speed machines with capacities of up to 35 or 45 tonnes, capable of stacking boxes three, four or five high. Container terminals are totally dependent on such expensive handling equipment; even a relatively modest terminal, with a throughput of 250,000 Twenty-Foot Equivalent Units (TEU), may have over $30 million invested in equipment – straddle carriers, rubber-tyred gantry cranes, rail-mounted gantry cranes, terminal tractors and/or lift trucks. The total life cycle cost of

one straddle carrier can exceed $3 million, while that of a quayside container crane can be as much as $16 million. This great variety of very expensive equipment poses particular problems for maintenance:

— First, fewer units are needed to handle the same volume of cargo as a break-bulk facility, and so it is essential that each unit of equipment is available for use for a very high proportion of its time;

— Secondly, the complexity of the electronic control and other systems installed in these machines requires new maintenance skills;

— Thirdly, the sheer size of the equipment, and their complex systems and components, have made it necessary to build new workshops, of novel design and equipped with new types of sophisticated maintenance, diagnostic and repair facilities.

4. Although most port investment and activity today revolves around bulk- and container-handling equipment, many ports – especially those in LDCs – still handle large volumes of general **break-bulk and neo-bulk** cargoes. They still rely on the traditional rail-mounted, level-luffing quay cranes for ship working and a range of mobile cranes, tractor-trailer sets and small lift trucks to move cargo over the quays and to transfer it to and from road and rail vehicles. However, even in these conventional systems loads have increased considerably in recent years, and lifts of 10 to 20 tonnes are not uncommon. Specialist equipment is also used to handle forest products, bagged cargoes and fruit, and railway rolling stock and a fleet of road vehicles may also be owned by the port. All this equipment has to be looked after by the engineers. Even though it is not as complex as much of that on a container or bulk terminal, it still requires a range of engineering skills to maintain it, and major ports typically have between 1500 and 2000 units of cargo-handling equipment in their inventory – a significant maintenance undertaking.

5. Backing up the cargo-handling equipment itself is a range of **ancillary equipment**, to enable the port to meet emergencies (fire trucks and tenders, ambulances, security vehicles) and to maintain the port's assets (mobile maintenance units, lubrication trucks, personnel vehicles, road-mending and cleaning vehicles and

machinery). This equipment, too, requires maintenance, of course.

The responsibility for carrying out maintenance and repairs on cargo-handling and service equipment depends on ownership and varies between ports, as will be discussed in Chapter 2. Maintenance will, nevertheless, be required, and the wide variety of equipment employed within the port ensures that the equipment maintenance function is the most demanding of the responsibilities of port engineers.

1.4 Equipment and its Maintenance

1.4.1 The Importance of Equipment Maintenance
Although the entire range of the port's assets – civil works, marine craft, utilities and services, plant and equipment – must be kept in good condition, particularly in a maritime environment exposed to such harsh conditions of wind and spray, humidity and salt, there is no doubt that it is the maintenance of equipment which merits the highest engineering priority and offers the major challenge. Paradoxically, it is in this area that maintenance difficulties are most apparent in LDC ports. While problems were observed, during this study, in the maintenance of civil works and, in some cases, of marine craft, it is the poor quality of equipment maintenance that undoubtedly presents the biggest obstacle to achievement of acceptable levels of efficiency. To some extent, the maintenance problems of LDC ports have been disguised until recently by their reliance on manpower, but recent technological change and the investment in fleets of expensive, complex equipment have thrown those deficiencies into high relief.

In this section, the background to this increasing reliance on equipment will be surveyed, the significance of equipment availability to the port's performance, profitability and competitiveness is considered, and the resultant importance of equipment maintenance is assessed.

1.4.2 The Impact of Technological Change on Seaports
The most important development in the shipping industry since the 1950s has been specialization, with the conventional general cargo liner or tramp vessel rapidly being replaced by a range of new ship designs, each carrying a particular commodity or type of packaging. First, the liquid-bulk trades acquired oil tankers, chemical products and gas carriers, and the dry-bulk trades adopted specialized carriers of grain, coal and fertilizers – in both cases vessels that have increased steadily in size to today's

giants. These developments were quickly followed by similar specialization in the break-bulk trades: fully cellular vessels, semi-container vessels (multi-purpose ships, combination carriers, conbulkers etc.), Ro-Ro vessels, deep-sea timber carriers, refrigerated ships and so on. Matching the right ship to the particular commodity and trade route characteristics has become an important decision for the shipowner in his striving for economies of scale and efficiency, and for maximum competitiveness.

In response to the specialization and technological developments in shipping, ports have had to adapt their existing facilities or build anew. Many of the all-purpose conventional berths have been replaced by new terminals, with very different designs, layouts, functions and facilities. Most significantly, new cargo-handling practices and procedures have had to be introduced, much more dependent on the use of expensive equipment, often with a high degree of automation, and relying less on manpower for the physical handling of cargoes between maritime and inland transport. The bulk trades were affected first; pipeline transfer methods have enabled a high degree of automation to be introduced in liquid bulk terminal operations, resulting in high throughput and speedy ship turnround. In the dry-bulk trades, gravity-loading systems, crane-mounted grabs, bucket wheels, chain buckets, spiral conveyors and pneumatic devices have been widely installed. Similar and equally impressive developments have taken place in the unitized trades, with enormous investments in heavy-duty equipment for the handling of containers, flats, pallets and other forms of unit loads.

As the technological developments in shipping make further advances, the mechanization of cargo-handling operations in ports will undoubtedly grow; seaports all over the world will become more and more dependent on cargo-handling equipment.

1.4.3 Seaports' Dependence on Equipment

Cargo-handling methods in ports changed little between the early 19th Century and the middle of the present century. Until about 30 years ago, port mechanization was restricted to quayside cranes; cargoes were moved manually between the quayside and storage areas, with hand-carts or barrows representing the extent of equipment use. Clearly, at that time equipment maintenance was emphatically not a problem. Then, in the 1950s (in the developed world) and 1960s (in LDCs) mechanization first appeared in the form of the pallet- or lift-truck. No longer had cargoes to be moved manually, piece by piece, but loads could be bigger, moved more quickly and stacked higher. The resulting great economies of scale rapidly overcame the problems

of the considerable financial investment required, and mechanization has since made possible speedier operations, improved output and productivity, reduced damage to cargoes and injury to the workforce, better use of storage facilities, and improved integration of port and inland transport operations. The result is that equipment is now an essential component of the inventory of resources at the port operator's disposal.

The past two decades have seen a prolific increase in the range and capacity of equipment available to port operators and the introduction of many special attachments for particular commodities and packagings. For example, over 1,000 ship-to-shore container gantry cranes have already been installed, and many tens of millions of dollars have been invested in more and more specialized equipment. A typical medium-sized LDC port may have a total investment of as much as $100 million in cargo-handling equipment, while a large port in Europe could have $200 million invested, with as much as $20 million a year being spent on routine replacement of cargo-handling equipment. The total investment in such equipment in the commercial seaports of developing countries alone could be more than $5 billion, at replacement cost value, with an annual operating cost estimated to be in the range of $1.25-1.5 billion.

Investment in equipment is likely to increase even further as mechanization proceeds. The World Bank – a major source of funding for port and harbour development – has in the past five years' lending supported 29 port and harbour projects with a total cost of $3,829 million, of which $1,109 million (29%) was for port equipment. In 1986 a further 31 projects were under preparation, amounting to $1,626 million of investment; again, a high proportion of this is intended for the purchase of equipment.

Today, then, ports have no option *but* to provide high-capacity mechanical handling equipment to meet the needs of their traffics and to remain competitive. Indeed, port planners predict further rapid developments in the range and capacity of equipment available to port operators, and envisage a time in the next decade or so when semi-automated and possibly fully automated terminals will be commissioned. The equipment management function, and particularly the management of equipment maintenance, is therefore likely to assume even greater importance in the future.

1.4.4 Service, Profitability and Competition

In recent years, changes in the geography of maritime transport and in shipping economics have increased inter-port competition and the importance of offering a high quality service to port users. The economies of scale achieved through the use of larger and more specialized vessels have effectively reduced the tonne-mile cost of sea transport, but these economies depend on the vessels being kept moving as much as possible and staying in port for as short a time as possible. The trend has, therefore, been for line-haul vessels to cover wider markets per voyage but to call at fewer ports on the way, maximizing the liftings per call. This has increased the use of transshipment services and has made traffics far less captive to traditional ports of call. Inter-port competition (the battle to become pivot ports for the new services) has intensified, making ports very conscious of the need to offer good service to shipowners.

What ship operators look for when selecting a port is a consistently high cargo-handling rate, guaranteeing a quick ship turnround. One Asian port has responded to this by setting as its performance objective that there should be literally no delay to container vessels arriving at the port; currently, it is 90% successful in achieving this objective. It also has a target of turning around each road vehicle delivering or receiving containers within 30 minutes of arrival; even at peak periods, it achieves this for 85-90% of vehicles. Clearly, these targets can only be reached if the port has a sufficient inventory of cargo-handling equipment, and if those machines are maintained in first-class, reliable condition.

Any decline in the quality of service offered (caused by frequent breakdowns of equipment in service, or long delays awaiting repairs) immediately reduces the attractiveness of the port to ship operators and cargo owners, ultimately leading to fewer calls and less cargo to handle. Since operating costs are largely fixed, the cost per tonne of cargo handled will rise. As prices are regulated by market forces, making it difficult for the port to raise its charges, port profitability will inevitably decline. On the other hand, if equipment reliability and availability can actually be improved, raising the quality of service to port users, ship operators may even be able to tighten their vessel schedules, improving vessel utilization and reducing transit times for shippers. They will be more disposed to concentrate cargo-handling operations at the port, increasing throughput and making a substantial contribution to greater port profitability.

Inter-port competition has become very much keener in recent years, and a port has to be competitive not just to attract new business but also merely to retain its existing customers. To be competitively attractive, the port has to establish and sustain a reputation for reliability and good service,

as well as being efficient and profitable so that it can keep its prices as low as possible. It is worth noting that the LDC container ports that have succeeded in developing major transshipment operations have in common a high reliability of service based on, among other factors, good equipment maintenance. This has even been achieved in some ports with relatively little indigenous, 'captive' traffic to attract shipowners.

Maintenance earns no revenues directly for the port, but it does most emphatically affect port profitability. Good maintenance is the basis for equipment reliability and high availability, on which the port's reputation for service depends. It also increases the utilization of equipment, reducing operating costs and giving the port the opportunity to reduce tariffs and become more competitive. It extends the life of assets and, by increasing availability, reduces the size of the equipment inventory required for any given operation; both of these factors reduce the need for capital investment. If equipment is kept in good condition, it breaks down less frequently in use and also performs more effectively when in use, again maximizing the effective capacity of port facilities with the minimum of investment. So the port's profitability and competitiveness are inextricably bound up with the efficiency of the maintenance function.

1.5 The Consequences of Poor Equipment Maintenance

1.5.1 Low Availability

The primary direct consequence of inefficient and ineffective equipment maintenance is that equipment availability (in the general sense of the proportion of the inventory in a serviceable, operable condition at any one time) is low. There will be too few units of equipment of the required type to meet the daily requisition demands of traffic officers, who will have to make do with fewer machines than they need. Berth or terminal output will be below the required level and ship's time in port will be higher than desired. Without the equipment they need, the operators may have to resort to unsatisfactory and unsafe methods of cargo-handling, increasing the risk of injury to port workers and of damage to cargo, vessels and port structures.

There are other consequences, too. If equipment is regularly out of service, undergoing repair or waiting for spare parts, for example, it will perform for fewer hours during the year than it was designed (and purchased) to do. In spite of this, it is unlikely that its working life will be thereby extended, as it will inevitably deteriorate during its periods of inactivity. So its total life's work will be lower than planned and its hourly operating costs over its lifetime will be higher; the return on that particular investment will be significantly reduced. This is particularly serious at a time when technology is changing so rapidly that a machine's economic working life may be much shorter than its physical life, and when it really needs to perform even harder, to 'earn' its capital cost sooner.

So low availability is perhaps the most damaging result of poor maintenance and the one with the greatest immediate impact on port performance and profitability.

1.5.2 Low Output and Performance
If, because of poor maintenance, cargo-handling operators are supplied with fewer units than they need or have to make do with the wrong sort of equipment, the amount of work performed per shift will be less than it should be. In the case of the ship operation and quay transfer operation, the consequence is that ship working time will be expensively extended. In the case of receipt/delivery equipment, the delays will be to inland transport vehicles initially, but ultimately the effects will spread to the storage areas and other cargo-handling activites.

Badly maintained equipment also tends to break down frequently, holding up work or even bringing it to a complete halt. Even while they are working, poorly maintained machines will not be able to work to their design specification; engine output will be reduced, affecting travel and lift speeds, and faulty hydraulic and other systems may well reduce the machines' ability to lift – they may have to be de-rated.

These are not hypothetical fears but observed facts: the standard of maintenance in many LDC ports is so much below acceptable norms that equipment performance is serverely limited and cargo-handling output seriously handicapped.

1.5.3 Additional and Unnecessary Port Investment
Some ports overcome (or disguise) the problems arising from poor maintenance – the low availability of machines for operators, their poor performance and reliability, and so on – by over-investment in equipment. They buy more units of each type of equipment than their planning calculations show is the optimum number, just to make sure that there will be sufficient serviceable machines available to operators when they want them. This is, of course, hardly a cost-effective solution. For example, if port operators need a fleet of 20 straddle carriers on each shift, to maintain a satisfactory level of service, but

the engineers can only achieve an availability rate of 60%, then the port will have to purchase 34 machines to guarantee that the operators have the number they want. If the engineers had been able to provide the reasonable standard of maintenance that would have produced an availability of 80%, a fleet of only 25 machines would have been needed – a saving of nine machines. At a purchase price of about $500,000 per unit, the port is thus investing an additional and unnecessary $4.5 million as a direct result of poor maintenance. If availability could only have been targetted at 90% – through the sort of maintenance quality that the port should have been aiming for – a further two machines (at $1 million) could have been saved.

Other maintenance practices may also increase the level of investment that a port has to make. Poor maintenance of roads, quays and backup areas can severely reduce the life of mobile cargo-handling equipment, forcing the port to replace those assets more frequently. In some LDC ports, such excessive wear and tear is estimated to reduce the expected working life of equipment by as much as 50%. It was not uncommon to find, during the port visits, forklift trucks and tractors that were initially estimated to have an economic life of five years to be almost unmaintainable and irrepairable after scarcely more than two years, ready for drastic refurbishment or, more likely, replacement. Apart from having a shorter than expected life, equipment damaged by road surface conditions may need additional corrective maintenance and damage repair, and will spend more time than it should in the workshops – more unnecessary costs on the port's budget. The already low availability figure will be reduced still further and this, in turn, increases the need for investment in reserve units. In some of the ports visited by the team, many millions of dollars' worth of capital equipment were lined up outside the workshops, either awaiting repair or refurbishment or destined for scrapping.

Another factor affecting unnecessary capital investment arises from low output (which, as has been explained, is a consequence of poor maintenance): its direct effect on ship's time in port. If ships spend longer in port than they should, berth occupancy will be higher than necessary and arriving vessels will have to wait for a berth to become vacant. If this persists, ship owners will put pressure on the port (through demurrage or freight rate surcharges) to construct new berths and facilities to eliminate ship congestion. This will entail large-scale investment, much of it in the form of loans from international banks and requiring interest repayments which will have to be met from scarce foreign exchange earnings.

Poor civil maintenance can have extraordinary consequences on equipment use and capital expenditure. In one port (certainly not unique), a container terminal surface is so uneven that the rubber-tyred gantry cranes purchased for it cannot be used in the export area of the container yard, only in the import and empties areas. That port has had to buy heavy-duty lift-trucks (front-end loaders) to handle exports, in addition to the already purchased full fleet of rubber-tyred gantry cranes. The lift-trucks are only able to stack boxes two-high, under existing surface conditions, whereas the gantry cranes would have stacked to four-high, and so the yard capacity has been severely reduced. Many containers now have to be regularly moved, at considerable expense, to off-dock premises for storage, because there is no room for them in the container yard. This is, in turn, imposing a social cost on the surrounding urban area through the significant extra traffic generated, and traffic congestion within the city is made much worse. The port is being pressed to build extra storage space within the terminal to overcome these problems – but that, too, would be the cause of additional expenditure, of course!

1.5.4 Additional Operating Costs

Poor maintenance has a direct and undesirable effect on equipment operating costs, for several reasons:

— If preventive maintenance schedules are not followed, so that equipment misses its routine services, any minor problems may turn into major defects, causing breakdowns and expensive repairs;

— If corrective maintenance is shoddily carried out, the machine will probably break down again very shortly, returning to the workshop for further repair;

— The combination of frequent breakdowns in service and inadequate maintenance procedures results in low availability and utilization, reducing berth output and putting up operating costs;

— If equipment spends frequent and lengthy periods in the workshop under repair, then utilization (in terms of operating hours) will decrease. Amortization charges have to be recovered whether a machine is in use or not, and those fixed costs will now be spread over fewer lifetime operating hours, so that the hourly operating cost of the equipment will increase significantly;

— If equipment has to be hired from contractors to meet operators' demands, operating expenditure again goes up;

— Some ports try to compensate for low availability by keeping equipment in use long after its economic life has passed. These machines will be unreliable and probably de-rated, so that their performance will be poor. They will also need more frequent engineering attention to keep them going than newer machines, and spare parts will become more and more difficult (and expensive) to obtain. All these factors will increase operating costs.

Increasing the effectiveness of maintenance will have a positive effect on equipment operating costs. This is not just a question of throwing money at the problem, however; the relationship between maintenance expenditure and the economic consequences on operations of breakdowns and substandard performance is not a linear one. Engineers in the most successful ports follow a maintenance policy which finds that optimal position where the sum of the maintenance cost and the costs resulting from breakdowns and delays is minimal. In many LDC ports, this compromise position has by no means been attained: maintenance is costly but of poor quality, and total costs are accordingly high.

1.5.5 Impact on Port Users

Ship operators can be adversely affected by the consequences of poor maintenance in a number of ways. Some of these affect their short-term decisions and levels of expenditure, while others influence their longer-term policy decisions and related costs. The direct (and potentially most damaging) consequence of slow cargo-handling arising from engineering deficiencies is that vessels are delayed in port. Voyage times are increased and so are vessel operating costs. Shortages of equipment, breakdowns and other disruptions of work also add to ship operators' port disbursements, particularly for stevedoring (e.g. charges for gangs standing by but not actually working) and for services based on time (e.g. berthage charges). Unless ship operators have uncommitted time available (as can apply in tramp trades) port delays will have knock-on effects on sailing and calling schedules at subsequent ports of call. Operators may try to catch up on time by increasing sailing speeds, with penalties in fuel costs. They might, instead, miss out a scheduled port of call, so that cargo for that port will have to be transshipped later, or might have to charter an extra vessel to maintain a set service frequency. All these are very serious actions for a ship operator to take.

On the other hand, if the port can increase its efficiency so that a few ship-handling hours can be saved, the ship operators may be able to tighten their schedules or reduce their sailing speed (and so fuel consumption) between ports of call. Either way, their vessels can be run more efficiently and voyage costs reduced. This is particularly significant for the large, specialist vessels which may cost up to $30,000 a day to operate, even while in port.

Cases have arisen where, because of the persistent unreliability of equipment, ship operators have resorted to flying out engineers and spare parts to a port (at their own expense) to ensure that the port's equipment is serviceable when their vessels arrive and to minimize delays to the ships. Some ship operators have even gone to the expense of supplying their own cargo-handling equipment in unsatisfactorily-run ports, complete with a permanently-based maintenance crew. In other cases, ship operators have decided to use only geared vessels on those routes, increasing investment and operating costs and reducing cargo deadweight. Many ports still charge the ship operator as if the port's equipment had been used (a less than tactful generator of ill-will), but most are resigned to losing potential revenue when the ship operator provides gear or equipment.

In the longer-term, of course, ship operators are likely to rearrange their schedules and miss out the unsatisfactory ports from their itineraries, particularly the smaller and less strategically important ones. Cargo will then have to be transshipped to those ports, in geared feeder vessels, from a relay port which has a better reputation for reliability. Alternatively, shipowners could put older, less efficient, ships onto those routes; these are more expensive to operate, which adds to the other cargo-handling problems of the ports.

Poor maintenance can also affect road transport operators, through delays to the loading and unloading of their vehicles. Such delays penalize cargo owners (through demurrage charges) and vehicle fleet operators (by reducing the level of use of the vehicles). Shortages of road and rail vehicles, resulting from their being held up in port, may cause freight to miss scheduled departure times, commodities to miss their markets and cargoes to deteriorate while they wait for transport.

If the port's operating costs increase because of poor maintenance and all its consequences, its operating surplus will be reduced and there could well be pressure for it to increase its tariffs to compensate – yet another economic blow for the port's users.

1.5.6 Impact on the Competitiveness of Ports

Poor maintenance can critically harm the reputation of ports, possibly to the extent that shipowners will decide no longer to serve those ports, or to serve them only by feedering. A port with a poor maintenance record will certainly be unlikely to attract a new, direct line-haul service in place of an existing feeder service. Ship operators are very unlikely to be interested in serving an uncompetitive port where there are alternatives.

In the vessel-load charter trades (e.g. a spot-chartered bulk carrier), a maximum loading/discharging period or a minimum daily rate of cargo working will have been agreed, and slow working by the port can lead to the charging of demurrage. For a 55,000-60,000 DWT vessel, as much as 60% of its $8,400 daily operating cost may be charged as demurrage. On the other hand, in deep-sea liner trades, operators tend to average freight rates across a geographically wide range of ports. Ship operators are accustomed to paying different charges at the ports covered by such averaging, without surcharging the high-charging ports. They are likewise loath to impose surcharges on ports for slow turnround, and only do so where delays are excessive and persistent. Maintenance is obviously not the only factor affecting vessel turnround, although shortage of equipment can be a major contributor to low output and to pressures on shipowners for general freight rate increases and, if disastrously bad problems arise from poor maintenance, the imposition of congestion surcharges.

In considering the impact of poor equipment maintenance on the competitive position of ports, it is also necessary to take into account the possible attitude and influence of shippers and receivers on port routing decisions. These will vary according to whether, for example, cargo is consigned in ship loads or in liner parcels. In general, shipper/receiver influence will be greatest in relation to ship-load traffics, though the operators of liner services (including containerized services) will also watch their customers' reactions, in case the use of any particular ports arouses their hostility. Shippers will obviously always be concerned when poor maintenance gives rise to service delays, and where the use of a particular port may increase freight costs.

1.5.7 Impact on the Country's Economy

Economic growth for many LDCs is closely linked to the expansion of foreign trade, most of which is carried by maritime transport. Export-led development has been a particularly important feature of the newly industrialized countries, where foreign trade growth has been reflected in significant increases in gross domestic product (GDP). Maritime trade is also important to other LDCs, which largely export raw materials and semi-finished products and import manufactures and foodstuffs from developed countries. Foreign trade is, for LDCs, a significantly larger share of the GDP than for developed countries; typically, it is equivalent to over 50% of GDP. Maritime transport costs, which can form a significant proportion of the value of the goods shipped, can act as a serious barrier to international trade. They can significantly reduce foreign exchange earnings, particularly for the relatively low-value primary commodities which make up the bulk of exports of developing countries. Since the costs incurred in port by shipowners (both direct and indirect) and shipper/receivers represent a significant proportion of maritime transport costs, increased port efficiency (contributed to by improved equipment maintenance) is very important to the lowering or containing of maritime and total transport costs. Reduced transport costs could subsequently be passed on in the form of reduced export prices, stimulating international trade.

As already noted, poor port maintenance, through unnecessarily high investment in the equipment inventory, substandard operating performance and increased infrastructure requirements, causes increased cargo-handling costs. If the port absorbs these costs (perhaps because of government controls on port charges, or because of intense local competition), its rate of return will be reduced. If, on the other hand, ports increase their charges against vessels, there are various possible consequences. Where liner services are concerned, the practice of averaging freight rates across a range of ports is likely to mean that the additional costs would initially be absorbed by the ship operators, but if that operator is a national of the country, the costs will ultimately be borne by the economy. In the case of chartered vessels, the cargo-handling and other shore costs not payable by the vessels will inevitably fall against the exporters and importers of the country (except for transit or transshipment cargoes).

As noted above, poor maintenance can slow down vessel turnround, so affecting vessel time costs. Here again, the freight cost implications depend on the basis of the shipping operations concerned. Short of very serious delays occurring, liner services would be unlikely to increase their freight rates or to surcharge them, and would absorb the additional costs in the short term. However, persistent high costs are likely to result in a general freight rate increase. In the case of chartered shipping, for example in the bulk trades, poor performance could give rise to additional freight costs (demurrage), where spot charters are involved. For vessels on a time charter basis, if turnround is seriously affected by poor maintenance, this could begin to affect the number of voyages vessels could make, so in effect increasing freight costs. These costs will be passed on in the form of higher freight rates.

So, in several different circumstances, irrespective

of contracts of affreightment, poor equipment maintenance will add to the nation's shipping bill and have a detrimental effect on the country's economy.

1.6 The Management of Port Maintenance

1.6.1 Elements of Maintenance Management
Although there is little doubt that inadequacies in port maintenance lie at the heart of the problems of inefficiency of LDC ports, it would be to oversimplify the case to see the problem as purely an engineering one, resolvable by upgrading workshop facilities and the technical skills of engineering staff. From the very early stages of this investigation, it quickly became apparent that these were by no means the sole – or, indeed, the major – root causes of port inefficiency. The deeper the study went, the more and more obvious it became that such symptoms as poor equipment maintenance and unsatisfactory supply of equipment to operators are largely the result of management and policy shortcomings, aggravated by government policies and regulations.

Clearly, it was essential to take the broadest possible view of the whole problem and to identify and investigate all the factors that could be contributing to the present unhappy state of maintenance in LDC ports. It was also felt vital to identify those conditions that have to be met in order to ensure that port maintenance is performed effectively. Accordingly, the study was designed to examine the crucial issues centring on the *management* of port maintenance and not just the activities of the maintenance workshops, and to investigate all the factors that must be taken into account when formulating appropriate maintenance management policies. But what constitutes port maintenance management? How should it be defined and what does it include?

Figure 1.6.1 shows the individual elements collectively making up the management of port maintenance, as proposed in this study. They are a set of strategies, procedures, practices, controls and activities, individually definable and describable but totally interdependent. Failure to establish, sustain or follow one set of activities leads inevitably to deficiencies or problems in others. The success of the overall management function is dependent on the strengths and qualities of the individual components. An understanding of the nature and inter-relationships of these components is fundamental to the effective management of port maintenance. The rest of this chapter briefly introduces each of these components, preparatory to considering each in turn, in much greater detail, in the remaining chapters of the report.

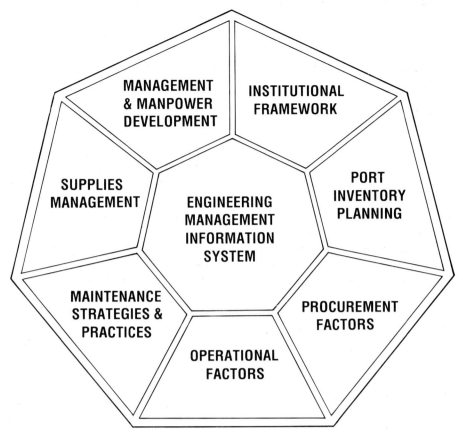

Figure 1.6.1: The Management of Port Maintenance

1.6.2 Institutional Framework

The policies and practices of maintenance management must be formulated within the framework of the institutional and organizational arrangements of the particular country and port. They will be influenced by the constitution, organizational structure and objectives of the port authority and the respective responsibilities, duties and authority of private and public operating companies. A major influence on maintenance management in LDCs is the relationship between the organizations in the port and central government. The nature and extent of central government regulations and controls imposed on the ports affect procurement of equipment and supplies, management and manpower career structures and many other vital areas. The degree of financial autonomy permitted to ports, particularly in terms of access to foreign exchange and freedom from investment controls, is of crucial importance to the port maintenance function. Institutional and organizational arrangements must be designed and developed so as to promote efficient maintenance policies and practices. This large and complex subject is discussed in Chapter 2.

1.6.3 Planning the Port Inventory

It has already been demonstrated that the efficient operation and maintenance of equipment (including cargo-handling, marine and other port plant and machinery) are the central concerns in port performance and profitability. Clearly, planning future equipment requirements must, therefore, be a central engineering function. The activity has become extremely complex recently, because of the growing range of equipment available and the rapid evolution in engineering design, equipment performance and specification. Ports must establish procedures for preparing an equipment plan that ensures that an appropriate inventory exists at all times to meet operational and other requirements. It must be based on traffic forecasts (taking into account all proposed port developments and the introduction of new traffics) and predicted operating and maintenance performance. Appropriate replacement strategies must be worked out, based on local conditions, on equipment reliability and on running and maintenance costs. The plan should determine the demand for each class of equipment in the port. To reflect the increasing importance of equipment to operators, the equipment plan must be incorporated within the port's corporate plan, to provide a framework for future acquisition policy. The port inventory plan is a vital input into the annual capital budgeting process and in longer-term port financial planning. It is considered at length in Chapter 3.

1.6.4 Procurement and Maintenance

Suitable procurement policies and strategies must be formulated and followed if the equipment plan is to be successfully implemented and maintenance facilitated. The objective must be to acquire the equipment that most appropriately meets operators' and engineers' requirements; it must serve its operational function to maximum efficiency while matching as nearly as possible the port's technical ability to maintain it. Effective procedures must be established and followed for writing technical specifications, preparing tender documents and administering the tendering process. Reliable techniques must be developed for evaluating bidding documents and for contract supervision. Finally, an appropriate organizational structure is needed for the procurement function and action taken to recruit, retain and develop competent staff. All these issues are dealt with in Chapter 4.

1.6.5 Operations and Maintenance

Crucial to efficient cargo-handling operations is the preparation of rules governing the allocation, deployment and safe operation of equipment. The aim must be the effective utilization of equipment, maximum operating performance and minimum demand on maintenance facilities. Operating manuals must be prepared, setting out safe and efficient practices, and adequate training and supervision provided to enforce them. Management must be more responsible, better informed about equipment deployment and more cost-conscious. There must be a new spirit of co-operation and collaboration between operations and engineering staff, to ensure that operators have the equipment that they need, while engineers have access to that equipment whenever it needs their attention. A key factor is an effective Operational Management Information System, including data on equipment costs. These operational factors are the subjects for discussion in Chapter 5.

1.6.6 Maintenance Strategies and Practices

The scale of port investment in equipment and the growing significance of equipment running and maintenance costs on revenue budgets and company profitability justify a considerable rise in the status of the maintenance function. This must be reflected in an increased level of authority for engineering managers within the organization and the allocation of greater resources to maintenance. There must be a fundamental change in management culture, with a much increased emphasis on customer service and performance-orientated maintenance. This can only be achieved through well thought out maintenance strategies, supported by reliable preventive and corrective maintenance procedures. Good workshop facilities and engineering practices must be established, within a framework of an efficient workshop administration and information system. Chapter 6 develops these ideas in depth.

1.6.7 Supplies Management

The port maintenance function cannot work effectively if it is not supported fully by an efficient spare parts and consumables supplies system. Supplies management is thus a vital component of the maintenance management structure, and needs to be developed to take full account of, and overcome, all the difficulties imposed by supply conditions, inventory costs and government controls. Effective reporting and administrative systems are needed to initiate the procurement process, to maintain accurate records on usage and stock levels, and to monitor and allocate costs. The Supplies Management Information System is a vital tool of the port maintenance function. The entire area of supplies management is considered in Chapter 7.

1.6.8 Management and Manpower Development

Human resources are a key factor in all components of port maintenance management. Manpower development policies and procedures must ensure that the port recruits suitably qualified personnel and that all employees are offered attractive career patterns. Training is of vital importance, and must be suited to the intellectual abilities and required skills of the individuals and to the needs of the port. Employee motivation must be fully developed, through financial and other incentives, discipline maintained and accountability established for each member of the port's staff. Salary, welfare and amenities must be reviewed to ensure that they serve to attract and retain staff of the right calibre for a modern, highly technological port. This very important area of management is surveyed in Chapter 8.

1.6.9 Engineering Management Information System

Central to the formulation of effective port maintenance (and all other) management policies is a reliable and comprehensive information system. This must contain continually up-dated records on operating performance, reliability, repair and maintenance schedules, and costs. It will then provide all the essential information necessary for monitoring operational and engineering performance and efficiency, and for making sound decisions on all aspects of maintenance management. A major revelation of this study has been the realization of how the Engineering Management Information System, which is described and discussed in Chapter 9, impinges on, and is the vital input for, almost all the other aspects of port maintenance management.

1.6.10 Improving the Management of Port Maintenance

Each of Chapters 2 to 9 deals, then, with one of the identified vital areas of port maintenance management – one of the segments of the structure visualized in Figure 1.6.1. Each chapter reviews the problems discovered during the study, discusses the various approaches to those problems adopted by the more successful ports – in both Europe and LDCs – and suggests protocols and models which the less successful ports should consider seriously in their attempts to improve the management of their maintenance function.

It is not the intention of the authors and team members to suggest that all the problems described are found in all ports, even in LDCs. Some of the ports visited manage their maintenance extremely well, in all, many or some respects, while others illustrate several aspects of the problems, to varying degrees. Indeed, just about all of the ports visited and surveyed have some valuable lessons to teach port maintenance managers and others concerned in the operational and engineering efficiency of ports worldwide.

The final chapter in this report gathers together the main recommendations to emerge, on the systems, organization, principles and practices on which good maintenance management depend. The recommendations are aimed as much at those involved in the provision of aid and technical assistance, through international projects, as port managers themselves. Implementation of many of the improvements so urgently needed in port maintenance can be considerably promoted if they are incorporated within technical assistance projects from the earliest stages, and monitored and guided by the technical consultants and experts involved.

It must be stressed, however, that this is essentially a discussion document. The authors acknowledge that the port sample is still a relatively small one, in spite of the efforts made to widen it by means of the questionnaire, and the port visits were inevitably brief. The team's observations were also inevitably coloured by their individual backgrounds and interests, however much they strived after objectivity. Nevertheless, it is hoped that it adequately serves its primary intention: to draw to the attention of readers the problems revealed or confirmed, and to offer possible solutions to those problems for wide discussion within the industry. The authors welcome feedback from those with practical experience in the various fields covered, as valuable input to the various documents and courses that will emerege from this and the other elements of the present project.

CHAPTER 2

The Institutional Framework

2.1 The Importance of the Institutional Framework

A most significant finding of this study is the extent to which institutional and organizational factors affect the ability of LDC ports to establish and sustain an efficient maintenance function. A central issue in this context is the nature of the relationship between central government (and relevant quasi-governmental bodies) and the port. In most of the LDCs surveyed, there are extremely close and strong links between relevant government ministries and organizations in the port transport industry, and these links greatly affect the ports' ability to manage their maintenance function. Government influence in the majority of LDC ports is omnipotent; governments maintain close control over all aspects of port development and scrutinize all management actions and decisions, however insignificant. It is, therefore, entirely appropriate to devote a complete chapter to the question of the role of government in port management affairs and how this affects port maintenance.

The form and degree of the government controls on ports are clearly influenced by the political ideologies and economic objectives of countries, and on established public administrative procedures. Some countries have centrally planned or *dirigiste* economies, and their governments require the ports to operate solely in the public interest, with all forms of inter-port competition strictly forbidden. These ports are closely supervised by the relevant ministries and, irrespective of any legislative enactments, are effectively managed as a branch of government, and are treated as public utilities. In other countries, ports are set public sector objectives but are given some degree of management autonomy to allow them to meet those objectives. Even so, there is still a strong government presence and influence on major decision-making, and rigid government control over most management decisions. In yet other countries, governments expect the ports to be operated commercially and require their managers to pursue a policy of profit maximization. They rely on competition and market forces to inspire constantly improving performance and an entrepreneurial management style. Clearly, considerable variety of governmental approach exists.

Most of the ports participating in the study are under some form of public ownership. The port authorities are either departments of government ministries, independent statutory or parastatal bodies (e.g. port trusts) or are under the direct control of local municipalities. A feature of these ports is the high degree of local or central government involvement in their management. In complete contrast, a few of the ports – and many of the independent terminal operators – are in private ownership and are largely free of government interference in their affairs.

Within these broad institutional arrangements, there are many different organizational patterns for the provision of port services. In some ports, especially in LDCs, the port authority is responsible for providing all port services and facilities. In others, the port authority provides only a limited range of services (usually those of a clear statutory nature, such as pilotage and conservancy), while other organizations are responsible for such services as cargo-handling and storage. In some ports, these independent port contractors are in the public sector (i.e. under some form of government control) while in others they are private companies.

These institutional and organizational arrangements clearly have a direct influence on port policies and objectives and on management style. They have a direct impact on the range and scale of the maintenance facilities and services, on the locus of responsibility for providing them, and on how the maintenance resources are managed. These are the issues that are considered in this chapter, under the headings of the organizational structure of the port, the relationship between port and government, and government controls.

2.2 The Organizational Structure of a Port

2.2.1 Role of the Port Authority

The role of port authorities varies greatly in different countries. At the one extreme is the totally integrated port authority, perhaps owning its own land, providing navigational aids, dredged channels and access to its berths, pilotage and towage services, and carrying out maintenance in respect of these activities as relevant. Such integrated authorities provide and maintain their infrastructure (quays and jetties for vessels to lie against, quay aprons and backup areas, roads, railway tracks, offices and transit sheds), quay cranes and a range of mobile cargo-handling equipment and vehicles. A port authority of this type may operate a single port or a group of ports; it may even be the sole authority operating all public-use ports in the country.

An integrated port authority may have a substantial marine department (owning pilot boats, tugs and dredgers), civil engineering responsibilities (in relation to the provision and maintenance of the quays, the surfaces of the quay aprons and backup areas, and for all the other civil works within the port) and mechanical engineering responsibilities (in relation to mechanical equipment – quay cranes, bulk handling equipment, mobile container and other handling equipment, and also transport vehicles). Port authorities of this type will be directly responsible for the commercial management and operation of their ports, and may also themselves provide labour for cargo handling and other functions.

At the other extreme is the purely regulatory port authority. This may plan and co-ordinate port development in a country, possess powers over port charges, and may have research functions for the ports industry as a whole. It is essentially a branch of government, and has no operational or engineering function in any ports.

Between these two extremes – the totally integrated port authority and the purely regulatory one – lie a range of different types of port organization, varying from country to country, and sometimes even within the same country. There are, for example, port authorities that are essentially landlords; they own the port land and water areas, provide and maintain navigational aids and related services, provide water access to berths of the necessary depth, provide the berth infrastructure itself (but not necessarily the surfacing) and generally co-ordinate port development. Other landlord port authorities may have slightly more active landside roles, including the provision of surfacing and possibly of some craneage (including both floating cranes and quay cranes), and may be involved in some general marketing activities in conjunction with independent terminal interests. In landlord ports, separate interests – perhaps only one company for virtually the whole of the port, perhaps several competing companies – develop the superstructure, provide equipment and manage and operate the terminals. Such terminal companies may be public or private sector in ownership, but often have the legal nature of a private sector organization.

Finally, there are situations in which there is formally no port authority as such, but where the obligations and functions of a port authority are undertaken directly by a government department. Here, again, there is no one single form. In Hong Kong, the Marine Department in practice takes on the role of a port authority, but its port role is largely confined to a regulatory function (especially as regards the co-ordination of new development), together with the provision of navigational aids and related marine services. In contrast, in one North European port, where there is no formal port authority, the port management provides navigational aids and related facilities, dredged access channels and water areas in the port, the entrance lock, berths and their surface, and also provides floating cranes. The operational and commercial management of the various terminals in that port is in the hands of private sector port companies.

2.2.2 The Role of the Port Operator

Just as the functions of different port authorities vary widely, so do the functions of port operators. There are three basic arrangements:

1. the operators may simply be part of an intergrated authority; in such cases, port managers may themselves be totally responsible for the commercial management of a port, for its operation (in terms of ship and cargo handling) and for providing and maintaining equipment necessary for the purpose. As operators, the port authorities carry out all cargo handling (on ship and ashore), using their own labour or that of another organization (such as a dock labour board).

2. As an alternative to the port authority operator, there may be public or private operators who lease berths or terminals and backup areas, possibly providing their own cranes, mobile handling equipment and buildings. Such companies may also be responsible for the provision and maintenance of quay aprons, backup area surfacing, roads and so on, as well as for maintaining their own cargo-handling equipment. They may not always own the quay cranes; these often remain the property of the port authority. In some ports, indeed, the mobile cargo-handling equipment, too, belongs to the port authority, is maintained by the authority and is hired out to the private sector handling

companies. This is, in a sense, a relic of the formerly common practice of cargo-handling companies investing very little in the ports in which they operated. This arrangement has become uncommon in major ports, but still continues in some ports with small operators. In another variation, operating companies manage and operate their berths or terminals but the port authority is responsible for civil works – the surfaces of quay aprons and backup areas, and roads within the port. Operating companies of this sort commercially manage their berths and terminals and provide the necessary port labour, either as permanent employees or drawn from some form of labour board. Other types of operator function solely as management contractors, operating container terminals or bulk handling installations on behalf of the port authority.

Such arrangements can give rise to maintenance-related problems. At one port, it is claimed that the life of (terminal operator-owned) cargo-handling equipment is much reduced by the poor state of the terminal surfaces; the poor civil maintenance provided by one organization causes problems for the mechanical maintenance function of the other. Indeed, the terminal operator in that port has successfully sued the port authority for the damage done to one of its expensive machines. The origin of such problems is often a question of finance: the need for an appropriate basis for payment of work carried out. Where such functional divisions of activity occur between different organizations within a port, there is a crucial need for appropriate contractual arrangements, e.g. maintenance leases for the terminal operators, allowing them to make their own decisions as to appropriate levels of expenditure on the maintenance of the roads and the surface of the cargo working areas within their leased sectors of the port.

3. There are also several hybrid arrangements. For example, a practice in some ports is to allocate some of the berths to one or more independent cargo-handling contractors (stevedoring companies or terminal operators), giving them exclusive rights for defined periods, while the port itself operates the other berths or terminals. In other ports, the authority performs all the the shore-based functions but contracts out the Ship Operation to stevedoring companies. Alternatively, berths

may be appropriated to ship operators, consortia or liner conferences, giving preferential or exclusive use of the facilities and allowing them to undertake their own cargo handling or to engage independent contractors to do that for them.

Such agreements affect responsibility for the upkeep of the berths' infrastructure and for the provision and maintenance of cargo-handling equipment. Under most such berth allocation or appropriation schemes, the port authority retains responsibility for maintaining the civil works and quay surfaces, but the provision and maintenance of equipment varies. Stevedores are normally required to provide all their own mobile equipment, even though quay cranes are usually hired from the port authority. In some cases, the stevedore is obliged to hire *all* the equipment from the port authority, who must, in return, provide all the facilities and resources for maintaining it. In other cases, the independent contractors hire equipment from suppliers and have no responsibility for maintaining it – though the port may insist on its staff inspecting it to ensure that it meets safety regulations. The arrangement adopted obviously affects responsibility for the provision and management of maintenance facilities.

A related complication arises from the recent emergence of off-dock container yard/container freight station operators and the growing importance of inland container depots in unitized trades. Many of these companies have port authority or cargo-handling contractor equity participation. The specialist cargo-handling equipment used at those centres to lift and stack containers creates a maintenance requirement often remote from port engineering facilities, and usually for relatively few machines. Port authorities often make arrangements to maintain those machines on behalf of the owners.

2.2.3 The Terminal Concept

In conventional general cargo trades, the functional unit of a port is the 'berth', its activity centred on the quayside at which the ship moors. The emphasis of the port's service is mainly directed at the ship and its owner. With the arrival of the bulk trades, with their mechanized facilities designed to transfer cargo as quickly as possible between the ship and inland transport, the emphasis moved away from the quayside to include also the landside activities. The name 'terminal' was introduced, implying an integrated activity providing services not just for the shipowner but also to importers, exporters and transport operators. The term 'terminal' has since been extended to unitized, and particularly containerized, facilities, which provide a comprehensive range of specialized services to all users.

If a terminal is to work smoothly and efficiently, its activities must be fully integrated and co-ordinated; this requires a high degree of management control and autonomy, a unified organizational structure. Independent terminal operators must be able to decide – in terms of their cost, revenues and viability assessments – how best to operate their terminals: how much equipment should be used, what types, when they should be replaced, and how they should be maintained.

This idea of the 'terminal unit' can be applied to individual sections of a port, even if they are all owned and operated by the same organisation. In effect, the port is divided into separate management units: the container facilities could be one functional unit, the bulk facilities another, the roll-on-roll-off berths a third, and the break-bulk berths a fourth unit. In a large port, there could be further divisions: the break-bulk berths could be grouped into two, three or more units, depending on how many berths there are, and there could be more than one container-handling unit. Each of these management units then becomes a 'terminal' in the sense of having its own financial and performance objectives, and functioning as a separate cost-centre (or, better, cost-sub-centres; the implications of the cost-centre approach are considered in several later chapters). The aim is to encourage maximum profitability consistent with the service objectives set for each 'terminal' by its management.

Each terminal management is then responsible for determining the appropriate best mix and volume of equipment, and the level of operating performance, that will allow the terminal to meet user requirements competitively. Of course, operators will wish to have sufficient equipment to cover all emergencies and peak demands, while engineers will wish to minimize the equipment inventory to reduce the demands on their facilities, and accountants will want to do it to reduce capital investment. Ultimately, it is a question of where responsibility should lie for determining the size of the fleet, its disposition and care, and the form of organization within the terminal must be such as to encourage careful operation, to minimize maintenance, and careful maintenance, to maximize equipment availability. Various ways in which such an arrangement can be arrived at are discussed in several later chapters.

2.3 Port Objectives and Maintenance

2.3.1 Setting Port Objectives
One of the more disturbing findings of this study is that many LDC governments have not set clearly defined financial or performance objectives for their ports. Even where governments are represented on the boards of port authorities (for example, by a senior civil servant from the Ministry of Finance), and where it would be expected that the port would be set clear targets acceptable to government, objectives may not be explicitly defined. Where some attempt has been made to set objectives, they are vague and poorly defined, and are certainly not consistently applied nor their attainment assessed. The situation is not helped by the very poor management and financial information systems existing in those ports; the 'annual' accounts of some ports are often four or five years late in appearing.

There are often inconsistencies between stated objectives and actual government practice. Inquiries by the project team into the details of port objectives and their implementation regularly evinced vague and often contradictory statements by senior port managers and government officials. Rarely do objectives appear in a formal document, and where they do there is considerable variation in the way they are formulated. For example, in some ports financial objectives may set a rate of return criterion on new investment, in others a return on net fixed assets; yet others demand a minimum cash flow; in many cases, no financial targets appear to be set at all.

The end result is that port managers rarely have a clear set of targets to aim for, and in turn have no incentive to formulate their own corporate and departmental objectives or any means of monitoring their achievement. This has important implications for the management of port maintenance. What *should* happen is that governments should establish an appropriate, clear set of objectives, and then allow executive managers to get on with their jobs. They should only interfere when targets are not met and when remedial action is needed. The changes in management culture and organization which this calls for will be considered in several later chapters.

2.3.2 Forms of Port Objectives
Port objectives, where they are set, are commonly defined in financial terms, in relation to Net Fixed Assets (NFA). Such calculations are often based on historic cost asset valuations; the consequences of this are very serious. For example, in one country with a relatively stable currency in terms of purchasing power, the rate of return on NFA

actually reported is 6%, which at first glance might appear satisfactory. In fact, this is the return on historic cost; on a replacement cost basis it turns out to be under 1%.

Elsewhere, ports may be set a basic objective of 'meeting operating costs and servicing capital charges'. In one country, the ports' obligations to service capital charges extend only to borrowings subsequent to their original (founding) investment, and their rate of return objectives are individually agreed with the government, according to their individual circumstances. Even so, the ports do not always meet those objectives.

Another approach involves some form of obligation to pay a proportion of profits to government. For example, one port authority pays 25% of its surplus to the government as a 'deemed dividend', on top of a tax payment of 50% of surplus *and* an obligation to service three substantial foreign loans. Notwithstanding the apparent severity of those impositions, they cannot be considered as effective financial objectives, as they embody no specific targets to motivate the port to increase its efficiency; indeed, they could be considered a distinct disincentive to profitability, as the port has little to gain by making a surplus.

Apart from financial targets, ports may be set other objectives, for example with regard to service levels to users; such non-financial objectives may be of overriding importance. In one such case, very high performance targets, in terms of waiting time for vessels and vehicle turnround time have almost certainly led to higher levels of capital investment than might have been undertaken on the basis of financial appraisals alone.

The choice of objectives, their definition and their burden can all have important implications for port authority finances and for port maintenance. The port authority in one LDC is set the objective of earning 15% of NFA at historical cost (equivalent to 7% after interest), but both domestic purchasing power and the foreign exchange value of the national currency have fallen greatly over the past few years, and such a target is consequently unduly low. The need in such a situation is to set more demanding obligations, such as a rate of return that takes into account currency depreciation, and that return should be calculated after depreciation, or on replacement cost, or at least after a rigorous revaluation of assets. In the case of the port just mentioned, there has been no asset revaluation since 1974!

There is also a need to avoid unduly high burdens on port authorities. The example quoted of the 25% deemed dividend after payment of a profit tax of 50% is a case in point; after meeting foreign loan servicing costs, it becomes very difficult for that port

to build up reserves. All government financial objectives and targets should aim at encouraging efficiency by allowing the port to benefit from its profits. For example, the port authority in one LDC is set an annual financial target and, if that target is bettered, the port is allowed to keep only 3% of the surplus for improvements, and *all* profits below the target are transferred to the government. If financial objectives are to be incentives for port management, they must be more generous than that; ports should be allowed to retain revenues to build up reserves, so that they can replace equipment and buy spares from their own funds, rather than applying to government for all significant expenditure.

In fact, most of the LDC ports surveyed are not allowed to keep even 3% of their revenues, even though, ironically, they make large operating surpluses. Taxation and dividend schedules, combined with restrictions on the ports' ability to retain funds and to transfer them to reserves, drastically reduce the sum available for investment. Ports are frequently seen by governments as major revenue-generators and net providers of funds to the exchequer. In cases where ports do have adequate funds (in local currency) for investment in new assets, they still have to apply to government for approval and for the release of foreign exchange. So, although these ports are profitable, they have to approach government for loans for equipment purchase and must compete with other sectors of the economy for scarce foreign exchange. Governments are frequently the only source of funds for investment, preventing ports from using internally generated profits for this purpose. Greater freedom should also be given to ports to review tariffs and to generate adequate revenues for this purpose. Given the economic and strategic importance of ports to the national economy, and the amount of foreign exchange they can – and do – earn, they must be allowed to retain sufficient funds to replace assets and to keep the asset inventory intact and in good condition. This is just one aspect of the greater autonomy from government control that ports should now be given.

2.3.3 Port Autonomy

One of the study's alarming impressions is that government interference in day-to-day port management, far from easing, is actually on the increase, further stifling what little initiative managers are able to exercise, and imposing a 'civil service' mentality on what is today a highly competitive and commercial, international, high technology industry.

Paradoxically, most port authorities have enabling

24

legislation which sets out their responsibilities and duties, and which apparently provides them with adequate autonomy to manage their own affairs with the minimum of government interference. In practice, of course, public administrative systems have evolved through which all aspects of port management come under microscopic government scrutiny. In an effort to reverse this trend, some LDC governments are now contemplating major structural changes, even to the extent of considering privatization of part or all of the ports sector. This would certainly be one way of introducing greater managerial independence, and should lead to greater efficiency, if modern management practices are imported within an organizational ethos of initiative, innovation, enterprise and managerial and technical professionalism. If port maintenance is to be improved in the way that current developments in the maritime industry demand, less, not more, government involvement in port management is needed.

In recent years, there has been a clear trend (in Europe, at least) to increasing autonomy in the ports sector. Historically, many ports were administered as or within government departments, and were closely bound by public service regulations. Even where separate port authorities existed, policy direction often remained very close to government, through the appointment of civil servants as members of port Boards. Indeed, in some countries port chairmen and chief executives have normally been chosen from within the higher civil service, even remaining within the civil service during their period of duty in the ports sector. Increasingly, however, ports have been seen as commercial organizations – at least in the sense of having to develop and exist within a commercial environment, responding commercially to the requirements of port users. Combined with this (and perhaps stemming from it) has been a widespread feeling that ports should be managed to a greater extent than previously as commercial enterprises, market-orientated to user requirements and able to respond quickly to those requirements.

This move towards increasing port autonomy has taken a number of forms, examples of which were observed during the mission visits. In some cases, port authorities have been set up to take over ports previously run as government departments, expressly to give greater autonomy to port managers. Elsewhere, new companies have been set up, with private sector status but owned by and answerable to a government holding company. Both these new types of organizations are markedly more independent than their predecessors, free to manage themselves with a minimum of government intervention.

In a third type of development, seen almost exclusively in developed countries so far, there has been increasing involvement of the private sector in the ports industry. This has taken various forms:

— Outright privatization of a whole port;
— Privatization of part of a port, with joint venture companies partly owned by public sector port and other organisations and partly by private interests;
— Management contracts with private sector companies to operate, for example, container and bulk-handling terminals;
— Leasing arrangements with private sector companies in respect of particular facilities within a port.

The various moves towards greater freedom of action within the public sector of the ports industry (particularly in Europe) have already had a considerable positive effect, not only on operational productivity and profitability, but also on the port maintenance function; increasing awareness of the central role of equipment to operational performance has stimulated improvement in the status of port engineers and in the resources provided for maintenance. It is rather more difficult to generalize about the impact of the various forms of privatization, but the same is probably true. Indeed, privatization has extended directly into the port maintenance field, through contractual arrangements for the maintenance of port equipment by private companies.

2.4 The Exercise of Government Control

2.4.1 Introduction

Central government has a pervasive role in port management in LDCs, as has already been described. Government controls are particularly conspicuous in the management of port maintenance, especially in relation to equipment, and range over many aspects of maintenance, from finance to conditions of employment. For example, in most LDCs, governments involve themselves directly and closely in the procurement process, for equipment and supplies, laying down public sector procedures for the preparation and execution of capital and revenue budgets, in fiscal management and tariff policies, and in employment schemes, manning levels and career structures. The way in which governments apply these controls has a direct influence on the efficiency of port maintenance.

2.4.2 Investment and Investment Controls

2.4.2.1 Institutional Structure and Government Control.

As already noted, there are wide variations in the institutional structure of the ports sector in different countries. Three broad categories of ports can be distinguished in relation to the exercise of government control of investment:

1. In some countries, the ports (whether public or private) are regarded by government as being essentially commercial undertakings, no different from commercial organizations in other sectors of the economy and subject, like those other sectors, to general planning (eg. environmental) controls; there are no controls aimed specifically at the port sector.

2. Elsewhere, ports are administered either as government departments (or as parts of departments) or *as if* they are government departments for capital investment/budgetary control purposes, even where they are nominally separate entities.

3. The largest group of ports are public corporations or 'parastatals'. They are administratively separate from government departments but are subject to port-sector investment and capital budget controls. Within this group, there is wide diversity in the extent and method of application of government control.

Each of these categories will be considered in this section, in relation to the exercise of government control of investment.

2.4.2.2 Ports Treated as Commercial Undertakings

The philosphy of regarding ports as commercial undertakings, without specific port-sector controls on investment or capital budgets, has largely been confined to developed countries so far. It has not spread to LDC ports primarily because of the perceived importance in LDCs of conserving their often scarce capital resources, but also because port development and operation are expected to meet non-commercial objectives of government, for example as part of a national development plan. Conversations with port managers in European ports which experience no governmental investment controls, and comparing their situation with those to which many engineers in LDC ports are subjected, leaves no doubts as to the value of that freedom in procuring equipment and spare parts, and in planning the optimum equipment inventory.

2.4.2.3 Ports Administered as Government Departments

The administration of ports as government departments, or as parts of such departments, is much less common than was formerly the case. Investment decisions in such ports are determined and controlled within the general framework of government accounting and budgetary practices, and within the availability of resources for all sectors of government activity. In one major port of this kind, it is not possible to segregate and cross-relate different port-sector expenditures and revenues from within the accounts of the state authorities concerned; it is difficult to see how the port can be expected to operate within set financial objectives under these circumstances.

In another port of this type, until recently no revenues were retained for the purchase of equipment and spares. Instead, all requests for such purchases were put to the appropriate branch of the Treasury for approval. That branch then decided on the amount of finance that it could provide, in the light of its assessment of priorities and of the availability of resources. Unfortunately, whenever the national financial position was tight, only very limited funds were made available to the port, even though it was (and is) profitable. The difficulties caused to the port by that procedure, whenever it needed to purchase new gantry cranes, straddle carriers and other equipment, as well as spare parts, have been taken into account during a recent general restructuring of the port, and it is now able to set aside reserves for future self-financing.

Tight government controls on many aspects of the activities of yet another port authority have been extremely constraining on the business development of a container terminal, for example. The solution adopted in this instance was to set up an independent company, partly owned by the port authority, partly by a holding company responsible to the Transport Ministry, and partly by other port and related state-owned enterprises. This company is far freer from government control, particularly as regards access to foreign exchange for the purchase of equipment and spares. Furthermore, the company is able to contract out quayside and rubber-tyred gantry crane maintenance to the equipment suppliers – an option that is not open to the port authority. There seems to be a distinct trend in LDCs to follow this route: away from government department status in favour of parastatal corporations with the necessary degree of autonomy to manage their operations and maintenance as they see fit.

2.4.2.4 Public Corporations and Parastatals

The extent and rigidity of government control of investment and capital budgets of the parastatal port authorities tends, not surprisingly, to reflect overall national policies as to the role of centralized planning and as regards flexibility and the detailed control of investment. In many countries, for example, port medium-term investment plans and capital budgets have to be developed in line with (and within the framework of) overall government periodic plans, such as their five-year plans. In addition, the approval of port investment programmes (e.g. for annual capital budgets for equipment purchase) may be affected by macro-economic government policies, such as Public Sector Borrowing Requirements.

The formulation of a five-year (or similar) capital budget starts within the port organization. From there, the plan will pass upwards in different ways in different countries; most commonly it goes through a single government department, but other departments can become involved as relevant to national circumstances. The number of government departments involved varies considerably and, when several different departments have to be involved in turn, the length of time required to approve the port capital budget (possibly with modifications) can be extremely prolonged.

Apart from this, there are very considerable variations in the degree of flexibility permitted to ports in their capital budgeting and in the amending and implementation of their investment programmes. In some countries, port authorities are able to maintain a rolling (typically five-year) capital budget, modified year to year in the light of developments. Elsewhere, the capital budget may be relatively inflexibly constrained within the originally agreed limits of the five-year plan. There may also be a requirement for specific sanction – after detailed examination – of projects within an agreed five-year plan, before their actual implementation is allowed.

On the other hand, there is often a mid-term review of a national five-year plan, and that might provide an opportunity for introducing additional items. The actual extent of such flexibility varies considerably. In one LDC port, the comment was made that requests for additional investment at an interim stage are liable to be met with the response that the port should have thought of that requirement when the five-year plan was originally formulated. Elsewhere, much more flexible policies are followed, and various possibilities exist for the introduction of non-Plan investment – sometimes to a substantial extent. For example, such items might be added to a port's annual capital budget, and approved by the relevant ministry or ministries. In some countries, it is possible for additional capital investments (needed, for example, for urgent commercial reasons) to be authorized at relatively short notice.

2.4.3 The Mechanism of Investment Control

2.4.3.1 Alternative Mechanisms

In principle, port organizations' investment programmes and capital budgets are generally controlled in either or both of two ways: from inside, through the appointment by government of Port Chairmen and Board members (and sometimes of senior management as well); and from outside, by the enactment of appropriate legislation and regulations (such as Ministerial directives) setting out investment and expenditure limits, above which government authorization is required. The nature of, and problems caused by, these control mechanisms are considered in the following paragraphs.

2.4.3.2 Control from Inside

The extent to which governments exert their control over ports from inside the port organization varies from country to country. In some countries, a majority of members of the Boards of port authorities are drawn from the public sector. Commonly, such appointees include one or more civil servants, usually including a representative from the ministry to which the port authority (or other parastatal body) reports; they also include representatives from other ministries or departments, for example those responsible for economic planning and finance.

The implications of civil service membership of the Boards of port parastatals are complex. As far as the control of investment programmes and capital budgets is concerned, much depends on the governmental institutional structures within which the port authority exists, on the organizations from which the civil servants are drawn, and on the seniority of the civil servants concerned.

Some port authorities with civil servants on the Board nevertheless have their proposed investment programmes and capital budgets scrutinized in fine detail by the various ministries concerned. However, the presence of senior civil servants on port boards does also mean that port authorities can shape their initial proposals in the light of likely government reactions, and that the ministries can be fully appraised by their Board representatives of the case for the proposals submitted. In some countries, this does seem to be an advantage: when the port's investment programmes and capital budgets are put forward, they are relatively quickly dealt with.

In one particular country, the process is carried even further: there is civil servant membership of the port authority Finance and Planning Subcommittees which examine all investment and capital budget proposals before they are put up to the Board. This is a double-edged administrative device. On the one hand, it should help ensure that port managers can take early account of likely ministerial reactions, while ministries can likewise be kept informed of port thinking on investment and capital budgets at an early stage; time is saved on both accounts. On the other hand, it does represent a significant extra involvement by civil servants in the direct managerial functions of port authorities.

Any time-saving benefit of having civil servants on port authority Boards is subject to important provisos: the civil servants involved must be of appropriate seniority, have appropriate background and experience, and be from the appropriate ministry or ministries. There are cases where civil servant members of the port authority Board are not from a ministry to which the authority ultimately reports; this is clearly of no help in quickening the passage of investment requests and capital budgets.

2.4.3.3 Control from Outside
There is wide variation, from country to country, in the pattern, flexibility, extent and depth of the control from outside of the investment programmes and capital budgets of port authorities and other parastatals, i.e. in the processing of their investment requirement and capital budget submissions by the ministry or ministries concerned. In some countries there is flexibility with respect both to projects outside (say) a Five-Year Plan and to rolling adjustments to forward capital budgets. Elsewhere, there may be far less flexibility, and there could be requirements for detailed appraisals, perhaps by several branches of government in turn. This imposes a far longer time-scale from the conception of the project to its actual implementation. The implications of inflexible port investment and capital budget controls for port maintenance (and, indeed, for port efficiency and competitiveness as a whole) are so significant that it is worth considering in detail one example of such a control system.

In the country concerned, port investments and capital budgets are determined within the framework of a Five-Year Plan. There is a very long gestation period. Once a port authority has itself decided its future requirements, it has to make a submission to its parent ministry, which considers its proposals conceptually. If agreed, the proposed investment programme is sent to the national planning organization, for consideration in relation to the totality of resource availability and the requirements of other sectors. If it is approved, the programme is then included in the national Five-Year Plan, and the projects involved are then returned to the port for detail to be added, before they are submitted again to the parent ministry for detailed programme appraisal. After this, the investment programme is sent on to a governmental organization responsible for public enterprises, is cleared with the ministry responsible for the control of environmental pollution, goes to the Finance Ministry, returns at high level to the public enterprises organization, and then is submitted to the cabinet. If any foreign equipment is involved in the scheme, there is an extra requirement for yet another organization to check that similar equipment is not produced in the country itself.

This is an almost incredibly involved and very time-consuming process – the epitome of bureaucratic inflexibility. Even if a bid for equipment successfully clears all the hurdles, it can take up to three years from first submission before the port actually obtains the required equipment. It is more than possible, of course, that circumstances will have changed by the time the machines are delivered, almost certain that the technology will have advanced, and inevitable that operators' demand for the equipment will have greatly exceeded, for some considerable time, the engineers' ability to supply.

In that particular country, if new equipment is required (for example, for additional or new traffic) which is not in the Five-Year Plan, it is – theoretically, at least – possible for its purchase to be sanctioned. The necessary resources would have to be found by the parent ministry from under-spending elsewhere in the ports sector, or (failing that) if the national planning organization can find funds from under-spending in other sectors. This is a slow and necessarily problematic procedure, hardly likely to be of much practical help in a situation where new equipment is urgently required to solve a newly-met operational or engineering problem.

2.4.3.4 Consequences of Inflexible Controls
Rigid and inflexible controls of the types described above have a number of direct and indirect consequences arising from the very long lead times between conception of an equipment requirement and its eventual commissioning.

Clearly, if equipment has to be requested several years ahead of its expected requirement, great weight has to be placed on accurate forecasting of needs. Unfortunately (as will be discussed in Chapter 3), long-term accurate forecasting of traffic, vessel types and sizes etc. is difficult, and it is not uncommon for it to fall far short of the accuracy required. Indeed, forecasting is often carried out in departments inappropriate for that task. Ideally, it should fall to personnel with marketing and planning functions – and their assessments should then be given full weight; in one port visited, forecasts produced by the planning department were in effect disregarded.

Where unforeseen traffics do develop, or where traffic grows much more rapidly than expected, the long lead times before new equipment becomes available will inevitably result in shortage of equipment for operators. Existing machines will be heavily used and there is a strong risk of their not being made available for maintenance, leading to rapid deterioration in condition and a further twist to the spiral of equipment problems. Ironically the delays in supply may be so severe that, in the words of one port manager, 'By the time the equipment has arrived, the traffic has gone' – no doubt to a more efficient port!

Where the regulatory constraints lead to long delays in acquiring spare parts (a common problem for engineers in many LDC ports), staff either come to accept the lines of out-of-service equipment outside the workshops or adopt a policy of holding very large stocks of spares. In one port, for example, import licences have to be individually obtained for spares costing more than a very modest amount; true, emergency items *can* be ordered in desperate cases on a 'lightning speed' basis – but this takes four to six weeks! Consequently, the port as a matter of policy holds sufficient spares for between one and two years' needs; when container gantry cranes were acquired, initial spares stocks were laid in to a value of 12.5% of the purchase cost of the cranes. Such stock-holdings impose a considerable capital burden on the port, as well as accommodation and management difficulties for stores personnel. Problems of this type are considered in greater detail in Chapter 7.

Relaxation of government controls on these aspects of equipment and spares management will also improve the efficiency of the maintenance function. Provided that ports prepare an effective equipment plan, approved by government, they should be free to replace existing equipment and purchase new when they need it, and to purchase all necessary spare parts and consumables to keep the equipment in good working order. This implies a significant reduction of present investment controls and of government interference in capital and revenue budgeting in many LDCs.

2.4.4 Aid Finance Projects

LDC Governments have a variety of roles in the financing of port investment, apart from controlling investment from domestic sources. Private sector sources are sometimes involved, either directly (e.g. where shipowners or terminal operators themselves finance the provision of port facilities and/or equipment) or indirectly (funding from commercial banking sources). However, by far the most important bases for the finance of port investment are multilateral funding by the international lending institutions and bilateral funding by foreign governments. Here, too, the national government often has an important regulatory role.

Such international funding may or may not be true aid funding; grants obviously *are* aid, but it is sometimes not easy to distinguish between aid and non-aid loans. Loans from international lending institutions can clearly be classified as 'aid', although some loans ('soft' loans, such as International Development Agency loans) will have a greater aid content than others. It is more difficult to assess the aid nature of bilateral government loans when (as is often the case) they are tied to the provision of resources sourced from the loan-providing country; it is not easy to distinguish between bilateral assistance to an LDC and assistance to the industries of the aid-providing country!

This latter point is relevant to government policy towards aid financing; there can be a danger that, through a bilateral aid arrangement, a national government may be encouraged to accept equipment that is either not needed or not appropriate to the conditions of its ports. It may, for example, be very complex and difficult-to-maintain 'state-of-the-art' equipment; simpler, more robust machines could be preferable. There can also be a standardization problem with tied bilateral aid, as well as when bilateral aid is received from several donor countries. There is a danger that the port will receive a multiplicity of types of equipment from the different donor countries, incompatible in terms of spare parts (with consequent spares and supplies inventory problems) and causing difficulties over the required maintenace skills and related training. These risks may be aggravated where bilateral aid also involves the provision of consultancy tied to the donor country, and where the aid arrangements substantially move control of equipment specifications from the beneficiary port organization to bodies in the donor country.

Governments of countries considering foreign aid for their ports will naturally wish to avoid such problems as far as possible (though not to the extent of foregoing that aid, unless an alternative source is available). A possible solution is for the governments to seek preparatory, independent (untied) consultancy advice as to equipment (or other) requirements. This possibility is discussed again later in the report, and is specifically considered further in Chapter 4.

In any case, the port engineers of the beneficiary countries should try to reduce problems of non-standardization as far as possible, by specifying the use of systems, assemblies and components (motors, engines, spreaders, etc.) that are common with those in existing equipment in the port. This should be possible, even when the aid is firmly tied to equipment manufactured in the donor country. Indeed, this principle of component compatibility (discussed in several later chapters) is probably more realistic – indeed, preferable, in some cases – to one of rigid standardization, whether in the context of aid or not.

There is also a clear need for governments to liaise closely with ports to determine whether equipment offered under an aid scheme is actually what the ports want – and whether they want it under the payment terms offered to them by their national governments. Although it might be assumed that this is always the case, it is far from being so. The port visits revealed several cases of inappropriate equipment being provided (in one case the machines provided on an aid basis were totally unjustified in economic terms) and of the port engineers having to maintain a vast variety of different, incompatible machines supplied under aid. On the other hand, one port authority had actually declined potentially available aid because of unsuitability of the offered equipment for local circumstances.

The exercise of a controlling role by governments extends not only to ensuring that their ports obtain appropriate types of aid-funded equipment but also – and, indeed, in the very first place – to determining aid priorities: between ports and other sectors of the economy; between the different ports sector projects; and between individual port projects. Governments have to make delicate decisions on project choice, bearing in mind that the potential volume of aid is necessarily finite; there is an opportunity cost to the use of aid for any particular purpose, in the foregoing of the opportunity to carry out alternative aid projects. This leads to the question of the internal pricing of aid by national governments to their ports. There is a need to set an appropriate internal price, even for grant aid.

Government practice varies with respect to the difference between borrowing costs (normally government-to-government) and relending charges (government to port). In some countries, especially where the foreign exchange value of the national currency is comparatively strong, there is no difference (or little difference) between government borrowing and relending rates. In other countries, especially where national currencies have been devalued, other arrangements apply. For example, some governments repay loans in the foreign currencies concerned but relend to their ports at fixed interest rates denominated in their own national currencies. Some of the ports visited have undoubtedly benefited from such arrangements (though comparisons are sometimes difficult, for example because moratorium arrangements on foreign loans may not be mirrored in relending schemes). Where this has not been the case (where there have been adverse parity changes and where ports have had to bear interest charges at the prevailing exchange rate), the finances of the ports concerned have undoubtedly been adversely affected.

Either way, adverse changes in external exchange rates can seriously affect the financial position of a beneficiary port. If the port is repaying the current national currency equivalent of their foreign currency denomination interest charges, its liabilities will suddenly increase at the same time as its revenues in foreign currencies are falling. On the other hand, if the port is repaying its government in the national currency, it is the government which is disadvantaged when it repays the full cost in the foreign currency. The problem is not, however, insoluble; possible solutions are considered in Section 2.4.8, in the context of the availability of foreign exchange and related tariff policies.

Aid is not something that should be automatically available to any would-be recipient. Indeed, such free availability can threaten the onset of a dangerous malaise: an attitude of leaving equipment (and, particularly, maintenance) problems unresolved, in the certainty that more machines will arrive from some benevolent source when needed. Such an attitude was certainly observed by the team in one port. Its consequence is poor motivation on the part of the engineers and inefficiency on the part of operators. Equipment tends to be badly maintained and becomes very unreliable; its economic life is short.

Furthermore, there is no point in giving aid to a port if, within a relatively short time, poor maintenance renders useless the equipment provided. It is surely reasonable for aid agreements to have conditionality requirements with regard to the maintenance of equipment. Certainly, there have to be guarantees that foreign exchange will be made available to make possible the continuing and satisfactory maintenance of the equipment. Some aid agreements – bilateral and multilateral – already lay down requirements in this respect, for example stipulating that initial purchases of aid-funded equipment must be accompanied by purchases of spares to the equivalent value of some set percentage of the original equipment cost. This approach has the drawback that it may entail the needless purchase of some spares that will not be required for a long time. A preferable approach (discussed in Section 2.4.8) is to earmark a proportion of the foreign exchange earnings of the port for the purchase of spares, and to keep that earmarked reserve free from all but the most necessary (to prevent malpractice) and trouble-free regulatory controls.

2.4.5 Depreciation

The choice of policies relating to depreciation and the disposal of assets has a vital role in the well-being of port organizations, not least in regard to port maintenance. A realistic depreciation policy helps to ensure that sufficient revenues are set aside to make possible the replacement of port assets (equipment or other) in whatever form may meet demand at the appropriate time in the future. To achieve this, the asset lives used for depreciation purposes should not exceed either the economic or the physical lives of the assets concerned. In fact, shorter depreciation lives are desirable, to leave sufficient margin for unforeseen developments (such as technological or commercial obsolescence) which would affect future demand for those assets or prompt their premature replacement.

If such policies are followed, with necessary flexibility permitted to dispose of assets, then the port can replace its assets whenever it is most appropriate from a cost standpoint, or when it is commercially desirable to introduce a new type of equipment. The costs of continuing to use existing equipment can be regularly compared with that of replacing it with new machines, and decisions to replace can be taken whenever appropriate. This makes possible the sort of flexible and reactive approach to asset disposal adopted by one major Asian port, where ongoing cost-benefit studies have led to a change in policy on forklift truck replacement, favouring truck disposal after five years rather than the six or seven years previously approved.

This is in complete contrast with the position in many ports where excessive depreciation lives are adopted. In one port visited, for example, the economic life of a forklift truck is five years, but the trucks are depreciated over seven years. In this sort of circumstance, various adverse consequences ensue:

— equipment may become uneconomic to use (in terms of running and maintenance costs) and unreliable – and may even have been scrapped,

well before the end of its depreciation life;

— equipment may have become technologically obsolete long before it has been fully depreciated;

— in spite of those realities, the port may follow rigid conventions which make it almost impossible to replace that equipment before the end of its depreciation life.

Apart from setting appropriate depreciation lives, a sound depreciation policy requires the adoption of a suitable basis for depreciation. Historic cost depreciation is still common, but often reflects monetary conditions which no longer prevail. Essentially, its use pre-supposes no fall in value of the national currency, either in terms of international purchasing power or in relation to relevant foreign currencies. Whenever this is not the case (and it frequently is not), there are strong grounds for replacement cost depreciation; use of this basis is, indeed, increasing.

Replacement cost depreciation has a number of advantages in relation to port maintenance:

1. Its use helps to make available the necessary resources to replace assets when required.

2. Its use also inevitably initially depresses apparent port profitability; this may, in fact, be beneficial in indicating that the port's earnings are insufficient to finance capital replacement, pointing to the need for improved earnings through, for example, higher port tariffs.

3. In many countries, there are rigid controls over at least some types of port charges (in the wider sense, i.e. including port dues), and port tariff revision may only be permitted at long intervals; when this happens, the real cost of port facilities to users inevitably falls in relation to the rise in other prices (particularly if the national currency is devalued against foreign currencies). In such a situation, the use of replacement cost depreciation ensures that the port continues to put aside sufficient monies to be able to continue to provide modern and efficient port facilities.

In contrast to the widespread rigidity of controls on port charges, government controls on ports' depreciation policies are generally relaxed – apart, of course, from the implications of any general national depreciation regulations in respect of taxation. Indeed, ports are often given wide latitude, subject perhaps to the approval of (say) the auditor-general or of a government-appointed auditor, and of any officials (e.g. from the Ministry of Finance) on their Boards. One port authority reported that its tax authorities were actually encouraging the use of shorter depreciation lives, specifically to encourage regular re-equipment and modernization.

Port authorities also often have wide latitude – at least in theory – in the disposal of their assets. In practice, however, time-consuming bureaucratic procedures often have to be completed before assets can be disposed of, seeming almost to be designed to *prevent* disposal happening. One port authority visited has (and admits to having) a large stock of old, unserviceable and even derelict equipment, but has not managed to dispose of any assets for more than seven years.

2.4.6 Budgets

The exercise of government control over capital budgets was discussed in Section 2.4.1. As far as revenue budgets and the control of expenditure on revenue items generally are concerned, there are differences between those ports operated as part of government departments and the other types of port organization. Where a port is operated as part of a ministry, then its budgeting process forms part of that of the ministry's; indeed, administrative procedures may require ministry authorization even for relatively small expenditures.

Apart from ports still in that category, government control over revenue budgets is usually only gently exercised. Public sector ports may have to submit their budgets to the ministries to which they report (eg. Transport or Communications) but not to ministries of Finance, Economics or Planning. Ministries may possibly query individual items, but generally the process is a trouble-free formality. Where ports have ministerial representatives on their Boards, they will in any case watch the interests of their ministries and keep them appraised.

Where ports are run by effectively autonomous bodies – even, perhaps, public corporations without any government representatives on their Board – the exercise of governmental control is likely to be minimal. More and more, the general principle is that autonomous ports should be left to run themselves – a principle that seems to have greatly assisted the successful operation of the more commercially profitable ports.

2.4.7 Port Charges

Many of the maintenance difficulties experienced in LDC ports arise from a shortage of funds, particularly of foreign exchange, for the purchase of vital supplies and rigid governmental constraints on overseas purchases. A major cause of ports' inability to finance such purchases themselves is that governments prevent them reviewing and, where appropriate, raising their tariffs to provide sufficient revenues; fear of inflation is usually given as the reason for such controls on port charges. Of course, ports may also wish to reduce their charges, to attract new business and to retain existing customers; here, too, rigid controls can make it very difficult for a port to respond to commercial pressures.

In many countries, there is a long tradition of governmental control of port charges, particularly those regarded as a port-imposed tax for the use of port facilities – ship dues, harbour dues, wharfage, etc. The situation has been changing recently in some countries (but not, unfortunately, in LDCs), and there is now a far higher degree of freedom with regard to the control of charges. This is largely due to the strong inter-port competition that now exists; there is less need for control, when ports have to keep charges down to remain competitive, and there may often be an urgent need to reduce charges to meet the challenge from nearby ports and to attract new business, e.g. transshipment traffic.

The trend towards increased freedom to set charges has, however, been very uneven. In some ports, freedom is total (subject, possibly, to user appeal) but at the other extreme it may take five years or more for a port charges proposals to be accepted, and changes in ship dues and wharfage still have to be gazzetted. Sometimes, however, there has been some relaxation, for example as to the granting of rebates, and some ports have also circumvented (legally) statutory controls on charges by consolidating such charges with other, non-controlled charges. Elsewhere, transshipment charges have been freed from control for competitive reasons, while control has been retained over certain charges deemed to be of national significance; for example, charges have been held down on imported foodstuffs and on exports.

The pattern of government control over charges varies. In some countries, complex bureaucratic processes prolong the making of decisions, with serious consequences on competitiveness. For example, when a particular port had to wait six months for a decision on a request for a reduction to attract major new business, while a rival port was able to make an immediate decision, that business was, not unnaturally, lost. Where government departments are represented on port Boards, such delays are inexcusable, and liaison over changes in charges policies should be close. Indeed, many ports are now required to do little more than to inform (say) the Ministry of Finance of a proposed change. Nevertheless, some ports are still subject to very tight control, largely because of the fear of the inflationary impact of higher charges.

Sometimes, paradoxical situations arise. In one country, wharfage charges (affecting the costs of both imports and exports) are charged on a value basis, so immediately reflect and accentuate any changes in the value of imported goods, whereas the charges payable by ship operators (ship dues, stevedoring charges) have remained unchanged since 1984.

Some ports have changed the basis of certain of their charges onto a foreign currency (in practice US dollar) basis. There are two reasons for this. When national currencies are devaluing against foreign currencies, the revenue from port charges in foreign exchange terms is decreasing. While this benefits foreign shipowners, the port's own foreign costs (e.g. for equipment and spares) are increasing in terms of its national currency. This is obviously unsatisfactory from the port's standpoint. If, however, charges are levied in foreign currency, the port doubly gains – in terms of its revenues (calculated in its own national currency) and of its foreign exchange earnings for the country concerned. This second factor may be beneficial, too, in improving its own access to foreign exchange, either directly (by some form of retention) or indirectly (by being helped to make its case to the relevant national authority for the allocation of foreign currency).

Some governments have permitted such denomination of specified port charges in foreign currencies (charges such as ship dues, stevedoring charges and landside charges payable by transit traffics), but others have not, even though such pricing is likely to have only helpful consequences. One government has declined to give the necessary consent, although pressed by its ports to allow it, allegedly because it fears that it would lead to pressure from the ports to earmark foreign currency earnings for their use.

2.4.8 Foreign Exchange

Foreign exchange constraints can directly affect port maintenance in several ways. Firstly, the procurement of spare parts and other essential supplies may be prevented by lack of availability of foreign exchange. Secondly, even if foreign currency is not totally unavailable, the lengthy process of obtaining authorization for its release can badly delay the acquisition of supplies. Thirdly, foreign exchange constraints can severely delay the purchase of new equipment, so necessitating the extended use of equipment that should be replaced and the over-use of equipment in short supply; both these factors increase the pressure on port engineers and their resources.

This is such a serious problem in some ports that it has led to two related developments. First, certain port charges (those payable or largely payable by foreign interests, e.g. ship operators) have been levied in foreign currencies; this has helped the ports to earn additional foreign currency, helping their case for the allocation of such currency. Secondly, a few governments have allowed ports to spend up to a certain proportion of their foreign currency earnings in foreign exchange; in other words, part of the ports' overseas earnings have been earmarked for use in the procurement of equipment and spares overseas.

The earmarking of foreign exchange can take various forms. For example, it can involve the lodging of monies in a special account on which the port can draw. One port is allowed to have 50% of its foreign exchange earnings lodged in a London account; this is a 'rolling' account so there is no undue pressure to spend all the funds within a particular accounting year. Another port organization – a commercialized, private-sector-type organization, albeit wholly owned by public sector interests – is permitted to spend up to 70% of its foreign exchange earnings (interestingly, the port authority in the same port does not share that privilege).

The benefits of earmarked foreign currency funds are clear: they make it unnecessary for the port to make a time-consuming case to the appropriate authorities, in competition with all other possible uses, for each release of foreign currency. This is a vital consideration in relation to spares and other maintenance supplies. It is, after all, in the national interest for there to be a quick and easy flow of spares to the ports, and this becomes clearly apparent when the port, by charging in foreign currency, can demonstrate the extent of its foreign earnings. Even where the port is not allowed to retain foreign earnings in a earmarked fund, it can make good use of a knowledge of those earnings. For example, one port authority keeps a very careful tally of all its foreign currency earnings and loses no opportunity to inform relevant ministers and civil servants of the extent of those earnings. It then has little difficulty in getting clearance for almost unrestricted access to foreign exchange – and not just for spares; typically, 75% of its capital budget is accounted for by foreign exchange costs, largely for equipment.

Present foreign exchange retention schemes are not well structured and often have inadequate control mechanisms. For example, in the case cited above of the port allowed to retain 50% of its foreign exchange earnings, those particular monies can only be spent on spares, and not on equipment; central bank approval is required for all use of the funds, to ensure that they are not used for purchases falling outside the definition of 'spares'. While the principle of such an account is admirable, it is justifiable to question the size of the fund for that restricted purpose, particularly as the port earns a considerable amount as foreign currency – about $34 million in 1987. Furthermore, not only does it *not* release the port from having to go through time-consuming administrative procedures before it can use the account, but the fund is also open to frequent 'raids' by government.

So, while this study supports the policy of quoting part of the port tariff in foreign exchange and allowing the port to retain a proportion of the related revenues for the purchase of vital resources and services overseas, it suggests that the use of an earmarked account should be subject to certain conditions:

1. The fund should be usable and sufficient for

   — the purchase of all prescribed spare parts and other vital consumable materials from overseas, to ensure that existing equipment can be maintained to full operating specification;

   — enabling the refurbishment of equipment to be carried out as appropriate;

   — replacing assets that have reached the end of their economic lives, as specified in the equipment plan approved by government;

   — for investing in new equipment (again as approved in the equipment plan) to meet growing or changing demands of the port's traffic and to continue to supply operators' requirements.

2. The level of the foreign exchange fund should be set at a level that

   — represents a realistic target, based on careful preparation of revenue budgets;

   — includes inducement for managers to exercise good cost control procedures;

   — includes provision for contingencies and serious unforeseen occurrences.

3. The management of the fund should

   — make the port responsible for administering the account, but with means of allowing its inspection by officials of the Central Bank or Ministry of Finance;

   — allow the port to prepare a prescribed list of spare parts, approved by the Central Bank, and to be able to import these free of further government import controls;

   — not allow it to be used for any non-prescribed item or for the purchase of items not concerned with port maintenance or equipment management.

2.4.9 Procurement

The extent and patterns of government controls on procurement vary from country to country, and with the type of port organization; at one extreme the port is completely free to purchase as it wishes, and at the other it is completely controlled by government rules.

For example, governments often preclude state-owned port organizations from purchasing direct from foreign suppliers, whereas an autonomous port may buy direct and use its own foreign currency immediately to do so. In one port, the container terminal operating company can buy direct from overseas while the port authority can only buy through local agents. These can be either public-sector, in which case the authority has to go through a bureaucratic procedure via an inter-ministerial committee (involving four ministries) and taking four months to obtain the necessary foreign exchange (if, indeed, granted) or it can purchase through local agents, using their own foreign exchange and paying a higher price.

Other government regulations may require ports to purchase the cheapest available product, or allowances may be made for qualitative, life-cycle-cost, standardization and other factors. 'Cheapest first-cost' rules obviously have implications for product life and maintenance costs, and possibly also for (non-)standardization. Even when such a requirement is not rigidly laid down, there may be psychological pressures to buy cheapest, unless the port can give a very convincing reason why an alternative product should be chosen.

In some ports, managers who wish to avoid these problems do so by minutely detailing the technical specification when preparing tender documents, so that only one or two acceptable machines fit the description exactly. Even this is not permitted in some countries, and the only remedy allowed is for engineers to make it clear to would-be suppliers that certain systems, components or assemblies should be compatible with equipment already standard within the port.

In the context of competitive purchasing, there will commonly be regulations specifying the circumstances under which port organizations are free to buy items 'off the shelf', by obtaining quotations or by going out to tender. Usually, if this is the case, the appropriate procedure to use is determined by cost levels. Tendering is not only time-consuming but also threatens the port's standardization or compatibility aims and so, in some ports, there is provision to apply to the relevant government body for waiving of the tendering requirement under certain circumstances. Often, however, procurement regulations are rigidly enforced and must be seen to be so, to the extent that, in at least one country, port tender boards cannot sit without a representative from the Ministry of Finance.

There may also be specific regulations on the procurement of imported equipment. In one country, for example, imports of more than a very small value not only require foreign exchange allocation but must also first be approved by a government organization which checks whether that type of equipment is manufactured in the country; if it is, import is almost certain to be refused. Apart from adding yet more delay to a long-drawn-out process, this can lead to standardization problems; a port may be allowed to import a foreign machine on one occasion but later applications to add to the fleet may be disallowed.

In a variant of this regulation in another country, ports can import equipment only if its cost – including import duty – is at least 20% lower than the cost of domestically produced alternatives. In certain countries, too, counter-trading may also be relevant in sourcing of imports and, in one case, if the port does not wish (or is not able) to import equipment on a potential counter-trade basis, it has to obtain a Treasury waiver. Counter-trading regulations can also, of course, cause problems of standardization.

A final illustration of the degree to which governments can regulate procurement involves restriction of supplier. In one country, Treasury circulars list the only agents and companies permitted to supply particular types of equipment. All suppliers must be firms registered in that country, and even so there are two lists – nationals and non-nationals – and there is more than a suspicion that approval of equipment purchase is easier via one list than the other.

In summary, it is clear that there are many reasons why a port may be found to be equipped with an odd assortment of cargo-handling and other machines, often incompatible and not ideally suitable for the jobs in hand. It is tempting to assume that the inventory is a consequence of less than well-thought-out planning on the part of its senior managers, but in many cases government regulations and controls have much to do with the situation, and are at least partly responsible for the consequential operational and engineering problems.

Nevertheless, procurement procedures need to be reviewed (see Chapter 4) to identify ways in which they might currently be contributing to excessive demands on maintenance and to the purchasing of equipment which is, in the long run, not best suited to the port's operating and maintenance capabilities. Present buying practices, such as the use of local agents and restrictions on importation, should also be critically examined.

2.4.10 Employment

The exercise of government control over employment in port organizations is usually external, in the form of the setting of the establishment framework in the ports, the determination of systems of promotion and career advancement, of salary scales and of pension arrangements. Governments may also, however, intervene directly in the appointment of chief executives and even, sometimes, of other jobholders. In certain ports, governments also intervene directly in personnel matters, through committees within the port authority. Some examples of these controls are discussed in this section, while the wider area of manpower development matters is considered in Chapter 8.

The appointment of port chief executives may be carried out on the proposal of port chairmen (and Boards, if relevant), subject to the agreement of the Minister responsible for the ports sector, or it may be carried out directly and solely by the Minister. In addition, the appointment of other senior jobholders may be determined by, or subject to the approval of, the Ministry concerned. In some countries, port chief executives may be chosen from outside the ports industry, and may (for example) be – and remain – civil servants.

The efficiency of the port organizations (and specifically of their engineering departments) can be markedly affected by the pattern of government control of employment; among these forms of control are the following:

1. It is widely the practice for public sector ports to have to adhere either to the same pay scales as those for government and related public sector organizations or to broadly similar ones. This often means that pay rates are below those in comparable positions in the private sector, making port management and technical posts markedly less attractive than those in competing engineering (particularly electronic engineering) companies. There may be compensatory factors, however, such as greater job security, and fringe benefits in the form of subsidized housing, for example. In at least one country, port employees pay no income tax!

2. The basis of promotion is commonly very different in the public and private sectors. There is, for example more stress on seniority in the public service and on merit and performance in the private sector.

3. There is sometimes a difference in the pension structure; in one country, port employees are in pension schemes linked solely to the one port authority for which they work and cannot transfer even to other port authorities in the same country. This is obviously a bar to job mobility. In the private sector of that country, employees contribute to a Provident Fund, which is not tied to any one employer. Portability of pensions is likely to add to the attractiveness of private-sector jobs to the more ambitious personnel, as do the better pay-scales and promotion arrangements.

4. In some ports, the shortcomings of public-sector port employment are aggravated by policies which limit career prospects. For example, it may not be possible for an employee to gain promotion by transferring from one port to another in the same country. In some ports, too, engineers are particularly penalized by career schemes which effectively exclude them from higher positions in general management. Such constraints can all too easily lead to vacancies in middle management, to demoralization of good engineers already in post and to lack of good quality management.

5. Although it is not easy to formulate incentives to encourage good maintenance practices and performance, it can be done (as is demonstrated in a few of the ports visited). However, public service regulations may not allow incentives to be awarded, whereas private-sector organizations regularly apply incentive schemes to get the best out of their employees. Indeed, in one country a port subsidiary of a public-sector holding company relies on a bonus scheme to circumvent the desperately low, controlled basic salaries (kept to national public-sector scales); in effect, the 'incentive scheme' is used to make the organization's pay competitive.

6. Public sector regulations can also affect performance and output in other ways. One country has a general public service directive restricting the number of hours any employee may work in a week, including overtime. Port authorities sometimes have to exceed such figures (if ship turnround demands it, for example), but must then be prepared to justify those excess hours either to the public service department or to auditors.

These and the other employment regulations do little to assist LDC ports in improving their recruitment, management and staff quality or operational and engineering performance. This report favours considerable easing of those controls, particularly with respect to factors encouraging initiative, skill and achievement at all levels of the organization.

Governments and senior port managements must improve employee accountability and personal discipline. All employees must be made responsible for their actions, and enterprise and initiative must be rewarded. This will involve altering the present rigid terms and conditions of employment and introducing appropriate incentive schemes. Changes in institutional and organizational arrangements are essential, to create a climate conducive to a far more dynamic and responsible management, to encourage initiative and innovation, and to develop greater efficiency and professionalism in the engineers responsible for port maintenance.

2.4.11 Complexity of Control

This section has demonstrated the very wide variations that exist in the degree and nature of governmental controls and regulations on ports and their activities. Observations made during this study leave the team in no doubt that the most successful ports, worldwide, are those experiencing the absolute minimum of government control and interference, while among the least successful – commercially, operationally and engineering-wise – are those on which the tightest governmental controls are imposed. Autonomy does appear to be functionally associated with commercial success.

Even where port organizations are not very autonomous, and where fuller autonomy is not realistically likely in the near future, it is possible to devise methods of exercising government control that are less onerous and certainly less time-consuming than is commonly the case. And time is, of course, of the essence, particularly when operators are so reliant on equipment and the maintenance function is so dependent on access to new equipment and spares. Some of the complex procurement and investment control procedures could well be streamlined to the considerable benefit of the port, allowing inventory levels to be reduced, time waiting for spares to be shortened and equipment availability and operating performance to be thereby improved.

Such simplifications should seek to reduce the number of different bodies that have to be approached, and to speed up the transmission and dissemination of documents to the few bodies still involved. It is much better for a port to have to deal directly with just one parent ministry than with several ministries, and particularly helpful if that ministry can then deal simultaneously and rapidly with any other ministries or departments that might have to be consulted. In one country, for example, the Ministry of Transport sensibly forwards duplicate documents simultaneously to the government's Planning Unit and to the Ministry of Finance.

Just as important as the streamlining of the procedures is the improvement of the authorizing processes, which is a matter of the quality and attitude of the government and civil service officials who ultimately handle the documents and submissions. The relevant departments must, at least, have sufficient staff to handle the quantity of work coming from the ports. Those staff must also have the appropriate skills, qualifications, experience and interest to assess the submissions intelligently and sympathetically, and to advise their ministers accordingly. They must appreciate that it is their function to assist the ports in handling the country's overseas trade as efficiently and profitably as possible, and not to impede that aim by applying regulations in the most restrictive and obstructive manner. If the ports cannot be given greater autonomy, then control must be practised wisely and well.

2.5 Recommendations

1. The governments of LDCs must review their present institutional and organizational arrangements, particularly as they affect the port maintenance function; they must not present barriers to the establishment of effective maintenance policies and strategies.

2. The working relationship between ports and central government must be improved, and regulatory and administrative procedures streamlined.

3. The efficiency of the maintenance function should be improved by operating ports as commercial enterprises that are market orientated and able to respond quickly to users' requirements.

4. The relevant ministry within central government must prepare an appropriate set of financial and performance objectives for all seaports under its administration, and must then ensure that senior port managers are fully aware of these objectives and of the need to pursue them single-mindedly.

5. The financial objectives, which should be reviewed periodically, must represent realistic targets, to encourage managers to strive constantly to improve port efficiency.

6. The performance of the port as a whole, and of its senior managers, should be monitored by government officials and assessed against the set targets, but they should interfere only if the targets are not met.

7. The port authority should prepare its own corporate objectives, taking into account the port's commercial, economic and operating conditions, and then should draw up specific objectives for each of its departments, ensuring that the principle of accountability permeates throughout the organization.

8. A clear set of performance and financial targets must be set for the Operations and Engineering Departments, and senior managers must establish monitoring procedures to see that these targets are achieved.

9. Where independent public companies operate in the port under government control, they should also be set realistic objectives.

10. Ports must be given greater autonomy and freedom to manage their own affairs, by relaxation of government controls, while still retaining sufficient government control to protect the national interest.

11. The financial objectives and fiscal treatment regime imposed on ports must not be burdensome, but must allow adequate reserves to be generated to allow replacement of assets when economically justified.

12. Depreciation schedules for civil works, plant and equipment must be realistically related to operating conditions and asset lives in the country; consideration should be given to applying depreciation on a replacement-cost basis.

13. Ports should be able to replace assets on economic grounds and be given investment freedom to develop an inventory of equipment which meets customers' needs.

14. Port assets should be revalued frequently, to provide a reliable means of measuring financial performance.

15. Greater freedom should be given to ports to revise tariff structures and levels so as to produce sufficient revenues to keep assets in good working condition and to replace them when necessary.

16. Ports should be allowed to set their revenue budgets without direct government interference.

17. LDC ports should be free to quote appropriate sections of their tariffs in foreign currency, as a protection against currency devaluations and to maintain revenue levels *vis-à-vis* overseas trading partners.

18. Given the economic and strategic importance of ports to the national economy, and the amount of foreign exchange they can – and do – earn, they should be allowed to retain sufficient funds in foreign currencies to replace assets and to keep the asset inventory in good condition.

19. Ports should not be required to bear the entire foreign exchange risks of externally sourced loans or grants which are re-lent at higher interest rates; such loans should be expressed in a basket of foreign currencies to protect against exchange rate fluctuations.

20. Provided that ports prepare an effective equipment plan, approved by government, they should be free to replace existing equipment and purchase new equipment when they need to.

21. There should be a reduction in present investment controls and government interference in capital budgeting for equipment and spare parts.

22. Flexibility must be introduced to speed up equipment planning and decision making.

23. Greater care should be exercised to ensure that equipment and other technical services provided as part of aid-financed projects are actually needed, and that they are appropriate to conditions in the port; independent and untied consultancy should be sought in such cases.

24. Procurement procedures need to be reviewed to identify ways in which they might currently be contributing to excessive demands on maintenance and to the purchasing of equipment which is, in the long run, not best suited to the port's operating and maintenance capabilities.

25. Present buying practices, such as the use of local agents and restrictions on importation, should be critically reviewed.

26. Government and senior port managers must improve employee accountability and personal discipline; all employees must be made responsible for their actions, and enterprise and initiative must be rewarded.

27. Ports should introduce improved career patterns, promotion prospects, salary levels, and other benefits and incentives, to encourage individuals' initiative, skill and achievement at all levels in the organization.

28. Changes in institutional and organizational arrangements are essential to create a climate conducive to a far more dynamic and responsible management, to encourage initiative and innovation, and to develop greater efficiency and professionalism in the engineers responsible for port maintenance.

CHAPTER 3

Planning the Port Inventory

3.1 The Need for an Equipment Plan

The primary reason for preparing – and using – an equipment plan is to ensure that the port always has an adequate inventory of equipment, of all types, to meet operational requirements. Operations staff must have access to the right types of equipment, of the right capacity and in sufficient numbers, to meet cargo-handling needs and to achieve their operational performance targets. The importance of such a plan has increased greatly as the degree of mechanization and dependence on equipment for cargo-handling have increased, and as break-bulk cargoes have progressively been replaced by unit loads. The growth in inter-port competition has led to a very strong emphasis on cargo-handling productivity and quality of service to customers – again increasing dependence on equipment when meeting corporate and financial objectives. The principle of planning applies also to marine equipment needs, of course – indeed, to all items in the port's asset inventory – but the problems are without doubt most acute for cargo-handling equipment, and it is on those assets that this chapter will largely, and justifiably, concentrate.

Planning future equipment requirements has become more complex because of the growing range of plant and machinery available for handling cargo and the rapid evolution in engineering design, equipment performance and specification. Further complicating factors have been the commercial and technical changes in shipping and international seaborne trade, such as changes of routes and developments in ship size and design. Again, equipment operating and maintenance costs have contributed more and more to cargo-handling charges, and the economics of owning increasingly expensive equipment has had a growing influence on ports' financial performance. All these factors combine to strengthen the case for devoting greatly increased management attention to the formulation of an effective equipment plan. Failure to develop such a plan will, as explained in Chapters 1 and 2, lead to operators not having the equipment they need, cargo-handling efficiency falling, and the port's reputation and commercial success being endangered.

The equipment plan is a crucial element in the port's corporate plan and is of particular value in formulating the annual capital budget. It must be an important consideration in port strategic planning. The significance of equipment in the financial management of seaports is well illustrated by the fact that one of the ports visited during this study spends about $50 million a year, out of its average annual capital budget of $150 million, on cargo-handling equipment alone. Other ports confirmed the growing importance of equipment acquisition and replacement in their capital and development budgets and the increasing proportion of their resources devoted to equipment. The growth in investment in equipment, at a time of capital rationing and cash-flow limits, makes it essential to prepare (and implement) a good equipment plan. This chapter, then, deals with the preparation of an equipment plan. It reviews planning procedures and proposes a model for the preparation process. By way of introduction, it first considers the nature of the investment decision and the alternative forms of investment.

3.2 The Investment Decision

3.2.1 The Importance of the Decision to Invest

The decision to purchase cargo-handling equipment for a port is a critically important management function. It is not just the level of the initial investment that is at stake but the recurring operating and maintenance costs throughout the life of the unit. Only if all the relevant factors are evaluated in this phase of the planning process is it likely that the port's stock of equipment will meet the operators' needs and that the overall least-cost solution has been achieved.

The extent of recent innovation in the equipment manufacturing industry has increased the rate of obsolescence and the degree of risk attached to the investment decision; when technological change is rapid, a great deal of background research and detailed pre-investment study is called for. The level of competition in the port transport industry increases the uncertainty over future market share and resulting demand for services – another element of risk. Other factors which contribute to the complexity of the investment decision are the total costs of the equipment package and its degree of technological sophistication. External factors such as international and national inflation rates, foreign exchange rates, investment incentives and the financial conditions attached to bilateral and multilateral aid or loan packages, can all add their influences to the decision and help to shape the environment in which the equipment plan is prepared.

The decision to invest in capital equipment is taken under one or more of the following circumstances:

— To acquire new types of equipment (or machines of different capacity or design to existing types), to meet the needs of new trades or changing commodity packaging;

— To add to the existing stock of equipment (with machines identical or very similar to existing ones), to handle an increasing volume of traffic;

— To replace existing equipment which is no longer economic to run, has been superceded by better equipment or has reached the end of its physical life.

Each of these investment decisions provides a different environment for the planning process, presenting differing degrees of risk and uncertainty, and resulting in varying amounts of research and preparatory work for the planning team. Before considering the steps in the preparation of the equipment plan, it is worth looking in rather more detail in the next three sections at these three circumstances in which equipment is purchased.

3.2.2 Investment in New Types of Equipment
The decision on buying equipment of a type new to the port, to meet the needs of new traffic, usually arises at the time of a major development programme, involving substantial investment in civil works (construction of new berths or terminals, or adaptation of existing berths) as well as the purchase of cargo-handling equipment. For example, one current new port development project involves a total expenditure of about $500 million, of which cargo-handling equipment (for bulk and container terminals) accounts for about $150 million. In the average development project, equipment investment typically represents about 30% of the total cost – an enormous single outlay.

If a port is constructing a new container terminal, the choice of handling system will have to be made early in the planning process, as it will directly influence terminal design and layout. Procedures and time schedules will be established for decisions on selection of equipment, tendering procedures and practices, evaluation, delivery and commissioning phases, to ensure that the equipment is on site, tested and ready to run when the terminal opens. The planners' duty is to ensure that arrival of the equipment does not cause delay in the opening of the terminal. In other words, the problem with planning for new types of equipment under these circumstances is deciding what type of equipment, and how many units, to buy, and not *when*. Only in cases where a change in traffic on an existing berth or terminal is gradual will there be an element of 'when' about the decision to buy new types of equipment.

So the decision on when to buy *new types* of equipment is sometimes easier than deciding when to *replace* equipment or to *expand* the present stock. Both of those decisions involve consideration of the level of demand for particular types of equipment and a thorough knowledge of the costs of owning and operating them. They are very important decisions (about 50% of all corporate investment is related to replacement) and rely heavily on a comprehensive and reliable Management Information System (see Chapter 9), monitoring the performance of existing equipment and recording full operating, maintenance and cost data for each unit of the port's equipment stock.

3.2.3 Expansion of the Existing Stock of Equipment
The constant objective of the port must be to ensure that its stock of equipment meets operational requirements, in terms of cargo to be handled and the nature of the work to be performed at the berths and terminals. That objective is not easy to achieve, because of the many different types of machine needed, the large number of units, the maintenance schedules that have to be met, and the possibility of unexpected breakdowns. A great deal of information is needed, on the current inventory, equipment performance, maintainability and reliability, and predicted future demand, if an appropriate decision on investment is to be taken – and that information has to be carefully interpreted. Nevertheless, it is essential for the port to plan the purchase of equipment and attachments to meet future demand: how much additional equipment will be needed, of what type, and when.

40

3.2.4 Equipment Replacement

The decision on when to replace existing plant or equipment is frequently encountered by port managers. The physical deterioration of equipment, due to wear and tear, making it unreliable and expensive to operate and maintain, inevitably means that it will some day have to be replaced. It may not necessarily be replaced by another machine of the same type, of course; design and manufacturing developments may mean that a newer design or model will perform more economically than existing machines, or could cost less to maintain.

Replacement decisions are more complex than those concerning expansion or new investment, primarily because they involve the sale, redeployment or scrapping of existing equipment. They therefore require very careful analysis. Regrettably, surveys of industry practice (Merret & Sykes, 1966) show that these decisions are often taken on the basis of inadequate data and selection criteria, and after applying poor investment appraisal techniques. Usually, cargo-handling operators initiate a request for new equipment when existing machines can no longer perform the particular cargo-handling tasks they were designed and purchased for; operating performance is the key factor, rather than an established financial policy or equipment plan. This is not surprising, given the usually poor maintenance record in many developing countries – the physical lives of equipment are often short, and machines have to be scrapped prematurely. In most cases, then, there is no feasible alternative but to scrap and replace, if the port is to be kept working. In a well-run port, however, the decision to replace, refurbish or overhaul should be based on a proper cost-effectiveness analysis of the equipment, its operating costs, and the cost-benefit of replacing or adding to the stock; the economic life should be the criterion, not its physical life.

The decision to replace existing equipment is taken for one or more of three reasons:

1. **Physical Failure:** The performance of all machines deteriorates with age and use, particularly in extreme climates and difficult operating conditions. Despite good maintenance, at some stage in its life the equipment will no longer be able satisfactorily and safely to perform its duties. For example, a quayside crane may, as a result of metal fatigue, have to be de-rated, i.e. it will no longer be capable of lifting the necessary loads. Under such circumstances, if the port is to continue to provide a safe and reliable service to users, equipment will need to be replaced.

2. **Reduced Efficiency:** Management often finds it beneficial to replace a unit of equipment while it is still in working order because, as it gets older, it becomes more and more expensive to run, through increased maintenance and operating costs. For example, the fuel consumption of a forklift truck rises as it gets older, and the major overhauls it needs and the increasing costs of repairing breakdowns may result in very high operating costs. It then becomes more economic to replace the machine than to keep it.

3. **Obsolescence:** Innovation, spurred on by competition in the equipment manufacturing industry and supported by research and development, has led to the increasingly frequent appearance of new and improved models, capable of performing more economically and effectively than their predecessors. As a consequence, it can be sensible to replace, by an improved type, a machine that has years of good working life left in it, to obtain lower unit cargo-handling costs.

In most of the LDC ports visited, the replacement decision (where there was a coherent policy) was taken solely on the basis of the *physical* condition of equipment. The physical life – that period during which the machine is capable of performing to specification – is clearly dependent on wear and tear in use and on the quality of the maintenance and repair services provided in the port. The physical life is at an end when the equipment can no longer operate and perform the duties for which it was purchased. However, this is invariably far too late, as it fails to take into account running and maintenance costs, performance efficiency and reliability. The replacement decision *should* be based on the *economic life* of the equipment (also called its Minimum Cost Life or Optimum Replacement Interval) – the period in which the average annual total costs (of ownership, running and maintenance) are minimal, and comparable and competitive with those of alternative replacement machines (procedures for evaluating the total costs involved in such investment are discussed in Section 3.5.10). Clearly, the rate of innovation in the industry – the obsolescence factor – will considerably influence the length of the economic life of existing machines. In practice, of course, the physical and economic lives are closely linked; as a machine ages, the cost of maintaining and running it rises and a replacement becomes an increasingly attractive option, even taking into account the capital investment involved.

3.2.5 Investment Decision Uncertainty

Although these three general categories of investment decision can be described, it is not always easy to distinguish them in practice – they tend to grade one into the other. This is likely to be increasingly the case, in fact, as engineering design and port traffic developments accelerate; even buying nominally the same type of equipment could, over the period of two or three years between successive purchases, generate the same sort of uncertainties over performance, maintenance and costs as a completely new type of machine. However, these purchasing environments do illustrate some of the difficulties encountered in equipment planning and justify the establishment of a formal planning procedure and framework. It is appropriate next to consider the planning procedures that exist in ports at present.

3.3 Present Planning Procedures

3.3.1 Planning Horizons

Most of the seaports visited and responding to the questionnaire reported that they apply some means of predicting and planning future cargo-handling and other equipment requirements. Three distinct contexts within which equipment planning takes place were identified during the study: as a response to a government-imposed five-year plan; as a contribution to the port's own medium-term plan (covering two to five years); and as a component of the port's annual plan. Although the time horizons may be different, the activities are complementary, and two or three of them may be current at a time. The three contexts are considered in turn in the following sections.

3.3.2 Government Five-Year Plans

In developing countries central planning of economic development is practised to a marked extent. The governments of most of the developing countries visited generally prepare five-year plans for all sectors of the economy (as discussed in Chapter 2). The transport sector features prominently in these plans, with proposals for major new port development projects, including the acquisition of plant and machinery. Senior port managers prepare forecasts of equipment needs for inclusion in these plans, which subsequently are taken as guidelines for the port's investment strategy.

3.3.3 Port Medium-term Plans

The second common planning practice is to develop medium-term plans (covering periods of two to

five years) for the port itself. There is a high level of unanimity among ports in both developed and developing countries in formulating five-year equipment plans. What distinguishes these procedures from the national plans is the fact that they concentrate on the acquisition of equipment to extend or replace assets in the port's current inventory, rather than taking a wider view of the country's economic development. Two sorts of five-year plans can be distinguished: one where the beginning and end of the period are fixed dates (e.g. a 1988-1992 plan) and the other a 'revolving' or 'rolling' plan, revised year by year and always covering the following five years. In both types, the first year can be planned in considerable detail and with some confidence, while the details for the later years are more tentative and are likely to change in response to commercial and technical developments. The plan is, then, a framework within which managers can prepare their replacement/acquisition strategy and budget appropriately.

3.3.4 The Annual Equipment Plan

The third planning horizon, covering the next year, features prominently in the planning strategy of most ports. The annual equipment plan is a major component of the port's annual capital budget planning, and is the most detailed level of planning. It includes specification of the type and capacity of the equipment to be purchased, complete with cost estimates, and is normally presented to senior management and the Board complete with detailed arguments supporting the case for acquisition. Although financial allocation procedures vary from port to port (in relation to whether they feature as revenue or capital budget items), the refurbishment of plant is also normally included in this annual equipment plan. The annual plan is, of course, normally a component of the five-year plan – particularly so in the case of the revolving or rolling plans, just as the port's five-year plan may well be devised in response to the government's requirement for a national development plan.

3.3.5 The Reality of Equipment Planning

When questioned on their equipment planning procedures, senior managers of nearly all the ports visited gave assurances that one or more of the planning processes described above were followed in their ports. On close examination, however, these seemingly comprehensive and elaborate planning procedures showed considerable variation in the degree of detail employed, the methodology adopted and the way the process was managed. In some ports the planning process is well established and duly followed, but in very many the procedures are either poorly defined (or practically non-existent) or are set down in more or less satisfactory fashion but are not, in practice, followed. There are considerable reservations, too, about the rigidity of some of the medium-term plans, restricting the port's ability to adjust the plans in later years in the light of changes in circumstances. The range of observed deficiencies in the equipment planning process are considered in the next section.

3.4 Deficiencies in Present Planning Procedures

3.4.1 Introduction
This study has revealed six principal areas of deficiency in current equipment planning procedures: excessive government controls; inadequate information systems; the lack of a coherent replacement strategy; reluctance and delays in the disposal of assets; failure to determine appropriate equipment inventories; and poor management of the equipment planning process. These six types of deficiency are considered in turn in the following sections.

3.4.2 Excessive Government Controls
One of the major conclusions to emerge from this study (see Chapter 2) is that government controls are often so strict as to interfere with the port's freedom to plan for and invest in new equipment. The controls take many forms, including restrictions on development plans and capital budgets, investment ceilings on foreign exchange, delays in the processing of applications for equipment purchase, loans, import licences, letters of credit etc., but the net result is severe discouragement of port managers in planning equipment purchase.

As was seen in Chapter 2, present procedures followed in many countries demand that development plans and capital budgets be prepared up to five years ahead, and must give details of all major items of expenditure; they become, in many cases, rigid planning guidelines beyond which the port must not stray during the lifetime of the plan. The imposed expenditure ceilings are often set so low as to ensure that just about *all* equipment purchases require government approval; they certainly take no account of the current replacement cost of plant and machinery (and even fairly modest spare parts may be caught in this financial trap in some countries). In most developing countries, in any case, government approval is mandatory for *all* purchases involving foreign exchange.

What these controls mean, in practice, is that the ports concerned are forced into preparing detailed forecasts of equipment requirements to cover unrealistically long periods, during which time considerable changes are likely to take place in their traffic and cargo-handling needs. While these constraints reinforce the need for effective planning, they unfortunately make it almost impossible for the ports to respond to short- and medium-term changes in market conditions, traffic and technology. Although scope exists in some cases for a mid-term review and modest revision, and while there may be opportunities to present supplementary capital budgets, these permit small adjustments only; unless the project or development in question actually appears in detail in the five-year plan, it will not be approved by government.

Government-imposed restrictions on the port's equipment purchases apply even in cases where the port will not need to borrow from the central bank or other sources. Most of the ports in the study generate sufficient operating surpluses to allow them to replace or add to their cargo-handling equipment (in domestic currency at least) from their funds, yet they are prevented from doing so. Admittedly, a case may exist for a government controlling port capacity and foreign currency expenditure, particularly when their foreign trade balance is unfavourable, but the sort of restrictions encountered in this study make it impossible for ports, however well-run, to respond adequately to users' needs and to keep their equipment inventory up to date and well stocked. This need is particularly galling when it is evident that the civil servants with these powers of veto on the equipment plan are insufficiently qualified to comment on it.

Government controls on the capital budgets of ports are made even more damaging by inordinate delays in processing and sanctioning requests for equipment purchase. It is not unknown for such procedures to take several years to complete, particularly if the port wishes to reject home-produced equipment in favour of overseas manufacture. Such delays have damaging effects on the implementation of the equipment plan; if the port is already feeling the effects of equipment shortage at the time of the request to government, operators will be desperately under-allocated by the time the machines actually arrive. It means that the planning procedure has to begin very much earlier than it should, at which time forecasts of need and technology are inevitably much less reliable and more prone to error.

3.4.3 Inadequate Information Systems

In most of the ports visited, there were inadequate records of present demand and utilization of equipment on which to base predictions of future equipment requirements. Consequently, decisions on investing in new plant were often rather makeshift. Managers frequently admitted that predictions on equipment needs were made on a 'hunch' and on past practices and experiences, rather than on the basis of a thorough and systematic examination of the factors affecting supply and demand. In some ports, the information system was very comprehensive (indeed, in one case the quantity of information presented to individual managers could be considered excessive) but in many it was grossly inadequate for planning purposes. Often, even where relevant information was regularly collected it was not collated or analysed for planning purposes. In several ports, the appropriate information was not even collected.

The deficiencies in the information available for predicting future equipment requirements can conveniently be classified into three groups, relating to traffic forecasts, operating performance, and running and maintenance costs. Although management information systems will be fully discussed in Chapter 9, it is convenient to consider here those aspects relevant to the equipment planning process, in the light of the deficiencies observed.

1. The first deficiency noted relates to traffic forecasts and the gathering of market intelligence for use in predicting future cargo types, volumes and handling systems. Although most ports prepare traffic forecasts, many of them for five and even ten years ahead, the predictions were often unreliable and insufficiently detailed for planning equipment needs, particularly in the unitized and conventional general cargo trades. One port visited had made a multi-million dollar investement in mobile cranes, based on a forecast increase in project cargoes; that traffic has not materialized and the cranes lie idle for most of the time.

   An important contributory factor in this context is the weakness of ports' commercial/ marketing departments and their failure to gather adequate commercial and technical information about market changes. The gathering of market intelligence on trading developments, ship routing and sailing schedules, ship types and sizes, and developments in cargo packaging and dimensions is poorly developed in many ports. Too often they rely on second- or third-hand information, picked up at random from ships' agents, rather than systematically collecting information published in the technical press and in reports prepared by international agencies and consultants, and then presenting them in suitably analysed form in planning meetings. As a consequence of not knowing the market, many ports have an inventory of equipment not matched to customers' needs. This is particularly noticeable in the case of heavy-duty plant; several cases were noted where alternative (and less efficient) means of cargo-handling had to be resorted to, causing delays and increasing costs.

   There should be a small unit responsible for collecting press-cuttings, abstracting from the technical press, maintaining contacts with leading authorities in the maritime industry, principals of shipping companies, etc., and assembling a regular Market Intelligence Report. This should be circulated to appropriate managers, to build up their knowledge of market trends. The port should also subscribe to relevant international information services (several now available online) to assist their marketing and planning functions.

2. The second category of information deficiencies relates to lack of reliable information on the operating and maintenance performance of equipment – as will be described in Chapter 5, the relevant data are either not collected, or are inaccurately and incompletely recorded, or are not analysed and presented in a suitable form. In many cases, information on the daily demand and supply of equipment is not recorded, and the distinction between deployment and utilization is not made clear. In many ports, it is not possible to determine from the available records whether there is a shortfall between operators' daily demands for equipment and the number actually supplied by the engineers; considerable evidence was collected in this survey to support operators' claims that there is a shortage of equipment. Even where daily records are available, they are not analysed periodically to compare supply and demand or to reveal trends in equipment use. In many ports, no data are regularly recorded on equipment availability, utilization and downtime. Without reliable data on these aspects of equipment management, it is not

possible to plan for future equipment needs with any degree of confidence.

3. The third category of information that is either missing or incomplete in many of the ports visited is knowledge of the operating (i.e. running and maintenance) costs of individual units of plant and equipment. The cost information that is available is usually presented in the form of broad estimates or predictions of expenditure for each maintenance workshop – largely for budgetary control purposes. Data are not disaggregated by category of equipment or to individual units, and they are insufficiently detailed to be considered a true cost control system. This makes it impossible to identify those machines that are expensive to run or maintain, and obstructs the establishment of an appropriate replacement strategy for use when planning future equipment needs.

3.4.4 Lack of a Replacement Strategy

Considerable evidence is available to suggest that some ports are retaining on their asset registers equipment that has greatly exceeded its working life. Operators are continuing to use machines (perhaps without option) long after their operating efficiency and reliability have begun to deteriorate significantly, and engineers are continuing to maintain that equipment (or perhaps are being expected to maintain them) when the cost of maintenance, in terms of spare parts and man-hours, is excessively high. In many cases, indeed, equipment is retained on the asset register for years after operators have stopped using it and only a shell remains after cannibilization! This is particularly strange since, in all the ports visited and contacted, the Accounts Departments have fixed depreciation schedules, often following World Bank recommendations.

The philosophy apparently adopted by some senior managers and engineers is that, if plant is still on the asset register, it must continue to be operated and maintained, whatever the cost. Because inadequate information is recorded on the reliability, operating performance and cost of maintenance of individual items of plant, the economic consequences of this management practice tend to be disguised. In one port (not one of those visited) a fleet of forklift trucks was refurbished using spare parts whose cost *alone* exceeded that of new trucks of the same model and capacity!

The extent of this problem is illustrated in Table 3.4.4A, which shows the age structure of selected equipment types as recorded in the latest census of the major ports of one country.

Table 3.4.4A shows very clearly that, in spite of the depreciation period being fixed (following World Bank guidelines) in relation to local climatic conditions, utilization rates, operating environment and driver skills, a very high proportion of the ports' equipment has been kept beyond that period: 83% of the forklift trucks, 100% of the tractors, 96% of the trailers, 98% of the mobile cranes and 50% of the portal cranes. Over 53% of the equipment was over 11 years old at the time, and nearly 16% was over 16 years old. A similar state of affairs is evident in a recent national survey of mechanical handling plant in the ports of a major Asian maritime country (NIPM, 1987), a summary of the data from which is presented in Table 3.4.4B.

This acceptance of excessive life spans is also illustrated by data collected during this study on equipment attachments (e.g. grabs), specialized items such as vacuvators, and floating craft – tugs, lighters, mooring boats, etc. In one port, out of 87 lighters owned by the port, 51 were over 15 years old and 10 were more than 20 years old. The retention of plant on the asset register well beyond reasonable life spans (in terms of age and/or hours of use) places considerable demands on the budget

Table 3.4.4A Cargo Handling Equipment Age Profile for an LDC's Ports

Equipment Type	Depreciation Period (Yrs)	Numbers of Units by Age (Years)						
		0-5	6-10	11-15	16-20	21-25	26-30	>30	Total
Forklifts	5	77	226	159	5	0	0	0	467
Tractors	5	0	45	36	17	1	0	1	100
Trailers	5	9	34	137	58	0	3	2	243
Mobile cranes	5	1	23	1	48	2	1	1	77
Portal cranes	20	0	32	2	0	0	20	14	68

Table 3.4.4B National Survey of Mechanical Handling Equipment

Equipment		Age Profile (Years)						Total
Electric wharf cranes	Age group	0-5	6-10	11-15	16-20	21-25	>25	
	Number	24	24	16	20	133	110	327
	%age	7.5	7.5	5	6	40.5	33.5	
Mobile cranes	Age group	0-5	6-10	11-15	>15			
	Number	51	48	7	41			147
	%age	36	32	5	28			
Forklifts	Age group	0-2	3-4	5-6	7-8	>8		
	Number	44	58	23	141	75		341
	%age	13	17	6.5	41.5	22		

and manpower resources of the engineering department, as well as adding to the difficulty of obtaining (or, more likely, having to make) spare parts. Moreover, preventive maintenance now becomes, to all practical purposes, corrective maintenance; as plant gets older, the frequency of breakdowns increases, upsetting the schedules of the maintenance engineers and complicating operational deployment.

Clearly, a realistic working life needs to be established for each type of equipment, reflecting local conditions, and this should form the basis for the Accounts Department's depreciation value. Then all items of equipment should automatically be considered for replacement towards the end of their depreciation period.

3.4.5 Reluctance and delay in the disposal of assets

Managers in a few of the ports visited reported difficulties in removing units of equipment from the asset ledger and of delays in their disposal. This does seem to be a deliberate policy, to make the port's inventory of equipment look more impressive than it really is. It has several unfortunate consequences, however, particularly in encouraging engineers to attempt to maintain (often at enormous cost) equipment that has exceeded its realistic life. It also makes it very difficult for operators and engineers to convince senior management of the real need for investment in replacement machines.

In some countries, the procedure set down for disposing of assets is burdensome, time-consuming and discouraging. This is particularly strange when written-down equipment could very well be sold as scrap or on the second-hand market, realizing income for purchasing new machines. A major contributory factor seems to be the existence in ports of internal committees which demand surveys and a great deal of paperwork before assets can be disposed of. Worse still, in some countries asset disposal requires central government approval, via the Ministries of Transport and Finance. Examples were cited of civil servants delaying approval for disposal for up to ten years after requests to scrap machines had been submitted by port engineers, even though the equipment was already, at the time of the request, completely unserviceable, heavily cannibalized and, to all intents and purposes, derelict. Such assets continue to remain on the port's register, supposedly still maintained but in fact totally unavailable for use by operators.

Although this reluctance to remove assets from the financial accounts and asset register was noted in several of the ports participating in this study, no entirely convincing explanation has been offered. The least implausible explanation offered is that parastatal bodies are extremely vulnerable to accusations of malpractice, and there is a fear that port or Ministry officials might be accused of selling off equipment at grossly below its value, for personal gain. Stories were told of equipment being sold off to private sector companies, at scrap value, and being very quickly refurbished and returned to operational use. Clearly, port authorities must be seen to be above suspicion, and must follow laid-down procedures scrupulously. They must ensure that a fair market price is paid for plant disposed of at the end of its working life. However, they should not use fear of criticism as an excuse to ignore the economics of equipment ownership and replacement; realistic replacement strategies must be established and adhered to.

3.4.6 Inappropriate inventory levels

The setting of optimum inventory levels for each major class, type and capacity of equipment used by a port is a complex and difficult calculation, even if accurate and complete information is available. Demand for port services is not easy to predict, and it shows wide fluctuations even during a shift. Furthermore, maritime trade is itself a dynamic phenomenon, with seasonal and cyclical variations. So the need for equipment also varies over many time-scales. Another factor is that current, intense inter-port competition for the available trade has tempted ports to over-invest in equipment, to ensure that they can satisfy the demands of ship operators for maximum daily output and cope with peak berth occupancy conditions.

Considerable economic and service benefits can be gained by improving the techniques used in determining optimum inventory levels, relating them to the port's corporate objectives, operational performance targets, and the maintenance strategy and capability of the engineering department. Clearly, a fundamental requirement in this activity is the availability of accurate and full information, particularly on the operating performance of individual classes and units of plant – data that were conspicuously lacking in many of the ports surveyed in this study.

3.4.7 Poor Management of Inventory Planning
There is considerable diversity in the way in which ports organize and prepare their equipment plans; in many cases, several departments or divisions are involved in the process, often with ill-defined and overlapping responsibilities, and the process appears uncoordinated, with self-interest much in evidence. For example, in some ports the plan is the sole responsibility of the Engineering Department, while in others the Finance Department takes on that task. More commonly, a number of departments are actively involved in the process – typically, the Planning or Management Services Department prepares the traffic forecasts, engineering and operations staff review equipment supply and demand (respectively) and the Finance Department sets the financial parameters and investment ceilings.

The practice of delegating equipment planning responsibility to a single department was criticized in several quarters. Engineers, it was claimed, allow equipment supply considerations to predominate, and 'ration' equipment allocated to operators so that utilization levels are lower than they should be; this is done, the critics say, to reduce pressure on them to improve the quality of maintenance and to minimize the required availability levels. On the other hand, Finance Department staff, when equipment planning is left to them, tend to consider the port to be over-stocked with equipment; they are intent on maximizing utilization levels and minimizing capital expenditure on new equipment, and are completely oblivious to the port's operational needs. Operations Department staff, of course, tend to over-invest, to make sure that they have all the equipment they need – or so the argument goes.

Clearly, the best balance between competing self-interests is to involve all the relevant departments in the planning process, but this inevitably increases the need for effective co-ordination. In some of the visited ports, there is evident confusion over the precise roles of individual units and their representatives, and this confusion weakens the effectiveness of planning. Given the importance of the equipment plan, it is essential to establish a clear organizational structure for the planning team and to apply firm and fair management to the process.

3.4.8 The Case for Improving Planning Procedures
The deficiencies in present planning procedures are widespread and quite apparent, yet the equipment planning process is clearly crucial to efficient port operations and maintenance. A sound planning organization, with the full involvement of the Engineering Department (through senior manager representation on a permanent Equipment Planning Committee) and working with clearly defined procedures, needs urgently to be established in many LDC ports; the lack of such planning is one of the diagnostic features of the less successful ports. The remainder of this chapter is concerned with the details of that equipment planning process, and the first consideration is the information that is necessary to provide a solid foundation for the equipment plan.

3.5 Information Needs for the Equipment Plan

3.5.1 The Range of Data Needed
Although ports generally collect and store *some* data on throughput and equipment use, in most cases they lack much of the information required for effective equipment planning (as was pointed out in Section 3.4.3). A major omission is a reliable measure of future demand – traffic forecasts to quantify future cargo-handling work, and what equipment will be needed to perform it. A range of operating data (utilization, downtime, availability, performance capability of equipment) is needed, to convert the forecast demand into numbers and types of machines. Information on the equipment in the current asset register needs to be analysed, to

determine the age and condition of the port's stock of machines, while data are needed on running and maintenance costs, to help to work out which machines should be replaced. Only when all this information is available and has been properly analysed is the planning group in a position to formulate a realistic and responsive plan. These are the information needs that will be examined in this section, beginning with the crucial, though often neglected, task of traffic forecasting.

3.5.2 Traffic Forecasts

A key activity in the preparation of an effective equipment plan is the compilation of comprehensive and reliable traffic forecasts. A 'revolving' five-year forecast is recommended, on which to calculate outline future equipment requirements, with more detailed and reliable predictions for the next year, on which the annual request for equipment can be based. The five-year forecast is itself revised regularly in the light of developments and as the reliability of the predictions improves.

In the context of equipment planning, the purpose of the traffic forecast is to quantify the amount of cargo-handling work to be performed by the port's plant and machinery – initially in global terms but ultimately in terms of individual types of equipment on the various berths and terminals. For this purpose, traffic forecasts of conventional form are not detailed enough; they predict the total volume of cargo passing through the port by commodity class (e.g. '250,000 TEUs', '500,000 tonnes of break-bulk general cargo') and take no account of double-handling, transshipment cargo and other significant factors. For example, cargo passing through the port via the direct route (handled directly to inland transport) will require little or no mobile equipment, whereas cargo following the indirect route through short-term storage may be handled three or even four times during its passage, needing equipment on each occasion. The importance of the relationship between cargo throughput and the actual amount of handling work to be performed is illustrated in Table 3.5.2, which shows that the predicted number of movements at a hypothetical container terminal with a design capacity of 250,000 containers (300,000 TEUs) is about 700,000 – a ratio of nearly three moves for each container passing through.

Obviously, it is the number of cargo *movements* through a port, and not the overall throughput, that determines equipment demand – how many units will be needed. It is predictions of cargo *movements* that the Equipment Planning Committee need to have before they can safely determine how much

extra or replacement equipment to purchase. For container traffic, the sort of calculations demonstrated in Table 3.5.2 are needed, while similar estimates are needed for bulk and general cargoes – for example, a 'double-handling ratio' to reflect the proportion of transshipment cargo, each item of which is handled once into storage and then a second time back to the quay for loading. The forecasting problem is particularly acute with break-bulk cargo, as the port is dealing with very large numbers of individual shippers, many of them dealing with small quantities of cargo in an unpredictable and variable way. For bulk cargo, predictions are easier, as here the port is dealing with a few, very large, customers, with regular shipments of large quantities of cargo of uniform types; equipment demand is very much more predictable.

Table 3.5.2 Annual and average daily in-terminal container movements for a terminal with a CFS and empties pool on terminal and an annual throughput of 250,000 containers (300,000 TEUs)

Quay Transfer Moves		
Import FCL	64,125	
Import LCL	42,750	
Import Empty	5,625	
Export FCL	33,750	
Export LCL	50,625	
Export Empty	28,125	
Transshipment	50,000	
Shifts via quay	12,000	
Total Quay Transfer Moves		287,000
To and From CFS		
Import LCLs to CFS	42,750	
Empties, CFS to pool	34,200	
Export LCLs, CFS to CY	50,625	
Empties, pool to CFS	42,075	
Total To and From CFS		169,650
Gate Complex Moves		
Import FCLs leaving	64,125	
Import LCLs leaving	0	
Import Empties leaving	5,625	
Export FCLs entering	33,750	
Export LCLs entering	0	
Export Empties entering	0	
Import FCLs recirc.*	44,888	
Empties recirc†	8,888	
Total through Gate		157,276
Total movements per year		613,926
Average movements per day		1,682

*Import FCLs recirculating into the terminal as Empties
†Empties recirculating from the Empties Pool to Shippers

So traffic forecasts prepared for equipment planning must be sufficiently detailed to quantify the amount of cargo-handling work to be performed. Not only that, however; they must also be divided into the major commodity groups (e.g. neo-bulks; general cargo) and then subdivided into individual cargo types (e.g. steel coil, packaged timber; bags, drums, crates). For each cargo type, the 'modal split' needs to be known – whether it is to be transported by road, rail or inland waterway (and what type of vehicle is to be used, its design, means of access and size) – to allow detailed calculations of the number of handlings or movements to be performed on its passage through the port. Again, Table 3.5.2 illustrates such a calculation, in terms of container status (FCL, LCL, empties), and terminal activity. At the end of all these calculations, the planners have estimates of the average number of movements generated per day (or shift); these will form the basis for working out the needs for particular types of equipment.

The predictions are, of course, in terms of the *average* amount of work to be performed each day; they do not take into account fluctuations in the amount of cargo passing through the port – daily, monthly and seasonal variations – which cause peaking problems. To predict these factors, the planners must refer to past traffic records and plot them to establish peaking cycles, as well as to discern gradual trends in cargo movements. They also need to discover any changes in cargo composition, and in unit or package sizes and dimensions; these will influence the design and capacity of the equipment to be purchased. Data on ship types and sizes, and on developments in inland transport vehicles are also of relevance in this context. For example, the number, type and size of vessels visiting the port directly affects the number, type and size of the equipment needed to handle their cargoes. Will the ships be geared or ungeared? What will be the size and load rating of ramps, the deck floor loadings, the principal dimensions of cargo access points? These and other structural features may restrict the use of equipment aboard the vessel.

One of the major challenges in equipment planning is predicting future commercial development and technological change in the maritime industry; both have a profound effect on future equipment needs. Given the current volatility of the marketplace, there is an increasing risk of equipment becoming obsolete soon after it is purchased. To make matters worse, the physical life of major cargo-handling plant and equipment is steadily increasing – recently purchased quayside container cranes are expected to have a working life of up to 35 years, given good maintenance and periodic refurbishment.

It is extremely important to choose such equipment carefully, to ensure that it will not require either early replacement or major engineering modifications because it cannot cope with changed cargo-handling circumstances.

Good market intelligence is absolutely essential to reduce these risks to a minimum, and is a vital input into equipment planning. So conventional traffic forecasting must be supplemented by a comprehensive and continuous gathering of information on trends in seaborne trade, changes in ship routing and scheduling, developments in ship design and cargo-handling technology, as well as related national, regional and global economic data. However, market intelligence research seems hardly ever to be done in the ports visited, and where it is done, it is generally badly done, so that severe problems have resulted in many cases. It is a difficult area, admittedly, but managers must take a more professional approach to it in their equipment planning.

3.5.3 Equipment Demand

The existing demand for each type of the port's cargo-handling equipment can be estimated in several ways. The easiest is to analyse periodically the daily Equipment Requisition Forms presented by operators, but these are unlikely to be reliable indicators, as operations managers rarely indicate precisely the amount of work the machines are to perform or the time they will be working. They often requisition a machine for a full shift when it is really only needed for a small part of it, giving themselves wide safety margins to cover miscalculations. So Requisition Forms give only the roughest estimates of time in use and may well disguise the true level of demand.

A somewhat better estimate can be obtained from the times of booking-out and booking-in of a machine from and to the equipment depot – its 'allocation time'. Even this only gives an approximation of its use, however, as it takes no account of idle time. A more accurate measure of demand is given by recording the number of hours that a machine actually works. Such 'Recorded Machine Hours' can be taken from a logbook carried on the equipment, filled in by a driver to note the time he started to use it, the time he returned it to its parking position and all periods of non-use (for whatever reason) in between.

Still better is the figure for hours of use indicated by an 'hour-meter' fitted to the engine of the machine (or indeed, to the motor of one or more of its constituent systems) and recording when the engine is working under load; it should not record time when the equipment is idle (though a separate meter recording *total* engine hours, including when it is just ticking over, is also useful, as are meters on other systems). The hour-meters are read on issue of the machine from the pool or engineering section, and the reading is taken again on return. If carefully recorded, the differences between readings give a complete picture of the actual use of the machine and, in combination with figures aggregated over time for that and similar machines, provides a realistic indication of the operators' demand for that equipment. The more successful of the ports surveyed all make good use of hour-meters, but they were not much in evidence in most of the LDC ports (nor, indeed, in some ports in developed countries).

3.5.4 Equipment Utilization

As a means of aggregating data on equipment usage, and to provide a way of comparing data and identifying trends in demand, the measure Equipment Utilization is commonly used. This value is calculated using the formula:

$$\text{Utilization} = \frac{\text{Recorded Machine Hours} \times 100}{\text{Possible Machine Hours}}$$

The most reliable figure to use for Recorded Machine Hours, as explained in 3.5.3, is that obtained from (adjusted) hour-meter readings, taken over a suitable period (day, week, month or year). The expression 'Possible Machine Hours' requires a little further explanation. It aims to indicate the maximum number of hours that a machine *could* have been used in the period under consideration, but opinion differs on the figure to use. Some ports insist that, in a week, the figure to use should be 168 hours (24 hours × 7), while others consider it more realistic to count only the number of hours that the berth or terminal in question is scheduled to work in the period. For example, if the berth works two 7.5-hour shifts each day for six days, then the possible Machine Hours would be 90 hours.

The drawback to this approach is that it ignores overtime and extra shift working, so the resulting value could be misleadingly high (whereas, in the example above, the 168-hour interpretation would yield a misleadingly low value for Utilization). The most useful value, in the context of calculating and comparing equipment demand, would seem to be one which reflects the hours actually worked, during the measured period, in the berth or berths to which that machine is normally allocated. So, for example, if a general cargo berth worked a total of 14 eight-hour shifts in a week, plus 8 hours of overtime, the Possible Machine Hours for that berth would be 120 hours. If the adjusted hour-readings for a forklift

truck allocated to the berth added up to 72 hours, the Utilization value for the machine in that week would be 60% (72 × 100/120). When this approach is used, planners have a useful measure of the demand by operators for equipment and of the 'slack' available to meet increased demand.

More realistically, of course, the planners will want to know the *average* Utilization value for all units of a particular type and capacity available to the operators on a group of berths or a terminal. For example, if the general cargo berth referred to above is one of four in the port, and between them they worked 60 shifts in a month, plus 20 hours of overtime – a total of 500 hours – while all the forklift trucks allocated to the berths had hour-meter readings totalling 275 hours, then the average Utilization for those machines is 55% (275 × 100/500).

If such a calculation is repeated weekly, monthly and annually, the overall level of demand for a class of machine can be determined, with seasonal and other variations in traffic flow taken into account. Such a Utilization value is an extremely important input to the planning of equipment purchase. A low level of Utilization (say 40%) for a particular class of equipment would indicate that the present stock of equipment is adequate – even generous – and that no further investment is needed, despite any claims to the contrary by operators. On the other hand, a high average Utilization (say over 80%) would support any request for additional machines. After all, this *is* an average figure, perhaps over a month, and indicates that Utilization was sometimes less than that and sometimes more. Indeed, there were almost certainly occasions when requests for that sort of machine could not be met. The need for extra equipment on those berths is even stronger if an increase in traffic has been predicted or if a larger proportion of cargo is expected to arrive in a form which that class of equipment is designed to handle.

3.5.5 Downtime

In considering equipment utilization, it was tacitly assumed that every item of equipment is accessible for use by operators during every hour that the berths work. This is, of course, an unrealistic assumption. Regular maintenance and service are essential, and all machines are put out of use through breakdown or accidental damage at some time or another. The technical term for periods when a machine is out of service and inaccessible to operators is Downtime. A high Downtime figure indicates that the machine is inaccessible to operators for long periods.

Downtime should, like utilization, be recorded for each machine in the port and then aggregated to provide a summary of the Downtime for each class and capacity of equipment. Managers involved in equipment planning need to know not only the Downtime value but also the causes of Downtime, and so the mechanical maintenance section should record all causes of Downtime for each machine in the port's inventory, not just under broad headings (such as 'preventive maintenance', 'breakdown repair', 'damage repair' or 'waiting for spare parts') but in detail – the precise nature of the fault, the components concerned, etc. (see Chapter 9). Such information will prove invaluable when deciding when equipment should be replaced and also for calculating reliability and maintainability values for particular manufacturers and models, for determining the performance record of specific components and for preparing technical specifications for new acquisitions.

3.5.6. Equipment Availability

The downtime records are also used in calculating a numerical measure of the proportion of time that a machine (or class of machine) is accessible to operators – its Availability. This is calculated from the formula:

$$\text{Availability} = \frac{\text{Available Machine Hours} \times 100}{\text{Possible Machine Hours}}$$

As in the case of utilization calculations, opinions differ as to the appropriate way of defining the Possible Machine Hours, but the same arguments support the use here, too, of the total number of hours actually worked in the period in question at a berth or group of berths. The 'Available Machine Hours' are then calculated by subtracting the total downtime of the machine or machines, in the period being considered, from the Possible Machine Hours. For example, in the case of the four general cargo berths referred to in the utilization calculation, if the total downtime recorded for that group of forklift trucks was 85 hours in that week, then the Available Hours were 415 (500 – 85) and their Availability was 83% (415 × 100/500). This is a relatively high value, indicating that the machines are being kept in a reasonable condition by the Engineering Department.

Taken in combination with the other operational measures (utilization and downtime), availability values can provide a considerable amount of useful information for equipment planning, as will be considered in the next section. Also useful – and complementary to Availability values – is Demand Availability, which is a measure of the percentage of time that equipment is available *when demanded by operators;* it is an indicator of any shortfall between demand and supply.

It is essential when preparing an equipment plan to study *all* equipment operational measures, for each category of machine, not just availability or utilization. By considering in combination indicators of demand (e.g. requisition form analyses, hour-meter readings), utilization, downtime and availability, planners can obtain much more reliable guidance in their deliberations than by examining them individually. For example, a low utilization figure may not necessarily indicate a low demand for that type or unit of equipment. It could be that the demand was there but that the equipment was not available to meet operators' demands; this would be confirmed if the downtime value was high and the availability figure was low. Thus, if utilization is 48% when availability is only 50%, purchase of new equipment need not necessarily be indicated; the first action to take should be to improve the quality of maintenance of the existing machines to increase availability. If this could be improved to, say, 80% there is every likelihood that the demand could then be met perfectly adequately. On the other hand, if utilization is high (e.g. 85%) and availability is also high (90%), then there could be a strong case for considering increasing the stock of that particular class of equipment.

So availability and the other operating indicators must be looked at together. It is also important to examine them in the light of measures of equipment performance – indicators of how much cargo-handling work the machines are capable of in a measured period. These are considered in the next section.

3.5.7 Equipment Performance Measures

The final group of operating data that need to be collected, analysed and taken into account when determining equipment needs are measures of the work done by the existing machines. Some of these are recorded for statutory purposes (e.g. the work done by the hoist ropes of cranes, in terms of the number of lifts performed) while others should be recorded as part of the Operational and/or Engineering Management Information Systems. For example, engineers will want to know the total number of hours of operation of a machine in a year, the number of movements made by a major assembly (e.g. the spreader of a straddle carrier, the traverse mechanism of a transfer crane), the running hours of a diesel engine, and so on.

In the context of equipment planning, such data need to be converted into a form which will indicate the rate of work possible from a particular type or unit of equipment. For example, the total number of lifts performed in a year by a gantry crane (as recorded on a trip-counter connected to a twistlock device, for example) can easily be turned into a performance rating as lift cycles per hour, to provide a basis for calculating the number of cranes needed to meet increased throughput. For quay transfer equipment, work study surveys may well be needed, to record over sample periods the average number of transfer cycles performed per hour, per shift and so on, and from that information the planners can calculate the average output rates or handling rates in tonnes (or other suitable units) per hour. However such rating values are derived, they can then be used to work out how many machines of a particular type are needed to handle a predicted throughput of cargo.

Clearly, all such data are extremely useful at the time of making decisions on purchasing additional plant or replacing existing equipment. Further information relating to the latter question concerns the age and condition of existing equipment, to which attention is turned next.

3.5.8 The Age and Condition of Existing Equipment

A very important function of the port's asset register is to record the purchase date of each unit of the port's equipment, to warn planners when it is nearing the end of its useful life. It will also contain data on each maintenance or repair job carried out on it, and when, giving a good indication of the condition of that piece of equipment. At the time of preparing the equipment plan, the engineers will refer to these records, to sort out any units that might need to be replaced within the period of that plan. Suspect items should then be surveyed thoroughly and reports prepared on their condition, in terms of the general state of their structure, condition of the motive power unit, assemblies and sub-assemblies. Taken with analyses, from the engineering records, of the machines' reliability and maintainability, this information may well indicate that particular machines are due for replacement. The decision to replace will also be greatly influenced by data on a unit's maintenance and running costs – a machine still within its physical life span might be considered for scrapping if it is costing too much to operate and maintain; it is this aspect of planning information that needs to be considered next.

3.5.9 Annual Maintenance and Running Costs

When a particular machine has been marked out for replacement or disposal during the preparation of the equipment plan, major determining factors in the final decision will include its current operating costs. If replacement is being considered, comparisons will be made between the predicted running and maintenance costs of that unit of equipment and those of the proposed replacement machine. In order to make those comparisions, detailed records must be available on the costs of operating every unit of equipment on the port's asset register during the whole of its working life. The records will include information on each maintenance activity performed on the unit, with costs apportioned to labour, spare parts, fuel and lubricants, and any other items of expenditure. They can then be converted into hourly running and maintenance costs (see Chapters 5 and 6) for planning purposes.

A characteristic feature of efficiently managed ports is the excellence of their costing systems and the wide use to which engineers put the cost information. In a well-run port, such data will be used when preparing technical specifications for new equipment (of similar type) and when evaluating manufacturers' bids. They will also be needed when considering the option of refurbishing the equipment instead of replacing it (as will be considered in Section 3.6.6) – they form an essential input to inventory planning.

3.5.10 Total Lifetime Costs

Deciding to replace an asset (or comparing bids for additional or replacement machines) would be simple if the future operating costs of new equipment could be reliably predicted and compared with the known costs of running the present machines. Replacement could then be timed when it is most economical, rather than when the asset is worn out. This important principle seems not to be followed – nor even to have been considered – in many ports; the almost universal practice is to operate plant, at whatever cost (in terms of running and maintenance), until it is no longer usable. This is partly explained by the difficulties experienced in many LDC ports in obtaining funds (particularly foreign exchange) to purchase new equipment, and partly by the general resistance to change detectable in many port managers – doing nothing is often an easier option than embarking on an apparently high-risk investment venture.

The rationale for replacing a functionally efficient piece of equipment is the reduced cost promised by its replacement. If the *total* annual cost of the replacement is expected to be less than the annual cost of continuing to operate existing equipment, then the old machine should be replaced or scrapped as soon as possible. If such a cost-benefit analysis indicates no economic advantage, then the existing machine should be retained until a later date, when the exercise should be repeated. When making that comparision, however, it is essential to take *all* relevant costs into account: all commissioning and installation costs of the new equipment, the utility or salvage value of the asset to be replaced, plus all running and maintenance costs through the life of the asset, as well as the initial and ongoing cost of the capital investment in the new machine (its 'ownership' cost). In essence, the task is to compare the future cash flows, the expected receipts (benefits) and outlays (costs) of the two alternatives, using some approved form of investment appraisal. The current expert opinion among procurement specialists is that Life Cycle Costing meets these requirements satisfactorily.

Figure 3.5.10 illustrates the theoretical basis for Life Cycle Costing by examining graphically the cost of operating a typical 3-tonne forklift truck over a life of ten years, by comparing : [a] its annual 'ownership' cost (calculated on the basis of an initial purchase cost of $40,000, spread over successive assumed lives of 1, 2, 3 etc. years; [b] the annual operating costs for each of the ten years of machine life (the actual cost of running the machine – including driver's wages, fuel and lubricant costs, maintenance and repairs); [c] its *average* annual operating cost – the actual costs averaged over successive years of operation; [d] the average annual *total* costs (the sum of [a] and [c]). The graphs show that the lowest average annual total cost of the machine occurs after six years of operation – the cost falls from year 1 to year 6 and then begins to rise. Beyond year 6 the actual annual operating cost exceeds the average annual total cost, and the most economic solution would be to replace the machine at year six. Note that this assumes that the truck is replaced by one of the *same type and performance*; it does not take into account any model improvement since the existing machine was purchased, which might yield better operating cost figures than for the original. The analysis also indicates that the average annual total cost rises relatively slowly beyond the optimum replacement time, which may suggest that the timing of the replacement is not too critical. However, this depends on the slope of the actual annual operating costs curve beyond this point. Provided the maintenance costs for the existing machine do not rise appreciably in that period, and given the uncertainty over the accuracy of predictions of operating peformance and costs, it would be acceptable to replace at some time

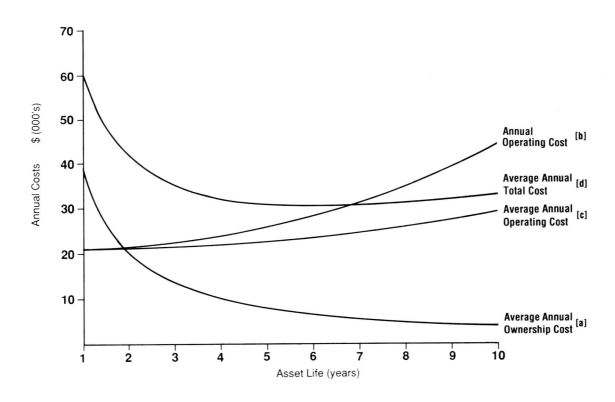

Figure 3.5.10: Operating Costs for a Standard Fork Lift Truck

between years 6 and 8. After that time, higher maintenance costs begin to assume greater significance in the model, and average annual total costs rise appreciably; continuing to operate the machine beyond that time is not the most economic or cost-effective solution for the port, even though the machine is still in working order.

Accepting this approach, and provided the port has reliable Operations and Engineering Management Information Systems, detailed enough to provide the necessary data, it is possible to determine approximate economic lives and target replacement strategies for each category of equipment in the port's asset register.

Having now considered all the various classes of information required by the planning group when formulating an equipment plan, it is appropriate to move on to discuss the process of preparing such a plan, in the light of the deficiencies observed in the less successful ports and the practices established in the successful ones. The next section describes the steps in that process in detail.

3.6 The Equipment Plan

3.6.1 Introduction
The discussions in the previous sections have provided a strong case, as outlined in Section 3.1, for a port formulating an equipment plan. This should have equal status, within the port's corporate or development plan, to such other activities as manpower development and financial planning. To summarize, the main factors justifying the time and effort necessary for preparing an equipment plan for a port in a developing country are:

— The utter dependence of the Operations Department on equipment for the efficient handling of the port's cargo;

— The high level of investment represented by equipment and plant, and the increasing proportion of capital budgets set aside for this;

— The importance of equipment planning decisions in determining the ease and cost of maintenance and of acquiring spare parts.

— The need in many countries to obtain government approval before investing in plant and equipment, and the inordinate delays resulting from that need;

— The length of time needed for negotiating loan agreements, commercial credits and other forms of funding to meet the cost of purchasing equipment.

In spite of the difficulties in predicting equipment needs well into the future, there is a strong case for preparing a five-year equipment plan (as a formal component of the port's strategic or development plan), to ensure that equipment acquisition is fully taken into account when planning future capital expenditure and projecting cash flow requirements. The plan should contain, in broad outline, predictions of the number and type of equipment that cargo-handling operators will need; the details will be worked out in the successive annual plans and capital budgets, and the long-term plan will be updated appropriately as the term of the plan progresses.

The preparation of the equipment plan (and the related capital budgets) must be delegated to competent staff, provided by senior management with the necessary resources (in terms of facilities, funding, time and data) to do an effective job. Not only must the team's predictions and calculations be accurate but they must also be backed up by detailed and persuasive arguments justifying the port's case, ready for vigorous defence of the plan in discussions with the ministries and other agencies which have the power of accepting or rejecting the port's requests.

The key to obtaining Board and government approval for requests for equipment purchase is a well prepared equipment plan; this section presents a set of guidelines on how such a plan should be prepared, step by step. The sequence of these steps is discussed in Section 3.6.10 and summarized in Figure 3.6.10. This scheme forms the framework for the description below, and reference to it when reading the description should prove helpful.

3.6.2 Preparation of Traffic Forecasts
The preparation of the equipment plan should be a joint effort between staff in the Operations, Engineering, Commercial and Planning Departments (or their equivalents), with each group providing their share of the data on which the plan is to be based. The starting point has to be traffic forecasts, and these must be compiled in ample time for the plan to be prepared and approved, and the procurement completed, by the time that equipment is needed. The actual lead time clearly depends on how long those processes take; if, for example, major investment in cargo-handling equipment is being considered, the plan might have to be submitted (first to the Board and then to officials of the relevant ministry) 18 to 24 months before the planned commissioning date, and the traffic forecasts will be needed some six months earlier than that again.

Responsibility for preparing traffic forecasts will depend on the organizational structure of the port; ideally, it should fall on the Planning Department or its equivalent. The task of converting those forecasts into measures of the work to be performed, by equipment type, category and capacity, should be the responsibility of staff in the Traffic or Operations Department who are familiar with cargo-handling techniques, users' requirements, modal split, fluctuations in demand and other operational factors.

The pace of technological and commercial change in the maritime industry makes it essential that representatives of the Commercial or Marketing Department be involved in the projection of traffic statistics, to contribute their market intelligence on trading patterns, ship routing and so on, while engineers should be able to contribute up-to-date information on developments in ship design and cargo-handling. Future traffic volume estimates must be based on a realistic assessment of the port's commercial prospects, taking into account:

— whether it plans to be a load centre or feeder port;

— its progress in multimodalism;

— local and regional interport competition;

— how much of its traffic is captive or volatile;

— the port's marketing and pricing strategies.

At the end of their informed deliberations, the planning group will produce reliable estimates of the quantity of cargo to be handled by the port in successive years of the Plan. As discussed in Section 3.5.2, the estimates should be expressed in terms of commodity groups, cargo types and modal split, to provide the basis for the next step in the planning process, the calculation of the equipment workload.

3.6.3 Calculation of the Equipment Workload

The next step is to interpret the disaggregated traffic forecasts in terms of the workload to be faced by the port's equipment. Initially, the forecasts will be in the form of estimates of the cargo, of different types, expected to pass across the individual berths (or related groups of berths) and terminals daily, weekly and monthly. The estimates will be expressed as tonnes/day, or containers/day, etc. as appropriate, and can now be related to the categories of equipment that will be needed to handle that cargo – break-bulk and palletized cargo to forklift trucks, containers to straddle carriers or rubber-tyred gantry cranes, etc.

These figures are, however, only *averages*; they will have to be adjusted to take account of peaking.

An equipment stock carefully calculated (on the basis of predicted annual throughput and the performance capability of individual units of equipment) to meet average daily and shift demands will not be adequate to match peak demands. These wide periodic fluctuations in demand present major difficulties to planners, particularly on single- or preferential-user terminals and where some form of berth appropriation scheme is in operation; on common-user terminals demand tends to be smoothed out.

The conflicting requirements of minimizing the expensive equipment inventory and meeting the needs of customers at times of peak traffic are extremely difficult to reconcile. If the port invests in sufficient equipment to handle peak cargo throughputs, machines will inevitably lie idle for several days in each week, when few ships are at berth. Equipment may be used intensively for short periods but will have relatively low average utilization. For example, in a recent survey (Thomas & Roach, 1988) of container handling systems, it was found that, worldwide, quayside gantry cranes had utilization rates of 25-40%, and other major plant (rubber-tyred gantry cranes, straddle carriers, etc.) had similar low utilization figures on many container terminals. There is evidence, then, that ports are tending to over-invest in equipment, to ensure that they can maintain a high standard of service to their customers, even at times of peak throughput, at the cost of having equipment idle for much of its time. To do otherwise (they believe) would be to risk loss of business.

One Asian container terminal illustrates the peaking problem well; most ships arrive at the port at weekend, when loading and discharge rates are up to three times as high as the *average* daily handling rate. Planners in that port have to apply a 'Peaking Factor' of 3 to the average rate when determining their maximum daily equipment requirements. While this may be an extreme case, it is not uncommon for specialized berths and terminals to apply quite high peaking factors, while factors in the range of 1.6 to 2.0 are frequently used at average berths.

The peaking problem is not confined to the Ship Operation; daily peaks in demand occur in the receipt and delivery of cargo and with in-terminal movements and transfer into and out of storage. However, *these* peaks tend to occur at different times of the day and week, particularly in modern terminal operations, and this can ease the difficulties to some extent, particularly if equipment can be deployed to different areas and activities as required.

Wide fluctuations in daily cargo-handling requirements make it difficult to plan investment in equipment. Should the port maintain a stock of equipment big enough to meet *all* peak demands, or should it set its equipment inventory at a level which meets operators' demands on all but a specified number of shifts or days in the year? Provided the necessary data are available, the port might set that level at, say, 90%, accepting that demand would not be fully met on about 36 days (108 shifts), if the port normally operates three shifts a day, 365 days a year. Such a decision will clearly depend on the operational performance targets set by the port and the ability of operators to supplement the equipment inventory, in emergencies, by hiring units from external sources.

A strategy of maintaining a minimum stock of equipment within the port and hiring-in to meet peak demands is clearly attractive, but does depend on the existence of reliable local hire firms. Even then, this could only be feasible for non-specialized equipment (such as forklift trucks), which has applications outside the port, and is impracticable for specialized machines such as straddle carriers. Nevertheless, some of the most successful ports rely on hiring equipment on a regular basis to cope with peak handling, and this strategy is worth considering when calculating the equipment workload, as should such options as transferring machines between berths or other working units.

3.6.4 Setting Performance Targets

Having determined a reasonable set of predictions for the equipment workload for the port during the period of the equipment plan, the next step in the planning process is to decide on the standards of service to be provided to port users: to formulate a clear set of minimum performance targets for the Operations Department. These targets should be established by senior management and included in both the port's corporate plan and the departmental objectives. They must be set at realistic levels, but sufficiently above current levels to provide an incentive to improve efficiency, and then should be reviewed regularly (at least annually, though some very successful ports review – and adjust – them as frequently as monthly).

Such a set of targets should cover:

— the maximum turn-round time for each class of vessel (e.g. cellular, multipurpose, dry-bulk, break-bulk), in relation to the type and quantity of cargo to be loaded and discharged;

— the maximum permitted waiting time for each class of vessel visiting the port;

— the minimum average hourly handling rates per working crane or hatch and per vessel, for each type of vessel and cargo, taking account of ship size and technology;

— minimum 'in-system' times for road vehicles delivering or receiving cargoes to or from storage in the port;

— maximum storage utilization rates and in-transit or dwell times, for each cargo type and status, and minimum delivery rates;

— maximum permitted downtime of equipment (particularly that resulting from accidental or driver-induced breakdowns or repairs);

— minimum safety standards to be maintained;

— general statements on relationships with port users and on staff matters.

Such a set of operational targets (a sample from an LDC port is presented in Appendix 3) provides the port with a yardstick against which to judge the performance of operational units, and should prove extremely valuable in providing motivation for staff in cargo-handling. Targets are considered to be crucial means of maintaining and improving efficiency in many of the most successful ports. Indeed, some of these ports have now established operational targets for each of their major customers, taking account of the type of ships used by them and of the type and quantity of cargo carried, so providing fair and realistic sets of targets for their berths and terminals to aim at.

In the present context, however, the targets of operational performance provide the planners with another category of information from which to calculate the optimum size of their equipment inventory. At one extreme, some major ports engaged in highly competitive trades are aiming to eliminate ship waiting time altogether, and so have set very high handling rates per working crane and vessel (e.g. a sustained rate of 25 containers/crane/hour for third-generation vessels) and assign three cranes per vessel. They have also set very ambitious service time targets for road vehicles; one port has the objective of servicing each road vehicle delivering/receiving containers in less than 30 minutes, and in others demurrage is now paid as compensation to the owners of delayed road vehicles.

Such high targets imply the need to maintain large (and expensive) equipment inventories, a measure of the stress that is now being placed on operational efficiency and customer service as a result of intense competition. The philosophy adopted by some major ports has been succinctly stated as: 'The equipment waits for the ships, not the ships for the equipment!' These ports recognize the economic conequences of shortage of equipment, and they promote and market their services on the basis of high operating efficiency. When preparing an equipment plan, it is obviously essential for the planners to take into account the service levels that operators are required to attain during the period of the plan. They are now in a position to convert the data on demand (in terms of the work to be done by the equipment), and the level of operating performance to be attained, into estimates of how much equipment will be needed to meet demand.

3.6.5 Determining the Optimum Equipment Inventory Level

Having arrived at a prediction of the work to be done by the port's equipment over the period of the equipment plan, and having set the standards of performance, in terms of customer service, it is now possible for the planners to calculate how much of each type of equipment will be needed. The remaining data needed to do this relate to the performance of the units of equipment involved in handling the particular types of cargo. Such measures as their output rate (in terms of container lifts per hour, quay transfer cycles achievable per hour, tonnes of cargo transferred per hour, etc.) will need to be extracted from the Operations Management Information System records, to convert the quantity of work to be done into numbers of units needed – taking into account, of course, those targets of turnround time, waiting time and peaking that have been set. An effective and reliable management information system is an essential requirement for this stage in the planning process.

The resulting calculated figures are, of course, minimum levels; they assume that all the equipment will be available when needed and that it will be deployed in ideal fashion. The planners must adjust them in accordance with past or targeted values (see Section 3.6.7) for availability and utilization, to ensure that equipment stocks will be large enough for operators to requisition what they want for every shift. Some form of statistical approach will probably be necessary at this stage. It is useful to analyse past data in the form of a histogram of the number of units of a particular type demanded per shift over a particular period. The total inventory level and the actual number of available units for each of those shifts are also plotted, so that it can be seen at a glance when demand exceeded supply. The plot can also be converted into a cumulative frequency distribution, which will enable planners to set their inventory safety margins appropriate to conditions in the port.

Another factor in setting optimum inventory levels is the allocation practice used in the port, particularly the number of machines normally deployed on specific tasks. Practices vary considerably in the ports investigated. In some ports – particularly those that set high performance standards – allocation is generous, with the aim of providing operators with the greatest flexibility to attain maximum berth/terminal throughput and to cope with short-term fluctuations in berth handling rates. They can then transfer units to different activities as needed, to ensure that all the berth operations are in balance (see Chapter 5). In ports where the equipment management function is less well developed and where there is a severe shortage of machines, some form of rationing is applied and operators have to make do with fewer machines than they need to sustain good cargo-handling performances. In yet other ports, a policy of over-investment is practised, ensuring that operators are allocated sufficient units each day, but resulting in more machines being purchased than are really needed.

Clearly, *some* reserve capacity is needed to cope with fluctuations in demand and to allow for servicing of equipment, but *excess* reserve represents costly unnecessary investment, often in scarce foreign exchange, which must be avoided. Much of the need for reserve equipment, covering short-term and seasonal peaking, can be avoided through careful allocation planning and deployment practice – moving equipment between activities, between berths, terminals or areas to match the need, hour by hour. There are difficulties, however, where the dock estate is divided into distinct and dedicated terminals or units, possibly with different ownership or management and with equipment 'captive' to particular areas. Nevertheless, even in these ports experience shows that it is possible to establish informal arrangements between operators that allow mobile equipment to be temporarily transferred between areas to meet peak demands. Only practical difficulties of incompatibility or manoeuvrability (e.g. of rubber-tyred gantry cranes) are major obstacles to the workability of such flexible allocation and deployment strategies.

The most common method of forecasting optimum stock levels uses traffic officers' 'rules of thumb' for allocating equipment. For example, many ports allocate two 3-5 tonne forklift trucks per working crane or derrick to the quay transfer operation in conventional general cargo trades. Other units are assigned to receipt and delivery and other berth activities, so that a total complement of equipment is identified for each berth. The maximum daily demand for each category is then the sum of those allocated to all berths. A realistic availability level is then applied to determine the minimum stock of equipment that will ensure the

Table 3.6.5 Ranges of typical performance values for container handling equipment

Equipment Type	Throughput (boxes/unit/yr)	Handling rate/hour	Moves/box throughput	Average Moves/ machine/year
Straddle carrier				
(older models)	8,000-10,000	12-15	2.5-3.0	20,000-30,000
(new models)	12,000-14,000	12-15	2.5-3.0	30,000-42,000
Rubber-tyred				
gantry crane	20,000	20	3.0-3.5	60,000-70,000
Rail-mounted				
gantry crane	35,000-40,000	25	3.0-3.5	105,000-140,000
Lift truck	6,000-8,000	7-10	3.0	18,000-24,000

average daily demand can be met, and then this figure is adjusted by the relevant Peaking Factor. Sensitivity analysis might be undertaken to assess the consequences of changes in availability etc.

An alternative approach is to estimate equipment requirements on the basis of the number of tonnes of cargo to be handled and the performance of a typical machine in terms of tonnes handled per year or moves completed per working hour. In some cases, more detailed calculations are prepared using average equipment travel and hoist speeds, in empty and loaded conditions, and travel distances for the berth or terminal in question. Such calculations contain a high margin of error, as the number of tonnes handled or moves completed per hour will depend on a number of factors: the activity being performed (quay transfer, storage, receipt/delivery), the layout of the berth or terminal, average equipment travel speed, the skills of the drivers, etc. However, it is possible to determine an average handling rate for individual pieces of equipment in this way. Table 3.6.5 shows a range of typical values, usable for planning purposes, for the main types of container-handling equipment (Thomas & Roach, 1988). The major uncertainty of calculating optimum equipment stock levels in this way is that it does not take into account peaking problems and actual (or planned) availability levels.

Some ports use even more sophisticated mathematical techniques to predict optimum equipment inventories. These can be of a variety of types, but they can be conveniently summarized as simulation techniques (e.g. using Monte Carlo risk analysis) and methods relying on queuing theory. For example, simulation involves the use of computers to model different operational scenarios, in which throughput, berth/terminal performance, equipment performance, utilization and availability, ship arrival patterns, and other factors can all be varied to investigate the likely outcomes. The

planners can, using such techniques, try out, as it were, the effects of different equipment inventories on the port's standards of service, to estimate the statistical probability of cargo-handling demand being met under different circumstances. The principal advantage of mathematical techniques in equipment inventory planning is that model parameters can be changed and proposed modifications to working practices can be simulated very rapidly, and economic and other benefits of alternative systems can be evaluated. They are particularly good at assessing the sensitivity of changes in the system behaviour. They are, however, totally dependent on reliable data and on the availability of carefully validated computer programs.

3.6.6 Reviewing the Port's Assets

At this stage in the planning process, the planning group will have arrived at a reasonably confident prediction of the numbers of each type of equipment that will be needed during the lifetime of the plan to handle the expected range and volume of traffic. The next stage is to review the existing equipment, for performance, age and condition, to determine which assets should be replaced or disposed of during the next plan period. The Engineering Management Information System will be able to provide most of the required data – e.g. the age of each item of equipment, its history of reliability, maintenance and repair – so that suspect items can be earmarked for further investigation. The engineers will want to inspect the targeted items in detail, surveying their condition and likely future problems. Just as important is to review the current cost of maintaining and running the machines; are there any which, although not nearing the end of their planned working lives, are becoming uneconomic to keep going?

Based on the results of the analysis, the Engineering Department should advise the planners on the units which they consider fully serviceable for the period of the plan, those which should be replaced (by either scrapping or selling) or transferred to lighter duties, and those for which an economic case can be made for refurbishment. The latter decision will be based on the estimated cost of overhauling and refurbishing, the expected life expectancy, performance, reliability, and running and maintenance cost of the refurbished machine, and the comparable figures for a suitable replacement machine. The analytical process ends up, then, with three lists of machines: those that will remain on the asset register as fully available to operators during the period of the plan, those that should be refurbished (and will be included for that purpose in the plan) and those that should be disposed of (this list should initiate the appropriate action without delay, to ensure that unserviceable equipment is removed from the asset register). To the latter list should also be added equipment that is, for various reasons, no longer needed by the port – perhaps because the cargo which it was designed to handle is no longer shipped through the port, or because the volume of that cargo has fallen substantially and there are surplus units. These items, too, should be disposed of appropriately.

The result of this stage in the process is a predicted revision of the port's inventory of equipment, indicating to the planners how many of the existing machines will be available to meet the estimated need. This list will, in due course, take its place alongside that summarizing the calculated optimum equipment levels when the supply and demand sides of the equation are reconciled. Before that stage, however, there is one more important step, in which the maintenance parameters for the period of the plan are set.

3.6.7 Setting Engineering Objectives and Targets

The tacit assumption in this outline of the planning process has been that utilization, downtime and availability statistics are known when the optimum equipment inventory levels are being calculated. However, 'availability' is not a fixed quantity; it can be increased, for example by taking on extra or better qualified maintenance staff, or giving existing staff further training, or by improving quality control, building new and better workshops, buying new maintenance machinery, improving spare part management, and so on. So the planning process offers a golden opportunity for reviewing existing maintenance quality and setting the Engineering Department new objectives and availability targets for the period of the plan, just as the operators can be set performance targets for their use of the equipment.

The Engineering Department objectives should include a statement of the maintenance policy and strategies to be pursued, and specific targets for the minimum availability figure to be attained for each category of equipment. To encourage cost-consciousness, the targets should also include maximum expenditure levels for each type of machine (calculated on the basis of a percentage of the capital cost of the machine, adjusted by asset age). The targets must be realistically attainable by the maintenance staff, providing motivation and promoting efficiency; they should be linked to an appropriate incentive scheme (see Chapter 8). A good example of such a set of objectives is reproduced in Appendix 4.

In the light of the agreed engineering targets (specifically those relating to equipment availability), the planners are now in a position to reconcile their demand and supply data.

3.6.8 Reconciling Demand and Supply

The final step in the calculation phase of equipment planning is to examine side by side the two sets of figures that have now been prepared: the list of equipment needed to meet the predicted traffic demand for the period of the plan (either for next year or the successive years of a medium-term plan), and the list of equipment that will be available from the port's inventory, in good working order, during the period. The newly revised engineering targets will allow the team to calculate, from the 'demand' list, how many of each type of equipment will have to be in the port's stock to ensure that the required number are available at any time; for example, if 25 5-tonne forklift trucks are estimated to be needed per shift to handle the expected break-bulk general cargo throughput (at the agreed 'risk' level with respect to peaking) and the agreed availability level will be 85%, then 30 machines of that type will have to be in the stock. If the inventory at that time (assuming that those machines recommended for disposal have been sold, and that those planned for refurbishment have been returned to full working order) will contain only 24 machines, then the provisional equipment plan should include the purchase of an additional six forklifts.

This is, however, just the first estimate of the shortfall between demand and supply. The planning team will need to discuss the provisional list of equipment purchases at length, in the light of the financial and other constraints to be considered in the next section. They must consider a range of alternative operational and planning strategies: could more flexible deployment reduce the need for additional equipment? Could peak demand be met by hiring as needed from local suppliers? Could the substitution of a new model of machine, with increased performance capability, reduce the number of replacement machines needed? The planning process is, therefore, not over at this stage; it is, as we shall see, a reiterative or recursive process, going through successive stages of revision before being presented to senior management and the Board.

3.6.9 Financial and Administrative Constraints

The equipment planning process does not take place in a vacuum, of course, and the recommendations of the planners will not necessarily be fully approved by the higher authorities. During the planning meetings, then, the team must take into account a number of potential constraints both on the timing of the acquisitions and on the nature and cost of the requested equipment. Three categories of constraints can be distinguished, all affecting the progress and outcome of the planning process:

1. **Financial Constraints:** Of obvious concern to the port when considering the equipment plan is whether sufficient funds are available in the capital budget for the year(s) in question and, in many ports, whether the necessary foreign exchange can be obtained. The capital budget will depend on corporate profitability, competing demands for finite resources, and any investment or budgetary limits set by government. The foreign exchange element may be avoidable, if the equipment is manufactured in the country or can be supplied through a local agent or distributor for local currency. Clearly, it would be wise in the later stages of planning for the team to consult with senior Finance Department staff on the availability of financial resources to cover the planned purchases. Top management will also be able to advise whether a foreign loan might be available or if the investment might be included in a current or planned multilateral or bilateral aid programme. Such discussions could very well initiate further discussions between operations and engineering staff on alternative types or models of equipment and sources of supply. It is also worth bearing in mind that the Finance Department's own figures for port profitability in the years in question will be directly affected by changes in the equipment

inventory; extra equipment could increase handling costs, but could also reduce demurrage payments and attract new business; replacing current machines with newer models could directly reduce handling costs while maintaining or improving throughput. Both of these possibilities would increase profitability. Clearly, *none* of the estimated figures used as input to the planning process is fixed and immutable; they all need to be revised as the planning proceeds, as they all affect each other to greater or lesser extent.

2. **Government Controls:** Even if the port finds that the equipment plan is attainable within its budget, there could be government controls that interfere with the implementation of the plan. Reference has been made earlier (Chapter 2) to the variety of controls commonly imposed by government ministries and central planning bodies in developing countries. They include limits on capital expenditure, foreign exchange limits, import duties, restrictions on trade with particular manufacturing countries (and positive discrimination towards others, e.g. with counter-trade agreements) and so on. Even if the controls are surmountable in the particular case of the current plan, they will inevitably take time to satisfy, and will have a profound influence on the timing of the planning process. It *must* be launched in good time to complete all discussions and clear all obstacles before the procurement process itself needs to start (Chapter 4). The control procedures also confirm the need for very detailed statistics and arguments to back up the request for equipment; the planners must be absolutely sure of their case and be able to justify the plan if asked to do so by senior managers, the Board and government representatives.

3. **Internal Procedural Delays:** As will be explained in Chapter 4, the procurement procedure may take a considerable time, particularly where there are stringent port and government regulations controlling the process, with a series of committees and tender boards within the port and review procedures in ministries, the central bank, customs and other agencies. The equipment plan itself may also have to pass through a sequence of reviews and committees before reaching the Board. So, to ensure that the required equipment is delivered and commissioned by the time it is needed, the planning process clearly has to be initiated at a very early stage in some ports.

So the planning process has to be very carefully sequenced and managed if all stages are to be completed in time and if its resultant plan will be still relevant to the port's needs when it is finally implemented. It is appropriate next to review that planning process in summary.

3.6.10 The Planning Process

The process of preparing an equipment plan is a complex and often long-drawn-out affair. Many months – even years – may elapse between the initial identification of the need for additional equipment and its purchase, delivery and commissioning. The earlier the process has to start, of course, the less reliable the forecasting can be; many elements of the basic data input to the process may themselves change as the plan develops. It is essential, therefore, for the planning process itself to be properly planned and managed, if it is to reach an effective and valid conclusion in good time. The steps in the process (summarized also in Figure 3.6.10) are as follows:

1. Forecast developments in cargo-handling methods for the major commodities handled by the port, particularly the wider use of equipment, taking account of commercial and other developments likely to affect equipment needs;

2. Prepare traffic forecasts for each major commodity class and cargo type, taking account of seasonal and other variations;

3. Convert the traffic forecasts into the quantity of work to be performed by cargo-handling equipment;

4. Review the performance levels of existing equipment, taking into account utilization data, and predict future equipment performance, in terms of hours of operation per annum, utilization levels, etc.;

5. Review and assess Operations Department objectives and the performance targets for each major trade and ship operator for the period of the plan;

6. Determine future equipment requirements by type and capacity;

7. Review present equipment condition, reliability and maintenance problems, and running and maintenance costs, to determine which units to retain, refurbish or dispose of;

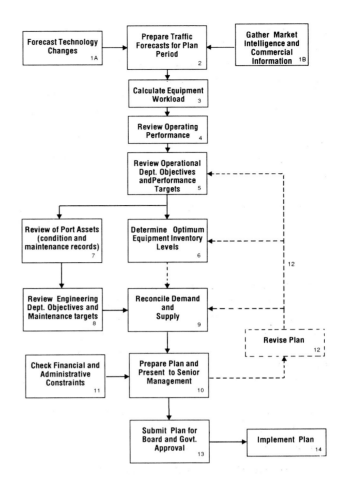

Figure 3.6.10: The Equipment Planning Process

8. Review maintenance performance targets (especially for availability) and maintenance budget limits for the machines which will remain on the asset register, and calculate the optimum stock of machines needed to meet shift demands;

9. Compare the calculated equipment demand with the current supply position to determine the predicted shortfall (or excess) during the period of the plan, for each type and capacity of machine;

10. Set out the plan in provisional detail, in terms of the number of machines of each type needed to be purchased, refurbished and disposed of for each year of the period in question, with brief notes justifying the need for each of these actions as well as first estimates of costs;

11. Present the provisional plan to senior management, including Finance Department representatives, to assess its financial implications in the light of port, governmental and other controls;

61

12. Revise the plan in the light of budgetary and other controls, reconsidering deployment and allocation strategies, alternative machines and models, and sources of supply as appropriate; these latter stages of the process may be recursive and reiterative (dotted lines in Fig. 3.6.10);

13. Present the plan, via senior management, to the Board with all necessary supporting documents and arguments (attendance at presentation meetings may be necessary, to defend the plan);

14. When the plan has been approved, take part in its implementation by working with procurement staff to ensure that the procurement process progresses smoothly and that the appropriate purchases are made; opportunity will also be provided in this stage to gain understanding of the problems encountered during specification, tendering and other activities involved in procurement, so that the lessons learnt can be incorporated in the next equipment plan.

The preparation of the equipment plan clearly involves considerable participation by senior and middle managers of the Operations, Engineering, Commercial, Planning and Finance Departments. Co-ordination of the various activities making up the planning process and good communication between all the parties are absolutely essential. To that end, some ports have placed in overall charge of the process the head of one of the departments involved – usually the Head of Planning or Management Services – and have encouraged a formal committee approach, rather than relying on informal contact between the contributing individuals. Given the vital importance of the equipment plan to the development and efficiency of the port (in terms of operations and maintenance in particular), proper management of the planning process is essential, and the information and views collected in this study give strong support for the establishment of a permanent Equipment Planning Committee, consisting of senior members of all the relevant departments.

3.7 Recommendations

1. The vital importance of planning future equipment requirements should be acknowledged by formalizing the function through an Equipment Planning Committee, consisting of representatives of the Engineering, Operations, Marine, Finance and Planning Departments.

2. Policy makers and senior port managers must establish formal procedures and devote adequate resources to ensure that an equipment plan is competently prepared.

3. The equipment plan should be included in the port's corporate plan and be a permanent and regular feature of the annual capital budget.

4. Ports should be given autonomy to develop and implement the equipment plan, within the budgetary or financial constraints imposed by central governmental and other regulations.

5. The plan should take the form of a revolving five-year plan, outlining future equipment and financial needs, and a detailed annual plan with more reliable estimates of investment.

6. Approval of the equipment plan and the sanctioning of equipment investment should be the responsibility of the Board of Directors, following simple procedures and timetabled to avoid delays in implementing the plan, and purchasing and commissioning the equipment.

7. Central government involvement in equipment planning, approval of investment, and the procurement process should be kept (or reduced) to the minimum.

8. The equipment planning committee must have available to them a comprehensive and reliable information system, providing them with all the data they need for their calculations, if an appropriate and reliable equipment plan is to be prepared.

9. The planners must have reliable traffic forecasts and related market intelligence reports, for use in estimating the amount of work to be performed by equipment, operating and performance data for existing plant, and information on current operating and maintenance costs.

10. A clear and tested procedure and timetable should be applied for the preparation of the equipment plans, strictly managed by the Equipment Planning Committee.

11. Annual and medium-term (five-year) traffic forecasts should be prepared and the data presented in suitable manner for managers to calculate the amount of cargo-handling work to be performed by equipment.

12. Methods must be established (and followed) for continuously gathering market intelligence and other relevant information for use in predicting future traffic levels and equipment needs.

13. Data should be recorded regularly on equipment operation, to allow utilization, availability and downtime to be calculated for individual units and for each category of equipment.

14. Periodic studies should be carried out to determine equipment performance for use in setting deployment practices and in equipment planning.

15. An appropriate equipment replacement strategy should be set for each category of equipment, based on current levels of use, local operating conditions and sound economic criteria, and depreciation schedules should be adjusted accordingly.

16. Procedures must be established for inspection and review of operating and maintenance records (including costs) of all units nearing the end of their working/economic lives.

17. Procedures must exist to allow ports to dispose of assets that can no longer fulfil their duties, are uneconomic to operate or maintain, or are surplus to operators' requirements.

18. The port must have an equipment cost control system, to supply data to assist managers in taking decisions on equipment replacement.

19. Departmental objectives must be established for the Operations Department, which lay down minimum performance and/or customer service standards, to which equipment needs must be related.

20. Maintenance performance targets should be set for all categories of equipment, stating minimum availability levels for each category of equipment and maintenance budgetary limits for each unit of plant.

21. Optimum inventory levels must be set for each category of equipment, based on established operating and maintenance objectives, the extent of fluctuations in demand, current deployment practices and relevant commercial information.

22. Predictions are required of the scale of the annual capital budget and estimates of the proportion available for the purchase of equipment.

23. The equipment plan, setting out the port's investment programme and the assumption on which it is based, should be distributed to all senior managers for information and comment.

CHAPTER 4

Procurement and Maintenance

4.1 Review of Existing Procurement Methods

4.1.1 Introduction

In Chapter 3 the importance was stressed of acquiring the right type of equipment, in sufficient numbers, to meet the needs of operators and to allow the engineers to follow good maintenance practices. Implementing the equipment plan involves the process of procurement, a vital part of the equipment planning process and one which can directly affect operating efficiency and the demand on the port's maintenance facilities.

The lack of appropriate procurement policies and strategies in many of the LDC ports surveyed in this study has caused considerable operating and maintenance difficulty, through the aquisition of unsuitable machines. Even where the inventory planning procedures have been carried out well, procurement practices (often as a result of government interference) have prevented ports acquiring what engineers and operators believe to be the most appropriate machines. What governments have decided was a 'good buy' has often proved to be an expensive mistake – poor cargo-handling performance, high downtime, problems with spare parts and even premature scrapping and replacement. The main problem has sometimes been that the port has insisted on purchasing 'state-of-the-art' technology, beyond the capability of the Engineering Department to service. Frequently, it's a question of government-imposed controls on investment levels and access to foreign exchange for equipment and spare parts purchase. At other times, difficulties are caused by inability to standardize (so that operators and engineers have to cope with a wide range of incompatible machines, systems and components), or poor technical specifications, or inadequate bid evaluation procedures.

All such mistakes and ill-considered decisions have profound effects on the workload of the engineering workshops and on the difficulties faced by technical staff. LDC ports must formulate a coherent set of procurement policies and strategies, so that the equipment plan can be properly carried out and so that all operational and engineering considerations are fully satisfied. This chapter reviews the problems arising from current procurement methods, and proposes changes to regulatory and management procedures aimed at improving procurement practices to the benefit of operational and engineering efficiency. This first section reviews the range of current problems and deficiencies that emerged during this study.

4.1.2 Absence of Coherent Procurement Policies

Many of the ports surveyed seem to have no clear, concise set of procurement policies and strategies; when questioned, port managers and government officials tended to give vague and contradictory answers about them. Often, senior managers seemed to be confusing 'procurement policies' with government or corporate regulations, and 'strategies' with internal procedures for preparing tender documents, evaluating bids, and so on. Clearly, many LDC ports have given far too little thought to strategic procurement decisions. No policies have been formulated on manufacturer and model diversity, on stock holding and supplies procurement, nor on the extent of technical assistance to be sought at time of purchase.

One of the most serious consequences of this lack of policy is that LDC ports often have a wide range of model types, purchased from a large number of manufacturers. Some engineers remarked that their equipment inventory is a 'mechanical zoo' of assorted machines; this presents major difficulties for the workshops and for supplies managers, who have to keep track of spare parts for many different types of equipment. Indeed, some ports with a declared corporate objective of minimizing spares stock-holding had a totally opposing equipment procurement policy which constantly expanded the range of models and manufacturers.

Other policy deficiencies complained of by managers concerned technician training (no arrangements included in procurement contracts for training workshop staff to service the new machines) and spare parts stocking (inconsistent and ill thought-out decisions on the quantity and range of spares and consumables to purchase along with a new machine). These and the other policy shortcomings bore heavily not only on the engineering staff, of course, but on the operators as well, as availability and reliability of the new equipment fell short of expectations.

In fairness to the ports, many of the policy difficulties result directly from government interference and the constraints imposed by public sector procurement regulations; these will be considered next.

4.1.3 Rigid Government Procurement Regulations

Most port authorities and many cargo-handling contractors are in some form of public ownership, and are accordingly subject to control by central, regional and/or state governments. As discussed in Chapter 2, the activities of public sector ports, and their freedom to formulate and implement policies, are to greater or lesser degree (in LDC ports usually the former!) regulated by central government ministries, parastatal agencies and local legislative assemblies, and such regulation is particularly common with regard to procurement of equipment and other assets.

Although procedures differ in detail, these ports follow long-established and basically similar procurement regulations when acquiring plant and machinery – regulations largely inherited from former colonial powers. Central government seems to have a pervasive influence on all aspects of the procurement process, regulating every action of these LDC ports. In sharp contrast, those ports visited in developed countries, managed under a mix of public and private ownership, have far less onerous restrictions placed on them and much greater autonomy when procuring assets. They can formulate procurement policies and strategies quite independently of government regulations, and acquire precisely the equipment that their operators and engineers recommend.

The regulations and restrictions imposed on LDC ports are primarily enacted to protect the public interest, rather than to achieve good economic results for the buyer. They are designed to fit in with national development objectives, national and international obligations, government-to-government relationships and trading agreements, and not the commercial and operational interests of the ports. Nevertheless, the ports have to comply strictly with them, even though they may have been given their own statutory powers (and a degree of – often spurious – independence) through Acts of Parliament or Presidential Decree. They are also subject to close ministerial scrutiny while they are carrying out their duties. It has been very apparent during this study that such close (even claustrophobic) government control is a major obstacle to the ports' ability to purchase sensibly with profitability and competitiveness the sole aims.

Government controls on procurement can take several forms. Through statutes and/or ministerial decrees they can dictate the procurement methods to be followed, and they can directly control the funding of purchases either by providing finance themselves, by sanctioning the use of funds, or by guaranteeing foreign loans. Ministries are often directly involved in the detailed management of the procurement process, even to the point of selecting the equipment supplier (often rejecting the recommendation of the port engineers and technical consultants). This is all the more remarkable when it is realized that those decisions are made by senior civil servants lacking any of the technical expertise needed to make informed decisions. Decisions are taken on political grounds, ignoring the interests of the port; it is hardly surprising in such circumstances that the equipment purchased is often quite unsuitable for local conditions. Under aid agreements (a major source of finance for equipment purchases in many LDCs), where the government is usually the contracting body and covers all aspects of procurement up to the transfer of the equipment to the port authority after commissioning, the engineers who will be responsible for maintaining the equipment may have had little or no involvement in preparing technical specifications, determining the workshop facilities that will be required, nor deciding what resources and staff training will be needed.

Regulatory procedures are used by many LDCs as a means of discriminating against foreign suppliers in favour of domestic manufacturers. Preference is given to indigenous manufacturers, irrespective of the quality and suitability of their products, and even if they are more expensive than imported machines would be if import duty were not imposed. Several instances were described to the team of equipment being purchased from local manufacturers which turned out to have much lower operating performance, higher downtime and higher maintenance costs than foreign machines. There were even cases where local industry had no suitable models in their ranges but import from overseas was prohibited, to encourage manufacturers to build those machines; ports were then forced to accept prototype machines, manufactured by companies with little or no experience in that field. Similar regulations often oblige ports to purchase locally-made spare parts; these are frequently of inferior quality, wear out quickly, and can cause damage to other components – increasing the amount of maintenance needed on all counts. These are extreme cases, but in many instances the port is required to make a very strong case before governments will even consider sanctioning the purchase of imported machines, and considerable lobbying of senior civil servants has to be carried out.

Another practice, apparently on the increase, is the preference given by governments to counter-trade or barter deals. As described in Chapter 2, these oblige ports to purchase from countries which are prepared to buy goods to an equivalent value from their own country. Several examples of this very restricting practice came to light in the survey. Although the national economic objectives lying behind the practice are appreciated, countertrade has resulted in some ports being forced to purchase inferior quality or unsuitable equipment, adding to their problems of model diversity and maintenance load. Indeed, there is little doubt that the apparent savings being made through such deals is actually a false economy, as the asset lives of these machines are often shorter than those of long-established and reputable manufacturers, so that they have to be replaced earlier than planned, and running and maintenance costs are frequently higher.

Another government regulation widely applied in LDCs forces ports, when evaluating competing manufacturers' tenders, to accept the lowest bid that meets 'a substantial part' of the technical specification – usually interpreted to mean about 80% of it. The port is thus not allowed to take into account the relative running and maintenance costs of the rival machines; these factors (and particularly the cost and ease of supply of spare parts) might well have prompted a very different selection. Even in ports where at least some attempt is made at such Life Cycle Costing (see Section 4.5.2), senior managers claimed that it is still extremely difficult to persuade government officials to agree to acceptance of bids that are not the lowest. It is widely understood that some major manufacturers take advantage of this to submit unrealistically low bids (hardly above manufacturing cost, it is suspected in some cases), with the intention of making all or most of their profit on the subsequent sale of spare parts and through engineering assistance and consultancy. In one verified case, a manufacturer charged $7,000 for a component available elsewhere for $500, and profit levels on spares of 350% are not uncommon. Manufacturers from one country are known to charge $10,000 a week to provide an engineer on site to carry out repairs; port engineers claim that the engineering manuals are deliberately undetailed and incomplete to ensure that such technical assistance will be required.

Engineers in some ports try to circumvent such 'lowest-price' regulations by specifying brand names in the technical specifications, perhaps insisting that a motor, engine or transmission matches that of equipment already on the inventory. Even this tactic is, however, prohibited by many government procurement regulations, and there is a great danger of a multi-model equipment fleet being purchased, against the engineers' wishes. The best that can be done, in those ports, is to specify systems, assemblies and components in such precise engineering detail that the suppliers will recognize what is being asked for, and so that it would be very difficult for them to attempt to match the specification with any less suitable or less desirable alternative.

Maintenance problems frequently arise where equipment is supplied as part of an aid programme or where loans are provided by donors at preferential rates of interest. Such agreements normally attach clauses restricting choice to equipment manufactured in the donor country. The recipient port has little or no option over choice of supplier or model, and there is a considerable risk that unsuitable machines will be supplied. Donors often take little care in investigating the operating and maintenance conditions in the port, or how easily spare parts will be obtainable. LDC ports relying on this form of funding are really adopting a policy of 'anything is better than nothing', and in effect are assuming that each wave of aid will be followed by another, to solve the problems that will inevitably result from having to operate and maintain unsuitable machines. This most certainly does not generate self-sufficiency and independence of outlook.

Among the problems cited as resulting from such aid programmes were:

— a port which had eight different makes of forklift truck of one capacity on the inventory, with no common assemblies or components;

— equipment designed and constructed for a temperate climate supplied without modification to a tropical port;

— a prototype, 'state-of-the-art' machine supplied to an LDC port with a notoriously poor maintenance reputation.

Clearly, ostensibly generous gestures by a donor country can generate maintenance and operating problems in a recipient port for years to come, unless care is taken at time of procurement.

4.1.4 Excessive Financial Controls

As explained in Chapter 2, many ports are unable to retain revenues for use in procurement; all funds must be sought from central governments, and these frequently impose strict and unrealistic limits on such finance. Capital budgets (and even, in some cases, revenue budgets) are closely scrutinized and limited, even where ports make substantial operating surpluses and are major earners of foreign exchange for the country. The imposition of capital rationing prevents ports from replacing assets that have reached the ends of their economic lives and from purchasing the vital spare parts needed to keep plant in good operating condition. It also places pressure on ports to accept 'lowest-bid' tenders, even where procurement regulations do not insist on that.

Another financial barrier that distorts the procurement process is the imposition of severe import duties and taxes on equipment and spares purchased overseas. Import duties on heavy plant and machinery regularly exceed 100% in some countries, and levels of 250% are not uncommon on electrical and electronic components. Such a barrier greatly increases the cost of spare parts and maintenance, as well as reducing the port's ability to select the most appropriate equipment for local operating and maintenance conditions.

Many governmental financial controls cause serious delays to the procurement process. For example, approval for foreign exchange spending often has to be obtained from relevant ministries and central banks, letters of credit have to be sought and other administrative requirements fulfilled – not just for expensive equipment but also for relatively inexpensive spare parts. Delays of many months and even years typically occur between the identification of a need by engineers and delivery of the items to the port. For example, in one country, a fund of about $80,000 is set aside for emergency procurement of spares – on the face of it, a very sensible arrangement (even though the sum is, in the view of management, grossly inadequate), but gaining access to that fund is an extraordinarily complex process:

— first, the port must obtain from the supplier a written or telexed quotation;
— on receipt, the quotation is given a technical scrutiny by the engineers, to check for suitability;
— if the item costs *less* than $7,700, the Controller of Supplies can approve purchase, but he then has to apply for an import licence from the relevant government agency; this can take a month or more;
— when the licence is granted, the controller has to apply for a letter of credit for the FOB cost, payable in foreign currency, and simultaneously issues a formal order to the supplier; the process can take many days or even months (average ten days); delivery is then awaited;

— if the item costs *more* than $7,700, clearance has to be obtained from the Ministry of Commerce;
— when permission to proceed is granted, a check has to be made on whether the item can be purchased in the country; the ministry responsible often queries the result of this search, and those queries have to be answered, possibly by visiting the ministry to defend the port's case;
— when the items have been cleared, the Controller of Supplies applies for foreign exchange release from the Ministry of Transport (based on a CIF quotation from the supplier) – another possible one- or two-month delay;
— when foreign exchange release has been obtained, the Controller can apply for an import licence and letter of credit. Altogether, there can be a delay of between four and six months before the order is written (by which time the purchase price of the item may well have increased, requiring a new quotation and the process has to start again!).

There are, in fact, further bureaucratic fences: open insurance has to be arranged, rules on paying freight followed, national flag vessels selected for transport, a freight-forwarding company has to be contacted to co-ordinate importation and to make payments, customs clearance has to be arranged, and so on. And this process, stretching over many months, is the 'emergency' procurement procedure, intended to enable engineers to respond quickly to the port's needs! While all that bureaucratic process grinds its way onwards, the equipment under repair sits, useless, in the workshop.

Although that may seem to be an isolated, extreme case, many other examples were collected of rigid financial and other controls interfering with procurement. In some ports, for example, elaborate tender procedures, involving the collection of six or more written quotations, have to be followed for the purchase even of items costing a few dollars. In many ports, totally unrealistic financial limits are placed on engineers and supplies staff, forcing them to get senior management (or even government) approval for relatively inexpensive, urgently required spare parts. All these obstacles make the management and implementation of maintenance that much more difficult.

4.1.5 Inadequate Technical Specifications
This survey has revealed two major deficiencies in the preparation of technical specifications for new equipment, both with a direct impact on the port's maintenance function:

1. Imprecision in the identification of the user (operator) requirements on which the performance specification should be based, allowing less conscientious suppliers to offer machines which, superficially at least, match the specification but in reality will not fulfil the purchaser's requirements. For example, the operator may specify a front-end loader 'to lift 35 tonnes', without stating that it is required to do so to a four-high stack; a supplier might well offer a machine that can lift a full 40-foot container only to a three-high stack, and be correct in doing so. Nevertheless, the machine will not do what the operator wants, and either operational efficiency will suffer or an unnecessary extra machine will subsequently have to be acquired.

2. Careless engineering specification can result in the purchase of equipment that the port cannot effectively operate and/or maintain. Examples were given to the team of engineering specifications so vague as to allow the purchase of equipment quite unsuited to tropical conditions (of temperature, humidity and salinity), and others of specifications demanding the latest technology, with complex electronic control and automation systems completely beyond the capability of the technical staff to maintain. Weaknesses in engineering specifications also make it more difficult for engineers to convince members of Tender Boards of the value of selecting equipment that is technically superior and has lower Life Cycle Costs, even though it is not the cheapest on offer.

Senior managers in several ports agreed that inadequate preparation of user requirements – the performance specification – was the primary cause of specification errors, a view endorsed by equipment manufacturers. Examples were given of:

— operators demanding features that they neither needed nor could use, raising the purchase price unnecessarily;

— equipment purchased with insufficient capacity to handle the intended cargo, because operators failed to specify all the lifting and stacking activities the machine was expected to do, and the conditions under which it was to work; they often did not take into account the de-rating necessary when attachments are fitted and when stacking high;

— vehicles specified with hard tyres (for economy and long tyre life), but which proved too uncomfortable to use on the quays and stacking areas;

— machines ordered with dimensions too large to allow them to enter enclosed storage areas or to move under overhead power cables, or with turning circles too large for the layout of the areas in which they have to operate.

Considerable scope clearly exists to improve performance specification procedures in LDC ports; suggestions for such improvement are made in Section 4.3.3.

An interesting finding of this study has been the variety of approaches adopted in the preparation of engineering specifications. Some ports prepare very detailed specifications, even for off-the-shelf purchases – specifying the construction materials to be used (e.g. steel plate and paint thicknesses), engine ratings, electrical installation standards, etc. In effect, their engineers participate in the design process. Other ports stress the preparation of a detailed *performance* specification, merely adding that the machine must meet stated national or international construction standards; it is then left to the manufacturers to advise on the unit which best meets the purchasers' requirements. Institutional arrangements, particularly the nature and extent of government procurement regulations, influence the detail required (or permitted) in the specification.

Many LDC ports now incorporate in the technical specification a requirement that the supplier should provide all necessary training of drivers and technicians, but this is often specified in far too little detail, with the result that the manufacturer (who often has little training skill, experience or enthusiasm) can get away with the minimum of training, of very inadequate quality. The sort of detail that should be specified is considered in Section 4.3.3.7.

4.1.6 Inadequate Spare Parts Procurement

A serious deficiency noted at many LDC ports is their inadequately formulated policy for the acquisition of spare parts, both at the time of equipment purchase and for subsequent stores replenishment. Problems in supplies management are endemic in developing countries (as will be discussed at length in Chapter 7) and are a major cause of poor maintenance. In the present context, the primary concern is with policy options at the time of equipment purchase.

There are two broad approaches to spares purchase when new equipment is being acquired:

1. The policy in some ports is to confine initial purchases to those consumable items (e.g. lube oils, filters) needed for routine preventive maintenance during the warranty period, leaving replacement parts to be supplied by the

manufacturers under the guarantee. During the period of the warranty (usually a year), the engineers prepare a list of the parts actually used, and those expected to be needed subsequently, and these are then added to the stores stock at the appropriate levels in readiness for the second year of operation. Clearly, this policy is only feasible where the port has ready access to spares, either through local agents of the manufacturer or direct from the factory, and where administrative and financial constraints are not a problem, so that there is little risk of delays in supply.

2. In other ports, a full manufacturers' recommended list of spares is acquired along with the equipment, either because the port is distant from all sources of supply or because of likely bureaucratic delays and difficulties in getting quick clearance of foreign exchange expenditure.

This study has shown that neither policy is appropriate for LDC ports, and that both contribute to the present difficulties experienced in supplies management. The second option, for example, frequently results in the wrong parts being stocked – some remaining in the stores, unused, throughout the life of the equipment – or the right ones being bought in insufficient quantities or not at all. There have been cases where about 20% of the cost price of equipment was spent on spare parts, many of which will *never* be used (e.g. gantry crane rail wheels, gear boxes, complete brake assemblies and complete electric motors) while parts that certainly *will* be needed were not stocked. Appropriate policies for spare parts procurement are discussed in Section 4.3.3.6.

4.1.7 Deficiencies in Procurement Management

A number of weaknesses identified in present procurement management could have a direct effect on maintenance. The most serious of these concerns the government regulations in most LDCs demanding that ports follow completely open national or international competitive tendering for equipment purchases. The consequence is often a very large number of suppliers bidding for the supply – thirty bids or more are not unusual in some of the ports visited. If the lowest bid meeting the specifications has to be accepted, it is very likely that the port will have to purchase from a new and untried source, with no consideration of makes and models already in the port's asset inventory, and with no account taken of standardization, compatibility or ease of servicing.

In two of the participating countries, procurement has to be arranged through local agents registered with the government. Most of these agents are factors who hold limited stocks but offer no maintenance services or technical support; few, if any, are dealers or distributors, who would provide such services. The disadvantages of this regulation are:

— the agents have neither the qualifications, expertise nor experience to advise the port on technical matters;

— the port's engineers are prohibited from going directly to the manufacturer to discuss their technical needs;

— purchase costs will be increased, since the agent will apply a commission to the manufacturer's price before selling on.

Even where regulations allow ports to purchase through international procurement agencies (e.g. the UK Crown Agents) or the country's own central purchasing agencies, there is still a limitation of direct contact between engineers and manufacturers, and a lack of opportunity for engineers to discuss maintenance factors in detail with suppliers.

The port's own bureaucratic procedures associated with procurement, particularly those defining tender document preparation and bid evaluation, often cause lengthy delays to the process, especially damaging in the acquisition of spare parts. Elaborate and time-consuming procedures have to be followed in many ports when selecting suppliers: hierarchies of Tender Boards, each restricted in the maximum value of purchases they can approve, and each supported by specialist committees that examine technical, operational or financial matters. In one port there are five Tender Boards ranging from a committee chaired by the Chief Engineer (with powers to authorize purchases up to $15,000) to the Cabinet of Ministers (needed to approve all acquisitions over $150,000 – effectively, all equipment purchases).

There was general dissatisfaction with current bid evaluation procedures and with the lack of thorough financial appraisal of competing bids. This was largely a subjective exercise, commonly applying a ranking system (giving an order of priority to such factors as price, delivery times, warranty periods), and in very few cases is there a detailed investment appraisal or life cycle costing approach. Senior managers complained to the team that there is a severe shortage of appropriately qualified and experienced procurement staff.

There are also grave shortcomings in the way bidding documents are prepared: in some ports the Chief Engineer is entirely responsible, in others the

Head of Purchasing/Supplies and in yet others the Head of Operations. None of these approaches is really satisfactory, as effective specification, bid evaluation and final selection should be a joint, consultative process if the right equipment is to be chosen.

Multi-donor projects involving the construction of facilities, purchase of equipment and provision of technical assistance raise particular problems in procurement management, demanding a clear management strategy and full co-operation between the several donors and port management. Examples gathered during the survey showed that such co-operation can be sadly lacking – donors competing with one another for the right to supply equipment, no overall plan (only a collection of uncoordinated sub-plans), duplication of facilities and training schemes, and general confusion in the minds of port officials and technical assistance experts. In one port, there were widely divergent views on the structure and location of workshops; the port authority had commissioned a sequence of six independent consultants' reports on workshop facilities, and still could not agree a plan with donors. There were similar disagreements over training philosophies, and the equipment being supplied by the various donors turned out to be incompatible with each other and with the port's existing stock, which must have stretched the maintenance capability of the port to the limits.

Complications can also arise when aid projects involve contracting and subcontracting to a series of 'third parties'. In one current example, the aid agency contracted by an LDC government to supervise (and fund) a project has itself contracted its own government's purchasing agency to procure container cranes, and that agency has then sub-contracted a national crane manufacturer – an extremely complex situation which is likely to cause considerable problems if disputes arise over the commissioned cranes! Another general criticism of aid projects is the comparatively short time for which technical assistance is provided as part of the procurement process – insufficient time to ensure upgrading of maintenance facilities of technical staff skills.

Clearly, management of the procurement process has many deficiencies, as have other aspects of procurement in the ports of LDCs. Considerable changes need to be made and new strategies and policies need to be devised. These improvements will be discussed in the next section.

4.2 Equipment Procurement Strategies and Policies

4.2.1 Strategies and Policies

Many of the difficulties and deficiencies described in Section 4.1 can be resolved by formulating and adhering to suitable procurement policies and strategies. (A procurement *policy* for capital equipment can be defined as a set of long-term goals or objectives which the port wishes to achieve, while *strategies* are the means of achieving those objectives.) To clarify the relationships between procurement policies and strategies, it is useful to picture a hierarchy of management objectives, each level in harmony with the others:

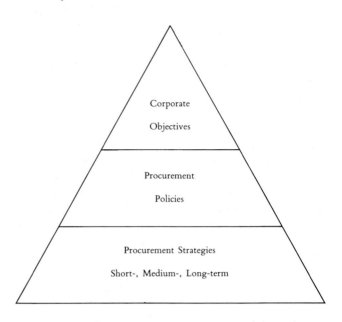

An example of a long-term procurement policy objective could be to reduce to a minimum the spare parts stockholding – perhaps as part of a wider policy of reducing the capital investment tied up in spares stocks and minimizing the cost of stock-holding. The objective can be achieved either by revising stock control strategy, or by buying on demand from local, stock-holding suppliers. The latter strategy might be precluded because local suppliers do not hold stocks of relevant spares, and the short-term strategy might have to be to revise the port's stock control, but this could be pursued alongside a longer-term strategy of encouraging the local suppliers to hold stocks of the spares that the port needs. The policy and its enabling strategies would fit within the port's corporate objective of maximizing profitability by reducing expenditure in each of the port's cost centres. Other procurement policies might be to limit the variety of makes and models of machines in the inventory, or to standardize on a particular make of engine or transmission – perhaps because local companies have experience in maintaining and overhauling them. To meet those policy objectives, appropriate strategies might be to amend procurement regulations, and to be more rigorous when preparing technical specifications.

The procurement policies adopted must be consistent with, and designed to promote, the port's corporate objectives and its development plans, and strategic questions that could provide the basis for the formulation of those policies are:

— What is to be procured?
— How should it be procured?
— When and why should it be procured?
— Who should be responsible for procurement?
— From whom should it be procured?

These questions will be considered in turn in the following sections, to illustrate the way in which an appropriate set of procurement policies can be formulated.

4.2.2 What is to be Procured?

Several policy matters need to be considered under this heading. First, should the port procure standard, off-the-shelf equipment or specially designed equipment? Generally, the former is preferable for cost, availability and spare parts supply reasons, leaving the latter as an option for specific, unique purchases, such as bulk-loading plant – in which case, port engineers may be involved in the design of the plant, collaborating closely with the manufacturer, or may need to employ a consultant (another strategic consideration). Indeed, engineers in more and more ports are now specifying systems, assemblies and components even for off-the-shelf purchases – engines, transmissions, electrical systems, etc. – to encourage standardization and compatibility, to allow simple component-exchange as a maintenance strategy, and generally to reduce demands on maintenance.

Other important strategy decisions concern items that may need to be procured at the same time as the equipment. For example, should the contract include a range of spare parts? If so, which spares, and what period of use should they cover? If not, is the supplier to guarantee prices and/or availability, and for how long? Can spares be obtained from alternative sources (e.g. the original component manufacturers) or will the suppliers provide line drawings and blueprints to allow local manufacture? Should the port encourage local suppliers, agents or stockists to hold spares? Will foreign exchange be available to purchase spares in the future? What delivery lead times are likely? How expensive will the spares be in a year or two? (Many ports complain of excessive markups on spares and of the difficulty of budgeting for likely price increases; both issues are best negotiated at the time of equipment purchase, when the position of the purchaser is strong.) The supply of spare parts is a crucially important issue in

many LDC ports, and it is essential to formulate a procurement strategy that suits local conditions, engineering and operational requirements, and the port's overall procurement policy.

Other elements that might be included in the procurement contract include training for drivers and technicians (see Section 4.3.3.7), and a maintenance agreement. Numerous examples of the latter were seen during this study, ranging from arrangements for specific tasks, e.g. engine overhauls or tyre replacement, to complete maintenance agreements. Supply of maintenance manuals, too, needs to be agreed and specified at the time of procurement – all part of the strategy decisions relating to What to Buy, and all considered in more detail later.

4.2.3 How should it be Procured?

The first issue here is whether the port is to acquire its capital equipment by outright purchase or by leasing/renting. In the past, the vast majority of acquisitions were by purchase, but there has recently been a rapid growth of leasing in ports of both developed and developing countries, and an increasing use of rental agreements. The major advantages of rental hire or leasing are the reduced initial capital investment (an advantage where funds for purchase are limited) and the reduced commitment of the port; short leases (one to five years) do not tie the port into use of equipment with long asset lives – particularly important when equipment design, ship technology and port traffic are changing rapidly. Leasing/rental contracts also contain maintenance agreements, reducing the port's maintenance responsibilities. This can be attractive where the port lacks the facilities or skills to maintain new equipment. Under such 'operating leases', servicing and overhaul are the responsibility of the leasing company, and maintenance costs are included in the agreed monthly, quarterly or annual payment. However, because ownership does not transfer in a lease, restrictions are sometimes placed on operating conditions, and these must be taken into account when considering leasing.

Other related considerations include delivery of the procured equipment. Is the equipment to be accepted in the supplier's country or at a local delivery point? Who will be responsible for transport from the factory and installation? It is common for buyers to require the supplier to supervise installation and commissioning – a sensible strategy, since the supplier knows the equipment, and his staff are experienced in installation and fault-finding. The port can then delay completion of payment until it is sure that the equipment is in good working order; the contract must have a comprehensive and tight set of clauses covering commissioning.

Another aspect of the decision on how to procure equipment concerns the procedural options available. When the port is free to do so, unfettered by governmental regulations or decrees, it has to decide:

— whether to use standing approved lists of suppliers or to carry out market surveys for each purchase;

— whether or not to use prequalification procedures;

— whether or not to use international competitive bidding.

These are important day-to-day issues, but they also have strategic importance, and are discussed in detail in Sections 4.3. and 4.4.

4.2.4 When should it be Procured?

The case for ports preparing an equipment plan covering, in outline terms, the next five years was made in Chapter 3. The Plan should set out a clear timetable for the procurement of equipment over that period and a set of guidelines for what specific needs should trigger off that action. The procurement process can then be carried out at the appropriate time to ensure that the equipment is purchased, delivered to site and commissioned by the time it is needed by operators. Where necessary, the timetable will also have built into it sufficient time for securing approval for the necessary expenditure and for negotiating the terms of this agreement.

4.2.5 Who should be responsible for Procurement?

Procurement is a specialized activity and so requires specialized skills and knowledge. If it is to be performed effectively, it requires not only the formulating of appropriate procedures but also the establishment of a dedicated organizational structure, manned with qualified and experienced staff. Among the strategic questions to be decided in this context are: will purchasing be undertaken by a central agency, purchasing for all the ports under a National Ports Authority, or will it be delegated to individual ports? To what extent will government be involved, through Ministries of Communications/Transport, Finance or Economic Planning? If procurement is to be carried out at the port level, what procedures will need to be established for preparing technical specifications, evaluating tenders and writing contracts? What investment ceilings should be set for individual managers and the Tender Boards or Committees?

Ports will then need to decide whether to establish a separate, permanent office or department, to take responsibility for all procurement, or to place that responsibility on an existing department. Although it would be unwise to suggest that there is only one possible form of organization – there is considerable variation in the ports surveyed, for example – there is certainly a strong case for a strengthening of the existing procurement function in many ports, where it has at the moment a relatively low status within the organizational structure. In many cases, responsibility for procurement is allocated to staff either lacking the necessary professional skills and knowledge or the time and resources to carry out their duties properly. It is becoming clear to port organizations around the world that effective procurement requires an organizational structure which recognizes that function as important in its own right. One approach that has been seen to work effectively is to have a Supplies Department, responsible for the mechanics of purchasing, but with technical questions and selection assigned to engineering and operations staff working together. The Supplies Department needs some staff at all managerial levels with procurement qualifications.

4.2.6 From whom should Equipment be Procured?

Procurement involves two parties: the buyer and the seller. The extent to which the buying organization is interested in the seller is a matter of strategic importance. There are two extreme positions:

— At the one extreme, the port views the seller as a supplier of equipment, a means to an end, and sees the equipment offered (its quality, price, maintainability, etc.) as the only factor of importance. The characteristics of the seller, in this view, are of no relevance and the buyer tries to achieve worldwide competition, evaluating bids strictly on non-supplier criteria, e.g. cost and value for money.

— At the other extreme, the seller is viewed as of importance and more than a means to an end – possibly an end in itself. The seller's characteristics are taken into account and given as much weight as, if not more than, the equipment being offered. The buyer gives preference to:

1. either a manufacturer of equipment or an agent, distributor or supplier;

2. either a domestic, regional or foreign supplier;

3. either a large company or a small one.

Such a stated preference may be justified politically (e.g. to build a strong economy by favouring national suppliers) or economically (e.g. to avoid spending foreign exchange) or administratively (to reduce a large number of potential suppliers, worldwide, to a manageable number). Preferences for supplier types can be expressed in quantifiable form (e.g. giving a 5% or 10% preference to national suppliers) or unquantified (using some such form of words as 'local suppliers will be given preference over foreign suppliers wherever possible').

In practice, ports will not need, or wish, to position themselves at either of these two extremes, but will be somewhere between them, perhaps changing according to circumstances. The procurement policy relating to choice of supplier will be established in the light of government regulation or advice. This important consideration will be discussed again in Section 4.4.

4.2.7 An Equipment Procurement Policy

There is, then, a wide and important range of strategic questions that the port needs to consider when establishing a policy for the procurement of capital equipment and other plant. Senior management must examine and, where appropriate, revise existing procurement regulations and methods to ensure that they lead to a sensible equipment inventory and meet the port's operating and maintenance capabilities. This policy should be set out in the port's corporate objectives and should be known to all senior managers. The following sections of this chapter look at some of the important strategies to be considered in this respect.

4.3 The Bidding Documents

4.3.1 Nature and Purpose of the Bidding Documents

The term 'Bidding Documents' – alternatively known as 'Invitations to Tender' or 'Tender Documents' – is given to the collection of informational and instructional materials that are prepared by the port and issued to all suppliers who are being invited to bid for the contract. They set out all the information about and technical specifications describing the equipment, convey all the necessary instructions for the bidders, and are designed to gather all the relevant technical, financial and other desired information about the potential suppliers. They include four broad classes of documents:

1. Sets of instructions that could be referred to as 'commercial' documents, detailing how the bid is to be prepared by the potential supplier and how it is to be submitted to the port.
2. Materials that can be grouped as 'legal' or 'contractual' documents, which set out the contractual terms under which the equipment is to be purchased, the warranties required, and so on.
3. A Technical Specification, which prescribes the operational and engineering requirements for the equipement.
4. A Training Specification, defining the nature of any training that the port requires to be provided for its operational and/or engineering staff – particularly if the equipment to be procured is of a type new to the port.

The importance of the Bidding Documents to the procurement process lies not only in the essential information and instruction to bidders that they contain but also in the way they set the 'tone' of the entire transaction. A badly prepared set of Bidding Documents gives a bad impression of the port, suggesting an unprofessional organization, as well as possibly leading to the purchase of inappropriate equipment. On the other hand, a well-prepared package ensures the gathering of all relevant information from bidders and should lead to better selection of supplier. The Documents serve four main purposes:

1. To tell potential suppliers that the port has an equipment requirement, and to explain what that requirement is.
2. To gather information from bidders about their prices, delivery dates, ability to meet specifications, etc.
3. To ensure that all bidders are given an equal opportunity to quote.
4. To indicate the Terms and Conditions on which the port is prepared to do business, and on which the Contract will be based.

In this section the place of the Bidding Documents in the procurement process will be considered in detail, beginning with a brief discussion of the responsibility for preparing the documents, and then dealing in turn with the commercial and contractual components of the documents, the technical and training specifications, and finally preparation of the documents.

4.3.2 Responsibility for the Bidding Documents

The Bidding Documents are obviously crucial to the success of the procurement process, and they must be clearly and unambiguously written to avoid any possible confusion. Yet, while all the ports participating in this study have a fairly clearly defined tendering procedure, it was not always obvious to the team who actually prepares the Bidding Documents. Generally, staff in the Engineering Department are responsible for preparing the technical content of the documents for equipment procurement, while the Supplies Department staff prepare those for spare parts and look after the procurement process itself. The involvement of other departments varies widely. In some ports, formal procedures exist for seeking the advice of operations and other departments, while in others the engineers claim that operations staff do not know what they want. In one instance (not one of the ports visited), the contract documents are prepared by a supplier and just vetted by the port; this is clearly a most unsatisfactory procedure, entirely open to abuse.

On balance, there is a good case for giving overall responsibility for preparing the Bidding Documents to the Supplies Department, but with the constant and close advice and assistance of the line departments concerned in the purchase – particularly the engineers and operators. The engineering and operations staff are the only people who can knowledgeably define the performance and engineering specifications for the equipment, but it is staff in the Supplies Department who have (or should have) the training and skills needed to prepare the documents, to negotiate the terms and conditions of the contract, to manage the tendering process and to handle disputes and possible litigation. The process of preparing the documents should, then, be a team operation; this will be discussed further in Section 4.3.7.

4.3.3 Commercial Components

The 'commercial' components of the Bidding Documents are those sections which provide instructions to the bidders on exactly how their bids are to be prepared and presented, and precisely how they are to be submitted to the port's Bid Evaluation team. Clearly, the port needs to establish formal procedures for inviting, receiving, opening and evaluating the bids and these must be strictly followed for each transaction. It is this information that forms the major part of the Commercial Documents.

These pages of the Bidding Documents will also give instructions on the pricing method to be used, the currency in which the bid is to be quoted, the last date of submission, the bid validity period and so on. They may also seek information on the supplier's standing and technical/financial competence, particularly if the port has not dealt with that supplier previously.

4.3.4 Contractual Components

The 'terms and conditions of contract' which make up the 'legal' or 'contractual' sections of the Bidding Documents serve two very important functions: they define as precisely as possible the rights and duties of the buyer and seller and they provide an agreed mechanism for settling any disputes which may arise between the parties during and after the contract period.

Most of the ports visited use internationally accepted forms of contract, or 'model conditions', with such minor variations as they consider desirable. The contract model issued by the Fédération Internationale des Ingenieurs-Counseils (FIDIC) is used extensively for major contracts, particularly for international tendering. In countries formerly under British Colonial rule, contract documents issued by the UK Institutions of Civil, Mechanical and Electrical Engineers are still used, although even in those countries the FIDIC contract seems to be gaining in popularity. No port expressed dissatisfaction with the international tender documents, though some conditions may be varied slightly to suit particular cases, especially those referring to terms and conditions of payment, insurance (with a national company named), sea transport (naming a national shipping line) and conditions of Letters of Credit (as approved by the National Bank). Alterations or amendments to these documents should, in fact, only be made if absolutely necessary, and then only after very careful study of all possible consequences; even the most minor of alterations to one clause can seriously affect the meaning of other, apparently unrelated clauses.

Most internationally accepted contract documents state clearly the country under whose laws the contract will be administered; before accepting such a term, both purchaser and seller must satisfy themselves that the laws can be evoked, and that they can be applied in any sub-contractors' countries. Arbitration under an international contract binds the participants to accept international law under, in the case of FIDIC, the International Chamber of Commerce. Although some managers commented that the port does not always get the equipment or services it thought it had specified, in terms of performance, quality, reliability or some other measure, the seeking of remedy through litigation does not appear to be a common occurrence. Most ports accept the standard arbitration clauses – and even these appear to be invoked only infrequently. One port, however, regularly strikes out all reference to arbitration in its contracts, and seeks resolution through litigation.

Not all port purchases will involve the drawing up of a formal contract document, of course, and the value of goods above which a contract document is required varies considerably from port to port. However, whatever the value of goods purchased, the purchase must be based on some clearly defined conditions of contract (for example, those stated on a supplier's order form or as part of the offer to sell). The majority of spare parts, for example, are likely to be purchased on normal traders' conditions, while cargo-handling equipment will almost always be purchased on a formal, specially drawn-up contract. Whenever purchases are made overseas, internationally accepted conditions of contract *must* be used.

Most of the ports visited engage consulting engineers to prepare contract documents for capital projects, particularly for civil engineering and related works. The powers accorded to consultants under FIDIC and similar contractual conditions are very wide-ranging, but the primary objective is to ensure that they act impartially. Unfortunately, this impartiality is sometimes seen by the port as favouring the contractor, and some port authorities now restrict the role of the consultant, particularly as far as authorization of expenditure is concerned; they must certainly define the duties of the consultant very precisely from the outset. LDC ports must also take into account the possibility that involving a third party (the consultant) in the contract negotiation process might lead to delays, and must timetable accordingly.

Warranty clauses are an essential part of the contract for supply of equipment; they typically extend for one year from the time of commissioning or acceptance of the equipment. No criticisms were made by any of the engineers interviewed of suppliers' provision of services required under a warranty clause of a contract. Clearly, clauses inserted in the contract to cover such services operate effectively and to the satisfaction of purchasers. In the case of aid projects, for example, donor agencies often provide the services of maintenance technicians or instructors during the period following handover, and these resolve most of the defects that occur, charging their work to the contractor.

A typical warranty arrangement for standard equipment, such as forklift trucks, is for the manufacturer to supply any replacement parts needed during the warranty period, for the port's maintenance staff to fit. For large pieces of equipment, it is quite common for the contract to require the manufacturer to provide, on site, the services of a guarantee engineer for a defined period (usually the defects liability period), and he will be responsible for making good any defects found during this period. Most contracts, furthermore,

allow the purchaser to retain a proportion of the purchase price during the warranty period, so that the cost of any repairs can be deducted directly from it. The residue at the end of the period is then paid over to the supplier. Alternatively, a bank guarantee can be provided for the same purpose. All such arrangements appear to work satisfactorily, and there seems little reason for the Bidding Documents to request alternatives.

4.3.5 Technical Specifications

4.3.5.1 The Importance of Technical Specifications
Preparing a technical specification is an extremely important activity in the procurement process, with a major influence on equipment selection, yet present procedures in LDC ports for preparing technical specifications are far from adequate. The result is that equipment is often purchased which does not meet operators' needs, is unsuited to local conditions, or cannot be properly maintained in the workshops.

A technical specification – a detailed description of the equipment to be procured – has four principal applications:

1. It provides a precise, accurate statement of the purchaser's requirements.
2. It allows comparison between competing tenders.
3. It provides data against which quality assurance checks can be made when the equipment is being commissioned and tested.
2. It forms an important part of the contract, and governs the conduct of both parties during all phases of the procurement process.

The specification is primarily an engineering and technical component of the Bidding Documents, but operating factors are of fundamental relevance and must be considered in its preparation. The preparation process should, therefore, be a collective effort involving representatives from the Operations, Engineering and Planning Departments, but co-ordinated by senior staff in the Supplies Department. The appropriate working-group approach has been described in relation to equipment planning in Chapter 3. It is the engineers, of course, who have the technical expertise for writing the detailed specification and must assume the major responsibility for preparing it, in discussion with the users – the operations staff. During the preparation of the technical specification, there must be continuous feedback between operations, mechanical engineering, finance and planning staff.

The objectives of the technical specification are to ensure that:

— the equipment meets operators' requirements for present and future handling needs for the particular class of cargo.

— the equipment's maintenance needs are clearly established, so that the engineers can prepare their facilities and resources appropriately.

— a uniform and comparable standard of product is offered by the tendering suppliers.

— minimum operating performance standards are met, while still allowing suppliers the opportunity to offer suitable alternative machines from their basic ranges of equipment.

— national and international standards and other statutory requirements (e.g. of safety, exhaust emissions) are complied with.

— maximum competition is encouraged in the supply market.

The rest of this section will consider the various elements of the technical specification and the process of preparing it.

4.3.5.2 Types of Technical Specification

Basically, there are two types of technical specification, one for purchase of equipment of standard design and capacity (for example, from a manufacturer's basic range) and the other for purpose-built plant.

Most major equipment manufacturers produce ranges of equipment, such as lift trucks, mobile cranes and tractors, each range constructed to a standard design and supplied in various sizes and lifting capacities. These 'range variables' are produced in volume and are often referred to as 'off-the-shelf' products, but buyers can make minor changes in the specification of these standard products, and can select from alternative power units, transmissions, steering systems, tyres, and so on. Some machines, such as lift trucks, can also be supplied with a range of attachments and special features, such as extended forks, side-shift, overhead-load guards and sun canopies. Producing a technical specification for this type of purchase is relatively straightforward, and most ports have a standard procedure for doing it – even to the extent of having standard forms on which to write the specification.

Indeed, many suppliers prefer ports ordering a 'standard' machine to restrict the specification merely to a statement of the desired operating performance, allowing the supplier to suggest which model within one of their standard ranges meets, or comes closest to, that specification. They like to discuss the specification with the client even before the operating performance requirements are finalized, feeling that their experience can often help to improve the specification and that they may be able to suggest points that have been overlooked. Discussing operating performance specification with several manufacturers before going out to tender certainly has advantages, and can result in a better choice of equipment – provided that the buyer is aware of the danger of becoming tied-in to a particular manufacturer.

The second type of equipment requirement, for 'one-off' purchases of custom-designed plant and equipment (such as a bulk-handling installation), demands a very detailed specification, including: technical drawings, general arrangements and dimension details, statements of design standards, performance standards, safety and control devices, structural, electrical and mechanical design requirements, an erection timetable, and inspection and testing procedures. These specification details are so specialized that ports often find it advisable to contract external consultants for the purpose.

Whether the specification is for standard or purpose-built equipment, and whether it is prepared by port staff or consultants, it is essential for considerable thought and effort to go into its preparation. Getting the technical specification right will make a major contribution to successful, cost-effective equipment selection. The process essentially has two components: determining the user or performance specification, and then using that as a basis for detailing the engineering specification. These stages are dealt with in turn in the next two sections.

4.3.5.3. The Performance Specification

The Equipment Plan (Chapter 3) will have determined the type of equipment and the number of units needed to meet operational needs, and the first stage in writing the technical specification is to check and refine those estimates through a series of pre-specification studies. The precise cargo-handling requirements need to be established by the operations staff, in terms of current and future demands, the nature and scope of the work to be performed and the full range of activities to be undertaken. Questions to be answered when deciding the machine's power, dimensions and capabilities include:

— Is the equipment to be used aboard ship or inside containers?

— Will it need to handle cargo to and from road or rail vehicles?

— Are there any overhead pipelines, conveyors or power lines that it will pass under on its route?

— Will it need to work under a gantry crane portal?

- What hours of work will it be subjected to, and at what intensity of operation?
- What type, size and weight of cargo will it handle?
- What terrain and ground conditions will it operate over?
- Are there ramps or inclines to traverse?
- What distances will it travel on each cycle or shift?
- What laden and unladen travel speeds are required?
- Are there restricted turning circles in its area of work?
- What are the environmental operating conditions, e.g. day and night temperatures, relative humidity, salt spray?
- With what existing equipment will it need to be compatible, in terms of dimensions, lifting capacity, interchangeable attachments, instrument and control layout, international symbols?
- What driver comfort requirements are there, such as visibility, ventilation, heating and noise levels?
- Are there safe access ladders, handrails, non-slip steps, guard rails, overhead-load guards?

Only when all the conditions and circumstances of the equipment's anticipated use have been detailed in this way can the engineers make informed decisions on the technical specifications and the suppliers be sure that their offered machines will be suitable.

4.3.5.4 The Engineering Specifications

When the engineers have been given the detailed performance specifications and have discussed them at length with the operations staff, they are faced with the task of balancing the range of facilities requested against factors of cost, ease of maintenance, reliability and safety, and of converting those requirements into detailed engineering specifications. A tight and accurate engineering specification will ensure that the users' needs are fully met while construction standards and maintainability are as high as possible. It will also eliminate the less suitable suppliers (and machines) from consideration and provide a firm foundation for any possible disputes. Writing the engineering specification also provides the opportunity for implementing the port's policies on compatability between machines and minimizing model and make variety (providing government procurement regulations permit; see Section 4.1.3).

The first task of the mechanical engineer is to convert the performance specification into principal dimensions and capacity. In doing so, he will want to ensure that the equipment supplied will be working comfortably within its capacity, rather than at its limits, and will take into account any de-rating necessary when attachments are fitted or when stacking cargo high or outside the given load centre. He will specify maximum dimensions that will allow the machine to pass safely under or between any potential obstructions on its working route, and power ratings that will let the equipment cope easily with any inclines that it will meet and with the operational demands and intensity of use that it will face.

The engineer will also be concerned with safety and durability factors, specifying stability standards (e.g. tipping loads, gradability) and adequate protection for components to reduce or prevent corrosion. He is unlikely nowadays to need to specify minimum thicknesses of steel or standards of welding and other fabrication techniques – most major manufacturing countries now apply appropriate national/international standards, prepared by panels of users, manufacturers and other interested parties, which ensure fitness for purpose – but the required standard should be named so that the port can be assured that the supplied equipment will meet agreed performance and quality criteria.

Manufacturers' engineering specifications may well serve as a satisfactory basis for the port's specification for standard equipment, but they may need to be modified to suit local conditions. For example, the unit may have to operate at high ambient temperatures, in exceptionally dusty conditions, or at high altitude (at Inland Container Depots). It may need to be fitted with special devices to allow it to work with hazardous cargo or in an explosives compound. The engineer will want to specify emergency stop devices, visible and audible travel warning devices, emergency escape systems, fire protection, limit switches and other safety features.

Even when specifying volume-produced equipment, the engineers will want to specify the type of transmissions, drive axles, steering and steer axles, hydraulic and electrical systems, and other such systems and components, primarily to maintain commonality with existing equipment and to standardize on components as far as possible. This enables the port to minimize the stock held in stores and offers maintenance staff the opportunity of becoming very familiar with a relatively small range of systems and assemblies. Engineers will also want to specify the fittings necessary to accommodate any particular attachments required by the operators, and will select the most appropriate tyres for the circumstances of operation: cushion or solid tyres for long life under hostile conditions and for machine compactness (but only where the surface over which the equipment will work is very smooth – solid tyres transmit damaging vibration when working over uneven surfaces), or pneumatic tyres for good traction on slippery surfaces and for assisting shock absorption on uneven quay surfaces. They will also be concerned with maintainability, and will specify easily removable engine covers, ample access and inspection doors and covers; all routine maintenance should be possible without removing systems and assemblies from the chassis.

Finally, the technical specification should specify the full extent of the inspection, commissioning and testing procedures required, both at the manufacturer's plant and on site at the port. The extent of these procedures will vary with the nature of the equipment; for volume-produced equipment of standard design, an on-site acceptance test will suffice, but for major units of equipment (e.g. quayside cranes), material and component testing may have to be performed at each stage of the erection on-site.

4.3.5.5 Procurement of Spare Parts

Clearly, if newly acquired equipment is to be kept in good working order throughout its life, arrangements have to be made at the time of procurement for the supply of the spare parts and consumables that the engineers will require to maintain it. One of the major problems identified in this study, in fact, relates to supplies management (see Chapter 7) and failure to manage properly the supply of spare parts and materials for maintenance. The procurement of spare parts forms, then, a vital element of the equipment procurement process, and discussions on what spares to purchase initially, and how to ensure a reliable supply of spares, must take place while the other components of the technical specification and the rest of the Bidding Documents are being prepared.

There are three broad policies that the port could pursue in this context:

1. It could buy a large quantity of spares at the same time as the initial equipment purchase, as part of that contract. Some ports purchase stocks that they estimate will be sufficient for as much as five years of service, while others buy, as policy, spares equivalent to 15% or even 20% of the equipment's purchase price. The advantage of this approach is that there should never be any difficulty or delay when engineers find that a part needs to be replaced –

providing the spares have been well chosen; this assumes that the engineers are familiar with the machine and its likely maintenance needs. The obvious *disadvantages* are that it ties up a substantial proportion of the port's capital, demands a large investment in storage space and management, and the spares may actually deteriorate to an unusable state before they are needed. Many of the purchased spares may, in fact, never be needed within the life of the equipment.

2. An alternative policy is to purchase a minimum quantity of spares, as recommended by the manufacturer and, possibly, modified in the light of experience by the engineers. Engineers in all the ports surveyed confirmed that they require suppliers to submit a list of spares that they recommend be acquired with the equipment, sufficient to cover a stated period of operation (say one or two years). In some cases, the engineers also prepare their own spares list, based on their own experience of local working conditions (possibly with similar machines, possibly by guesswork only) and then use this to produce a modified supplier's list for inclusion with the technical specification. Any such modification does, of course, rely on good engineering records, and these are sadly not available in many LDC ports (as will be discussed in Chapter 9); the engineers' list may not then, be very reliable – but neither are the suppliers' lists in many cases. In one recent project, tenders from a number of international manufacturers for a particular type of cargo-handling equipment showed wide variations in the tenderers' perceptions of the reliability of their equipment, as revealed by the spares that they recommended would be necessary. Some manufacturers have a tendency to submit a very short list of spare parts, making their bid look much more attractive than their more realistic (honest?) competitors. Clearly, the Bidding Document must be extremely precise in its instructions in this regard, specifying the exact period which the spares are intended to cover, asking for clear indications of which supplies are consumables (and therefore determinable) and which replacement parts (and only statistically estimateable), and requesting a statement of the basis on which the tenderer is making his assessment.

3. A third option is chosen by some ports, particularly those in developed countries: at the time of procurement of new equipment, only consumable items (filters, spark plugs, etc.) are included in the contract, and purchase of all

substantive items is delayed until the end of the warranty period. These are ports which experience no difficulty in obtaining spare parts, even in emergencies, and have a guaranteed, rapid supply line direct from the manufacturer or from a local stockist. Ports fortunate in being able to do this can reduce their initial supplies stockholding to the bare minimum, while allowing engineers to monitor the equipment in operation for a sufficient time to determine the appropriate schedule of spare parts to stock for their own conditions. For an LDC port, this option is almost always ruled out, not just by their distance from the sources of supply (even distant ports *can* be supplied in an emergency within 48 hours or so) but, more importantly, because of administrative delays in acquiring approval for expenditure, for import licences and so on, and because there are no local sources of supply. They are also unlikely to know from experience which of the supplier's listed parts are consumable (and therefore should be stocked) and which replacement parts (and left until after the warranty period).

There is no doubt that the third option has many attractions, if it could only be adopted in LDC ports. To make it feasible, however, major changes would be needed in government and central bank control procedures. One possibility would be for the port to set aside sufficient funds (in foreign currency) in their annual capital equipment budget for the procurement of supplies (as discussed in Chapter 2), or they might maintain funds overseas to avoid any delays in obtaining approval for foreign exchange expenditure. At the time of procurement of new equipment, the strategy could be to lodge a particular sum (perhaps 10% or 15% of the equipment's purchase price) in an overseas bank in readiness for spare parts purchase. Alternatively, a credit line could be established with the supplier, topped up periodically to avoid payment difficulties.

As it is, however, LDC ports are almost bound to adopt option 1 (which avoids problems of long lead times) or option 2 (in which case stock control and management have to be carefully performed, adjusting stock levels and always allowing sufficient time when restocking for completing all the administrative and financial formalities). When equipment is made available as part of a bilateral or multilateral aid package, ports should insist that sufficient funds are set aside from the initial equipment purchase for spare parts and other supplies. If finance is severely limited, the only way to increase the provision of spare parts is to buy fewer units of equipment; this is certainly preferable to buying a large fleet which cannot be properly maintained. Funds set aside for the purchase of spares should not necessarily be used up at the time of procurement; it is preferable if most of it could be set aside until the port has had experience of operating the new equipment under local conditions and has a clearer idea of what items should be stocked.

Many port engineers complained to the team of the poor spare parts service given by many manufacturers, and of their reluctance (or refusal) to provide the information requested. As an illustration of this secrecy, instances were quoted of suppliers preferring to send their representatives to fit a new part rather than supplying it for the port's technicians to fit. So that the port can make its own assessment of how and where to purchase, the tenderer should be required to provide a detailed list of the spares needed to cover maintenance for, say, two and five years, with the name of the manufacturer of each part and its country of origin. Detailed drawings should also be supplied, so that parts could be repaired or even manufactured in the port or locally if necessary. Port engineers complained that manufacturers are very reluctant to do this (while manufacturers countered that such drawings would be passed to local manufacturers who would copy the component to sell cheaply, but as an inferior item that could well damage the supplier's reputation). The supplier should also have to state the procedures and financial obligations required of the port when seeking to order additional spares.

4.3.5.6 Maintenance Manuals

Port engineers from both developed and developing countries frequently criticized, to the team, the quality of the maintenance manuals provided as part of an equipment purchase. This applies particularly to manuals supplied with specialized equipment (e.g. container-handling equipment); those for standard, volume-produced machines are generally considered adequate. However, close examination (and discussion with consultants) suggests that even some of these manuals are less than ideal, and do not seem fully to take into account the circumstances in which they are to be used. Here are some of the critical comments received:

— Manuals are not well organized, contain too much information (relating, for example, to other models in the same range or to alternative systems and components to the ones actually supplied), and are not designed to be easily understood by technicians unused to reading technical documents (or, indeed, any other material) and possibly with cultural difficulties affecting understanding of two-dimensional drawings of three-dimensional objects.

— Presentation is frequently poor, juxtaposing original material with pages copied from component or system supplier's literature, and mixing operating and maintenance instructions in such a way that the wrong person might be induced to attempt a job.

— Translations into the local language also leave much to be desired; indeed, some manufacturers do not attempt this, either providing the original manuals or having them translated into a third language, supposedly common to both supplier and buyer.

— Those compiling the manuals are not always aware of the conditions in which the equipment will be operated and maintained, and there is more than a suspicion that manuals are carelessly assembled from previously used editions. In one instance, where a Northern European manufacturer was supplying equipment to a tropical port, operating instructions for the engine stated that antifreeze should be changed annually; the port engineers realized, of course, that antifreeze was not required and filled the radiators with plain water, but did *not* realize that they should have added an appropriate inhibitor (normally contained in the antifreeze) to safeguard the engine and cooling system against corrosion.

Clearly, much more attention needs to be given to the manuals when preparing the Bidding Documents, and the port's requirements in that respect must be spelt out. The main points to be considered for inclusion in the contractual requirements are:

— the port should be allowed to approve the (separate) maintenance and operating manuals before finally accepting the equipment;

— it would be very helpful if engineering and operations staff could be involved with (or at least consulted by) the contractor while the manuals are being compiled;

— the manuals must be produced on durable materials, allowing them to be used in workshops and outside, preferably with frequently-consulted pages protected by plastic film;

— the text should be translated into the local language(s) and expressed in the simplest possible way, with clear, simple and well annotated diagrams illustrating every maintenance activity;

— the manuals must be logically organized into sections and subsections, for easy reference – in the case of marine craft, for example, the maintenance manual should consist of separate sections for propulsion machinery, auxiliary machinery, deck machinery, and so on, with subsections for each, covering mechanical, electrical and hydraulic sytems;

— every system, assembly and sub-assembly should be clearly and accurately illustrated, and each diagram should identify, by name and reference number, the components illustrated;

— a general section should be provided at the beginning of each manual, listing all data which need to be referred to frequently: rope sizes and lengths; valve tappet clearances; tyre pressures; conveyor belt types and lengths, and so on;

— finally, the manuals must be supplied *before* handover of equipment, and failure to do so should result in the supplier being penalized.

4.3.5.7 *Preparing the Technical Specifications*

The technical specification is the most individual part of the Bidding Document. It is written to convey a unique set of instructions and particulars to the tenderer. A well-prepared technical specification smooths the management of the procurement process and makes it much more likely that the equipment supplied will suit both operators and engineers to the maximum, but there is considerable evidence that the preparation of technical specifications in many LDC ports is far from satisfactorily carried out. The high cost of purchasing, operating and maintaining the port's assets, and the heavy dependence of ports on the use of equipment in cargo-handling, fully justify the investment of considerable time and effort in the preparation of good technical specifications. Careful pre-specification research will be amply rewarded by the selection of reliable equipment that exactly meets operators' and engineers' needs.

The time and effort needed to develop the technical specification depend on the nature, value and degree of specialization of the equipment. Routine, inexpensive purchases may not require a specification; it may be enough to quote a model number or an international standard. However, complex and detailed specifications are needed for major works and for expensive or technologically advanced equipment, including a full description of the performance requirements, a set of drawings with technical explanations, and statements of the quality of materials and workmanship demanded. For unique, custom-built plant or equipment, there may be a need for design specifications – a detailed technical description supported by blueprints, dimension sheets, structural and finish standards, and so on. This work is so specialized that consultants will almost certainly be engaged to carry it out, in full collaboration with the port's engineers.

Consultants are also sometimes engaged when preparing specifications for technologically advanced equipment new to the port, but in the majority of ports surveyed the technical specifications are prepared by the Engineering Department. In many LDC ports, however, the engineers do not have the knowledge or experience (particularly shop-floor experience) to prepare good specifications, nor do they appear to have sufficient interest in the operation of the equipment that is purchased. They are only faced with the need to write technical specifications infrequently, after all – perhaps every two or three years – and it is often not easy for them to keep abreast of technological developments in the meantime. They do not have regular contact with other ports or with equipment manufacturers (presumably because it might be construed as favouring one contractor against another), nor do they appear to have easy access to technical publications. In some ports, the mentioning of manufacturers' names in technical specifications is prohibited; this, too, tends to dissuade engineers from discussing their requirements with suppliers. While many LDCs send port personnel overseas to observe operations in other ports and to visit manufacturers' premises, those people are frequently not the engineers who will subsequently write specifications for new equipment and maintain it after commissioning.

In the ports of developed countries, in contrast, the engineers maintain very close links with colleagues in other ports and with manufacturers. Senior engineers in European ports usually visit other ports – even their competitors – once a year, to exchange views, compare equipment operation and maintenance, and to observe new developments in equipment design and performance. Regular contact is also maintained with the major manufacturers, through visits, telephone conversations and regularly distributed technical literature. Attendance at conferences and subscriptions to the technical journals also help them to keep abreast of developments. All these experiences are used to improve constantly the engineers' knowledge and the specification and choice of new equipment.

All these opportunities need to be made available for engineers in LDC ports, too, but until their knowledge, skills and experience in this context are fully equal to those of engineers in developed countries, one way of improving specification quality may be to rely more on the advice of manufacturers. Many are prepared to assist port engineers in the writing of specifications, and this in itself may not be detrimental to the contract. They may suggest new ideas and features which will improve performance or maintenance; many manufacturers do, in fact, collaborate closely with their customers in developing their products, incorporating improvements on the suggestion of users. Such manufacturers are well placed to advise on the most suitable model. There is a risk, of course, that manufacturers will try to write a specification that favours (or even uniquely matches) one of their own models, and the buyer needs to be on guard against this. If the port's engineers are not fully qualified to vet such specifications, a consultant should be employed to do so.

4.3.6 Training Specifications

When a new type of equipment is procured, the port is often totally reliant on the manufacturer or supplier for training its operators and maintenance personnel; the port's own training unit, even where this is reasonably well staffed, resourced and accommodated, is rarely able to undertake detailed technical training for an unknown type of machine. These training requirements need, then, to be specified, in detail, in the Bidding Documents. However, the study showed that in many cases the training needs are very inadequately presented in the contract, and the extent and quality of the training are left almost entirely to the tenderer. He, on the other hand, can claim that he is given almost no guidelines as to what training is required. The result is that the contract contains little more than a vague reference to the number of staff to be trained, and it is not surprising that what training is given is very inadequate. One port which is investing millions of dollars in new equipment has demonstrated its commitment to training by appointing just one, part-time training officer to the project, and by arbitrarily halving the funding originally set aside from the project for training, to 'reduce costs'! This degree of interest in training is not exceptional, and it was fairly obvious during this study that many departments are reluctant to release personnel for training.

This shows remarkable lack of foresight; the investment in new equipment could be largely thrown away unless drivers are trained to operate it properly and engineering staff are trained to maintain it. So the training specification should be given as much attention in the preparation of the Bidding Documents as the technical specification. The background, previous training and current skills of the relevant personnel should be presented in as much detail as possible, so that the tenderer can structure his programme and teaching methods accordingly. Some instruction (e.g. for driver-instructors and workshop foremen and supervisors) might well take place at the manufacturer's plant, but much of the training must be given on site, using the actual installed equipment – the trainee must experience real operating conditions. All training must include appropriate assessment of progress and attainment (few programmes have done so in the past), and the tenderer's programme should state the basis of such assessment. It should also describe how the training will be presented and what materials, facilities and staff they will provide.

Most contractors use their commissioning personnel for on-site instruction, but this is far from ideal; while those staff may be very good engineers, they are not necessarily good teachers, and are in any case unlikely to be suitable for training operators. The Bidding Documents should, therefore, require the tenderer to provide details of all staff proposed as instructors, giving particular attention to their instructional qualifications and experience, and their ability to communicate in the language of the port.

All these details must be provided *at the time of submitting the tender for the equipment*. Too often, discussion of the training to be provided is left to the last minute, long after the successful bidder has been selected – often just before the equipment is delivered! By this time it is far too late for the port to approve or to ask for amendments to the suggested programme. Suppliers' programmes also leave far too little time for training realistically to be completed before the equipment is handed over and the contractors leave the site. This is certainly one area of the Bidding Document procedure which demands urgent and significant improvement in many LDC ports.

4.3.7 Preparing the Bidding Documents

The preparation of the Bidding Documents must be a team effort, involving staff in the operations, engineering, supplies, finance and commercial departments. It must be well organized and managed and follow a firm timetable; it has to start early enough to ensure that the equipment is commissioned by the time the operators need it. The process involves the following steps:

1. Senior staff in the operations department prepare their performance specification, based on the already approved port Equipment Plan and a series of pre-specification studies.

2. The performance specification is then passed to senior Engineering Department staff so that they can prepare the engineering specification. They convert the performance data into detailed technical form, using their own pre-specification research to guide them.

3. Operations, engineering and other interested staff then critically review the separate components of the technical specification together, to check that it fully satisfies the port's requirements. Any necessary amendments are then made to the written specification.

4. The approved technical specification is then incorporated, with the legal, commercial, financial and other information and instructions, in the Bidding Documents.

5. Before the Supplies Department issues the Bidding Documents to potential suppliers, all interested parties should examine the details once more, discussing them fully until they are satisfied that the Documents define exactly the equipment that the operators need, and that it complies with the port's procurement policy and development plan.

4.4 Tendering Practices

4.4.1 Supplier Selection Methods

Supplier selection, preparatory to inviting bids, is an extremely important part of the procurement process, and one that can have a very significant influence on port maintenance. The survey has shown that, although ports vary considerably in the ways in which they draw up Bidding Documents and invite tenders for the supply of equipment and other items, there are just three primary methods for selecting potential suppliers: open tendering, prequalification and selective tendering. Each has its advantages and disadvantages, and these are considered in turn below.

4.4.2 Open Tendering

In open tendering, the port invites bids from all companies that wish to submit them, using newspaper advertising (both national and overseas) and announcements through embassies and consulates to notify as many eligible firms as possible. This is the most common method adopted by public bodies and is the one applied by most of the ports surveyed in this study.

The principal adavantages of open tendering are:

— It gives equal opportunity to all suppliers to take part in the bidding process;

— It ensures the widest possible competition, which should result in the best possible deal for the port;

— It allows suppliers unknown to the port to offer their services;

— It forestalls any charge of favouritism or bias, and satisfies the need for public accountability;

— It minimizes the risk of collusion (and price-fixing) between bidders.

There are, however, a number of serious disadvantages to open tendering, which the port must consider very carefully:

— A very large number of bids may be received, making bid evaluation time-consuming and administratively expensive;

— Many of the bidding companies may well be unknown to the port, and a great deal of investigation may be necessary to establish their merits;

— They may turn out to be quite unsuitable as suppliers, in terms of experience and capability;

— The principal disadvantage is that (particularly if it is coupled with a requirement to accept the lowest-cost bid) open tendering can lead to ports acquiring a very diverse range of makes and models, adding greatly to the engineers' maintenance problems;

— Open tendering for procurement of spare parts and other supplies (surprisingly common in LDC ports) leads to lengthy administrative delays, with comparatively small benefits in terms of cost savings.

With all these serious drawbacks, open tendering is really only justified if the port has not previous knowledge of a particular equipment market and cannot otherwise gain that information quickly, reliably and economically. It can, at least, reassure the port's senior managers that they have made every effort to contact all potential sources of supply.

4.4.3 Open Invitation to Prequalify

In this method, bidding is a two-stage process. In stage one, the buyer advertises details of its requirement, inviting applications for prequalification documents designed to gather information about the suppliers' capabilities and characteristics. In stage two, the buyer classifies the suppliers, on the basis of analyses of the returned forms and previous knowledge or experience of the companies, as 'approved' or 'non-approved'. Formal bids are invited from the 'approved' group only. Prequalification is permitted by most major lending agencies, including the World Bank and the Asian Development Bank.

Prequalification is normally more satisfactory than open tendering, particularly for large or complex works and the procurement of purpose-built equipment and specialized services. It enables the buyer to reduce the range of potential suppliers to a manageable number – those that are most likely to be able to complete the contract satisfactorily, provide proper after-sales service and supply the necessary spare parts. The list of 'approved' suppliers can be kept from one procurement process to another, revised and updated as supplier circumstances change and as the port gains experience with those companies.

The principal disadvantages of prequalification are that it can be time-consuming and, however much care is taken in establishing criteria for approval/non-approval, it can lead to some unsatisfactory companies being invited to tender and some suitable ones being eliminated. The latter risks can be minimized if engineers and supplies managers keep abreast of developments in the marketplace and take every opportunity to meet representatives from reputable suppliers. Regular contact with colleagues in other ports also provides useful information on the quality and performance of manufacturers and their products.

Prequalification is the appropriate supplier selection method to adopt where:

— the port has not previously purchased that particular type of asset, but is familiar with the market and the main manufacturers;

— where the equipment is non-standard, complex or of high value;

— where the supplier is being asked to provide additional services such as installation and training.

— where procurement regulations demand acceptance of the lowest-priced suitable bid.

It is generally considered that five to eight 'approved' tenderers will provide adequate competition and allow the buyer to choose a contractor with the necessary technical capability.

4.4.4 Selective Tendering

This method differs from the other two in having no element of 'openness' about it; the port directly invites companies either to submit to prequalification or to bid immediately for the contract. Selective tendering is the preferred method of supplier selection in European ports, but is only used in one of the LDC ports surveyed. In many European ports, it is now the policy to invite just one or two suppliers to bid for a contract. While this undoubtedly fits in well with the objective of equipment standardization, there is the danger that it might tie the port to a very small number of suppliers for a long time.

Clearly, the success of selective tendering depends almost entirely on careful initial choice of potential bidder. Inviting selected companies to prequalify is certainly helpful in this regard, particularly when the port is aware of the likely suppliers but lacks up-to-date information on their current capabilities, or when the port is sufficiently familiar with the equipment to make open tendering or open invitation to prequalify unnecessary. Engineers and supplies managers in European ports are well informed about the activities of leading equipment suppliers and make a point of continually updating their knowledge, so that they are in a good position to operate the selective tendering approach.

When a port becomes a regular purchaser of a particular type of equipment, it does not need to carry out even a limited selective prequalification exercise for every purchase – indeed, it should avoid this wherever possible, in the cause of inventory standardization and compatibility. The 'approved list' thus becomes very valuable: all suppliers approved during one prequalification exercise are placed on the list, and names are selected from that list for future contracts. The Approved List is revised from time to time, as new suppliers become 'approved' and demonstrate their ability to give good service, and unsatisfactory suppliers are deleted.

4.4.5 Tendering Regulations

Regulations and practices affecting procurement often prevent LDC ports from acquiring equipment which best meets their operating and engineering needs, as was described in Section 4.1. Open tendering is a major contributor to those difficulties. There is considerable evidence that, although open tendering may be the safest approach from the point of view of public accountability, it often results in selection of equipment which is not the most suitable for the port. Open invitation to prequalify and selective tendering are much more appropriate methods, provided the port has good market intelligence and reliable data on the operation and maintenance of its existing equipment.

LDC tendering regulations should, therefore, permit these methods, or be amended to allow them to be used, and ports currently affected by regulations prohibiting those methods should discuss possible changes with government representatives.

4.5 Bid Evaluation

4.5.1 Present Selection Procedures

Tender selection practices vary from port to port, but certain common features have been identified in the participating ports. For example, selection usually proceeds in two phases: *Bid Analysis*, in which all the bids are examined individually, and those that are obviously unsuitable are weeded out; and *Bid Evaluation*, in which the remaining bids are compared with each other and the best one selected.

Bid analysis and bid evaluation are normally carried out by a group (or groups) of individuals from the various interested departments, and their recommendations are then submitted to the appropriate Tender Board or Committee for approval. Individual members of the groups usually concentrate on specific aspects of the bids, within their own sphere of competence (e.g. commercial, technical or legal issues) before coming together as a team to select the successful bidder. The most common method of comparing the bids, in the Evaluation stage, is to apply a system of weighting or ranking to previously-agreed factors considered important in that particular purchase; technical specifications, purchase price, delivery time, training offered, spare parts supply, warranty period and other factors are given rank-order and a weighting factor, so that bids with varying strengths in these areas can be compared. In spite of the apparent rationality of such ranking/weighting systems, it must be remembered that they are very subjective, and may not provide appreciably more reliable means of bid comparison than a more synoptic approach.

The major criticisms of present tender selection procedures in LDC ports are the superficiality of the bid analysis and evaluation and the reliance on purchase price as the major choice determinant. These both deserve to be considered more fully:

1. There is a lack of depth in the analysis of supplier performance (particularly the supply of spare parts and other after-sales services) and the technical aspects of competing bids (especially maintainability). In some ports, for example, operations managers are not involved in examining offered performance specifications to check that they meet operating needs. Component/system compatibility is often not considered by engineering managers, nor are likely problems of equipment maintenance. All these factors *must* be researched in considerable detail, and all operational and engineering aspects must be discussed in depth – possibly with experienced users in other ports.

2. In many ports, investment appraisal is not applied to the bids, to compare their true costs. The evaluation teams rely on initial capital cost and take no account of the costs likely to be incurred during the life of the asset. In reality, the purchase price is often only a small proportion of the total lifetime cost of the equipment, and certainly should not be the *only*

cost factor considered in the purchase decision. Reliability, running costs, maintenance costs and spare parts costs are among the many factors that *should* be taken into account, and it could well be that a machine with the highest purchase price will turn out to be the better value in the long run. In other words, some form of Life Cycle Costing should be applied in the bid evaluation process; this is considered in the next section.

4.5.2 Life Cycle Costing

Life Cycle Costing is a means of quantifying the total cost of asset ownership and use. Its primary aims are to determine the economic replacement time for an asset (as discussed in Chapter 3) and to compare the true costs of competing tenders when procuring new assets. The costs that must be taken into account when making the latter assessment include:

— the cost of preparing the specifications (including consultancy and other fees) – this can be significant where one or more of the bidders is requesting phased or staged payments;

— design and development costs (where applicable – for most asset purchases these will be supplier costs, incorporated in the purchase price, but again needing to be considered if payments are to be staged);

— acquisition, installation and commissioning costs;

— estimated running costs throughout the life of the asset (including fuel, drivers' wages, etc.);

— maintenance costs throughout the life of the asset (including engineering labour costs, spare parts and consumables costs, periodic overhaul and refurbishment costs, cost penalties for production losses through breakdowns and services, etc.);

— 'ownership' costs – the depreciated capital investment and opportunity costs;

— the cost of disposal of the asset.

Life Cycle Costing is particularly relevant to equipment procurement because it places appropriate emphasis on engineering considerations. It takes account of the economics of engineering, particularly the importance of good design and maintainability, and also pays due attention to operating performance, in terms of total lifetime output (which takes into consideration downtime and utilization of the asset). An initially cheaper machine may well have poorer lifetime operating performance and higher lifetime maintenance and repair costs, and Life Cycle Costing allows these to be estimated and

compared. Most of these costs will have to be estimated by staff in the operations and engineering departments, on the basis of data supplied by the manufacturer (and these will have to be specifically demanded in the Bidding Documents) and recorded in their own management information systems. Discounted cash flow techniques then need to be applied to the flow of likely costs over the life of the asset, to convert them to present-day values. This procedure allows the evaluation team to take into account the terms and timing of payment of the purchase cost (perhaps spread over a series of phased instalments). The objective, at the time of procurement, is to choose the supplier whose product meets the specified requirements at the lowest life cycle cost.

Applying life cycle costing has many benefits, allowing true comparison of competing bids and helping to reduce operating expenditure, to maximize profitability and to increase the competitiveness of the port. However, surprisingly few ports apply the technique consciously and formally in bid evaluation. A few engineers claimed that they use estimates of future maintenance and operating expenditure when comparing bids (in some cases applying investment appraisal, too) but in most ports, particularly in LDCs, no attempt is made to apply life cycle costing, and investment decisions seem to be based almost entirely on comparison of initial capital cost. There are, admittedly, certain difficulties in applying life cycle costing. For example:

— The information supplied by bidders is rarely sufficiently detailed to allow future maintenance and operating costs to be estimated. Manufacturers do not supply data on equipment running costs or performance levels under port operating conditions – in many cases, they just do not have such data. Maintenance manuals are not organized in such a way that preventive maintenance can be costed, nor do they give guidance on when major overhauls and refurbishment might be required, what amount of work is likely to be involved, nor what it might cost. Even future spare parts expenditure cannot be forecast accurately from the manufacturers' information. Yet *all* that information is needed for calculating Life Cycle Costs.

— Most ports do not have sufficiently comprehensive or reliable Operational and Engineering Management Information Systems to use for Life Cycle Costing. Where operating performance data are recorded, they are often incomplete, unreliable and not relatable to specific models. Few ports record the work done by particular machines, in terms of annual or lifetime output, nor are figures available for lost production due to equipment shortages or breakdowns. Few records are kept on the frequency and cause of breakdowns, accidents and repairs for individual machines, models and brands, and so it is almost impossible to calculate the amount of maintenance work that has been performed on the different types and makes of equipment in the port's inventory.

— A major problem is that most LDC ports do not have good financial reporting and cost-control systems in their operating and maintenance departments. It is, therefore, impossible for engineers to work out the maintenance costs of currently owned equipment or to calculate standard costs for the routine maintenance and repair tasks undertaken in the workshops. Also missing is reliable cost information on the spare parts and consumable materials used to keep equipment in good working order, on drivers' wages and fuel/power consumption. There is little or no factual basis available, then, for calculating current equipment costs and for forecasting future running and maintenance costs for the equipment being offered by bidders.

— Managers in many LDC ports also referred to the difficulty of predicting future national and international inflation levels and movements in exchange rates which might occur during the life of the asset to be acquired. Major devaluations have taken place in the recent past of LDC currencies against the major international currencies – the US dollar and the Japanese yen – in which many bids are quoted. This makes it very difficult to predict accurately capital recovery charges, the future cost of spare parts and of technical assistance that might be required from the supplier.

— The final reason why Life Cycle Costing is not used in LDC ports is that senior port managers and governmental officials are not aware of the technique and its value. Most managers involved in the evaluation of bids have received little or no training in procurement and are unaware (or at least unconvinced) of the merits of applying Life Cycle Costing.

There are, therefore, undoubtedly difficulties in using Life Cycle Costing in bid evaluation, but the benefits to the port – in terms of much improved confidence in selecting a supplier and of the likelihood of a more appropriate choice of equipment – are so great that it is well worth while trying to overcome those difficulties. Many of them are, in fact, problems which must be tackled for other reasons, and their solutions are discussed in other chapters of this report. Even going some of the way towards estimating Life Cycle Costs – for example, just making realistic estimates of likely running and maintenance costs – can make an enormous difference to the success of the bid evaluation process, even if the more complicated calculations of opportunity costing, lost production costing and so on are omitted until management information and other systems are better developed.

4.5.3 Improving Selection Procedures

Action is clearly needed in a number of areas to improve tender selection procedures in LDC ports.

1. The content and quality of technical specifications must be improved and greater attention paid to performance specifications and to the maintenance features of purchases. More detailed information should be demanded from manufacturers on typical running and maintenance costs in a representative environment, and on the relationship between costs and hours of operation. Recommended preventive maintenance schedules should be supplied, with estimates of the number of man-hours required by the different trades, of the quantities of spare parts needed for each type of service for, say, one, two and five years of operation, and of the costs of those parts and materials. Estimates of the frequency of major system overhauls and of equipment refurbishment, with costs, should also be supplied. All that information then needs checking through discussions with colleagues in ports that are using machines of the type being procured.

2. Managers must improve their information systems, so that they have available the data needed for comparing operating and maintenance performance of equipment currently in the inventory; the essential features of such systems are discussed in later chapters.

3. Ports must improve their bid evaluation procedures and introduce some form of Life Cycle Costing to compare the full costs of ownership and use of an asset throughout its working life. Particular attention must be paid to the likely demands that new equipment will make on maintenance facilities and to running and maintenance costs.

4. Managers directly involved in procurement must be given adequate training in the planning of procurement, the preparation of technical specifications and other components

of the Bidding Documents, and in bid analysis and evaluation.

4.6 Management and Supervision of the Procurement Process

4.6.1 Organization of Procurement

Given the wide range of activities and procedures involved in procurement, and the variety of skills required, an important question to consider is how best to organize the procurement function for capital equipment purchases. The broad aims should be to:

— allow all interested parties to take part in and contribute to the decision-making process, as appropriate;

— use the skills and expertise of all relevant personnel to improve decision-making;

— ensure that the decision-making process is carried out smoothly, efficiently and in accordance with the policies and procedures of the port.

As discussed briefly in Section 4.2.5, there is considerable variation in the organizational framework within which procurement is carried out, but a strong case can be made for it to be managed within a Supplies Department by staff qualified specifically for that function. Procurement is an important function in its own right, and it requires an organizational structure which recognizes that. There is much evidence to indicate that this has not been recognized in many LDC ports; responsibility for procurement has often been allocated to staff either lacking the necessary skills and knowledge to perform the function professionally or who lack the time needed to perform it properly, as their other responsibilities and duties (mistakenly) claim priority. This needs to be remedied urgently, and an appropriate organizational structure set up, within which the various activities of the procurement process (including the co-ordination of the various teams and committees responsible for preparing Bidding Documents, evaluating bids, etc.) can be carried out in an efficient, effective and integrated fashion.

Most of the elements of the management of procurement have been covered in various earlier sections (particularly Sections 4.3.5.7 and 4.3.7), but a few aspects of supervision remain to be considered, and they are discussed in this section: general supervision, timetabling, independent inspection and performance tests.

4.6.2 General Supervision

All contracts for the supply of physical assets or services must be supervised, but the extent of supervision needed depends on the confidence that the port has in the contractor. If the port has a large staff, including personnel with the appropriate skills, it may be possible for the contract to be supervised entirely in-house, but many projects require very specialized skills (often for a short period only) and in these cases it may be best to employ third-party supervision.

As well as covering such routine contractual matters as certificates of payment, timetable adherence and approval of technical issues, contract supervisors must pay particular attention to quality assurance and quality control. These are usually best supervised by specialist firms. Statutory regulations may also require government bodies to be involved, particularly during load-testing and similar commissioning operations.

4.6.3 Timetabling

During the survey, no criticisms were made of contractors' failing to keep to a programme for the supply of equipment or the completion of civil engineering works, although it is known that at least two current (1988) port projects, each with major capital equipment and civil engineering contracts, are running late. In one of these instances, delays have been caused by changes required by the client, and additional civil works have proved necessary because of unforeseen obstructions. It is suspected that LDC port managers do not complain because they would not be ready to operate the plant or equipment even if it were to be commissioned on time! They need the extra time to appoint and train personnel, set up documentation systems and organize operational and engineering procedures before the equipment or terminals can be operated.

When civil, mechanical and electrical works are undertaken within the same major project, delays in the civil work (possibly for quite justifiable reasons) tend to mask delays in the mechanical and electrical contracts. For example, equipment cannot be installed until the quay is ready to receive it, and in this way delays in the supply of equipment appear insignificant to the port. In reality, such major projects are often disastrously badly managed, with little or no co-ordination between the various components. In one current project, the equipment has been installed but no workshops have been completed, while training programmes for a very large workforce has still not been agreed and few staff have yet been recruited, just a few months before the first vessel is due to arrive. Timetabling and management of procurement projects clearly need considerably more attention in many ports.

4.6.4 Independent Inspection

Independent inspection services are often employed to cover quality control, non-destructive testing and chemical analysis of materials, inspection of welds and the witnessing of trial runs of components at the contractor's (or sub-contractor's) premises. Inspection companies are also often employed by LDC buyers to check goods, including batches of spare parts and other supplies, at overseas suppliers' premises before they are packed and dispatched to the port. This not only prevents possible mistakes in supply and variations in quality of goods, but also helps to smooth import and customs difficulties when the supplies arrive in the country. Some government and port regulations demand this type of inspection.

Even if consultants are employed to undertake independent inspection in their special fields, it is important for the port's engineering and procurement staff to retain full control of the project, and appropriately qualified staff will have to be recruited and/or trained to do this.

4.6.5 Performance Tests

It is important for those involved in procurement to remember that the supplier of capital equipment is only contractually obliged to supply equipment *in accordance with the specification*. This means that any tests (such as performance tests) which are carried out on delivery, by the port's operations or engineering staff, must refer to specific points in the agreed contract. Even if, as is sometimes the case, equipment is found to be unsatisfactory when tested, in that it does not perform quite as the operators would like it to perform, this is irrelevant unless the contract explicitly requires that performance. So a port has no right to reject equipment that does not meet its expectations, unless they are clearly and un-ambiguously included in the technical specification section of the contract. This underlines the importance of careful preparation of the technical specification; it must cover *all* the technical and operating characteristics which the port requires in the equipment.

The port and supplier should agree, at the pre-contract stage, on a detailed inspection and testing procedure, perhaps based on the standard testing procedures of a professional body, such as the Institution of Mechanical Engineers, and the details must then be explicitly included in the contract. Such an agreed procedure prevents problems arising during the acceptance phase of procurement.

4.7 Recommendations

1. LDC ports need to formulate and implement suitable procurement policies (long-term objectives) and strategies (the means of achieving the objectives) to improve their equipment management.

2. Improved procurement policies and strategies must be adopted by LDC ports, consistent with, and designed to promote, the port's corporate objectives and its development plans.

3. Senior management must examine and, where necessary, revise existing procurement regulations and methods to ensure that they lead to a sensible equipment inventory that suits the port's operating and maintenance capabilities.

4. Greater attention needs to be paid to the preparation of Bidding Documents, to improve supplier selection.

5. Responsibility for preparing the Bidding Documents should rest with the Supplies Department, but with the constant and close advice and assistance of the line departments concerned in the purchase, particularly the engineers and operators.

6. Bidding Documents must be clearly and unambiguously written to avoid possible confusion, wherever possible using internationally accepted documentation and conditions of contract.

7. Preparation of the technical specification must be well organized and smoothly managed, ensuring successful, cost-effective equipment selection and following a firm timetable to ensure that the equipment is commissioned by the time operators need it.

8. Preparation of the technical specification should be a collective effort involving representatives of the Operations, Engineering and Planning Departments, co-ordinated by senior staff in the Supplies Department.

9. Operations staff must be given responsibility for preparing a detailed performance specification, setting out the precise cargo-handling requirements in terms of current and future demands, the nature and scope of the work to be undertaken, and the full range of activities to be performed.

10. Engineers must be responsible for preparing a detailed engineering specification, taking into account equipment design, capacity, safety and durability factors, and ensuring that users' needs are fully met and that construction standards and maintainability are as high as possible.

11. The engineering specification must support the port's policy on equipment and component compatibility, minimizing model and make variety and striving for commonality with existing equipment.

12. Engineers in LDC ports must maintain regular contact with other ports and with equipment manufacturers, to exchange views, compare equipment operation and maintenance and to observe developments in equipment design and performance.

13. Engineers must receive regularly technical publications to keep abreast of technological developments and take every opportunity to increase their knowledge of new equipment and its engineering and operating features.

14. As the purchase of spare parts forms such a vital element of the procurement process, decisions on what spares to stock, and on how to ensure a reliable supply of spares, must be taken while the technical specification and Bidding Documents are being prepared.

15. LDC ports should try to follow the policy of only purchasing consumable items at the time of procurement of new equipment, delaying the purchase of replacement parts until the end of the warranty period; major changes in government and central bank control procedures will almost certainly be needed.

16. LDC ports must be allowed to set aside sufficient funds (in foreign exchange) in their annual capital equipment budget for the procurement of supplies, if possible retaining it in an overseas account to avoid delays in obtaining supplies caused by waiting for approval for foreign exchange expenditure.

17. At the time of procurement of new equipment, the strategy should be to lodge an agreed sum (preferably equivalent to 10-15% of the equipment purchase price) in an overseas bank in readiness for spare parts purchase.

18. When equipment is provided as part of a bilateral or multilateral aid package, LDC ports should insist that sufficient moneys are set aside from the initial purchase fund for spare parts and other supplies.

19. LDC ports should demand from suppliers a detailed list of the spares needed to cover maintenance for, say, two and five years, with each part's original manufacturer and source of supply indicated.

20. Detailed drawings of systems, assemblies, sub-assemblies and components should be provided by the equipment supplier, so that parts can be repaired or even manufactured in the port if necessary.

21. The training specification should be given as much attention as the technical specification when preparing Bidding Documents for procuring new types of equipment.

22. When specifying training requirements in the Bidding Documents, the background, previous training and current skills of personnel must be stated in detail.

23. Suppliers must, in their tenders, specify the objectives of their offered training, how they intend to present the training, how progress is to be assessed, and what materials, facilities and staff will be provided.

24. The Bidding Documents must state clearly that the maintenance manuals to be supplied must take into account local conditions and circumstances, must be provided in the local language(s) and be specifically related to the model of equipment purchased.

25. Great attention must be given to choice of the appropriate method for selecting potential suppliers, preparatory to inviting bids.

26. Open tendering should only be adopted for supplier selection if the port has no previous knowledge of a particular market and cannot otherwise gain that information quickly, reliably and economically.

27. Prequalification should be used for supplier selection where the port has not previously purchased a particular type of asset but is familiar with the market, where the equipment is non-standard, complex or of high value, where the supplier is being asked to provide additional services, and where procurement regulations demand acceptance of the lowest-priced suitable bid.

28. Selective tendering should be the supplier selection method adopted where the port is aware of likely suppliers, has purchased equipment of the type previously and is familiar with the market, and where the engineers and supplies staff have kept themselves well informed about the activities of leading suppliers.

29. Bid evaluation procedures in LDC ports must be improved through in-depth analysis of supplier performance and of the technical data provided.

30. Life Cycle Costing, using discounted cash flow techniques, should be applied in bid evaluation, based on costs estimated by operations and engineering staff from their own management information systems and from data supplied by the manufacturers, to make true comparison of competing bids.

31. Bidding Documents must request bidders to supply sufficiently detailed information to allow future maintenance and running costs to be estimated and compared.

32. Ports must maintain comprehensive and reliable Operational and Engineering Management Information Systems to use for Life Cycle Costing.

33. General supervision and independent inspection practices should be reviewed and, if necessary, improved to ensure good quality control and conformity with statutory and other regulations during construction, installation and commissioning of new equipment.

34. The port and supplier should agree, at the pre-contract stage, on a detailed inspection and testing procedure, to ensure that the procured equipment will meet operators' and engineers' requirements and to prevent disputes during the acceptance phase of the contract.

35. The procurement function must be organized within an appropriate managerial framework, recognizing its importance to equipment management, and be given appropriately qualified staff and adequate resources.

36. Timetabling and management of procurement projects must be given full attention, to minimize delays and to ensure that all activities are completed on time.

CHAPTER 5

Operations and Maintenance

5.1 Significance of Operational Factors to Maintenance

Information gathered from the questionnaire distributed as part of this study and observations made during the port visits confirm that there is a strong relationship between the way equipment is operated and the effectiveness of maintenance services. Ports that have major maintenance difficulties invariably have deficiencies in equipment operating practices and control procedures; indeed, these were frequently a major cause of additional and unnecessary burdens imposed on the engineering services. The ways in which equipment operating practices contribute to maintenance problems vary from port to port, but a number of common elements can be identified:

— Operators do not predict their future demand for equipment, so that engineers cannot prepare maintenance schedules and workplans in advance; even when demand *is* predicted, the information supplied is often unreliable, frustrating the efforts of engineers to plan the use of their workshop resources.

— Lack of co-operation and communication between engineering and operations staff often leads to poor control of allocation procedures and to related difficulties in keeping to preventive maintenance programmes.

— Equipment frequently misses preventive maintenance because operators do not return it to the workshop at the due time; when it is eventually released, pressure of urgent engineering work may prevent the engineers from carrying out the full service, or work may be rushed.

— Once the planned maintenance programme begins to fail, the port tends to rely more and more on the emergency repair of breakdowns; repairing broken-down machines takes longer than preventive maintenance, and this reduces the number of units available to operators.

— The fewer units there are available, the more intensively those machines have to work; the equipment is subjected to greater wear and tear and the amount of maintenance required increases.

— Inadequate equipment allocation procedures may prevent equipment being regularly inspected by engineers, particularly if the port is relying on a repair-on-breakdown maintenance strategy; fault detection and notification are then entirely dependent on drivers' pre-shift inspections — often a misplaced reliance, as drivers skimp or overlook these tasks.

— If warning signs are ignored by drivers, minor problems escape detection and grow into major ones; equipment is kept operating until it fails comprehensively.

— Careless driving and lack of attention to safety rules and procedures lead to accidents and damage to equipment, directly and unnecessarily increasing the workshops' workload.

There is no doubt, then, that the efficiency of the maintenance function depends to a great extent on the observance of good operating procedures, effective management and supervision of equipment use, and on sound and safe driving practices. In particular, the study demonstrated that drivers do not look after the equipment that they are operating. In many ports, bad driving causes frequent accidents and breakdowns, creating an enormous amount of unnecessary fault-finding and repair work for workshop staff. Careless and reckless driving can also cause damage to civil works, breaking up the quay and road surfaces; unless potholes and other defects are repaired immediately, they will in their turn cause extra wear and tear to the equipment. Poor 'housekeeping' by operations staff (including drivers) can also cause immense damage to machines — litter, packing materials and other debris left on the working surfaces are accidents waiting to happen, and are particularly damaging to tyres and to lower surfaces of mobile equipment. All these examples of poor operating practices and of misuse and abuse of cargo-handling equipment can be accounted for by poor recruitment, inadequate driver training and lack of supervision.

Another aspect of the influence of operations on maintenance concerns record keeping. Failure to maintain comprehensive and accurate records on equipment performance (particularly cost data) causes great problems for the engineers. Without detailed records of the hours worked by equipment, it is impossible to determine precisely when a preventive maintenance service is due; either over-maintenance (expensive) or under-maintenance (dangerous) is the likely consequence. Lack of data on running hours and costs can also result in plant being maintained well beyond its economic life; these data are essential for the development of appropriate replacement strategies and other equipment planning decisions. As far as operations managers are concerned, of course, such deficiencies in the Operations Management Information System (OMIS) lead to a lack of cost-consciousness and managerial accountability – one of the major concerns to emerge from this study. Operations staff, just like engineering and all other port employees, must begin to base their decisions, policies and practices on economic criteria.

These then, are some of the deficiencies in operating procedures and practices identified in this study as diminishing the performance of cargo-handling equipment and intensifying the demands placed on the resources of the engineering department. They will be examined in more detail in Section 5.2, before going on to consider the control of equipment allocation (Section 5.3), the management of equipment operation (Section 5.4), operating costs (Section 5.5) and operating records (Section 5.6).

5.2 Review of Operating Problems Affecting Maintenance

5.2.1 Control of Equipment

The study revealed considerable variation in the delegation of managerial responsibility and in the procedures for the control and daily allocation of cargo-handling equipment. In the majority of ports visited, the equipment is notionally 'owned' by the operations department, and operations managers control its requisitioning and deployment. In a few ports and terminals, on the other hand, engineering staff are directly involved in those duties and even, in one or two cases, have notional 'ownership' of equipment and control its deployment. In yet other ports, it is ships' agents who decide what equipment should be requisitioned for a shift and how these units are to be deployed on their vessels. In one of the ports surveyed, the operations managers effectively control the equipment but allocation and deployment are carried out by an Equipment

Foreman assigned to each terminal. He reports directly to the terminal manager at the 'operational' level, but at the 'functional' level is responsible to an Equipment Manager, whose task it is to co-ordinate the movement of units from one berth or terminal to another, as necessary. The Equipment Foreman liaises between staff in the operations and engineering departments, to determine future equipment requirements, and plans and adjusts maintenance programmes.

Assigning responsibility for the control, allocation and deployment of equipment to Operations staff frequently causes problems in maintenance. Operations staff tend not to release plant to the workshops when it is due for planned maintenance, or when minor faults are first detected – even when they have no urgent need for the units. In some cases, equipment is only handed over to the engineers when it fails in operation! Under such circumstances, preventive maintenance programmes are almost impossible to sustain, and it is hardly surprising that some ports affected by such problems have given up all pretence of practising that strategy. Moreover, because the engineers are unable to inspect plant regularly, they cannot monitor its condition and repair any bodywork or structural damage (nor, indeed, can they immediately trace the cause of damage and apportion blame). When equipment eventually reaches the workshop, the engineers are commonly faced with a large number of faults and defects to remedy – not just the one causing the immediate breakdown – and the equipment may then be out of service for many days or weeks being repaired. While that item of equipment is unavailable to operators, the remaining units are overworked, adding to their normal wear and tear. Not surprisingly, the failure rate of those units is high, adding to the maintenance workload. In ports where such a vicious circle of operational mismanagement was observed, equipment deteriorates rapidly, creating engineering problems that plague the maintenance department throughout the machine's (much shortened) life.

A major disadvantage of placing control of equipment in the hands of the Operations Department is that it can create difficulties when the engineers are planning maintenance. If operators do not forecast their demand for equipment a few days ahead, engineers cannot prepare an effective maintenance workplan. Unreliable forecasts are almost as bad, as they cannot be used for detailed resource planning and for evening-out demand on the workshops. Without such a maintenance plan, work will come in irregularly and often the workshop will be overloaded, with routine work having to be carried out at night or at weekends – at expensive overtime rates. The resulting pressure on maintenance staff can lead to sub-standard work, low morale and a poor attitude to the job. If that sort of situation is allowed to persist, preventive maintenance work will be dropped and the engineers will only respond to breakdowns and accidents.

Another consequence of Operations managers' control of equipment is that they are less likely to be cost-conscious than if they have to 'hire' units, as needed, from Engineering or from a central pool. They are also likely to be less than diligent in their collection of operating and financial information for the Operations Management Information System (OMIS), and will have little incentive to be rigorous in their allocation procedures. A frequent complaint to the team was that operators retain equipment on their berths or terminals when they had no genuine need for it, even when other sections of the port were suffering a shortage of plant. This is particularly common where there is a general shortage of cargo-handling equipment in the port, for some reason or another; operators hold onto machines as a defence against not being allocated units when they really need them. In the event, of course, they only make the situation worse by retaining the machines – particularly if such retention causes equipment to miss its maintenance 'slot'.

Of course, present cost-control procedures (or the lack of them) mean that operators face no financial penalties in holding on to equipment beyond their needs. Indeed, if cargo-handling equipment is in short supply, and its allocation to the berth when needed is by no means certain, an operator may be forgiven for being over-cautious. There is no excuse, however, for not recording (and making use of) reliable data on demand, utilization and availability of equipment. Without such information, it is practically impossible to forecast equipment needs and to prepare an equipment plan (Chapter 3). It is also not possible for managers to combine operating and financial information in developing equipment performance indicators or measures as part of the OMIS and EMIS (Chapter 9).

5.2.2 Allocation and Utilization

Preventive maintenance programmes are almost always based on equipment operating hours: machines are due for servicing every 500 hours, 1000 hours, and so on. This is, on the face of it, a good principle to follow, but only if the 'operating hours' are accurately known; in most cases the figure is taken from allocation records, rather than from records of the actual hours worked, and this could lead to over-maintenance of plant and unnecessary extra workloads for the workshops.

The problem is that, in most ports surveyed, the practice is to allocate equipment to a particular berth or task for a complete shift, whether or not it will be required to work the whole time. The daily operating record (where one is kept) registers the time the machine leaves the central workshop or parking area, notes the location and nature of its intended work, and the time of return to the workshop or parking area on completion of the job – usually the end of the shift (though in some ports the operators may actually keep the machine for several shifts before returning it). If these data are used for determining the hours of work of that machine, and subsequently for calculating its utilization (over a week or month), inaccuracies will be introduced into the OMIS. For example, a machine allocated to the berth for an 8-hour shift may only actually work for 2 hours; it lies idle for the rest of the time – or may even have suffered a temporary breakdown (unrecorded because of inefficiencies in the OMIS). So the operator's equipment needs are overstated, equipment operating hours inflated, and resulting equipment performance indicators miscalculated. The effect on engineering is to cause the machine to be given its periodical preventive maintenance long before it needs it.

What is needed, clearly, is a more accurate measuring and recording of machine working hours, as well as a more honest requisitioning system. There must be a true record of the time that each machine has actually worked on the berth, rigorously excluding all times when the machine was idle. This is most accurately done by fitting one or more hour-meters to record the engine running hours under load, the work done by hoist motors, traverse etc. (as described in Chapter 3). If hour-meter readings are taken at the beginning and end of each shift (or period of allocation), both operators and engineers can have a realistic indication of the hours of work performed by equipment.

The difference between utilization as measured by allocation (calculated from requisition forms and time-out: time-in records) and as revealed from hour-meter readings is dramatically demonstrated in Table 5.2.2, which presents data on a fleet of tractor units at an Asian container terminal. It shows that utilization calculated on the conventional basis of allocation records averaged 59% for the year (362 working days, with three 6.5-hour shifts per day: a possible 8,688 working hours), while 'true' utilization, on the basis of hour-meter readings, was only 18%. This illustrates not only how much more efficiently machines can be allocated when working hours are accurately predicted (provided that operators can re-deploy machines to different operating areas during a working period, or that machines are returned to a central pool as soon as they are finished with) but also that planned maintenance based on 'requisitioned hours' is likely to be far too frequent. In the case illustrated, the tractors would have received five '1,000-hour' services during the year on average, when they would in reality have merited just two.

Table 5.2.2 Utilization of prime movers at an LDC container terminal, 1987 (possible machine hours = 8,688)

| Unit | Utilization | | | |
| | 'Requisition' basis | | 'Hour-meter' basis | |
	Hours	%	Hours	%
1	4,176	48	996	11
2	7,059	81	420	4
3	7,059	81	1,406	16
4	7,059	81	906	10
5	3,694	43	2,146	24
6	3,694	43	2,250	25
7	3,694	43	2,119	24
8	3,694	43	1,833	21
9	3,694	43	2,032	23
10	4,176	48	925	10
11	4,176	48	1,657	19
12	3,694	43	2,604	29
13	4,176	48	1,635	18
14	3,694	43	2,920	33
15	3,694	43	2,784	32
16	3,694	43	2,070	23
17	3,694	43	1,880	21
18	7,059	81	1,554	17
19	7,059	81	1,469	16
20	7,059	81	821	9
21	7,059	81	1,340	15
22	7,059	81	1,069	12
23	7,059	81	1,204	13
Total	117,175	—	38,040	—
Average	5,095	59	1,654	18

5.2.3 Bad Driving

A frequent and very expensive cause of equipment downtime is accidents. They may involve personal injury to employees, damage to cargo or ship and, of course, damage to the cargo-handling equipment. Management's primary concern in this context must be the safety of its workforce, and it is essential that all precautions are taken to avoid personal injury and fatalities. Customer care is also of major importance, of course, and the port will wish to avoid any damage to cargoes and vessels. However, care of

cargo-handling machines is also of very great importance, given the large sums invested in equipment in a modern port. Accidents often result in severe damage, involving the need for repair to bodywork, structure and mechanisms. Expensive spare parts may have to be purchased, requiring the quite avoidable expenditure of foreign exchange. The equipment is often out of service for weeks or even months as the engineers try to obtain vital spare parts from manufacturers and suppliers; this can be very difficult when there are strict foreign currency controls, import and customs licences and other procedural constraints (Chapter 4). While the machine lies idle at the workshop, particularly where the climate is hot and humid, it will begin to deteriorate, giving further maintenance problems and, in severe cases, possibly premature scrapping.

Although the ports surveyed regularly record accident statistics, they do not distinguish those caused by or involving equipment. This is a serious omission; safety officers need those data to determine where procedural improvements have to be made and where extra training is required. The port transport industry in general has a poor record over safety, and accident rates in many developing countries are unacceptably high. Technological development and increasing use of machinery are making the working environment progressively more dangerous; accident rates could rise even higher unless stricter safety measures are introduced and regular (and repeated) training is provided in safe working practices. The magnitude of this problem is illustrated in Table 5.2.3A, which summarizes recent accident statistics for one African port, with a working population of about 2,000 operations staff. The majority of the accidents involved equipment of one sort or another; what driver training was provided was of poor quality in that port, and little direct safety training was given.

Table 5.2.3A Recorded accidents at a small African port, 1985-87

	1985	1986	1987 (Jan-Sept)	1987 (projected)
Total accidents	448	857	1,771	(2,361)
Accidents involving insurance claims	273	215	311	(415)
Fatalities	4	7	2	(3)

Many of the ports visited have recognized the safety problems created by increasing use of equipment and have allocated additional resources to safety training. The value of such training has been demonstrated by statistics published by the UK

National Dock Labour Board: between 1970 and 1986, during which time the Board (supported by Government legislation) undertook a safety awareness and training programme, the number of medical treatments in UK ports – a useful indicator of the industry's accident rate – fell from 3.12 treatments per registered dock worker to 1.75. The benefits of a policy focussing attention on equipment and operational safety are also illustrated in Table 5.2.3B, which shows a substantial reduction in the reported accident data for a major LDC port in the five-year period 1982-1986, during which time the port pursued an active safety policy and upgraded its safety training; the labour force remained virtually constant over that period. Senior managers at the port estimated that over 60% of accidents involve cargo-handling equipment; it is clearly extremely important to improve safety awareness and training for all drivers and operators.

Table 5.2.3B Summary of reportable accidents at a major LDC port, 1982-1986

| Year | Reported Accidents | | |
	Aboard ship	Ashore	Total
1982	107	579	686
1983	107	567	674
1984	78	100	178
1985	81	118	199
1986	91	83	174

However many safety features are built into a piece of equipment, it will only be as safe as its driver. About 45% of all forklift truck accidents are caused wholly or partly by operator error. Furthermore, bad driving is a frequent and major cause of equipment failure and breakdown; drivers subject their vehicles to unnecessary wear and tear, by misuse of the controls and non-observance of traffic regulations. They ignore the warning sounds of machinery under stress and do not recognize them as indicators of imminent mechanical failure. Admittedly, this is not always the drivers' fault; they may not have been given any instruction on the basic principles of diesel and i/c engine function, gear box and transmission operation, etc., and they may not appreciate the difference between good and bad driving practices because of the poor quality of the training provided.

Driver abuse and misuse of cargo-handling equipment, which was observed not infrequently during the port visits, is also a consequence of poor supervision and management. In many ports, the absence of well established operating rules and regulations,

and their continuous and effective enforcement by managers and supervisors, lie at the heart of this operating problem. In an extensive survey by the UK Production Engineering Research Association (PERA) of equipment maintenance problems in UK seaports (Anon, 1986), driver abuse was identified as the biggest single contributor to plant failure. No fewer than 36 categories of operator misuse were recognized, including: overloading; driving too fast; violent acceleration and braking; towing trailers with their brakes full on; driving machines with punctured tyres; accidental and intentional impact damage; over-revving, immediate forward-reverse direction changes and other bad practices; smashing of controls (hour-meters, ammeters, ignition switches, etc.) and vandalized horns, lighting and batteries. That study found that, for example, 30% of repairs to cranes and 15% of those to tractor units were caused solely by driver negligence, and concluded that, overall, the majority of breakdowns are due to deliberate abuse or carelessness on the part of drivers. Clearly, then, without good training, discipline and supervision of drivers and operators, it is extremely difficult to implement an effective maintenance strategy.

Although studies and statistics on the scale and in the detail of the PERA survey have not been carried out in developing countries, maintenance engineers in many of the ports visited reported that a large proportion of equipment defects and failures are the result of driver misuse. Repairs to vehicles damaged in accidents (often the direct result of driver negligence) were also cited as causes of excessive and avoidable demands on the skills of engineering staff, with equipment being out of service for long periods as a consequence. Engineers, supported in the main by traffic officers, recited a catalogue of bad driving practices, ranging from damage caused by exceeding the rated capacities of equipment to engine seizure resulting from omission of pre-shift inspections. Managers even reported that it is not uncommon for equipment to be sabotaged, to allow drivers to finish work early (or to ensure that they will have to work overtime – it is a question of choosing carefully when the 'breakdown' should occur!). In cases where driver abuse and misuse of equipment are endemic, it is impossible for engineers to sustain an acceptable level of availability, because of frequent breakdown and damage to machines and the time needed to repair them.

The proper operation of cargo-handling equipment is, of course, a very important aspect of port management. Much of the bad driving described above is the result of inadequate supervision by those managers responsible for controlling day-to-day operations. Managers and supervisors on the berths pay too little attention to the conditions of the equipment in their (possibly temporary) care and to the driving practices of their operators; they often ignore the blatant misuse and abuse of the equipment. The subject of management is considered in greater depth in Section 5.4.

The direct consequences of inadequate care of plant and negligent operation are reduced availability and a shortage of equipment for cargo handling. Breakdowns during operation, frequently the result of bad driver practices, often cause labour and other equipment to be idle on the berth and lead to delays to the vessel. Breakdowns also disrupt the planning and scheduling of cargo-handling operations, affect maintenance schedules and the demands on engineering, and generally reduce the quality of port service to users. They also lead to equipment shortages in operations; these will be considered in the next section.

5.2.4 Equipment Shortages

It was not always possible to identify the true extent of equipment shortages in the ports surveyed, partly because some ports do not record daily demand accurately and partly because of inadequacies in allocation procedures. So it has not been possible to establish a direct and general relationship between equipment operation and the quality of maintenance services, nor to determine the impact of equipment operation on the port's optimum equipment inventory. However, there is considerable evidence that many ports with a demonstrably poor maintenance capability experience serious equipment shortages. For example, Figure 5.2.4. displays the demand and supply statistics for a fleet of standard forklift trucks over a 19-day period at a port where equipment shortages were prevalent. It shows that on nearly 70% of days supply fell short of operators' requirements, and on some days the shortfall was over

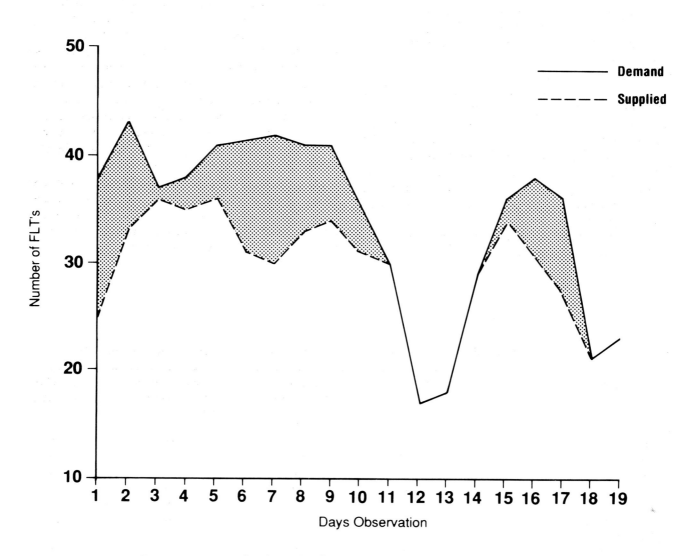

Figure 5.2.4: Demand and Supply of Cargo Handling Equipment (Standard FLTs)

96

30%, even though the number of units requested on each berth was well below international norms. In this port, the equipment that was allocated to the berths frequently broke down during operation, making matters worse. Cargo-handling output was, at best, low and, at worst, nil, as operations ground to a complete halt and labour was sent home. So the imbalance between supply and demand at that port was in practice even worse than Figure 5.2.4 indicates. To overcome these impossible conditions, ship operators have begun to import their own equipment (and, incidentally, maintenance staff) to work their vessels, bypassing the port's equipment allocation and maintenance systems. This has caused further operational problems, involving driver allocation and training, as well as increasing the range of plant operating in the port.

The principal cause of equipment shortages is not necessarily failure of the port to purchase enough units (although this is certainly the case in some ports; see Chapter 3). It is often that equipment is not adequately maintained, so that it is not available when needed. Poor operating practices (particularly bad driving) add to the problem of inadequate workshop service, by increasing unnecessarily the need for maintenance. Table 5.2.4A demonstrates the magnitude of this problem. It shows average daily 'availability' data for ports in one of the countries surveyed in this study, arranged under four headings (the terms used are those of the ports concerned): the inventory level (units currently listed in the ports' inventory); units 'serviceable' (considered by the engineers as being – notionally, at least – capable of being maintained and used); units 'under maintenance' (either currently in the workshops or awaiting spare parts); and those 'available for work' (units fit for allocation to the berths).

The most striking point to emerge from Table 5.2.4A is the extremely small proportion of inventoried units that were listed as 'available for work'. For example, only 15% of the total stock of forklift trucks were, on average, available for use at any one time during the period surveyed, and only 42% of them are actually still considered capable of being maintained ('serviceable'). The explanation for these extraordinary figures is that equipment is retained on the asset register well beyond its physical life (see Chapter 3), and that a very high proportion of the rest of the stock is undergoing repair, often because of accidents resulting from bad driving. Many of the 'unserviceable' units had been heavily cannibalized in an attempt to keep other units in at least a maintainable state.

In ports like these, with a high proportion of the inventoried equipment either under repair or awaiting repair, often for months at a time, the allocation of equipment to the berths is determined almost entirely by supply considerations, instead of by operator demand. Every unit that is in working order (or something near it) is put into operation and is worked to exhaustion, missing its preventive maintenance and storing up more problems for the workshops in the future. Unless new plant is purchased, the shortages and pressures on engineering get worse and worse, and operators are unlikely ever to receive the type or number of units that they need to handle the cargo entering their berths. Equipment shortages reduce handling output, making the port less attractive to users and less profitable. Thus the cycle continues: less usable equipment, more pressures on remaining units and on engineering, less effective maintenance, more breakdowns and fewer available machines.

Table 5.2.4A Equipment inventory and average availability of equipment in the ports of a developing country, 1988

Type of equipment	Inventory Level	Number 'Serviceable'	Number 'Under Maintenance'	Number 'Available'
Portable cranes	70	53	24	29
Mobile cranes	77	36	25	11
Forklift trucks	467	199	127	72
Tractors	100	65	51	14
Trailers	243	94	40	54
Berthing tugs	8	6	5	1
Lighters & pontoons	107	71	56	15
Lighter towing tugs	14	10	6	4
Labour launches	17	14	9	5

Equipment shortages can also occur in ports which have invested in an apparently adequate stock, and where a reasonable maintenance capability exists. Such is the case in a few of the ports where engineers notionally 'own' the equipment and control its allocation to operators. In those ports, daily equipment allocation is based on what the engineers determine to be the number of available units, rather than on operators' requisitions. In effect, the engineers keep equipment in the workshops and garages, 'rationing' its supply to operators, with the claimed objectives of reducing wear and tear on plant and minimizing demands on maintenance! There is, of course, a certain twisted logic in the argument, as equipment is undeniably kept under close surveillance and is almost guaranteed to be at the workshops when it is due for its regular service. On the other hand, it is totally at odds with what should be the port's (and engineers') primary objective of maximizing cargo-handling output. The practice appears to pass senior managerial scrutiny purely because the operators have become resigned to 'requisitioning' only the number of units that they know will be made available to them for a shift, and never exceed that number, even though the underlying demand for equipment is regularly much higher. To all intents and purposes, the daily requisition figures are manipulated to equate with the available units as predetermined by the engineers.

Data illustrating this singular equipment control procedure, as recorded during January and February, 1988, are presented in Table 5.2.4B; they clearly show how attractive the engineers' 'utilization' and 'availability' figures can be made to look. It would appear that availability was high at that port, and utilization low, indicating that there were no allocation problems and effectively concealing the underlying shortfall between demand and supply. The port's stock of equipment seems, on the face of it, to be more than sufficient for operators' needs, and allocation and control procedures appear satisfactory. In practice, the operators were frequently short of equipment in the months surveyed, and the number of units allocated to them was well below international norms for similar trades and throughputs.

In fact, the ports visited exhibited wide variations in the amount of equipment allocated for similar cargo-handling tasks. At some ports and terminals, little equipment was operated and there were frequent delays to cargo-handling, whereas at others operators appeared to have an ample supply, with units also held in reserve ready to meet peaks in demand or breakdowns. These differences can be partly explained by variations in inventory level and partly by maintenance capability, but there are also considerable discrepancies between the allocation 'norms' set by traffic officers:

— For example, the practice in some ports is to allocate one forklift truck for quay transfer to each working hatch or crane, while in other ports handling similar cargoes two or even three units are allocated. These allocation 'rules' are often rigidly applied, taking no account of the type of cargo being handled, while in other ports the number of units allocated is varied to suit anticipated ship loading/discharging rates, quay transfer distance and other factors. Not surprisingly, perhaps, the more rigid rules are applied in those ports where the engineers are responsible for allocation or where they exercise a strong influence over the operators.

— In some ports, equipment is commonly deployed aboard ship, while in others this rarely happens, either because of a shortage of suitable machines or because dockers insist on their traditional working practices. The latter ports also tend to rely heavily on manpower for receipt and delivery of cargo.

— The practice of one major container terminal, supply permitting, is to allocate the maximum number of quayside gantry cranes to each working vessel – up to five at a time, in the case of third generation vessels. At other

Table 5.2.4B Utilization statistics for a port, January-February, 1988

Equipment type	Inventory level	Units supplied /shift	Fleet hours worked	Utilization	Available hours	Availability
Wharf cranes	29	25 (80%)	24,994	60%	38,842	93%
FLTs (3 t)	49	25 (51%)	40,090	45%	79,359	89%
FLTs (5 t)	12	6 (50%)				
FLTs (25 t)	1	1 (100%)				
Electric FLTs	10	6 (60%)	N/A	N/A	N/A	N/A
Mobile cranes	9	6 (66%)	5,705	44%	11,096	86%

terminals visited, only one or, at most, two cranes are allocated; naturally, loading/discharging times are much longer at those terminals.

— Similar variations in allocation procedures were observed for straddle carriers, rubber-tyred gantry cranes, mobile cranes and other cargo-handling equipment.

The principal explanation for these port-to-port differences in allocation levels is that management pursues contrasting operating philosophies. In ports where allocation norms are high, traffic managers are very conscious of the role of equipment in achieving high cargo-handling performance, reducing ship turnround time and maximizing their ports' competitiveness. Those ports have fully embraced mechanization and have set high performance targets, both to attract new traffics and to retain existing customers. The allocation strategy in these highly efficient ports is to provide sufficient equipment for operators to maximize cargo-handling output. In other ports, particularly those still relying heavily on labour-intensive practices and those experiencing maintenance problems, mechanization is still considered complementary, not central, to cargo-handling operations. The equipment inventory in those ports is generally inadequate and its supply to operators is rationed. Cargo-handling performance targets are set at low levels, as output is largely determined by manpower, and traffic officers seem not to appreciate the economic balance between equipment operating costs and the cost of ships' time in port; the objective of those operations departments seems to be to minimize port operating costs rather than shipping or total maritime transport costs.

When unrealistically low equipment allocation norms are set, not only do operators have insufficient resources to handle cargo but they also have no reserve machines to meet peak demands or to redeploy as operational needs fluctuate. The resulting low output and long ships' time in port have a serious impact on total maritime transport costs. The correlation between equipment allocated and output achieved is indicated in Table 5.2.4C, which shows the number of forklift trucks allocated per working hook and the tonnes/gang/hour achieved at the berths of four ports handling similar conventional general cargo. Clearly, where operators are given realistic equipment allocation, they have the flexibility and resources to maintain high levels of output.

Some ports overcome their poor maintenance capability, and avoid the risk of equipment shortage, by investing in a larger than normal inventory. In this way they can guarantee that operators have the equipment they require, with generous reserve capacity to meet peak demand. In these ports, both availability and utilization are low. Although this strategy allows operators' equipment needs to be met, by disguising rather than solving the underlying maintenance deficiencies, it does so at considerable cost in unnecessary capital investment – and, incidentally, adding to the engineers' difficulties by increasing the number of units to be maintained!

Table 5.2.4C Forklift truck allocation and output at four LDC ports

Port	Units allocated per working hook	Ship output in tonnes/gang/hour
A	1	10-12
B	1	6-8
C	1.5	12-15
D	2	20-22

5.2.5 Allocation of Drivers

Despite the large number of employees in LDC ports, operators reported that there are occasions when equipment lies idle during a shift because of a shortage of qualified drivers. This often resulted from a combination of absenteeism (a serious problem in some ports), sick leave and holidays. Clearly, sufficient drivers should be recruited, trained and allocated to ensure continuity of work for all plant and machinery, without resorting to the dangerous practice of drafting in untrained drivers in emergencies, risking accidents and extra maintenance work.

Two main driver allocation strategies have been adopted. In some ports, it is the responsibility of the Operations Department to allocate drivers at the same time that equipment is requisitioned for a shift. Commonly, the drivers are selected from a central pool, particularly in conventional cargo-handling areas. For more specialized driving and operating, it is more usual for the drivers, too, to specialize and to be semi-permanently allocated to a terminal. In one port, however, the operator of a specialist terminal has to take drivers from a central pool of casual labour; not surprisingly, accidental damage accounts for over 80% of the total maintenance costs on that terminal!

The alternative arrangement is for the Engineering Department (or its mechanical engineering section) to be responsible for driver allocation, with the men allocated, along with the equipment, from the central workshop or a satellite workshop. The main benefit of this approach is that drivers become familiar with, and are semi-permanently assigned to, particular types of machine. They also come under the direct surveillance of the engineers, encouraging them to take interest in the technical performance and maintenance of their equipment. On the other hand, they are in a sense servants of two masters, administratively under the engineers but, while working the equipment, under the control of operations staff.

Whichever administrative approach is adopted, most ports support the principle of assigning drivers to a particular type of equipment wherever possible, to maximize familiarity and skill. Indeed, many ports try to keep a driver attached to a particular machine, to promote a feeling of responsibility for and pride in the operation and appearance of the machine. However, three-shift working, holidays and unscheduled absences tend to interfere with this arrangement. Nevertheless, a few ports have been successful in forming small teams of drivers permanently assigned to particular machines on a three-shift working system, and there have been considerable benefits to productivity and equipment condition.

5.2.6 The Working Environment

This study has revealed a significant relationship between equipment maintenance and port working conditions. Mechanical and electrical engineers in several of the participating ports reported that a major cause of corrective maintenance and damage repair is the poor condition of quays and other working surfaces. Two principal reasons were identified. First, civil engineers do not properly maintain the port infrastructure – particularly the quay and other surfaces. Second, operating staff do not follow good housekeeping practices, and fail to keep the working areas clear for the movement of equipment. These will be discussed in turn here.

In some ports, the condition of quay surfaces, roadways and storage areas has been allowed to deteriorate to such an extent that it has become a major cause of equipment failure and damage. Mobile equipment has to travel continuously over rough and uneven surfaces, with many potholes, and this significantly increases the occurrence of suspension, transmission and mast assembly failure. Drivers often make matters worse by swerving to avoid potholes or over-revving to overcome surface resistance. The team noted many cases where remedial civil maintenance work had been left unfinished, with open trenches, rubble and other materials littering the working area, apparently for many months. Differential subsidence of quay surfaces had also been left uncorrected. All these defects are hazards to drivers as well as imposing unnecessary wear and tear on machines.

Engineers reported that failure to maintain the quay and other surfaces to a satisfactory standard not only increases demands on the mechanical and electrical workshops but also severely reduces the working life of equipment. It was common to find standard forklift trucks scrapped within three or four years of delivery and, in extreme cases, taken out of service within eighteen months of commissioning. In one port, a fleet of 60 forklift trucks, supplied with hard tyres, had to be disposed of within months of delivery; drivers refused to use them because of the discomfort experienced when travelling over poorly maintained quay surfaces. Inadequate lighting of working areas was also mentioned as a cause of accidents during night shifts. Clearly, greater attention to the design of working areas and to the maintenance of civil works, including rail tracks, is essential to eliminate these major contributory causes of poor equipment reliability.

The second major cause of damage to and breakdown of equipment within working areas is failure of berth managers and supervisors to ensure good housekeeping on the berths and terminals. Loose dunnage, discarded cargo strappings, stevedoring gear, pieces of cargo and general debris scattered about the quays frequently cause damage to manoeuvring equipment. Tyres are especially vulnerable to such damage; more than one port reported that damage resulting from contact with debris is the commonest cause of replacing tyres, not wear. Tyres are also expensive items to replace: in the case of a front-end loader, one tyre costs about $1,000, while a rubber-tyred gantry crane replacement tyre costs about $1,600. Oil and hydraulic fluid spillages which are not cleaned up or properly treated also contribute to damage to tyres and equipment, as well as increasing the risk of accidents. All working surfaces *must* be kept clear of obstructions and debris, and oil and other spillages *must* be removed immediately. Operations managers and berth managers must be made directly responsible for keeping their working areas in good condition; they must make regular inspections to ensure this.

5.2.7 Conditions of Employment

By no means all of the ports surveyed acknowledge, through appropriate pay levels, the special skills required by drivers and the pressures they work under. Salary structures and payment systems in many ports have not been set at levels high enough to attract and retain the most capable people, and there are either no differentials or only slight ones between the salaries of equipment drivers and those of basic dockworkers. However, in other ports drivers and operators are paid considerably more than dockworkers, appropriately reflecting their additional skills and responsibilities.

A major obstacle to the attainment of good cargo-handling performance is that equipment drivers are in many ports excluded from incentive schemes. Ports claim that it is difficult to devise a scheme that is both equitable and easy to apply to operators. Reservations are also expressed about the danger that incentives may encourage hasty and careless work, so increasing the accident rate. However, in spite of these apparent difficulties, some ports have successfully introduced group or individual incentive schemes for drivers, often linked to Ship Operation gang output or to terminal performance (see Chapter 8). This approach is certainly to be encouraged; the setting of realistic performance targets and the introduction of a fair and simple to operate incentive scheme will provide motivation to equipment drivers and encourage them to produce their best work.

The incentive schemes should not, however, be allowed to lead to restrictive practices; in some ports visited, drivers refuse to move between one operating area (at which bonus payments apply) to another (where they do not), and even prevent their equipment being so redeployed. Both driver and machine are kept at the berth to which they were allocated, even though operations have been completed there before the end of the shift and there is a demand for extra equipment elsewhere. There are even cases where drivers refuse to transfer between tasks on the same berth, because of differentials in bonuses. For example, they will not transfer, with their equipment, from one hatch to another because their incentive scheme is linked to hook output, or refuse to move from the quay transfer operation (carrying a bonus) to the receipt/delivery operation (which does not). In one port surveyed, there are two distinct groups of drivers: those on incentive schemes, who are non-transferable between tasks, and those on day-work, who are. Clearly, incentive schemes must be devised so that they apply widely and fairly, and must not be allowed to restrict managers' flexibility in redeploying equipment and drivers as necessary.

A most disturbing revelation of this study has been the extent and scale of corrupt practices in cargo-handling operations, in particular the way these influence the performance of drivers. Several ports and users (clearing and forwarding agents, ships' agents, etc.) reported that unauthorized and illegal payments to equipment drivers, amounting to extortion, are widespread. The increasing dependence by port users on equipment to move their cargoes is being exploited by drivers, to the extent that demanding such payments has become a deeply entrenched practice. In some ports, the situation has deteriorated to the extent that cargo will not be moved until drivers and supervisors are bribed appropriately. A particularly worrying aspect is that senior managers appear to condone, or at least turn a blind eye to, these practices. Although there is little doubt that the very low salaries and lack of incentive schemes in these ports are major contributory factors, there is no excuse for senior management to allow them to continue. They do nothing to improve cargo-handling efficiency, port profitability or the port's reputation with its customers, and allowing drivers and other operations staff to break port regulations (not to mention national laws) in this way must undermine any attempts at discipline, accountability and self-respect as management policy.

5.2.8 Hours of Work

Although most ports now adopt seven- or eight-hour shift working for equipment drivers, there are a surprisingly large number imposing working periods much longer than this, particularly in the second or night shift. In one of the ports visited, the 'evening' shift lasts from 16.30 hours to 06.00 hours the following day, and during this time operators are fully employed in their vehicles. Not surprisingly, this port reported that the majority of accidents occur after midnight and are primarily the result of driver fatigue! In another case, drivers are continuously employed in their vehicles, except for two one-hour meal-breaks, from 08.00 to 24.00 hours each day. Although such grossly over-long shifts are exceptions, many ports allow drivers to work overtime beyond their normal working hours and even, in some cases, to complete a second shift.

Little formal research has been undertaken into fatigue-related problems in port equipment drivers, but several managers interviewed reported that accident rates increase towards the ends of shifts, particularly the night shifts, and it was generally agreed that long shifts increase the strain on operators, particularly in hot conditions or at night time. Managers in several ports also reported that long or late shift working is the most common cause of employee absenteeism.

Another stress-inducing practice is common: drivers are required in several ports to operate their equipment continuously for the complete shift with only the briefest of refreshment breaks. In one case, drivers are actually encouraged to work right through their meal-breaks and are paid overtime rates for those periods. As an inducement, they are provided with free food which they are expected to eat while keeping their equipment working. Alarmingly, such practices (which surely contravene all safety rules) are now spreading from conventional equipment, such as forklift trucks and tractors – where they are dangerous enough – to the larger and more complex machines used on bulk and container terminals. These demand the highest levels of driver concentration and skill, are the most dangerous machines in the port and are used in operations where the cost consequences of accidents and equipment downtime are the highest.

The more enlightened ports have now introduced job rotation schemes: drivers can transfer to different tasks during the shift to relieve stress and to provide work variety. For example, quayside gantry crane drivers can interchange with their checkers; each pair of men work alternate two-hour periods at each task. Some such form of sensible job-switching to alleviate pressure on the drivers of high-powered, fast-moving and dangerous equipment would seem to be essential on present-day berths and terminals. As well as being considerate to the drivers, sensible working hours, with adequate relaxation, realistic manning and provision for job-interchange, have beneficial consequences to port productivity: high levels of concentration and performance can be sustained throughout the shift and the risk of accidents is minimized. A reasonable shift for a driver or operator of modern high-capacity cargo-handling equipment would consist of no more than four 2-hour sessions, with adequate refreshment breaks between the sessions and one or two job-switches. If overtime is worked after the shift, it should be for no more than two hours.

5.2.9 Inadequate Cost Information Systems

Many of the LDC ports visited do not record detailed and reliable information on equipment operating costs, so that it is impossible for managers to know the annual operating costs of individual units or a fleet of one type of machine. Although some form of estimated cost is entered in the annual revenue budget, this has little relation to the actual costs incurred and does not relate to particular categories of machine nor to specific operational cost centres. The lack of detailed costing procedures also casts considerable doubt on the accuracy of annual expenditure estimates.

In contrast, the more efficient ports – certainly those visited in Western Europe – have in recent years developed comprehensive and detailed systems for recording operating expenditure. In the most advanced (computerized) systems, expenditure can be assigned to individual units of equipment and even to each assembly, sub-assembly and component

within that unit. Computerized systems can also be interrogated to extract detailed cost information for equipment operation and cargo handling – by vessel call, by ship operator or consortium. They can provide a complete history of operating costs for each machine on the asset register. The availability of this type of information – continuously and instantly – has revolutionized the decision-making ability of managers in both Operations and Engineering.

Without such a record system, managers are totally unaware of the cost of operating cargo-handling equipment, and how much that contributes to total cargo-handling costs. They cannot appreciate the extravagance of requisitioning more equipment than they need and of not returning equipment to the pool immediately they have finished with it. They do not understand the cost consequences of not ensuring the safe and correct operation of the machines, of breakdowns and accidents, and of not releasing equipment for regular maintenance and inspection. Without cost-consciousness there cannot be individual accountability, and operational performance targets and objectives cannot be set for terminals, berths, working units and individuals. All these shortcomings were apparent in many of the ports surveyed during this study, and contribute significantly to the poor engineering and general performance of those ports.

5.2.10 Poor Operating Records

Although most of the ports surveyed record some data on equipment operating performance, the extent and reliability of the information collected varies considerably, as does the use to which that information is put by management. Some ports have excellent systems, recording detailed information on daily operating performance of every unit of plant and equipment, shift by shift. The data are analysed regularly within an Operations Management Information System to assist all managerial decision-making. At other ports, only fragmentary operating data are recorded – often unreliable – and these are seldom analysed and presented to managers in a useful form. Many managers seem uncertain as to what data should be collected and how it should be analysed, and there is considerable confusion over terms and definitions. Worse, there was evidence of deliberate mis-information: data are altered or presented in such a way as to conceal the true state of operational affairs, e.g. on equipment demand and supply.

In most ports where operational information is regularly collected, the OMIS is paper-based, but recently more and more of them have been developing computer-based systems. At one major Asian port, a fully computerized system records in great detail daily allocation, deployment and performance of equipment. The computer prints out a daily equipment and personnel allocation form, showing the allocation of every unit of equipment (identified by its unique inventory number), and its driver, to every berth or terminal working area (also coded). At the end of each shift, the actual operating performance (hours of work, times and causes of delays, fuel consumed etc.) is entered into the system and a set of performance indicators is immediately calculated. All operations managers and engineers have direct online access to these data through their own terminals, giving them up-to-the-minute knowledge of the current deployment situation, reserve units and performance. Most ports have yet to develop such a complete OMIS; a few are moving towards that goal, but many have still to begin the process, still lacking even the most basic data-collection forms and procedures. The question of Management Information Systems is considered at greater length in Chapter 9.

Without a competent OMIS, operations managers and engineers have little knowledge of the performance of individual machines, and senior managers are unaware of equipment problems. For example, preventive maintenance schedules are usually (and mistakenly – see Chapter 6) based on fixed time intervals rather than actual hours of operation of equipment; the latter data are just not available. The life expectancy of equipment components, on which cost-effective preventive maintenance schemes are based, cannot be determined. Senior managers are unaware of the operators' true equipment needs, and cannot formulate a realistic replacement strategy or optimum inventory levels. Operating data cannot be combined with cost information to produce the financial performance indicators needed for setting budgets, for determining pricing policies and for monitoring the operating costs of individual units. Managers cannot know the cost of using equipment in cargo-handling nor how this is affected by availability and utilization levels. They cannot pinpoint where scope exists for improving allocation and deployment efficiency, and the port is unable to adopt in full the much-needed principles of managerial responsibility and accountability. The full relevance of operational cost data to management is considered in Section 5.5.

5.3 The Control of Equipment Allocation

5.3.1 Scope for Improvement
In many of the ports visited – particularly those with poor maintenance and equipment shortages – present allocation and deployment procedures give inadequate control over the condition of plant and equipment. Changing the traditional methods of allocating machines, and strengthening the management of the procedures will make significant improvements to the amount and nature of the maintenance and repair work to be performed, to the management of maintenance and to the efficiency of use of workshop and other engineering facilities.

The principal objective of equipment allocation and control should be to ensure that traffic officers receive the right type of equipment, in sufficient quantities and at the right time to meet operational needs and to maximize cargo-handling performance. Good allocation also ensures that equipment is maintained to full specification, that preventive maintenance is carried out as prescribed and that the most efficient use is made of maintenance resources. Efficient allocation and control lead to high equipment reliability and utilization, and maximize asset life, thereby minimizing the port's capital investment in plant. Increasing equipment working hours reduces its hourly operating costs and improves its revenue-earning capability. The principal advantage, in the context of this study, is that good allocation procedures allow full control over the scheduling of preventive maintenance, so that engineers can spread the workload efficiently over their workshop facilities and resources.

5.3.2 Responsibility for Equipment Control
The study has revealed considerable variation in equipment allocation, in terms of managerial responsibility and control; it will be useful to review some of those approaches first:

— Traditionally, staff in the Operations Department control the requisitioning and deployment of the equipment, subject to availability as reported by the Engineering Department. The equipment is notionally 'owned' by the operators, with the engineers merely providing the services necessary to keep the machines in good working order. In this approach, engineering is solely a cost centre, and is not revenue-earning.

— In one port, equipment allocation and deployment at each terminal (as well as terminal workshop schedules) are controlled by an Equipment Foreman. He reports directly to the Terminal Manager on a day-to-day or operational level, while being functionally responsible to an Equipment Manager within the Operations Department. It is the latter's job to co-ordinate the supply of equipment over the port as a whole and, in discussion with senior engineers, to control maintenance schedules.

— In some ports, in contrast, staff in the Engineering Department are directly involved in allocation and, in a few cases, effectively control it, rationing the supply of equipment and often taking little notice of operators' demands or current machine availability.

— In a few ports, the equipment is notionally 'owned' by engineers in the workshops and is allocated to operators on request.

— In yet other ports, ship operators or their agents decide what equipment to requisition and how those units are to be deployed on the vessel.

— In another case, responsibility for control, allocation and deployment of equipment rests with the operators, but engineering staff have the right to forbid the use of individual units on technical grounds (e.g. unsafe condition, overdue maintenance).

Although all these management systems appear to work (with varying degrees of success, perhaps), there is evidence that the most effective approach is to give responsibility for the control of equipment to engineers. In effect, the equipment should be 'owned' by the Engineering Department, which is then fully and unconditionally responsible for its condition and upkeep. The equipment is, as it were, 'hired out' to the operators by the hour, on request. This strategy has several advantages:

1. The Engineering Department (or, ideally, the individual terminal or area workshop) becomes a cost/revenue centre; not only does it have its own expenditure – in the form of spares and supplies purchase, labour salaries and overheads – but it also has its own income, as notional hire-charges to the operators. The Engineering Department can now set appropriate financial as well as performance targets for the workshops, encouraging greater accountability and cost-consciousness right down to shop-floor level. This will promote efficiency in service and repair work (keeping costs down) and improve workshop turnround time, availability and reliability (equipment out of use generates no income).

2. With the engineers in control of equipment use, they can better plan and schedule maintenance programmes for maximum efficiency, taking into account operators' needs (known in detail in advance, through the requisition forms). They will also be in a better position to monitor maintenance costs in particular and equipment costs in general. With equipment under their constant care, the engineers can continually monitor the use and cost of each machine, can inspect it daily (taking immediate steps to put right any defect, however minor it might appear) and can take disciplinary action in the event of damage or faults arising from driver negligence.

3. The strategy has benefits from the operational viewpoint, too. Each traffic manager is still free to determine the type and number of units of equipment required, and will requisition them from the engineers for the appropriate period (preferably by the hour, rather than the shift, to encourage prompt return to stock). The cost of equipment hire is subsequently debited against the operational cost/revenue centre – either the Operations Department, the relevant port section or the individual berth or terminal; it could (indeed, should) ultimately be debited against the particular ship call or cargo-handling activity (e.g. storage). Such an approach will encourage operators to requisition and deploy equipment efficiently, and to be generally more cost-conscious.

Establishing and sustaining such an equipment control system is conditional on several factors. First, an effective budgetary control system is needed, with operational and engineering cost/revenue centres clearly identified. Secondly, good OMIS and EMIS systems are essential – not least in order to set appropriate hourly 'hire' rates for the equipment; these will have to be agreed, to mutual satisfaction, between senior managers in Operations and Engineering, and set at levels that will encourage efficiency in both provider and user centres. Thirdly, allocation procedures will have to include a means of recording accurately the actual hours of work of equipment units, so that these can be charged to the appropriate cost/revenue centre. There also has to be, of course, extremely close liaison between engineers and operators, to make sure that maintenance schedules and allocation are planned equably, as well as collaboration with the port's marketing and planning departments to assess likely future changes in traffic and equipment requirements.

Even with equipment control in the hands of the engineers, daily equipment requisitioning and deployment must remain, of course, the province of the operations staff involved. The procedure for doing this will depend on where the equipment is held and controlled from; this is discussed in the next section. Exactly how the process of allocation is managed depends on the procedure followed in the particular port, which will be considered in Section 5.4.

5.3.3 Equipment Holding Policies

5.3.3.1 Factors Affecting Holding Policy

The management procedures set up to control and allocate equipment to the various operating areas will depend on where equipment is held in the port. This is influenced by institutional factors (particularly whether there are independent terminal operators within the port), on the size and geography of the port estate and on the location of workshops. This study has identified three principal methods of managing the daily distribution of equipment to operational areas: central, sectional and berth/terminal holding. These will be considered in turn.

5.3.3.2 Central Holding

In some ports, all equipment (or all equipment of a particular type) is held at a central workshop or parking area and is distributed from there to individual working areas throughout the dock estate. Requisition forms prepared by traffic officers at the individual berths or terminals are sent to a central control unit, where they are collated and analysed. The demand for each type of machine is worked out and compared with the list of available units, as presented by the engineers. The allocation plan for that shift is then prepared, so that each traffic officer is given – as far as possible under the circumstances – the machines he needs.

The principal benefit of this centralized holding system is the degree of control over equipment allocation that it offers to the engineers. It also gives the planning managers the ability to apply rational priority ranking to working areas if total demand exceeds available equipment supply. It also allows machines to be transferred from one task or area to another as soon as it is freed from current duties.

On the other hand, the system can lead to delays to startup of operations, particularly in a port with a large dock estate, where equipment has to travel long distances from the central holding area to some of the working areas. It is also argued that it is less easy than with some other arrangements to ensure individual managerial accountability for equipment operation and condition, and to apply close cost control. However, if the central pool of equipment is itself designated as a cost/revenue centre and an hourly rental charge is applied, there seems no reason why it should be administratively difficult to allocate costs equitably to the operational cost centres.

In general, central holding of equipment works well in a relatively small port, where an efficient distribution system between the depot and the working areas can be established, and where the equipment fleets are not very large. It is not so sensible where the port is large, where equipment is difficult to move about, and where the operational areas are specialized.

5.3.3.3 Sectional Holding

An alternative strategy is to distribute the port's stock of equipment over several depots, located within different zones or sections of the port. For example, small 'fleets' of machines can be held at or near the satellite workshops (see Chapter 6) serving sections of the port, to be allocated daily from there to the individual working areas. Most ports are already administratively divided into groups of related operational areas, each section consisting of two or three berths, and these sections offer the obvious basis for a sectional equipment depot.

One problem of such an arrangement is that operations managers often jealously guard against transfer of equipment from their section to another, even if they have a temporary surplus and a neighbouring section is experiencing peak demand. They even go so far as to disguise their true needs to excuse equipment retention. This difficulty is overcome if allocation responsibility is assigned to the Engineering Department and equipment operators are charged directly for each hour of equipment use.

In some ports, the central depot and sectional depots exist side by side. Conventional equipment in everyday use, such as forklift trucks and tractor units, are held on a sectional basis, as are units whose use is functionally restricted to a section, such as straddle carriers and rubber-tyred gantry cranes. Other specialized units, such as mobile cranes and heavy-lift machines, are more usually held at a central depot. The sectional holdings allow the rapid deployment of equipment to the local working areas at shift startup and to be transferred quickly to nearby working areas as needed. It is often argued that cost-assignment is easier than in a centralized system, and can give traffic officers more direct control over operational priorities.

There are problems and dangers in sectional holding, however. There is a tendency for operators to use all the equipment within their section, whether or not there is a genuine need for it. This might lead to misjudgement of the total port requirement for equipment and to over-investment. Sectional allocation also means that parking areas have to be provided in several areas of the port, at or near the section's satellite workshop; pre-shift inspections and minor repairs of the section's machines are carried out at that workshop. Some duplication of workshop equipment and facilities is inevitable, and careful check has to be kept of the cost-effectiveness of the strategy.

5.3.3.4 Terminal Holding

An increasingly common pattern of equipment holding is to allocate it permanently to terminals. Where berths and terminals are dedicated to specific and specialized traffic, particularly containers and other unitized cargoes, they have their own specialist equipment requirements, and it is sensible – indeed, natural – to hold that equipment on the terminal, at or near the terminal's own workshop. Operations staff have practically complete control over allocation and deployment (though there is no reason why the engineers should not still 'own' and 'hire' the equipment, for the purposes of cost control), while maintenance is easily taken care of by the on-site workshop. All operating and maintenance costs are specific to the terminal, and costing and budgeting are relatively easy. Indeed, costs can be allocated to specific users or traffics, allowing the full cost of each ship's call and cargo-handling activity to be calculated separately and increasing managers' awareness of costs, revenues and operational profitability.

Evidence gathered during this study suggests that terminal holding, with allocation and deployment controlled from the terminal, provides the most effective means for planning and controlling equipment use. It offers full scope for co-operation between operations and engineering staff, and allows efficient planning of maintenance. It provides excellent opportunities for applying managerial accountability principles and cost control. Although there is the danger (as in the case of sectional holding, with its related satellite workshops) that terminal workshops can lead to duplication of engineering facilities, this can be avoided by restricting the terminal workshops to routine preventive maintenance and minor repairs, while substantial repair work, overhauls and refurbishment are carried out at the central workshop.

The 'terminal concept' is, of course, more appropriate to specialized terminals handling unitized, container and bulk traffics, and is less easily applied to conventional break-bulk, general cargo facilities. It assumes 'unity of command', with one organization (a public or private terminal operating company) being responsible for all activities.

5.3.4 The Management of Equipment Allocation

5.3.4.1 Management Procedures

This study supports the practice of staff in the Operations Department being ultimately responsible for equipment allocation. It is the operators who know the types of ships to be worked and the cargo to be handled, and they who have first-hand experience of the suitability of particular machines for different traffics and cargo-handling activities. It is also Operations Department staff who have to meet operational performance targets and who are best able to predict demand for equipment. However, allocation must be subject to equipment being available for use, and this has to be controlled by the engineers.

Responsibility for calculating daily equipment needs and for completing the shift Requisition Forms should rest with traffic officers directly involved in planning and supervising cargo-handling operations. They will determine the type and number of machines to be requisitioned for the next work period on the basis of the nature and amount of work to be performed, and the type of cargo to be handled. It has emerged from this study that appropriate allocation procedures do not exist in many ports, that the information needed for the process is not available, or is unreliable, and that equipment requisition procedures are, in some cases, inappropriate or inefficient. Data on equipment demand and supply are not recorded or collated for use in equipment planning in those ports.

It is the responsibility of senior port management to ensure that proper planning procedures are established and followed. Those procedures must not be in the form of rigidly fixed allocation norms per berth and per shift, but must take into account the (carefully) predicted level and nature of demand for that shift. Operations staff must study all available data on the next ships' calls (from stowage plans, vehicle appointment schedules and other documents) to work out the types and quantities of cargoes to be loaded and discharged, to be received at or delivered from the storage areas and to be moved within the port. They can then prepare detailed shift-by-shift operational plans. In the efficient berths and terminals visited, this process had been developed to a high degree of precision and detail; operations staff prepare detailed work schedules, forecasting the precise times that individual consignments will be handled in a particular shift – in some cases days or even weeks ahead. Not only does this allow operators to requisition exactly the equipment that they will need, in ample time, but also helps engineers to forecast equipment demand accurately and to schedule preventive maintenance comfortably.

In many cases, operators can now plan their operations in outline, including equipment requirements, for a month ahead. This allows maintenance engineers to plan their maintenance programme with considerable confidence. The plans may have to be adjusted, of course, as forecast ships' movements and shippers' predictions become firmer, but forward planning of this sort is extremely beneficial in allowing peak demand to be prepared for and engineering workloads to be spread. It also encourages co-operation and good relations between operations and engineering staff, and contributes to efficient equipment allocation and utilization, maximum cargo-handling productivity and good control over plant maintenance.

- Crucial to the success of the requisition-allocation procedure is precise information on what equipment is (or will be) available. An accurate, up-to-date list of all serviceable units must be prepared for the daily equipment planning meetings, at which traffic officers and maintenance engineers confer to organize allocation. Also listed should be the units that have been designated for routine maintenance in the work period in question; the engineers must be prepared to compromise on these if unexpected cargo-handling needs arise that cannot be met from the proposed allocable stock. Sudden surges in demand or reduction of serviceable units (because of breakdowns or accidents) will need prompt action on the part of both operators and engineers. Substitute machines will have to be brought in from the holding areas, or from other work areas where they are undertaking less urgent tasks, or machines waiting at the workshops for routine servicing may have to be withdrawn temporarily. The wider use of computers in operations planning and maintenance scheduling makes it much easier to change plans at the last moment, as circumstances demand.

A practice followed successfully in some ports (and discussed at greater length in Chapter 6) is to make maintenance staff directly responsible in their day-to-day work to the terminal or section manager. The organizational structure at those ports includes a line relationship between terminal manager and workshop staff while still retaining the traditional functional relationship within the Engineering Department. Those ports claim an improved relationship between operations and maintenance staff, and improved planning and scheduling of allocation and maintenance. The arrangement is said to ensure that operations and workshop staff follow similar objectives and to improve management accountability.

However, a feature of *all* successful ports is the good co-ordination and co-operation between operators and maintenance staff. Constant communication between staff in the Engineering and Operations Departments is essential for ensuring appropriate equipment allocation and cargo-handling efficiency – and it must take place at three levels within the organization. At the lowest level, there must be daily planning meetings between traffic supervisors and workshop staff to consider equipment demand, to plan preventive maintenance schedules and to review current repairs. At the next level, weekly meetings should be held between engineers, traffic officers and supplies staff, to review maintenance and operating performance and to consider possible improvements. At the top level, the Chief Engineer should chair monthly meetings of all heads of departments involved in operations, maintenance and supplies, to discuss policy and long-term development issues. At all meetings, comprehensive and accurate data must be available to assist in discussion and decision-making; it is here that efficient OMIS and EMIS systems come into their own.

Co-operation and co-ordination are not helped in many of the ports visited by a lack of an adequate communication system on the berths; often even the telephone system was out of action and hand-held radio sets inoperable. Poor communication systems cause delays to both cargo-handling and maintenance, by preventing that frequent communication between operators and engineers that is such a notable characteristic of the successful ports. Traffic officers and engineers need good two-way radio systems to inform each other immediately of equipment shortages and surpluses, of breakdowns and accidents, and of the need to transfer machines between working areas.

5.3.4.2 Requisition Forms

Another prerequisite for efficient equipment allocation is a good requisition procedure, with a well-designed Requisition Form. The more detailed the information provided by operating staff, the more effective will be the port's equipment control, allocation and deployment. In most of the requisition procedures observed during the study, traffic officers do not indicate precisely the nature or amount of work the requested machine is required to do. They tend to requisition for a full shift on each occasion, and include large safety margins, so that units are often idle on one berth while a genuine need for them exists elsewhere in the port. The Requisition Form should be so designed that traffic officers *have* to record the type of work to be performed, the type and capacity of equipment (and attachments) needed, and the estimated times of starting and finishing the work. When the equipment is issued, the time of issue is entered on the Daily Equipment Record (a register or set of forms), along with the other details of the requisition. Then, as soon as the planned work has been completed, the unit must be returned to its holding position and 'signed off' the Equipment Record ready for other duties.

The data recorded on the Requisition Forms by traffic officers and that on the Daily Equipment Record as recorded by the engineers (or whoever is responsible for issuing and receiving back the units at the holding point) should be collated daily and regularly analysed and presented to senior managers in a form suitable for interpretation and use in equipment planning (see Chapter 3). It is particularly important to record the daily demand and supply of each category of equipment. This information is then combined with data on operating and performance (hours of work, availability and downtime) to provide a reliable measure of equipment demand – especially trends in demand – for use in planning. Information needs and systems, in which operations and engineering needs overlap considerably, are discussed at length in Chapter 9.

5.3.4.3 Allocation Priorities

Whenever operational demand for equipment exceeds supply, some form of priority rule must be applied. In most cases (particularly at specialized terminals), priority is given to the Ship and Quay Transfer Operations, to minimize ship's time in port. The next priority is to allocate equipment to receipt and delivery operations and after that to in-terminal movements. Activities associated with the CFS are usually given the lowest priority. However, some flexibility must be preserved; if storage areas are congested, activity there might have to take precedence over the Ship Operation temporarily. Similarly, priority might have to be given to berths where dangerous, fragile or delicate cargoes are being handled at a particular time. Berths at which ships are loading or discharging large or heavy indivisible loads cannot handle those cargoes without heavy equipment, and so will be given allocation priority over those handling loose cargoes, where conventional equipment or extra labour could manage.

However carefully demand and supply are balanced, and in spite of applying sensible priority rules and re-deploying between work areas, there will be occasions when the demand for a particular type of equipment may be beyond the ability of the port to supply. Under such circumstances, it might be possible for operators to manage with alternative, albeit less suitable, machines, or for equipment to be hired from external companies or even (in the case, for example, of a major item such as a floating crane) from another port. If that sort of situation arises

more than very occasionally, of course, it indicates that the port's inventory is inadequate, and the planning group should review plans for acquisition of new units.

5.3.4.4 Allocation of Equipment Drivers

The ports surveyed have adopted two distinct approaches to the allocation of drivers. In some ports drivers are selected and trained by Engineering Department staff, come under their direct control and are allocated with the equipment from the central and/or satellite depots. In other ports, drivers are allocated, with other categories of labour, by operations staff. Although either method can work satisfactorily, there is evidence that equipment control and maintenance procedures are more likely to be effective where driver allocation is the direct responsibility of the engineers. That arrangement offers a more reliable means of regularly inspecting and monitoring the condition of equipment, as well as of monitoring driver performance and taking any necessary disciplinary action.

In such a system, drivers come under the line authority of operations staff, being directly controlled by them while carrying out cargo-handling duties, but their functional responsibility is with the Engineering Department. This organizational structure allows drivers to be considered as first-line maintenance staff. They are expected to carry out pre-shift inspections of equipment and to monitor its performance during operations. They are responsible for filling-in the equipment log-books and for promptly reporting any faults or defects. All their activities will be carefully monitored (by traffic officers and berth supervisors while under their control and by the engineers at other times) to ensure that they are properly operating and looking after their equipment.

Driver allocation practices need to be reviewed in several of the ports visited. One port reported that equipment is often idle because of driver absenteeism, even though the total workforce is extremely large – indeed, far bigger than it need be. That port needs to recruit (preferably from the existing labour force) and train sufficient additional drivers to cover absenteeism, which is particularly damaging to port performance when it affects large and technically advanced equipment. It would also help considerably if the 'integrated gang system' were to be adopted, with each man pre-trained to take over any of a range of duties; backup for absenteeism is built-in to such a system.

There is also scope for improving driver allocation procedures for each shift. Many ports complained that delays occur at startup of cargo-handling, because drivers and machines are not allocated in advance to a particular berth; they take a significant time to arrive at the berth after allocation. This is, of course, particularly the danger if equipment and drivers are allocated from a central holding area. Some form of prior allocation of men and machines should be introduced, to ensure a prompt start to the shift – perhaps involving a form of overlapping of shift working hours, allowing drivers to start a little earlier than the end of the previous shift. However, this should not involve unreasonable working hours, and salaries must be adjusted to compensate, so that drivers are well motivated to maintain high standards of output and to have a flexible approach to allocation and to re-deployment during the shift.

In fact, a major obstacle to effective equipment deployment is the existence of employee restrictive practices which prevent traffic officers from transferring equipment and drivers between different operating areas or tasks. In some ports, equipment which has been allocated to a particular berth *has* to remain there for a complete shift, even if operations are completed there before the end of the shift. Where drivers are participating in an incentive scheme, they may refuse to transfer from area to area, even from one hatch to another, if the move would take them to a non-bonus activity. Such restrictive practices can tie the hands of traffic officers to such an extent that cargo-handling performance and equipment utilization are significantly reduced.

5.4 Management of Equipment Operation

5.4.1 The Need for Improved Management
Good management of equipment operation minimizes the risk of accidents and breakdowns, and contributes significantly to keeping equipment in good condition. In so doing, it helps to hold down the demands on maintenance facilities and resources, maximizes equipment reliability and utilization, and improves cargo-handling productivity. This study has identified many bad operating procedures and practices which demonstrate the need for immediate improvements in equipment management. New operating regulations and safety rules must be defined and strictly implemented, equipment drivers need closer supervision and better training, and disciplinary procedures must be tightened up. These measures are discussed in this section.

5.4.2 Operating Regulations
An important component of good management of equipment in operations is a set of detailed operator

manuals for all types of equipment operated in the port. Each manual should set out, in a clear, concise and easily understood style (and in all the languages used by employees), the detailed operating procedures for all activities performed by that equipment: safe operating speeds under different conditions; cargo lifting and stacking rules; safety considerations; technical data on the lifting capacity, controls, instruments and facilities available. For example, a standard forklift truck manual should give the lifting capacity of the machine at different load-centres, and show how to de-rate that capacity when handling awkward or bulky loads, when stacking cargo high and when using special attachments. Wherever appropriate, the manuals should use charts, tables, diagrams, cartoons and photographs to illustrate good and bad practices.

The operator manuals supplied with equipment by the manufacturers *should* be adequate for this purpose – a few are excellent – but in most cases, they will have to be edited, adapted or even completely rewritten to suit local conditions. When they have been prepared and approved, copies should be given to all traffic managers, supervisors and drivers, and they must be read thoroughly and carefully by all. There should be no doubts or uncertainties as to how all tasks are to be carried out.

Since equipment operating procedures may need to be changed in time (for example, as new cargo types or attachments are introduced), it is sensible to produce the manuals in a format suitable for regular up-dating. A loose-leaf, ring-bound format is one approach, allowing amendments and additions to be produced, circulated and inserted easily and quickly. The main 'dos and don'ts' should also be reproduced as posters, job-aids and other visual media for use in port safety campaigns. They will also form the basis for driver training schemes.

5.4.3 Supervision
Traffic officers and supervisory staff directly involved in cargo-handling operations must be made more aware of their responsibilities regarding drivers and equipment, they have a primary duty to ensure that equipment. when under their control, is operated safely and correctly. It is quite possible to reduce significantly the incidence of bad driving and accidents if managers and supervisors do their jobs properly. They need to be better trained and made to understand clearly that they are accountable for the condition of plant and equipment allocated to their working areas. Whenever they see bad driving they must take immediate action to discipline the driver. If they detect signs that equipment is developing a mechanical fault or is unsafe to operate, they must immediately stop using it and report the fault to the

engineers. Any accident involving damage to equipment must also be notified without delay. The corollary of this is that, if the engineers find, when inspecting equipment on its return to the workshop at the end of a shift, evidence of damage or misuse, the operations managers and supervisors at the berth can be held responsible and accountable for it. Those staff will then be called to account in the investigation which should follow immediately.

The key to improving equipment care is to make each driver directly accountable to his superior for the condition and operating performance of the machine in his charge. Disciplinary procedures must follow any incidence of negligence or deliberate abuse. In ports where drivers are now required to sign for their equipment at the beginning of the shift, thereby accepting it as being in good condition, equipment misuse and abuse have been significantly reduced. They are responsible for carrying out pre-shift inspections (under supervision), for undertaking minor adjustments and repairs during the shift, and for immediately reporting any defects. All defects, symptoms of developing faults, and breakdowns are also recorded in the machine's log-book (kept within the cab). At the end of the shift, the driver 'signs off' in the logbook, signifying that he is returning the machine in good condition (or with certain faults reported), and the logbook is then checked by the engineers. In this way, both engineers and operators have a complete record of exactly who was in charge of the machine when any accident, breakdown or fault occurred.

Another good practice, though not always easy to implement, is to allocate a team of three drivers semi-permanently to a particular machine, each driver operating it for a single shift in a three-shift schedule. One cab and/or ignition key is signed over to each driver, preventing anyone else from driving the machine. Although this practice introduces an element of inflexibility into driver deployment, it has led to significantly improved driver care and to a reduction of accidents in those ports adopting it. It seems not just to be a case of increased driver accountability but also of inducing a strong sense of 'ownership' in those drivers.

5.4.4 Safety

In all ports, safety awareness programmes are essential to reduce or eliminate the number of accidents involving cargo-handling equipment. Some of the ports surveyed have recently made significant improvements to safety in their dock estates, and the steps they have taken should act as models to others.

The first essential is to provide regular safety courses for all employees involved in equipment operation. Indeed, safety factors must be included in *all* operational training schemes (see Chapter 8). A full-time safety officer must be appointed, responsible for reviewing cargo-handling activities and proposing plans and projects designed to improve safety. He should be given authority to implement agreed new safety regulations. The safety officer should discuss equipment accidents with the engineers and operators, and suggest where design improvements might have helped to prevent them; any modifications identified should be incorporated by workshop staff, wherever possible, or manufacturers could be asked to assist; modifications proved effective in use should be incorporated in the specifications for any new acquisitions.

The role of the safety officer within the port organization is of increasing importance as the working environment becomes more dangerous and as governments enact ever stricter legislation on safety and health in the workplace. In the United Kingdom, the Health and Safety at Work Act has imposed stringent responsibilities on ports; every port must have a Safety Officer, printed safety rules booklets, handouts and posters. One of the overseas ports visited has established safety committees in each work area. These meet regularly to discuss faults and deficiencies, they produce and display prominently charts on area accident rates, and are generally active in promoting safety in the workplace.

Safety awareness must be developed in *all* personnel, and must be seen to be actively supported by senior management. Many ports have a long way to go in this respect, particularly in equipment operation and maintenance: speed limits are not set; traffic flow patterns are not defined; vehicles do not stop at intersections; indiscriminate parking is permitted in operational areas; rear-view mirrors are not used or may even be missing; direction indicators and horns are not used – the catalogue of dangerous practices is a long and dismal one. Management must also pay greater attention to safety aspects when preparing technical specifications for the procurement of new equipment, noting those design features that give improved driver control and reduce accident risk, such as safety warning devices, limit switches and overhead load guards.

Finally, as part of the safety awareness programme, the safety officer and operations managers should collaborate in the preparation of a safety guide to be distributed to all port personnel. This should set out the port's safety policy and all its safety regulations: safe practices, accident prevention procedures, accident reporting procedures, and so on.

5.4.5 Disciplinary Procedures

An important finding to emerge from this study is the positive contribution that strict but fair disciplinary procedures make to driver attitudes and performance. Although all the ports surveyed have established some forms of disciplinary procedures, their effectiveness and implementation vary considerably. A feature of those ports with exemplary operating records is the vigour with which severe – even punitive – disciplinary procedures are applied to errant drivers. These ports have strict operating rules and regulations and make each driver responsible for the care and operation of his equipment. Random checks ensure that the driver carries out such essential duties as pre-shift inspections, log-book completion and accident reporting. Drivers are made responsible for keeping the cabs of their machines clean and for monitoring the performance of equipment during the shift; in some cases, they are even expected to correct minor faults arising during operation. Clearly, if disciplinary procedures are to be fairly applied, all rules and regulations governing drivers' duties and responsibilities must be clearly set down and given to every driver.

The study suggests that a disciplinary procedure should have certain vital components. In the event of an accident, the procedure should begin with the writing of an accident report by an operations or engineering manager (depending on the location and timing of the accident), followed by a formal enquiry into any rule-breaking, carried out by the relevant Head of Department. If he considers the driver has broken any of the rules, a charge sheet should be made out and a hearing held before a committee of senior managers, with the Head of Department in the chair. The accused driver may be accompanied by a 'friend' (normally a Union official) as he defends his position. If the accusation is proved, the committee should have the authority to recommend disciplinary action – the imposition of a fine, suspension from work or even dismissal.

In several of the surveyed ports, disciplinary committees can impose penalties of fines equivalent to seven days' pay, suspension from work of several days up to many weeks, and, as a last resort (for very serious offences or repeated misdemeanours), dismissal. In one port, there is also the possibility (not infrequently used) of imposing a surcharge on the driver to recover in full or part the cost of repairing the damage caused in an accident. Typically, the fine amounts to 20% of the cost of repair but on one occasion a penalty of $2,000 was imposed. The accident rate at that particular port has dropped markedly recently, and no accidents at all had been reported in the six months preceding the team's visit.

Disciplinary proceedings of that degree of severity must provide for a right of appeal by all employees found guilty of breaking operating rules or regulations. The appeal should be heard by a panel of representatives of the port authority and a trade union or other employee organization. In some ports, panel membership is equally divided between management and trade union representatives, but this has often made it difficult to reach firm conclusions, and the disciplinary procedure has fallen into misuse there. A balance in favour of the employers, but with adequate safeguards and defendant support, appears to be the more successful approach.

Whatever the difficulties of setting up and using strict disciplinary procedures, particularly where industrial relations are dominated by powerful trades unions, it is essential for the achievement of good operating and maintenance practices that such procedures be adopted.

5.4.6 Driver Recruitment and Training

Although the majority of ports participating in this study claimed that they provide equipment driver training, the observed form and quality of the courses varies considerably. In many cases, traffic officers and engineers questioned made it clear that they considered the training to be of poor quality. The effects of inadequate training are often made more serious by inappropriate recruitment practices, poor salaries and an unattractive career structure for drivers. Every port must select men carefully, making sure that they have the right aptitude and attitude for operating equipment, and must then train them thoroughly using the most appropriate methods and materials. A number of policies and strategies relating to those aims are pursued by the ports surveyed, and will be discussed here.

As far as **recruitment** is concerned, the traditional and most widely practised method is to select potential drivers from the existing labour force, by screening and testing employees having a current vehicle driving licence. Alternatively, driving posts are advertised locally, and filled by men holding public driving licences, preferably heavy goods vehicle licences. Initial recruitment is almost always to basic driving posts – operation of small forklift trucks or tractors. Operators of larger and more complex equipment (such as heavy-duty lift trucks, straddle carriers, rubber-tyred and rail-mounted gantry cranes, and quayside container cranes) reach those positions through a process of gradual promotion after experience and training. A model career development pattern, designed to attract and retain good equipment drivers, is illustrated in Figure 5.4.6.

Two distinct strategies were observed for driver **training:** specialization and the Integrated Gang System (IGS). In the first approach, an individual is trained to operate one specific type of machine and will then operate that equipment exclusively until selected for promotion and given training for a more technically advanced machine. In the IGS strategy, all operators are given a range of driving skills by being trained to operate all types of equipment used on a particular berth or terminal. On a general cargo berth, for example, all members of a gang will be trained to operate winches, shipboard cranes, quay-side cranes, mobile cranes, forklift trucks and tractors, as well as to carry out such related duties as tallying and cargo security work. Clearly, the IGS gives maximum deployment flexibility to operations managers, and covering for absenteeism poses few problems, but there is the danger that gang members will not work consistently enough at any one task to master it thoroughly. In practice, even in an integrated gang, special aptitudes soon surface, and there is a tendency for individuals to specialize for a large part of their time.

Both training strategies appear to work satisfactorily, given good management and the appropriate circumstances and environment. Ultimately, the most appropriate choice depends on local conditions, though there is a distinct trend towards increasing specialization in container terminals and other areas where unitized cargoes are handled. Indeed, there has recently been an interesting – and undoubtedly significant – move towards recruiting as drivers staff with engineering qualifications or at least a technical background. For example, at one of the LDC ports visited, engineering graduates had been recruited as container crane operators, although they alternated six-monthly between crane operation and maintenance workshop supervision. This experiment has successfully integrated operations and maintenance and has led to improved equipment reliability. Another port was considering employing technicians as gantry crane drivers, the only doubt (expressed by the Personnel Manager) being that technically qualified staff would find the work insufficiently interesting to stick to it for long, and that staff turnover would increase. Despite such reservations, there is little doubt that the trend in driver recruitment is towards more technically qualified staff, and that salary and conditions of employment will have to improve to attract recruits with the desired qualifications.

Many of the most successful ports acknowledge driver training as a vitally important management function; their philosophy is that only improved driver skill can reduce the very high costs of accidental damage to equipment. One major European terminal operator reported that the inadequate training of a new batch of twelve drivers resulted in a threefold increase in the accident rate, causing maintenance expenditure to rise by $450,000 in that year. With very few exceptions, the general standard of driver training observed was very poor, and instruc-

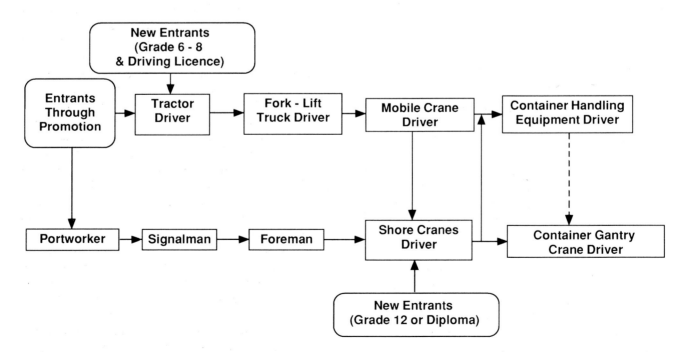

Figure 5.4.6: Model Career Development Structure for Equipment Operators

Table 5.5.2A Equipment running costs at selected ports, and their relationships to port operating costs and revenues

Port	Annual Equipment Running Cost ($ millions)	Running Cost as %age of Port Operating Cost	Running Cost as %age of Port Operating Revenue
A	5.1	12%	7%
B	30.0	10%	8%
C	15.0	10%	6%

Table 5.5.2B Average equipment running costs at an LDC port (in $ equivalents)

Equipment Type	Driver Costs (estim.)	Material Costs	Fuel & Power Costs	Annual Running Cost	Annual Operating Hrs (est.)	Running Cost/ Hour
Container crane	52,500	2,315	44,967	99,782	3,500	28
Rubber-tyred GC	41,000	237	13,312	54,549	2,000	27
Straddle carrier	41,000	90	3,734	44,822	1,400	32
Front-end loader	25,000	314	4,709	30,023	1,500	20
Tractor	27,500	341	3,982	31,823	1,800	18
Forklift truck	18,000	346	960	19,306	1,200	16

tional methods and materials were inadequate; rapid action needs to be taken in the majority of ports to improve matters. Driver attitudes must be changed, so that they operate their machines safely and to maximum performance levels under all conditions. Their knowledge of the mechanical and electrical systems of the equipment they operate must be improved, so that they become more aware of the need for good equipment care. Training is a vital element in this strategy, and it will be considered again in Chapter 8.

5.5 Equipment Operating Costs

5.5.1 The Nature of Operating Costs

A cost control system which records, analyses and interprets the operating costs of individual units of equipment is essential to an effective equipment management policy. The system is used to determine hourly operating costs, to set 'hire' rates to be charged against operational cost/revenue centres, to prepare annual revenue budgets, to revise port tariffs and pricing policies, and to assist in equipment planning.

Operating costs can be divided into running costs (drivers' earnings and the cost of fuel and/or power) and maintenance costs (workshop staff earnings, the cost of spare parts and materials, and workshop and other engineering department overheads). Maintenance costs will be considered in Chapter 6, but the nature and significance of equipment running

costs will be discussed in this section, together with approaches to allocating and controlling costs, and the need for cost-consciousness in operations managers.

5.5.2 Running Costs

5.5.2.1 The Significance of Running Costs

Although very few of the ports surveyed keep records of the running costs of individual units of equipment, it has been possible to extract estimates of total expenditure on running cargo-handling equipment from their various annual reports – but without, unfortunately, being able in most cases to relate those costs to equipment types, operating areas or cargoes. Even in ports which keep detailed records of maintenance costs of individual equipment units and types, drivers' incomes and fuel costs are very rarely apportioned; all port or departmental labour costs tend to be combined, and equipment fuel costs are also pooled. Senior managers were also reluctant about releasing what might be commercially sensitive information, and so detailed cost figures were difficult to obtain.

Nevertheless, some estimates of total annual equipment costs are derivable, and those for three of the ports visited (two in LDCs, one in Europe) are presented in Table 5.5.2A. It is interesting that, although the ports are very different in size and handle very different types and volumes of cargo, the proportions of total port operating costs and of port operating revenue represented by equipment running costs are remarkably similar – and relatively small. This relationship will be discussed further in Chapter 6.

Some more detailed figures relating to particular types of equipment were provided by a major (and very efficient) LDC port, and these are given in Table 5.5.2B. Even here, however, some data have had to be estimated, as full details were not available. Fuel and power costs were accurately recorded for each equipment type, as were the costs of consumable materials such as lubricants. The operating records also gave equipment 'utilization hours', but these are really 'allocated hours' rather than actual running hours (as would have been recorded on hour-meters). They have been converted into estimates of running hours on the basis of engineers' assessments that the machines operate, on average, for 30% of the allocation times. Drivers' employment costs have also been estimated, on the basis of known manning and salary levels at the port. In the table, all these recorded and estimated costs have been summed to give estimated annual running costs of the various equipment types (excluding the Operations Department's overhead costs). By dividing these by the estimated operating hours per year of each equipment type, it has been possible to estimate average hourly running costs for those categories of equipment.

The estimated running costs per hour may, on the face of it, seem quite modest, but in fact still represent a significant cost and one in which considerable savings can be made – provided the port keeps good operating records within its management information systems. The fact that so many estimates have had to be made to complete Table 5.5.2B demonstrates that even the best-run ports still do not keep a complete record of all the relevant costs. What is also immediately obvious from the table is that driver costs are by far the largest item in equipment running costs, and it is that aspect which will be considered next.

5.5.2.2 Drivers' Salaries

Not unexpectedly, this study revealed substantial differences between equipment driver employment costs in developed and developing countries. In Western European ports, total driver employment costs (including salaries, pension contributions, social security payments, etc.) varied from $25,000 to $55,000 a year; individual rates depended on the type of equipment operated, and also varied to some extent from country to country. Equipment drivers in the ports of developed countries have become among the highest paid port employees and frequently earn salaries equal to – even higher than – those of middle or quite senior managers.

Table 5.5.2C Driver and dockworker incomes (in $ per year) at sample LDC ports

Port	Equipment driver income range	Basic dockworker income range
A	1,500-2,000	1,500-2,000
B	1,550-2,000	1,550-2,000
C	380-500	250
D	6,600-7,200	4,000-5,000
E	2,800-5,000	1,680-2,200

In the LDC ports surveyed, drivers' salaries are very much lower than this, as is demonstrated by Table 5.5.2C. This shows income ranges (salaries and bonus/incentive payments, housing allowances and other welfare payments included) for five LDC ports, averaged over drivers of all equipment types, from forklift trucks to quayside gantry cranes; basic dockworker salaries are included for comparison. The table suggests that developing countries adopt different policies when setting employee payment schemes. In some ports, quayside gantry crane operators can earn up to 2.5 times the salary of a basic dockworker, as part of a deliberate policy to attract the best men to that job, while in other ports dockworkers earn similar salaries to drivers, notwithstanding the extra skills and responsibilities involved in driving. In spite of this variation, no shortage of applicants for driving posts was reported in any of the ports surveyed.

There seems to be no consistency in the application of incentive schemes for equipment drivers; they are totally excluded from them in some ports, while in others only a few equipment-based operations (e.g. quay transfer) carry incentive or bonus payments. Certainly, there is resentment where drivers – or, worse, *some* drivers – are excluded from incentive schemes available to other employees.

Where incentive schemes are in force in LDCs, they tend to be based (as in many European ports) on group performance – the tonnage or number of units handled per shift at a berth or terminal, or even total port throughput in a measured period – though some schemes reward individual performance. In group schemes, the driver is treated as a member of (for example) a shipboard gang and is paid a bonus at the same rate as the other members. Typically, such payments come to about 10-20% of gross salary, though in one port the average total bonus, incentive and overtime payments for port employees amounted to up to three times their basic wage!

Those ports that do not operate incentive schemes claim that it is too difficult to devise a scheme which is both equitable and easy to administer, basically because they cannot establish reliable performance standards to cover the wide variety of ships calling at the port, the varied commodities handled and the resulting differences in cargo-handling output. There is some truth in this (as there is in the expressed fear that bonus payments might encourage dangerous driving practices, in the effort to maximize output), but it is significant that several of the most successful ports have managed to surmount those obstacles. In one of these ports, there is a three-tier incentive scheme; on the container terminal, for example:

— Category 1 drivers (of quayside gantry cranes) receive individual incentive payments based on achievement of standard work values, established for each type of vessel calling (e.g. one set for feeder vessels, another for a second-generation cellular vessel, yet another for a multipurpose ship).

— Category 2 drivers (employed on rubber-tyred gantry cranes and tractors involved in ship loading/discharge operations) receive bonuses based on piece-work rates and overall Ship Operation performance.

— Category 3 drivers (operating machines employed in moving cargo within the terminal and on receipt/delivery operations) receive bonuses relating to overall terminal performance only; it is considered too difficult to set and measure individual performance values for these activities, as they all involve idle periods outside the control of the drivers.

All categories of drivers also have to work set minimum hours in the month in order to qualify for the incentive schemes – the more hours worked, the higher the rate of incentive that is available; this is so that drivers are not tempted to work excessively hard on a few successive shifts and then take days off. So, although incentive schemes are not easy to devise and administer, they can be successfully applied, and there is considerable evidence that the successful schemes do make significant contributions to cargo-handling efficiency. There is no doubt, either, that computerized management information systems (OMIS, EMIS and personnel/administrative systems) make them very much easier to administer. The potential dangers to operational safety arising from the encouragement of drivers to operate their machines at high speeds and for long periods are overcome in several ports by the incorporation of 'disincentive' or 'demerit' systems; instances of careless, negligent or dangerous equipment operation can be penalized by deducting sums from that month's bonuses, or even by removing those individuals from the incentive scheme for that period.

Certainly, accidents resulting from bad driving should trigger immediate exclusion from the scheme, and instances where equipment has been operated while unsafe or when showing signs of needing maintenance should be similarly 'rewarded' by demerit points.

5.5.2.3 Fuel Costs

Fuel costs in the LDC port figured in Table 5.5.2B are relatively low; diesel fuel in that country carries almost no excise duty. Nevertheless, fuel accounts for up to 25% of the running cost, while power for the quayside gantry cranes contributes 45% of running costs for those machines. A recent survey (Thomas & Roach, 1988) of costs in the ports of developed countries, where labour costs are far higher, shows that fuel still accounts for 12-25% of running costs (quayside gantry crane power in those ports only amounts to about 15% of running costs). Clearly, significant savings in running costs are possible through attention to fuel consumption figures.

In European ports, certainly, considerable emphasis is now being placed on fuel economy when specifying and selecting new equipment. The success of this strategy is demonstrated by figures given for one major European port by Jerusel (1988), showing that there has been, between 1972 and 1987, a reduction of 35% in hourly fuel consumption of its straddle carrier fleet, in spite of a 60% average increase in weight of the machines and a proportional improvement in lifting capacity. Clearly, fuel and power consumption must be recorded for every item of cargo-handling equipment, so that the success of all fuel-economy measures introduced can be assessed, as well as for calculating total running costs. One European port has individual metering at the fuel supply station, for each of its fleet of straddle carriers, and the system is linked to the machines' hour-meter records. Some such system should form a component part of the OMIS at all ports; it could well be assigned as a Supplies Department responsibility.

5.5.3 Cost/Revenue Centres

If equipment operating performance in LDC ports is to be improved – as it urgently needs to be – it is essential to establish effective cost control and to make managers and supervisors more cost-conscious. Costing procedures must be introduced, covering all the activities of the engineering and operations departments, and allowing equipment costs to be allocated to the relevant cargo-handling activities. Deficiencies in cost recording and budgeting must be eliminated as a matter of urgency.

The most effective approach is to make each terminal, berth or operational section a separate cost/revenue centre. All the costs incurred in handling cargo – specifically the costs of running, servicing and repairing the equipment, of paying dockworkers and drivers, foremen and tally clerks, and of overheads – are charged to that centre against a particular vessel call. Similarly, all income received from the ship operator, shippers, agents etc. is credited to the centre. In this way, the operations managers at that cost/revenue centre have an immediate and striking measure of the profitability of their own unit, and the contribution it makes to the profit (or loss!) of the port as a whole.

There are some difficulties in applying this cost/revenue centre principle. First, it is not always easy to allocate the fixed costs of labour and overheads; dockworkers are typically transferred between a number of berths and are rarely assigned to one work area for any length of time, and equipment also moves from area to area. However, in the latter case the problem is relatively easily solved by making the Engineering Department the 'owners' of the machines (as suggested in this study), 'hiring' them by the hour to the operational cost/revenue centre. There seems no fundamental reason why labour should not be treated similarly, 'hired' by the operators from a central pool by the hour. An alternative approach is to make a group of berths the cost/revenue centre, with labour and equipment assigned to them as a group, but this has the disadvantage of making it difficult to relate costs to a particular vessel call or cargo-handling activity – and this is an extremely useful exercise when reviewing performance, setting targets (see Chapter 8) and fixing pricing schemes.

Fewer problems arise where a *terminal* is identified as a separate cost/revenue centre. Equipment, labour and other resources are often permanently assigned to a container, bulk or similar terminal, so that total costs are relatively easily apportioned to the terminal, to vessel calls and to individual cargo-handling activities. In some of the most successful terminals, each separate activity or function is identified as a cost/revenue sub-centre, e.g. there is one for the Ship Operation, one for Quay Transfer, one for container yard stacking, etc. This allows very precise scrutiny of performance, productivity and efficiency.

Establishing a complete mosaic of cost/revenue centres and sub-centres within the Operations Department (and, indeed, within the Engineering Department, as will be discussed in Chapter 6) allows managers and supervisors to have reliable, detailed information on all the activities performed in their operational unit, on which much better-informed

and secure decision-making can be based. Departmental objectives, berth or terminal performance targets and other management tools can be created, and valuable data can be made available for a host of decisions on financial and pricing policies and port development strategies.

5.5.4 Cost Control
A common weakness in many of the ports surveyed is the inadequacy of their management information systems (see Chapter 9) and particularly of their cost control. In the present context, what is needed is a much more accurate, reliable and consistent recording of fuel consumption and drivers' employment costs (basic salaries and wages, overtime payments, incentive and other bonus payments etc.), hour by hour and shift by shift, for each individual unit of equipment. These data can then be aggregated for the year and linked to the hours worked (by hour-meter record) and other performance data, with the maintenance costs for that unit and with its capital cost (based on assumed asset life and the port's depreciation schedule) to give the total annual and hourly costs of operating that machine. The latter will then be the basis for charging operators for use of the machine.

Not only will this procedure allow standard costs to be established for operating the plant and handling different types of cargo, which will be needed for budgetary control, but it will also be of enormous value to managers (particularly the engineers) when considering the economic life of the asset and equipment replacement strategy.

5.5.5 Cost Consciousness
One of the most serious deficiencies detected in LDC ports is the almost complete lack of cost-consciousness in operations and engineering staff. They are totally unaware of the nature or level of equipment running and maintenance costs, of the operating revenue and expenditures of their units and of the contribution they make to the profitability (or otherwise) of the port. Key managers – the ones directly responsible for the operation and maintenance of plant – are being bypassed when cost information (however little is available) is distributed, and they are rarely involved in the budgeting or cost-review processes.

In complete contrast, the striking features of the most successful ports are the completeness and accuracy of the cost information systems, and the extent to which cost data are distributed to employees at almost all levels in the organization. Workshop and traffic managers and supervisors are aware of departmental objectives and targets, are expected to monitor performance closely, and take part in regular weekly or monthly meetings to examine how closely they have achieved their targets. There is continuous pressure to improve performance and to identify ways in which equipment costs can be reduced, so that targets can be set at ever higher levels.

It is clearly important for managers and supervisors to be involved in the financial reporting system, in the preparation of budgets (by estimating expenditure on the basis of forecast traffic flow) and cost targets. They must have regular feedback on actual cost and operating performance of their sections and should be made responsible for constantly up-dating the operating performance data of the equipment in their control. The performance of individual managers should be assessed regularly, making them accountable for their section's achievement of its financial and performance targets; the question of accountability is considered again in Chapter 8.

5.6 Operating Records

5.6.1 Operating Data

The importance of information systems as a basic tool of effective management has been, and will be, repeatedly stated throughout this study. Operating records relating to equipment performance are an essential component of the port's information systems (both OMIS and EMIS), as they have four main applications:

— they provide operators and engineers with the data on equipment use that they need in order to schedule and control the preventive maintenance and statutory (and other) inspections for each unit of plant and equipment in the inventory;

— they are used to review and, if necessary, amend the daily equipment allocation and deployment procedures;

— when combined with other operational data (on cargo handled etc.) they provide a means of calculating a range of performance indicators relating to port productivity and costs, including equipment operating costs;

— they are an essential input to the equipment planning process (Chapter 3).

LDC ports need to establish systems for recording an array of equipment and other operating data, including:

— information on the demand and supply of equipment, per shift and per day, in terms of

the number of each type of equipment requisitioned, the number supplied and the means by which any shortfall was met;

— daily records of the number of units of each equipment category available for use and the number out of service, with the causes of all downtime;

— shift and daily records on the use of each unit of plant – hours of work (preferably by hour-meter readings), type and location of work, and any breakdowns, faults or accidents reported while in operation;

— records of the fuel, power and lubricants used by each piece of equipment.

This information should be collated and analysed daily, weekly and monthly, to provide a running record of the demand, supply and utilization of the port's equipment inventory, allowing managers to identify fluctuations in supply and demand, and any trends that will be helpful in estimating future equipment needs. The data should be used as the basis for a set of important performance indicators – weekly and monthly availability, utilization and downtime values (as discussed in Chapter 3) – to be amalgamated within the OMIS with Berth Occupancy, Tonnes per Gang Hour, Tonnes (or Containers) Handled per Ship Hour in Port and other indicators. In the best developed of current OMIS systems, operational information is now available in terms of performance relating to individual vessels calling at the port, and a comprehensive array of productivity and cost data is available on demand, from each manager's desk – right down to the level of total equipment operating cost per vessel call and per tonne or container handled, average hourly running and total operating costs per unit of equipment, and even costs relating to the major assemblies, sub-assemblies and components of that equipment.

5.6.2 Collection of Data

The collection of information on equipment performance and cargo-handling operations occurs in a series of stages. Equipment requisitioning (a measure of **demand**) takes place during pre-arrival planning or daily work scheduling; at that time, operations staff will assess ship working and other cargo-handling activities and thus calculate the necessary resources. Data on the equipment **supply** situation should be recorded daily by engineering staff, including details of units out of service. The information on supply and demand should then be collated centrally by senior staff responsible for equipment allocation.

The performance of equipment should be recorded for each shift or day by engineers in charge of the workshops or parking/holding depots. The times of equipment departure from and return to the depots should be noted in the Daily Equipment Record, which should also contain data on the running hours of engines and other systems, noted from hourmeters at the beginning and end of each shift or work period. Delays resulting from breakdowns or accidents during the shift, initially recorded in the equipment logbooks by the drivers, will be transferred to the Daily Equipment Record at the end of the shift, so that the Record ultimately contains a complete history of the operating performance of that unit of equipment. Total working hours data should periodically be collated from the Daily Equipment Record to calculate utilization of individual machines, categories of machines, and the full equipment inventory.

Data on the fuel and/or power consumed by each unit of equipment should be recorded by engineering staff and indicators of fuel economy regularly prepared. Records of drivers' hours of work should also be kept on the equipment record card, to assist in calculating running costs. Standardized values should be developed for driver employment costs for each category of equipment, for cost control purposes. The running costs should be periodically combined with the maintenance and capital costs (amortization) entered by the engineers, to provide a record of total equipment operating costs.

5.6.3 Use of Operating Data

The regular preparation of equipment operating records will assist managers in controlling maintenance schedules, amending allocation practices and planning future equipment needs. The OMIS can help identify operating or maintenance problem areas, which goes a long way towards solving them. It can help to increase productivity and make managers more cost-conscious, particularly since operating costs form the highest proportion of total port costs. It can also improve pre-arrival planning procedures and enable comparisons of operating performance to be made, shift to shift, ship to ship. It provides the basis for setting performance and cost targets for managers, against which to assess actual performance.

It is essential, then, that operating information is regularly collected, collated and presented in a suitable form for distributing to all relevant senior, middle and junior managers, on a weekly or monthly basis. The data will then form the agenda for discussion at all meetings at which port operating performance and maintenance performance are reviewed. In this way, managers can constantly aim to improve the performance of the operations and engineering departments, gradually achieving higher and higher targets and maintaining or advancing the port's commercial success in an increasingly competitive market.

5.7 Recommendations

1. Equipment operations management in LDC ports urgently needs to be improved, by the introduction and observance of good operating procedures, the effective management and supervision of equipment use, and the strict insistence on sound and safe driving practices.

2. Equipment allocation procedures should allow engineers to spread the workload efficiently over their workshop facilities and resources, so improving equipment reliability and utilization, extending asset life and maximizing the port's capital investment in plant.

3. Responsibility for the control of equipment, as well as for its condition and upkeep, should be given to engineers, allowing them to 'hire out' units by the hour to operators, as requisitioned.

4. An effective budgetary control system should be established, with each berth, terminal or operational section designated as a separate cost/revenue centre.

5. Appropriate management procedures and well designed forms should be developed to control and allocate equipment to the various operational areas and to record accurately the actual hours of work performed, so that these can be charged to the relevant cost/revenue centre.

6. Equipment holding policies should be chosen in relation to institutional factors, the size and geography of the port estate and to the location of workshops.

7. Whichever equipment holding pattern is adopted – central, sectional or terminal – it must ensure managerial accountability and effective cost control.

8. Responsibility for calculating daily equipment needs and for requisitioning machines must rest with the traffic officers directly involved in planning and supervising cargo-handling operations.

9. Efficient operational planning and equipment allocation procedures must be established and followed.

10. Traffic officers should be responsible for equipment deployment on their berths, and procedures must be developed to facilitate the transfer of equipment between berths to meet sudden surges in demand or equipment breakdowns.

11. Co-operation and co-ordination between traffic officers and engineers are essential to achieve maximum cargo-handling productivity and good control over plant maintenance.

12. Constant communication is essential between staff at all levels in the Engineering and Operations Departments to ensure appropriate equipment allocation and cargo-handling efficiency, and a continuous two-way flow of information between berths and workshops.

13. Data recorded on the Requisition Forms should be collated daily, regularly analysed and periodically presented to senior managers in a form suitable for simple interpretation and use in equipment planning.

14. Priority rules must be established for equipment allocation, and contingency plans must be prepared to cover occasions when demand exceeds supply.

15. Allocation of equipment drivers should be the direct responsibility of engineers, as this offers the most reliable means of regularly inspecting and monitoring the condition of equipment and driver performance.

16. Detailed operating manuals should be prepared for all types of equipment owned by the port, each setting out in a clear, concise and easily understood style (and in the language used by employees) the details of the operating procedures for all activities performed by that equipment.

17. The management skills of traffic officers and supervisory staff should be upgraded, to make them more aware of their responsibilities for ensuring that equipment is operated safely and correctly when under their control.

18. Each driver should be made directly accountable to his superior for the condition and operating performance of the machine in his charge.

19. Safety awareness programmes, supported by the appointment of a port safety officer, must be run regularly for all those involved in cargo-handling operations, and drivers and operators must attend safe driving courses every year.

20. A strict but fair disciplinary procedure must be followed, with precisely specified accident enquiry rules, range of penalties, and driver appeal arrangements.

21. To improve driver skills and attitudes, ports must adopt appropriate driver recruitment policies, establish attractive career structures, set good salary levels and conditions of employment, and provide good training schemes.

22. Ports must adopt a cost control system which records, analyses and interprets the running costs of individual units of equipment, so that appropriate hire rates can be charged against operational cost/revenue centres, and so that annual revenue budgets, port tariffs and prices can be set.

23. Data on the running costs of individual units of equipment, detailing drivers' earnings and the cost of fuel/power and consumables separately, must be regularly recorded for costing purposes.

24. Individual and/or group incentive schemes should be applied to equipment drivers, based on output and hours of work, to improve cargo-handling efficiency, but with disincentive or demerit elements to discourage drivers from operating their equipment unsafely.

25. The fuel/power consumption of each unit of equipment must be regularly monitored, and greater emphasis needs to be placed on fuel economy when specifying and selecting new equipment.

26. All the costs incurred in handling cargo (including running and maintenance costs, the labour costs for dockworkers, drivers, tally clerks and foremen, and all relevant overheads) must be charged to the appropriate cost/revenue centre against a particular vessel call.

27. Operations and engineering staff must become more cost-conscious and be made directly accountable for operating performance.

28. Operators must be set appropriate financial and performance targets for their berths, based on the type of cargo and vessel handled and the resources available to them.

29. Operators' actual performance should be recorded, fed back to them, and regularly compared with their set targets, to provide a stimulus for improving efficiency.

30. Operating data must be regularly collected, collated and distributed in suitable form to all relevant senior, middle and junior managers, as a means of improving the performance of the operations and engineering departments.

CHAPTER 6

Maintenance Strategies and Practices

6.1 Review of Maintenance Problems

6.1.1 The Nature of the Problems

A striking feature of this study has been the enormous gap between the competence of the engineering services in efficient ports and those where there are major equipment management problems. Indeed, maintenance is now undoubtedly the biggest obstacle to achieving satisfactory cargo-handling performance standards in many LDC ports. The more efficient ports have devised appropriate and effective maintenance strategies, constructed suitable workshop facilities and fully stocked them with machine tools and other equipment, have developed the technical and managerial skills of their staff and have established good maintenance planning and control procedures. In contrast, in some LDC ports, many of these organizational and management procedures and facilities are missing or poorly developed, and the engineers are unable to fulfill their duty of providing an adequate maintenance service for civil works, marine craft, and cargo-handling equipment and plant.

Those ports experiencing serious maintenance difficulties face an array of problems, and no single cause can be identified as explaining the generally poor quality of their maintenance services. The major difficulties identified during the study, and which are the prime contributors to poor maintenance, can be categorized under eleven headings. These are briefly reviewed in this section, before considering, in Sections 6.2 to 6.7, various aspects of the organization, policies, facilities and practices of port maintenance.

6.1.2 Insufficient Maintenance

The engineering departments in many LDC ports are incapable of meeting the demands for maintenance placed upon them. It is not just that the departments cannot handle the sheer volume of work coming in but also that they are faced with an increasing variety and complexity of work. So routine preventive maintenance is often neglected as technical staff concentrate on the urgent repair of breakdowns. Cargo-handling equipment, marine craft and civil works do not get the regular, routine

inspections that they should, and so minor problems tend to go undetected and are allowed to grow into major defects, resulting in more frequent breakdown of plant and machinery. The few units left serviceable get over-used and neglected, while the engineers struggle to keep up with repairs, until those, too, break down. The vicious circle of neglect and breakdown constantly increases the workload and pressures on the maintenance workshops and technical staff, and the situation inevitably gets worse and worse.

Part of the problem is that engineering staff take a very long time to locate and diagnose the cause of equipment failures, and then to decide what action to take to correct the fault. They then fail to plan their work effectively and, inevitably, take much longer to finish it than they should. They take hours or even days to respond to breakdowns, and it all results in equipment being out of service and unavailable to operators for very long periods. A common sight in these ports is equipment sitting in the workshop, often for many months, awaiting repair.

It is not just cargo-handling equipment whose maintenance is neglected, either. In some of the ports visited, the civil works had not been properly maintained, particularly the quays and the surfaces of the operating areas. Surfaces had broken down, often to the hardcore, and differential subsidence had not been rectified. All these failures to maintain civil works in turn contribute to a high frequency of plant and equipment breakdown. In some ports, too, little or no maintenance had been provided for floating craft, so that many of them had become unseaworthy and beyond repair; craft had actually sunk at their moorings through lack of hull maintenance.

Failure to carry out adequate maintenance programmes results in a rapid deterioration in the condition of civil works, floating craft, plant and machinery, and to severely shortened asset lives. Replacing assets prematurely scrapped because of insufficient maintenance has placed considerable extra and unnecessary burdens on the limited financial resources of the ports and on the foreign exchange reserves of these developing countries.

6.1.3 Inadequate Maintenance

A major deficiency in many LDC ports is the poor *quality* of the maintenance work. Many instances were cited during the survey of work not being properly performed. For example, machines are frequently allowed to leave workshops in poor condition, supposedly having received a full service but without inspection and with jobs uncompleted; little attention seems to be paid to quality control. Not surprisingly, the equipment is soon returned to the workshop because of failure in operation. Indeed, cases were reported of maintenance staff deliberately not servicing or repairing equipment properly, because they 'knew' it would be abused and misused by drivers and would quickly return to the workshops! The result of sub-standard maintenance work is, of course, the fulfilment of their prophecy: the equipment quickly fails again and is back in the workshop, adding to the maintenance workload. And so the vicious circle continues.

On the civil engineering side, the sign of inadequate maintenance is the skimping of surface repairs: at best numerous holes are carelessly filled in, instead of the whole surface of an area being renewed. The holes are, in any case, filled with inappropriate materials. Inevitably, the constant movement of heavy cargo-handling machines over the surface causes the repairs to break up again very quickly, and the problem returns.

Technological change and the increasing sophistication of plant and machinery are adding to the problem of inadequate maintenance. Engineers in many developing countries are finding it more and more difficult to maintain the electric, electronic and hydraulic systems which are increasingly commonly fitted in equipment – complex systems which were not common when those engineers were trained, perhaps, and for which no further training has been given since. Substandard maintenance particularly follows the commissioning of new plant, again a sign of a training failure. It is also evidence of poor quality inspection procedures in the workshop; LDC ports often have no established routine for inspection before equipment is released from maintenance, and it is very rare indeed for the Engineering Department to have an independent inspectorate section.

6.1.4 The High Cost of Maintenance

Although technical staff salaries are generally very much lower in LDC ports than in the ports of developed countries, total maintenance costs are just as high overall – sometimes higher. In fact, if the time cost of plant being out of service is included, or the cost of hiring plant during that time added, then the cost of maintenance often greatly exceeds that of developed country ports. Three factors contribute to this situation:

1. The engineering departments in many LDC ports are grossly overstaffed, imposing enormous overhead costs on maintenance. Admittedly, salary levels of technical staff are only about 7-15% of those of equivalent personnel in ports in Western Europe (Jerusel, 1988) but, as this study has confirmed, manning levels are often 10 to 30 times as high.

2. Excessive overtime payments are frequently and regularly made to technical staff, in spite of the high manning levels; they often amount to as much as 25-30% of total salary expenditure. This probably reflects the amount of emergency repairs that have to be undertaken out of normal workshop hours, because management is unable to match technical staff working hours with peak maintenance demand.

3. Developing countries have to pay very high prices for spare parts. LDC ports are largely dependent on foreign manufacturers for equipment and, consequently, for spares and supplies, and so inevitably incur high transport costs for them. The lack of a competitive market and the imposition of agents' and other commissions add to the delivered costs of spare parts. A recent study (Jerusel, 1988) estimated that LDC ports pay between 1.4 and 1.8 times the prices paid by ports in developed countries for the same spare parts, and one Supplies Department manager reported being asked to pay three times what a colleague in another country paid for the same component.

All these factors contribute to the problems of controlling engineering costs in LDC ports, adding to the general difficulties of equipment management.

6.1.5 Inadequate Maintenance Facilities

Reference was made in Chapter 1 to the range of maintenance services carried out by ports and the facilities needed to provide them – from slipways or dry docks for servicing marine craft, and heavy plant for the upkeep of quays and civil works, to delicate apparatus for testing electronic components on cargo-handling equipment. Although a few of the ports visited rent or hire maintenance facilities when required, or use the services of outside contractors, most ports, for policy or other reasons, undertake maintenance in-house and so need the relevant workshop and other facilities. However, the location, size and design of those facilities are not always appropriate, and the tools and equipment provided within them are often inadequate.

In general, the LDC ports visited have reasonable facilities for the maintenance of marine craft – slipways, drydocks and related workshops – or have made suitable arrangements with external contractors, but the provision of facilities and equipment for civil maintenance is less satisfactory in many ports and in some cases the work is totally non-mechanized. Stones are broken by hand, surfaces are repaired with picks and shovels, and compacted manually.

The situation with respect to the maintenance of cargo-handling equipment is also less than satisfactory, with poor siting, layout and resourcing of workshops and other facilities. In many ports, bad location of workshops leads to delays in engineers' responding to breakdowns, and to long travel distances for plant moving between the workshops and operational areas. In some cases, workshops are outside the dock estate altogether, and in others are right in the operational areas, where they interfere with cargo-handling operations and traffic flows. In one port visited, a major maintenance facility is located near a bulk ore-handling terminal, resulting in severe dust pollution, to the detriment of men and machines. In another port, a workshop is frequently flooded during the monsoon season, making its use virtually impossible in those months. Some ports with large dock estates have only a central workshop with long travel distances to and from many of the operational areas, instead of having satellite workshops around the dock estate. Others have no mobile maintenance facilities to deal with equipment which breaks down in operation and which cannot be moved to the workshops for repair. All they can provide is men with hand tools, and it is not uncommon for heavy machines to be pushed back to the workshop (using cargo-handling equipment), often causing further damage in the process.

Most ports have, of course, constructed buildings specifically to house the workshop facilities, but in some cases existing buildings have been converted for use as workshops, and many of these are unsuitable for the maintenance of modern cargo-handling equipment. They are poorly laid out, inconvenient to work in, and have inadequate services – heating, ventilation, lighting, power, water and gases. Indeed, some of the surveyed ports reported that they have no maintenance workshop facilities whatever. For example, a modern container terminal has been constructed without a workshop, while at another port a makeshift facility has been provided on a piece of waste land, using old, empty 20′ containers. One senior maintenance engineer, responsible for the upkeep of new container-handling equipment, remarked that his overall pocket was his 'workshop' and that all maintenance work has to be performed out on the quays.

In fact, many of the participating ports reported that the buildings in which workshops are located are unsuitable for carrying out maintenance, particularly of modern tall equipment. They are often of inappropriate design and are poorly laid out inside, with poor lighting, inadequate ventilation, and no water or other services. Where those services are installed, they are often inconveniently sited. Inside the workshop, the locations of the various specialist operations (welding, engine overhaul, etc.) are not always suitable, and the siting of the workshop stores creates long delays in obtaining spare parts. Frequently, operations requiring a clean atmosphere are positioned among those producing dust and toxic fumes.

A major deficiency observed in the workshops at many ports is the shortage (even complete absence) of work-benches, shelving and storage space. Maintenance equipment – lathes, drills, test apparatus and hand tools – are often in very short supply and very old. There is often a severe shortage of lifting devices, ramps and service pits. Toilet and washroom facilities, changing rooms, canteens and other amenities for employees are entirely inadequate.

6.1.6 Bad Workshop Practices

A common observation in very many ports is that staff do not observe good 'housekeeping' practices within and around the workshops: working surfaces are coated with oil, grease and dirt; hand and machine tools are not properly looked after – they are covered in grime and grease, are not sharpened, adjusted or maintained; tools are not put away in lockers and storerooms, and are lost or pilfered; equipment awaiting spare parts is parked indiscriminately in the workshop areas, and parts that have been removed from machines under maintenance are scattered about, unlabelled (in one extraordinary case, a complete fleet of forklift trucks had been stripped down by unskilled workshop staff, and all the removed parts had been piled up together in the centre of the workshop; there was no chance whatsoever that those machines would ever be reassembled or used again). Portable gear and equipment, such as acetylene welding gear, are not looked after, and are not returned to their storage positions. Little or no attention is given to encouraging safe engineering practices within the workshops, and first aid and other medical services are entirely inadequate.

Another aspect of bad workshop practice is the failure of workshop managers and supervisors to control the flow of work into and through the workshops. Effective and comprehensive planning, scheduling and supervising procedures are needed, otherwise work is uncontrolled, the workshop area becomes congested, and important tasks are overlooked. Quality control is an important element of this control procedure; much of the dissatisfaction expressed by operators at the state of equipment allocated to them can be put down to the lack of inspection of equipment before it leaves the workshop – indeed, each stage in a service or repair job should be thoroughly checked by a foreman or supervisor before the technicians are allowed to carry on to the next stage. This sort of control is conspicuously lacking in many LDC workshops.

6.1.7 Shortage of Skills

A common feature of ports with deficient maintenance capabilities is the shortage of suitably qualified and experienced managers, supervisors and technical staff. Poor recruitment and training practices, and inadequate salaries and conditions of employment, have contributed to the low level of technical skills of mechanics, electricians and other craftsmen. This no doubt accounts for many of the problems outlined in previous sections – the generally poor quality of maintenance work and the many bad engineering practices so commonly observed.

Of particular concern is that managers and supervisors seem not to be fully qualified in either their technical or managerial fields. In most LDC ports participating in the study, the engineers are university or polytechnic graduates, but have received little or no training in management skills and have scant appreciation of modern management methods. Middle and junior grade engineers and supervisory staff have little knowledge of financial management, budgetary control, man management or scheduling and planning. Equally important, professional engineers and supervisors have received no shop-floor training since their appointment (indeed, the managers have rarely had any practical training at all) and are consequently unaware of the detailed day-to-day problems that arise in maintenance. Junior- and middle-ranking engineers are firmly office-based, venturing very infrequently (if at all) into the workshops or onto the quays. They fail conspicuously to keep a close watch on maintenance standards, to identify maintenance problems and requirements, and to take the necessary remedial action. Yet these are the essential hands-on skills and responsibilities of engineering managers in the equipment-dominated present-day port.

Technical skill shortages were also observed in such key personnel as workshop superintendents, in stores management and in the supervision and clerical work related to engineering and technical services.

All these aspects of management and manpower development will be discussed further in Chapter 8.

6.1.8 Lack of Spare Parts

Delays to the completion of maintenance and repair work resulting from the lack of spare parts and 'consumables' are endemic in LDC ports. They occur everywhere, even in ports that in other respects have a good reputation for maintenance, and 'waiting for spare parts' was the commonest complaint made by engineers in this survey. The causes of these delays (which are many, varied and always serious), and the various deficiencies in the procurement, storage, issuing and management of spare parts and other supplies are considered at length in Chapter 7.

The direct consequence of poor spare parts management is that many units of cargo-handling equipment (and, indeed, marine craft) are often out of service for many months or even, in extreme cases, years. While awaiting spares, equipment is frequently not protected against the weather and sea spray, and the condition of the chassis, bodywork, systems and components deteriorates severely. The equipment also regularly suffers the ravages of workshop staff: a common practice is to remove parts from out-of-service machines to repair similar units, with the consequence that, when the originally required spare part is eventually delivered, the machine still cannot be made serviceable – it is now lacking other parts! This practice of 'cannibalization' often results in many units being laid up and eventually prematurely scrapped, permanently reducing the number of serviceable units available to operators. This has an inevitable impact on cargo-handling rates, of course, and in the long run greatly increases operational costs, as the port has to buy a larger number of units just to keep sufficient units serviceable; this also puts greater demands on engineering services, of course, as there are now even more machines queuing for maintenance.

6.1.9 Unnecessary Demand for Maintenance

As equipment ages, more and more maintenance will be required until a point is reached when the most economic choice is to replace it with a new machine. Retaining equipment beyond that point will not only be uneconomic for the port but will also place increasingly heavy demands on maintenance facilities and resources. As indicated in Chapter 3, many ports retain assets on their register well beyond their economic life, and they continue to maintain that plant despite the high cost involved and the disproportionate amount of time that has to be spent by engineering staff in keeping it (just) serviceable.

Purchasing an unsuitable type of equipment can also contribute to excessive demands on a port's maintenance capability. Several cases were cited of ports specifying the wrong type of equipment for the prevailing conditions, leading to early failure of components and long periods out of service under maintenance. For example, tractor units built for a temperate climate will be unsuitable for use in the tropics; they need to be supplied with additional engine cooling systems, transmission and oil coolers, and tropical air filters. This might sound obvious, but mistakes have been – and continue to be – made in specifying and supplying new machines.

Another cause of excessive demand on maintenance (as discussed in Chapter 5) is the high incidence of damage resulting from accidents. Incorrect use of equipment, poor driver skills, careless attitudes towards equipment operation, lack of discipline and inadequate supervision – all these combine to increase the wear and tear on plant and the risk of damage and failure, and to add unnecessarily to the burden of the port's maintenance facilities.

6.1.10 Poor Organization of Engineering Services

In many LDC ports, the organizational structure of the Engineering Department has not evolved in step with changing demands for maintenance. Organizational structures that were designed when the port authority was exclusively concerned with the maintenance of civil works and marine services, with cargo-handling performed by separate stevedoring companies, have not changed even though the port has now become directly involved in cargo-handling operations. The expansion in the type and amount of equipment acquired by ports as their dependence on mechanization has grown, and the impact of that on the mechanical and electrical maintenance functions, has not been acknowledged by senior management in terms of changes in the organizational structure. Similarly, organizations that were developed to suit the needs of break-bulk general cargo trades have not been adjusted in response to the technological and institutional changes that have accompanied the move to unitized trades.

A direct consequence of these failures to adjust is that the organizational structure of the Engineering Department does not reflect the relative importance of different disciplines. It lacks an appropriate blend of skills in the individual engineering disciplines. In some organizations, insufficient status and authority are given to mechanical and electrical engineers, and there is often confusion over the division of work between sections within the Engineering Department.

Communication often breaks down in cases where there are overlapping responsibilities for maintaining one piece of equipment. For example, in many cases ships' crews are responsible for day-to-day maintenance and minor repairs aboard ship, whereas major overhauls and repairs come under the jurisdiction of a marine workshop engineer. Unless there is the closest co-operation between the two groups, co-ordination of maintenance is threatened and the vessel may well experience more downtime than necessary. In one country visited, confusion and conflict arise because the national ports authority involves itself directly in the daily activities of the individual ports under its control. Although notionally non-operational, the engineers at Port Authority Headquarters interfere in the day-to-day scheduling of maintenance work within the ports.

Other organizational problems observed included failure to establish clear lines of responsibility and to delegate authority to staff at the lower levels in the organization, particularly in the workshops. There is in some ports a complete tier of management missing: key staff with appropriate engineering and managerial qualifications and with shop-floor experience are missing from workshop management, so that supervision is ineffective. Planning and scheduling are haphazard, as workshop staff lack the authority to demand release of machines from Operations for preventive maintenance. In one port, the situation has reached the stage where the engineers have no idea where within the port estate particular items of equipment are, and cannot retrieve them for maintenance (even if they had a clear idea of when that maintenance is due). Many of these aspects of management and organizational stucture are considered again in Chapter 8, as well as later in this chapter.

6.1.11 Lack of Co-operation and Co-ordination

A frequent observation in LDC ports is that appropriate functional relationships have not been established between staff in the engineering and operations departments. This has led to poor communication between operators and engineers, frequently resulting in conflict between staff at all levels in the two departments, to the detriment of operational and maintenance performance. Planning and scheduling of maintenance are particularly affected. Typically, operators will not release equipment when maintenance is due, and engineers hold on to equipment when it is urgently needed on the berths.

Similar problems also arise within the Engineering Department, where there is poor communication between the various sections of the Department and among workshop staff. Cases were cited where major electrical work was undertaken on a unit of equipment and the machine reassembled, only to find shortly afterwards that mechanical work, which could easily have been carried out at the same time, was also needed. Opportunity maintenance should be a valued element of the engineering strategy of the port, but can only be taken advantage of if there is regular and close communication between department staff.

It must be acknowledged that co-operation and the dovetailing of maintenance work with operational needs are often hindered by poor communication systems. Several ports suffer from exceptionally unreliable telephone systems, and have no internal radio communication systems, linking operational areas, workshops and mobile maintenance units, to overcome the problem. Notification of breakdowns and accidents takes a great deal of time at these ports, and leads to considerable delays in the response of workshop staff. In some managers' offices, the duplication or triplication of telephones on their desks looks impressive, but is in reality an attempt to ensure that at least one is working; this is often a forelorn hope!

Organizational barriers also impede good communication. On many occasions during this study, evidence appeared that staff in the operations and engineering departments avoided communicating directly with one another. Indeed, even within departments there is considerable scope for improvement in communication, and there is often a particularly serious communication gulf between office-bound professional engineers and the craftsmen on the shop-floor. The main reason is that missing tier of management at that level, referred to earlier – the skilled, experienced, practical engineer at workshop manager/superintending engineer level. The result is a lack of work supervision and little or no quality control.

6.1.12 Lack of Financial Control

In many countries, maintenance budgetary and costing procedures are unreliable, lack the required detail and do not provide for effective managerial control and accountability. Appropriate costing procedures have not been developed, and procedures for forecasting workshop expenditure can at best be described as *ad hoc*. Even when a contingency allowance of 10-25% is added to the engineers' estimate of expenditure, the budgeted sum is still exceeded.

That is not to say that the engineering budget should be treated as a rigid limit on maintenance expenditure; the successful ports all agree that equipment and facilities *must be maintained* if the port's function of handling cargo as efficiently as

possible is to be supported. The budget should be a financial target, just as Mean Time Between Failures and Mean Time To Repair should be set as performance targets. Some ports do, however, fix engineering budgets as ceilings, which can lead to absurd consequences. In one case, maintenance of a port's fleet of dredgers was suspended because of a shortage of funds, despite the fact that dredging is an essential port service. Other cases were reported of the engineering department being unable to order spare parts because its budget limit had been exceeded for the year.

The opposite extreme is, of course, just as indefensible. In many ports, no performance or fianancial objectives are set for the engineering department, and engineers have no budgets to work within. The expenditure estimates used in the port's annual budget are unrealistic, and there is no means of detecting excessive expenditure on maintenance. Clearly, the Engineering Department, just like any other cost centre in the port, must have some means of controlling its expenditure and of being controlled within the port's overall budget.

6.2 The Organization of the Engineering Department

6.2.1 The Status of Engineering

The efficient port authorities and terminal operators visited during this study reported that the status of engineering, particularly the maintenance function, within the organization had been upgraded in recent years in step with the increasing dependence of cargo-handling operations on equipment. In those ports, the scale of investment in plant and equipment, and the growing significance of equipment operating and maintenance costs in port expenditure and profitability, have made managers in all disciplines more conscious of the importance of the maintenance function. Operational performance is almost totally dependent on equipment, and this has been reflected in the increasing support for and resources given to engineering. Stimulated by increased inter-port competition and the need for improved operating performance and efficiency, all managers in those successful ports seem to be fully aware of the significance of equipment costs and of the importance of engineers to the profitability of the port.

The improved status and importance of engineering in port and terminal management in the most efficient ports are demonstrated by the increased authority of engineers within the company's organization. Several of the organizations visited reported that engineering had relatively recently been raised to full departmental status. The Chief Engineer (or Director of Engineering Services) is now commonly a Board level appointment, and engineers – including maintenance managers – are members of policy-making bodies. The establishment and management structure of the Engineering Department have been strengthened, and managers directly involved in maintenance – the practical engineers with their offices 'over the shop' – have been given increased status.

In those successful ports, there has been an accompanying change in management culture, with an increasing emphasis on customer service and performance-orientated maintenance. More resources are being devoted to engineering's own capital and revenue budget allocations and to equipment planning and replacement strategies. So engineers now commonly control a larger proportion of the port's revenue and capital budgets – another indication of their raised status within the organization.

6.2.2 Existing Organizational Structures

Several factors influence the way engineering services are organized within a port's administrative structure, among them: the type of port authority controlling it, and its statutory responsibilities; the extent of any involvement of private or public companies in port operations; and the range of services offered to port users. The organizational structure within engineering services will also vary, depending on such factors as the range of services undertaken 'in-house' and the degree of dependence on outside contractors. In the light of the considerable diversity of administrative structure displayed by ports (as discussed in Chapter 2), and the wide range of engineering and technical services required (outlined in Chapter 1), it is hardly surprising that ports exhibit a wide variation in organizational and administrative structures in their

engineering function. No 'model' structure can be pinpointed, even within the most successful European ports.

Perhaps the most common current arrangement is to group all the specialist engineering and technical services functions within an Engineering Department (called a Division in some ports), which has equal administrative status to that of other staff and line departments. The head of the department is a Chief Engineer (still, very often, a civil engineer, though increasingly now he may be a mechanical or electrical engineer, as well as possibly having had operational experience), who is directly responsible to the General Manager or, in a very large port, his Deputy General Manager. Increasingly commonly, the head of the Engineering Department has a seat on the Board. Such an organizational structure is summarized in Figure 6.2.2A.

Within the Engineering Department, the traditional method of grouping activities is by function – a series of Sections (confusingly, also known as Divisions in some ports) related to specific disciplines. The usual arrangement is to have separate Civil Engineering, Mechanical Engineering, Electrical Engineering and Marine Engineering Sections, though there may also be a Technical Services Section (responsible for the port's electrical supply, lighting, water supply and drainage, telephones, etc.), and an Estates Section looking after employee housing and similar functions. In many ports, however, these specialist services are part of the responsibility of the Electrical Engineer and Civil Engineer respectively. The heads of the Sections report directly to the Chief Engineer in this model, which is summarized in Fig.6.2.2B, together with some indication of the major functions within the Sections.

Within the Sections, further subdivision follows lines of functional responsibility. The lower tiers within the Mechanical Engineering Section, for example, reflect the organization and responsibilities

Figure 6.2.2A Example of a Port Authority Organizational Structure

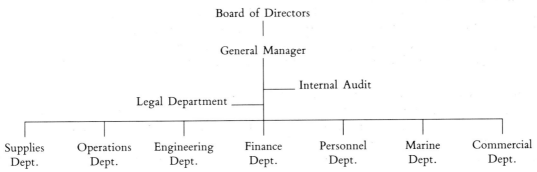

of the workshop or workshops, their locations and the equipment being maintained there, as well as the staffing and shifts worked. There has to be, for example, a Foreman Mechanic for each maintenance shift. Figure 6.2.2C shows a rather traditional organizational structure for the Mechanical Engineering Section of a large, multi-purpose port, in which a central workshop carries out the bulk of the maintenance work.

Although this is a convenient way of subdividing the Engineering Department and the Sections within it, there are several disadvantages with respect to modern methods of equipment maintenance:

1. The managers directly responsible for port maintenance are found at the lower levels of the organization, lacking status and with too much of the 'overall culture' connotation to the posts to attract the best people. Good graduate engineers tend to go instead for posts in the design, construction, planning and procurement branches, when what ports desperately need is engineers with a commitment to 'hands-on', practical engineering.

2. The traditional structure, with its split between mechanical and electrical engineering, at Branch level and even within the workshops, tends to make co-operation and co-ordination of maintenance work more difficult than it need be.

Figure 6.2.2B Example of Organizational Structure of Engineering Department

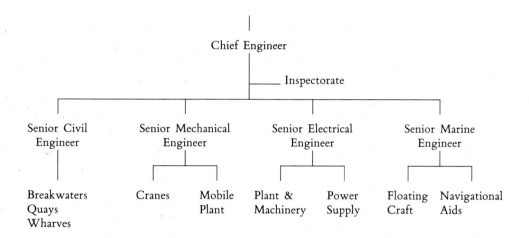

Figure 6.2.2C Traditional Organization of a Mechanical Engineering Section

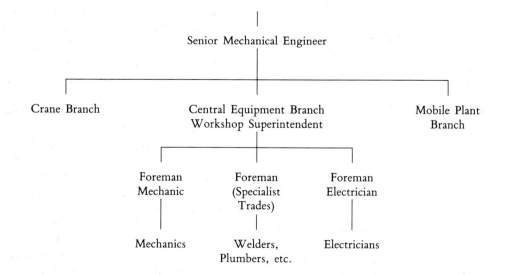

3. The structure is 'bottom-heavy' in that it puts greatest weight in the area of short-term maintenance responsibilities, and finds no firm place for staff planning work for the medium and long term. It neglects the need for engineers in staff functions responsible for planning and co-ordinating the port's maintenance work.

4. The various branches of the Engineering Department have overlapping functions, leading to duplication of staff skills and workshop facilities. For example, the marine workshop employs mechanics, electricians, welders and other specialist trades, skills which also exist in the mechanical and electrical workshops.

5. Rigid functional groups tend to erect barriers between branches, perpetuating the restrictive practice of skill or craft demarcation and making technician deployment and the development of multidisciplinary teams more difficult. For example, the traditional division between mechanical and electrical engineering branches makes the planning of maintenance more difficult and increases the number of employees in these two disciplines.

There is much to be said for reviewing and revising the organizational structure of the engineering services within the port, and for introducing a degree of flexibility, to ensure that the structure (and the objectives of the units within that structure) reflect fully the nature of the traffic handled, current operational needs and the geography of the dock estate. Some of the possible changes are discussed in the following sections.

6.2.3 Decentralization of Maintenance

The detailed organizational structure of the Engineering Department must take into account the geography of the port, the number of workshop units needed, their functional nature and their location. The traditional practice in the context of mechanical/electrical maintenance has been to establish a central workshop, responsible for the maintenance of all the port's equipment. This gives the senior maintenance engineer maximum control over this workforce and allows specialist facilities to be provided most economically, in just one location. It also makes data collection for the EMIS and OMIS much easier than if facilities are spread around the port. However, there is the profound drawback that all equipment has to be brought back from the operational areas to one location, inevitably some distance from many of the berths and quays. The constant flow of many different sorts of equipment through the workshops also makes it difficult for staff to specialize in, and become extremely familiar with, one category of machine.

With the growth in the range, capacity and sophistication of cargo-handling equipment, and with the trend towards specialization of traffic in port sections and terminals, it has become more appropriate to decentralize the maintenance function and to establish a series of distributed workshops. For example, a container terminal is given its own specialized workshop, dealing with the day-to-day maintenance and minor repair of straddle carriers or rubber-tyred gantry cranes. Dry-bulk, forest-product or multi-purpose terminals will also have their own workshops. Indeed, the principle is now frequently extended to conventional berths, too, by grouping them into functional 'sections', with an attendant workshop.

The advantages of such 'satellite' workshops are that:

1. they are near to the operational areas, minimizing travel distances for equipment and workshop staff, and maximizing the engineers' response rate;

2. they can specialize in one or two types of equipment (to the benefit of the technicians' diagnostic and repair skills);

3. they greatly improve the co-operation and collaboration between engineering and operational staff;

4. they are also ideally placed to carry out routine pre-shift inspections of equipment, which is allocated from a depot near each workshop.

Even when satellite workshops are set up, there is still a need for the central workshop, to carry out maintenance work on general-purpose equipment allocated throughout the port (e.g. mobile cranes, heavy lifting machines), for major repairs, overhauls and refurbishment, for bodywork repairs and fabrication, and also for the care of specialized equipment owned in small numbers. For example, quayside cranes at conventional berths are usually maintained from a central workshop (although in this case most of the work will be performed out on the quays, of course).

The important principle in the decentralization is that the satellite workshops are restricted to *routine* maintenance and minor repairs; they should not be equipped with more specialist machine tools and other rarely used facilities. All specialist services and major works, which would not be economic (in terms of both staff and facilities) to duplicate at several satellite workshops, are provided for at the central workshop: overhaul of engines and transmissions, rewinding of electric motors, fabrication, refurbishment of components, casting and machining, and so on. The complete range of necessary skills have to be provided at the central workshop, and an effective system of communication and co-ordination needs to be set up between the central and satellite workshops, to ensure that planning and scheduling of maintenance are efficiently organized.

6.2.4 The Organization of Maintenance Services

Modern organizational structures reflect the increasing importance of maintenance within the Engineering Department. Figure 6.2.4A shows one approach to the revision of the structure of the combined Mechanical/Electrical Section; the same principles apply to the organization of civil and marine sections.

The structure shown in Fig.6.2.4A illustrates several good principles:

— The organization combines the mechanical and electrical functions within the one branch, reducing the risk of conflict, improving communications between staff and increasing the scope for improved planning and co-ordination of maintenance.

— It includes the appointment of a maintenance manager having overall responsibility for all maintenance and reporting directly to the senior mechanical/electrical engineer (though in a small port this post is probably not justified).

— The staff function within the branch is strengthened by the inclusion of a planning

engineer and a maintenance engineer. The planning engineer is responsible for medium- to long-term planning of equipment needs and for research and development work. The maintenance engineer is responsible for medium- to long-term planning and scheduling of maintenance (day-to-day planning is carried out by a lower-tier group within the workshops, as will be explained shortly).

— The division of the maintenance work is now between operational areas, rather than between engineering skills, with the setting up of terminal/sectional workshops and a base or central workshop (Section 6.2.3).

— The organizational structure within the workshops is streamlined, with few tiers of authority; this is illustrated in Fig.6.2.4B.

Five excellent management principles have been illustrated in this section. There is another principle that needs to be incorporated within the maintenance organizational structure: line relationships with other departments. This is discussed in the next section.

6.2.5 Line and Functional Relationships

A principal objection to the traditional grouping of activities on functional lines is that it does not provide clear lines of reporting between the engineering and operations departments. In European ports there has been a subtle but distinctive change in port philosophy in recent years, in a move to create a partnership of engineering services with operations. The handling of cargo is considered a team effort in which staff in operations, engineering and other departments co-operate fully to achieve high levels of performance.

Figure 6.2.4A Model Organizational Structure of a Mechanical/Electrical Section

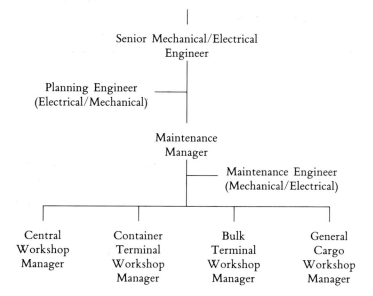

In one port, this has been achieved by the introduction of a new branch of management within the Operations Department – the Equipment Division – with responsibility for co-ordinating the roles of engineers and operators. However, at the terminal level another approach has been successful, in which a line responsibility has been introduced between the terminal manager and maintenance staff; the workshop manager reports directly to the terminal manager (in a miniature version of the port's organizational structure), while retaining his functional relationship with the Chief Engineer at port headquarters.

Another important line relationship is that between the Workshop Storeman and the Workshop Manager (Fig.6.2.4B); the storeman's primary task is to provide a service to the Workshop Manager and his technical staff, but he reports functionally and administratively to a superior within the Supplies Department.

6.2.6 Management Style

At senior management and executive levels, two discernible developments have been the advance of mechanical and electrical engineers and the emergence of multi-disciplined and more broadly qualified line managers in engineering. The Senior Mechanical/Electrical Engineer almost invariably has a mechanical engineering background, although in some ports and terminals managers with both operational experience and engineering qualifications have been appointed to such senior positions; this has

certainly been the trend in some European ports. Another significant development has been the growing emphasis on managerial skills of engineering staff; some now have both engineering and management qualifications.

In the more efficient ports, the management structure of the Engineering Department has been brought into line with current management theory, with a relatively broad (but still manageable) span of control and very few levels of authority. The emphasis is on 'hands-on' engineering, with a relatively small core of administrative managers, responsible for maintenance policy and planning, and a majority of practically-biased engineers.

Of particular significance is the way authority is delegated to workshop staff. A key appointment within the Department is the Workshop Manager (also called, in some ports, the Workshop Superintendent or Superintending Engineer, and in Europe known as the 'Meestergastr'). He is responsible for planning and scheduling maintenance (through the workshop Routing Desk) and controlling maintenance workloads and workshop activities. He is the principal employee in the day-to-day maintenance function. In Europe, the Workshop Managers have often had extensive engineering and management experience in heavy engineering before coming into the port. Even though many of them have risen from the shop floor, they are generally at least diploma-qualified engineers. The Workshop Managers provide a vital link between the policy-making, planning and workshop levels, and are involved in all equipment management activities.

Figure 6.2.4B Model Workshop Organizational Structure

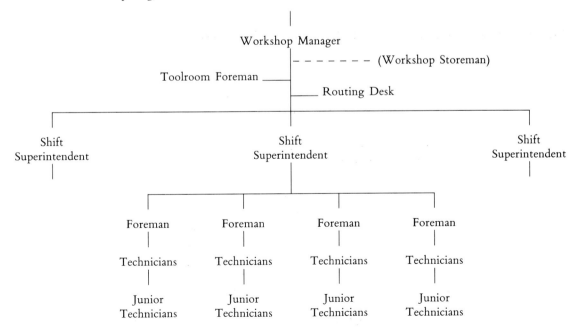

Of course, most LDC ports have a Workshop Manager post (or its equivalent) within the Engineering Department, but the holders of those posts are generally quite different from the 'meestergastr' ideal. They have the wrong background (in 'theoretical', rather than practical, engineering), the wrong status (as 'managers', rather than engineers) and the wrong approach (desk-orientated, instead of sleeves-up and hands-on). They cannot, because of their training and philosophy, act as that vital link between day-to-day maintenance activities and forward planning and policy-making, and apparently lack all interest in the practicalities of maintenance engineering. This is one area of the organization of maintenance where LDC ports need to make urgent and drastic improvements.

6.2.7 Accountability

Another important trend emerging in the organization of the Engineering Department is the strengthening of the principle of accountablility at all levels. Efficient ports have developed organizational structures with clear lines of authority, each employee made fully aware of his individual responsibilities and accountable to his immediate superior for his performance, which is carefully monitored. The principle of accountability is discussed at length in Chapter 8.

An important development in this context has been the setting of clear departmental and individual performance objectives, against which targets the achievement of employees, workshop teams, the workshops themselves and the Engineering Department as a whole can be assessed. Indeed, the principle of accountability depends on such performance targets. Realistic shift, daily and other periodic targets, defined in performance and cost terms, must be set for each unit and employee, and the actual performance must be measured constantly and fed back. Every employee must have the necessary authority to carry out the tasks set him, and there must be an appropriate way to reward him when he achieves his set targets. (The questions of employee motivation and incentive schemes are considered again in Chapter 8.) Appendix 4 reproduces an indicative set of objectives for an Engineering Department, taken from the complete series for an LDC port.

6.2.8 Employee Skills

One of the consequences of technological change and increasing dependence on cargo-handling equipment is the need for ports to employ engineering staff with an ever broader range of specialist technical skills – in terms both of more skills per technician and of more specialist technicians. However, severe skill shortages exist in many developing countries in most technical and craft disciplines. In particular, staff are urgently needed with appropriate qualifications and experience in the electronic, refrigeration and communication fields.

The steadily increasing technical complexity of plant and machinery is placing great pressure on the Engineering Department to upgrade the skills of existing mechanical and electrical staff and to recruit more highly qualified technicians. Among the craft and technical personnel in particularly short supply are welders and fabricators, electronics and communication specialists, instrumentation and control technicians, and specialists in condition monitoring and automation. Strategies for developing the skills of engineering staff are discussed in Chapter 8.

6.2.9 The Development of Technician Teams

The increasing use of complex assemblies of mechanical, hydraulic and electrical (more recently, electronic) components in cargo-handling equipment has strengthened the need for multi-skilled teams of technicians to perform a range of maintenance and repair tasks. Having such teams of technicians, regularly working together as a close-knit group, gives the maintenance manager a great deal of flexibility when planning and allocating work, and also allows adoption of the valuable strategy of assigning a team to a particular category of equipment for an extended period; the group thereby acquires considerable collaborative fluency and also becomes very familiar with the construction and working of that type of machine.

There are, of course, two ways to achieve such a multi-skilled team: by assembling a group of specialist technicians, each an expert in just one craft or trade, or by training each technician to be an expert in a range of trade skills – the multi-skilled technician. However, it is unreasonable to expect any technician to become equally skilled in *all* the trades needed in a workshop team, and so the ideal technician for the multi-skilled team is one who has been trained specifically in one skill (e.g. as an electrician) but has also received general training in other skills (e.g. mechanical and hydraulic maintenance) and is able to undertake 'non-specialized' work in those areas, too. It is a team of such specialist-generalists that gives maintenance managers and planners that flexibility that they need.

6.2.10 Staffing Levels

In many LDC ports, too many staff are employed in the Engineering Department, so that output per man is low, maintenance costs are high, and the teams employed on a job are too large, causing interference and inefficiency. This contrasts starkly with the small, close-knit teams of technicians employed in European ports, highly efficient and easily supervised.

Engineering managers in LDC ports must tackle the question of appropriate manning, using the recent experience of the ports of developed countries as a guide. The starting point must be the volume of work passing through the workshops and the setting of work values for those jobs. Engineers should make a point of asking, whenever they visit another port, what work values are applied there, and look for published information on the times needed to complete routine maintenance tasks. Work-study techniques will probably have to be applied locally to establish or confirm such values, in association with the Engineering Department's own records of work productivity. Manning levels for technical staff can then be set accordingly, reflecting European practice but taking into account local conditions (of available facilities and technical skills). A suitable team size for a workshop would be about three or four men, and perhaps two teams would be needed per shift in a medium-sized workshop; the actual numbers needed will, of course, vary considerably according to circumstances.

Then appropriate supervisory staff levels must be set, sufficient to ensure efficient and safe engineering practices, effective control of the work in progress, and good quality control. It is important not to over-supervise – it is the technical staff, after all, who will be performing the bulk of the maintenance work – but a suggested ratio would be one supervisor to two technician teams (i.e. to 6-8 men). The foremen will report to a Shift Superintendent – at a ratio of perhaps three or four foremen per Superintendent – and the three Shift Superintendents at a workshop will be directly responsible to the Workshop Manager.

Such a staffing level results in a lean, efficient and well-supervised maintenance operation, and illustrates good principles of management organization, in that the span of control is reasonably compact and there are few hierarchical levels of authority. Each employee is close to his immediate superior, and accountability can easily be practised and assessed.

6.2.11 Hours of Work

There are ways of improving the present efficiency of engineering services by revising the organization of shifts and staff working times in the maintenance workshops. Some LDC ports have a very long way to go in this respect, as this study has revealed. In some ports, maintenance staff are reluctant to work night shifts or at weekends, even though cargo-handling operations are offered on a 24-hour basis, 7 days a week. Not surprisingly, there are frequently delays in response to equipment failures at these ports, and units are regularly out of action for long periods. Because engineering staff work day shifts only, any emergency call-out at night or at weekends, for essential maintenance and repair work, has to be paid at overtime rates, which reduces the cost-effectiveness of maintenance.

Another problem of organizing engineering shift-working to match that of operations is that, when operations staff are particularly busy (usually the day-shift) cargo-handling equipment is under its heaviest use and is least available for maintenance, so workshop staff are often idle. Then, when cargo-handling is slackest and the equipment most conveniently available for maintenance (normally the night-shift or at weekends), the workshop staff are off-duty and there is, at best, skeletal manning. Clearly, a better balance of shift-working is needed, with maintenance staff hours matched to the slackest cargo-handling activity. If flexible working hours were to be introduced, engineering efficiency would be very much improved. For example, if vessel arrivals are known to 'bunch' towards the end of the week, engineering shifts should be biased to the first few days. If operations staff regularly work two shifts, workshops staff should be at their most numerous during the third, unworked shift. It should also be possible for the Workshop Manager to call in maintenance teams when there are unexpected breaks in cargo-handling activity, e.g. if a vessel is delayed or a call is postponed, or when it is known (from the Ship Arrivals Planning desk) that there will be a lull in activity.

The overall aim must be to ensure that, when equipment is available for maintenance work, technicians are on hand to take advantage of it; maintenance work must be scheduled for when it is least likely to reduce equipment availability to operators. That is not to say, of course, that workshop staff should not work during peak cargo-handling hours; obviously, equipment inevitably breaks down occasionally when operating, even in the best-run port, and accidents will also occur on times. So stand-by teams of technicians must be available whenever the berths and terminals are working. In this context, it is worth considering the advantages of staggering workshop and operations staff working hours; peak demand for emergency repairs are likely to arise later in a shift rather than earlier, and there might be benefits in starting the engineering shifts an hour or two later than operations shifts.

So the general message is to examine carefully the peak demands for engineering services as they occur during the day and over the week, and to arrange workshop hours accordingly. Managers should try to organize flexible working, so that they can offer to operations staff the ideal service and meet their one main objective: to provide operators with the equipment they need, in first-class condition, whenever they need it.

6.3 Maintenance Policies, Strategies and Tactics

6.3.1 Maintenance Policies

A feature of the visits made to the various organizations in this study is the diversity of their maintenance policies and strategies; no two ports seem to follow exactly the same approach to maintenance. The differences are just as marked between European ports as they are between those and LDC ports. Some ports adopt a uniform policy for all their equipment, others are more flexible, varying their policy for different types of equipment or different circumstances, and yet others appear to have no formal policy whatever. The evidence accumulatated during the survey, and summarized in Section 6.1, indicates that port maintenance in LDCs is generally in a very poor state, and that these ports urgently need to review their approach to maintenance, consider the options and formulate an appropriate maintenance policy.

It is possible to divide the different approaches to maintenance into three broad categories of policy options:

1. *Preventive Maintenance*, based on routine inspection of equipment at prescribed intervals or at set times, is designed to take action before failure occurs;

2. *Corrective Maintenance* involves the carrying out of repairs when equipment has failed – a policy of repair after failure;

3. *Designing-out Maintenance* is a longer-term policy which attempts to eliminate (generally through a succession of small improvements) the need for maintenance.

These approaches to maintenance will be considered in turn in this section, and then their role in the development of maintenance plans, strategies and tactics will be discussed.

6.3.2 Preventive Maintenance

6.3.2.1 Introduction

Preventive maintenance systems attempt to predict when equipment assemblies and components are likely to fail and to replace them (or adjust them) before failure actually occurs. This can be achieved in several different ways. For example, components can be changed at set time intervals (Fixed Time Maintenance) or when inspection indicates that they are beginning to deteriorate (Condition-Based Maintenance). They can also be changed when the equipment is under maintenance for another reason, or when it becomes unexpectedly available for examination (Opportunity Maintenance). All these approaches have in common the aim of taking action before the equipment begins to cause problems, and the desire to plan and schedule maintenance in advance, rather than to react to an unexpected emergency.

In this section, these three varieties of Preventive Maintenance will be discussed in turn.

6.3.2.2 Fixed Time Maintenance

Most ports adopt a policy of preventive maintenance based on fixed time intervals, either as the sole method or in combination with others. Maintenance schedules are usually established on the basis of manufacturers' recommendations: parts are replaced, or lubricating oil is changed, after a stated period of life – say, every month or every three months. Such a schedule also specifies regular inspections and checks on the condition of systems, sub-assemblies and components, the most familiar of which are the daily pre-shift inspections of radiator water level, battery electrolyte level, lubricating oil level and tyre pressures and condition.

There are considerable benefits in such a policy, particularly in ports where the level of engineering skill is limited:

— It is completely deterministic;
— It is simple to follow;
— It is particularly easy to plan;
— It allows a maintenance programme for a fleet of machines to be scheduled without difficulty.

Fixed Time Maintenance or Systematic Maintenance (Gonon, 1987) is, perhaps, the ideal way of achieving good maintenance with the minimum of diagnostic and planning skills and with limited resources, and should result in high availability of equipment and few breakdowns in service. The only difficulty reported in applying such a scheme in LDC ports is that some technicians have problems in reading and interpreting the manufacturers' maintenance manuals; this needs to be determined when a machine is delivered, and the manufacturers should be requested to provide a simplified maintenance schedule in the local language (as discussed in Chapter 4).

However, there are significant shortcomings in adhering rigidly to Fixed Time Maintenance of this type. First, it does not take into account the degree of use of a machine; on the same berth, one forklift truck may work for 100 hours in a week while another may only be active for 50 hours, yet both would receive their three-monthly service at that prescribed interval. It would be more economical, clearly, if one were to be serviced at half the time interval of the other. While this might not matter a great deal if the components and materials exchanged at the Fixed Time Interval services are low-cost items that can be changed quickly, it will certainly make a difference if they are expensive (particularly if they have to be purchased overseas, in foreign currency) or if there are several man-hours of technician's labour involved. Obviously, in either of those cases it is very desirable that parts be changed only when they need to be. There is also a persuasive argument that it is preferable not to open up systems and assemblies and to dismantle them unnecessarily; while removing an inspection cover to examine, say, the brush gear of an electric motor, should cause no problems, provided it is done carefully, there is a tendency in some LDC ports for dismantling for inspection to be taken to extremes. Such an approach to 'maintenance' can *cause* problems as well as curing them.

A more logical and effective approach is to base the Fixed Time Intervals on hours of work, rather than hours of life. That would, at the very least, overcome the problem of the differentially worked forklift trucks, mentioned above. As discussed in Chapter 5, the most reliable data on which to base such periodic maintenance are those derived from equipment logbooks or, still better, from hour-meter readings. This approach certainly reduces the danger of 'over-maintaining', and applies considerably less pressure on the workshops than the rigid hours-of-life policy. The main difficulty of applying it is, as described many times in this survey, the paucity of reliable operational data in many LDC ports, making it almost impossible to be sure when a machine has completed 500 hours of work; in such cases, Systematic Maintenance based on the calendar is safer.

Another objection, repeatedly mentioned by engineers in Europe, is that scepticism about the basis for the manufacturers' recommended intervals appears well-founded. They are, it is commonly believed, unnecessarily cautious. So, while they may be accepted provisionally when a new type of equipment is procured, they should be treated as the basis for experiment and modification in the light of experience. Several European engineers reported that they have gradually increased maintenance intervals without giving rise to reliability problems; in one case, straddle carrier service intervals were progress-

ively lengthened from 250 hours to 500 hours, 750 hours and eventually to 1000 hours, without detrimental effect. At another port, service intervals (for a different model of straddle carrier) were increased from 250 to 350 and then 500 hours, before compromising in the light of operational experience at 350 hours. In a well-run port, then, with a good Engineering Department, it is quite possible to adjust the Fixed Time Intervals to a realistic and safe set of hours-of-work schedules, for each category of equipment, taking into account local working and engineering conditions. This makes the policy far more cost-effective than relying unquestioningly on manufacturers' schedules.

The adoption of such an adjusted Fixed Time Maintenance (or Predictive Maintenance – Gonon, 1987) policy depends, of course, on having a very comprehensive and reliable EMIS; it cannot be operated without a full set of operational and engineering records, constantly updated with engineers' observations on the state of the equipment under the various maintenance regimes, and of data on the unexpected failure or deterioration of systems and components, and periodically adjusted in the light of experience. It also needs to be backed up, particularly during the initial investigative phase, by an efficient and rapid repair-on-breakdown system, as there is undoubtedly an element of risk in it. To a large extent, the time intervals chosen have to reflect a nice balance between the cost of a particular service and the cost of disruption to operations caused by a breakdown.

There is also the objection that Fixed Time Interval maintenance is, to some extent, based on a fallacy: it assumes that component or material deterioration and failure are perfectly time-dependent, when in practice no component can be guaranteed to *need* replacement after a pre-determined period of working. Inevitably, Fixed Time Maintenance errs on the side of safety, and on many occasions items will be changed before they show signs of deterioration. An alternative policy, which overcomes these objections, is Condition-Based Maintenance.

6.3.2.3 Condition-Based Maintenance
A recent innovation which is gaining acceptance in many industries, and which has been introduced by some of the more successful ports, is maintenance based on condition monitoring. The aim is to inspect all components and systems regularly (with as little disturbance as possible, e.g. via inspection covers), checking on the state of particular items or parameters, and noting any signs of deterioration. The component or system is then changed, adjusted or repaired *just before* it is about to fail. The

advantages of this approach (also known as Conditional Preventive Maintenance – Gonon, 1987) are that:

— the working life of the systems and components is stretched until almost the last moment, and items are only replaced when they need to be;

— intervention is minimized, systems are only dismantled at long intervals, and unintentional damage caused by the maintenance procedures is avoided;

— pressure on the workshops and technicians is as low as possible;

— maintenance scheduling is simplified, as the condition monitoring gives advance warning of the need for servicing;

— equipment reliability is high (providing the condition monitoring is accurate and carried out systematically and reliably) and break-downs in operation are infrequent.

There are two principal difficulties in applying Condition-Based Maintenance, however. The first is the need for an extremely efficient and comprehensive EMIS, to hold and analyse the large amounts of data that have to be recorded; Chapter 9 goes into these factors in some detail, so that all that needs to be said here is that such systems exist, are in routine operation in many of the most successful ports, and there is no genuine obstacle to their widespread use. The second problem is a more serious one: the need to identify parameters which can be routinely and easily monitored (without disturbing systems and assemblies) and which provide a reliable and relevant indicator of the condition of the systems and components that need to be constantly checked.

Some effective forms of condition monitoring have been used, of course, for a very long time. The most obvious is that series of pre-shift checks which are (or should be) undertaken by workshop technicians and/or drivers before any machine leaves the parking depot for work on the berths. Tyre pressure and tread condition checks are perfect examples of condition monitoring, allowing remedial action (tyre inflation or tyre replacement, if tread depth or sidewall condition have reached dangerous levels) on the spot and preventing breakdown in service. Oil, water and battery electrolyte levels can be equally easily checked and faults put right.

Another, equally simple and equally valuable, form of condition monitoring is carried out by the expert driver/operator while cargo-handling or other machinery is being used; he listens for odd noises, watches for undue smoke emission, notices unusual vibrations, observes the instrument panel for meter readings or warning lights. The cabs of recent models of container gantry cranes, rubber-tyred gantry cranes and straddle carriers are particularly well-fitted with diagnostic warning lights and meters, all of which are giving the operator a continuous report on the condition of the engines, motors, ropes, hydraulic systems and electronic control systems. As pointed out in Chapter 5, drivers must be trained to *use* all these monitoring devices, noting any signs and symptoms in the equipment log-book and reporting them to the engineers – immediately, if the warning signal warrants it.

The major advances in condition monitoring in recent years (and which are now taking place at an accelerating pace) involve automatic and semi-automatic systems, either permanently installed within equipment and systems or temporarily attached to them while instrument readings are taken. Whereas driver-based and mechanic-based observational monitoring have been relatively commonly used in developed countries' ports for some time, and are not totally unknown in LDC ports, instrumental and automated monitoring is a much more recent innovation, and is only now beginning to be accepted in European ports. Few examples of its application were noted during the LDC port visits, but one of those ports, at least, has recently purchased a set of monitoring devices and is in the process of establishing baseline data preparatory to implementing the system on a regular basis.

Several on-load and off-load techniques are now available, measuring and recording thermal, vibration and noise parameters in mechanical equipment and components, and current testing in electrical machinery. Detection transducers can either be permanently fitted into a system (for example, vibration detectors in bearings in a conveyor-belt at a bulk terminal, temperature transducers in a gear-box) or temporarily attached to or pressed against an 'anvil' or fixed sensing point when a measurement is taken. The measuring instrument is then attached to the transducer lead and a reading taken, preferably while the machine is working under normal load. In the most recent systems, the complete measuring device can be installed in or near the machine, and its signals transmitted regularly and automatically to a central computer, where they are recorded, analysed and printed out. However, most existing condition monitors depend on a technician taking readings on-site and recording them in a log-book, or recording them in a hand-held computer for transfer to the main system on return to the workshop.

However the readings are taken, the fundamental initial step is to establish a set of bench marks or 'fingerprints' – the 'normal' readings of temperature or vibration/sound frequency – against which changes can be detected. This can take many months of readings and graph plots, but has been found to be perfectly practicable, in both European and LDC ports. The graphs show up clearly and unmistakably any changes in performance. All that then remains is for the engineers to correlate these changes with component condition; this is where the skill comes in, and where experience counts. It is to be hoped that a body of published information will quickly accumulate, to inform engineers of what constitutes the 'norm' for a range of monitored parameters. Manufacturers, too, should provide data on component performance indicators, to provide at least a starting point for port engineers to base their analyses on.

Another form of condition monitoring, which some see as of particular benefit to LDC ports, where diagnostic skills and information systems are poorly developed, is oil analysis. Samples of engine and other oils are taken from significant points at regular intervals and sent or taken for analysis at specially equipped laboratories (in Latin America and North America, independent laboratories have been set up for this purpose, and the major international oil companies are setting up some laboratories in the Third World currently). The analysis not only informs engineers about the condition of the lubricant, and warns of the need for oil changes, but – much more importantly – can provide a great deal of information about the state of the engine or system from which the samples were derived. Chemical analyses and microscopic examination for metal and other particles can, with experience, reveal a vast amount of information about the condition of the equipment, and the resulting report can pinpoint exactly where adjustment is needed, and which components need replacing.

The only drawback of oil analysis is that it is expensive at the moment, and would not be cost-effective for relatively inexpensive equipment (conventional forklift trucks, for example); figures of $7,000 a year per machine are quoted currently for three tests per month, which might restrict its application to the higher-powered, more complex and more expensive equipment used on container and bulk terminals. Even so, if the system resulted in the prevention of major damage to a heavy-duty engine or hoist, avoiding a straddle carrier or gantry crane being out of service for an extended period, oil analysis could well prove cost-effective. Even savings on lubricants themselves could be sufficient incentive; one Latin American port has saved 25%

of its engine oil consumption in one year by using an oil analysis service. If, as seems likely, the service can be provided more cheaply as it becomes used more widely, or if a 'packaged' version of it can be made available for port workshop use, then it is likely to assume increasing importance in the preventive maintenance armoury in the future.

So far, the application of condition-based maintenance in the port transport industry is patchy. In the more efficient ports (particularly in developed countries) and at terminals using expensive and technically sophisticated equipment, it is gaining acceptance steadily. Although some engineers (without firsthand knowledge of condition monitoring) expressed considerable doubts as to its usefulness and cost-effectiveness, others are increasingly enthusiastic. At one bulk terminal, the senior mechanical/electrical engineer reported savings of many tens of thousands of dollars in the first nine months of conveyor-monitoring, in terms of downtime saved by timely replacement of bearings, adjustment of bearing angles and other relatively simple procedures.

Overall, there seems no reason to doubt that condition monitoring will become more and more common in the future. Cargo-handling equipment will be specified with built-in monitoring devices, both intrument- and warning-light-based and automatic. Monitoring devices will be fitted at an increasing rate to existing plant and equipment, and hand-held computers will be used increasingly to record data on site. The improving reliability and reduced size and cost of electronic devices are already making it more and more easy and economic to apply condition monitoring in the field, without the backup of electronic engineers and with the minimum of training. Paradoxically, it could well be argued that the most sophisticated condition monitoring techniques are even more suited to use in LDC ports, where engineering (particularly diagnostic) skills are least well developed and where equipment downtime and repair costs are disproportionately serious, than in developed countries, where engineering facilities and skills are widely available, and where new equipment, parts and manufacturers' help are easily accessible.

6.3.2.4 Opportunity Maintenance
As its name implies, the policy of Opportunity Maintenance is merely that of taking every available opportunity to apply preventive maintenance to the port's equipment – not a complicated principle to grasp, but a very useful one to follow in a busy port. It can be applied in two rather different contexts.

First, it describes the practice of taking advantage of every non-operational period (for example, the delayed arrival of a vessel, or a gap of a few hours or a day between planned vessel arrivals) to rush a maintenance team onto the equipment and to carry out as much preventive maintenance as possible in the time available. It is in this context that Opportunity Maintenance is commonly (almost unavoidably) applied to equipment which has a high or continuous operating time and where the costs of breakdown and unavailability (in terms of labour, parts and delays to ships and cargoes) are high. For example, the policy is the one pursued at bulk terminals, where the cost of ships' delays following equipment breakdown, commonly recovered through demurrage, is very high. Some of the bulk terminals visited experience extremely high berth occupancy – often over 90% – which leaves very little time for scheduling maintenance. When the berth is vacant, maintenance has to be started without delay and completed very quickly.

The type of maintenance practised under such circumstances is a mixture of Fixed-Time Maintenance (the next due preventive maintenance schedule is applied) and Condition-Based Maintenance (any components that have deteriorated sufficiently to make them likely to fail before the next opportunity might arise are replaced). Under these circumstances, it is almost certainly cost-effective to replace *any* doubtful item, unless it is very expensive, as it is impossible to predict when the next 'opportunity' will arise, and breakdown in operation is extremely costly to the port.

The other context in which Opportunity Maintenance is practised relates to more conventional cargo-handling equipment. Basically, the principle is that, whenever a machine is brought into the workshop for, say, repair of accidental damage or a breakdown in operation, the workshop manager or his routing desk officer checks whether that machine is due for a routine preventive maintenance visit within the near future. If it is, the 'opportunity' is taken to carry out that service while the machine is stripped down and under repair. This is a simple concept, easily put into practice (provided there is an effective, easily accessed EMIS to tell the routing desk when a service is due), and one that can be very cost-effective, saving out-of service time for the operators and economizing on workshop staff time.

6.3.3 Corrective Maintenance

Corrective or 'Palliative' (Gonon, 1987) Maintenance is that which is carried out when equipment fails in operation. In itself, it hardly merits being considered as a maintenance *policy* –

after all, every port maintenance facility must include resources and plans to ensure the prompt repair of faults and breakdowns. However, when there is a deliberate decision on the part of senior engineers to 'operate to failure', i.e. to continue to operate machines on the berths, without routine inspections or preventive maintenance, until they break down, then 'Repair on Breakdown' can be thought of as an optional maintenance policy. It cannot be denied that, for one reason or another, many ports (particularly in developing countries) rely largely or completely on corrective maintenance to keep their equipment fleet in (relative) action.

Such 'emergency' or 'fire-fighting' maintenance is practised for several reasons. For example, in ports where engineering skills, management and resources are inadequate, pressure on the workshops is often so high that it is impossible to follow any preventive maintenance schemes, even if there were a will to do so. Again, many LDC ports have either no EMIS or a very unreliable one, so that data on which scheduling should be based are just not available.

The only circumstance under which repair-on-failure is really justified is where an item or component is extremely cheap, has a long (but unpredictable) life and is quick and easy to replace. It is hardly worth building the inspection of such an item into a preventive maintenance schedule, and the penalty of having to repair it during operations, in terms of cost and downtime, is negligible. It is difficult to find any other circumstance under which repair-on-failure can be considered a rational and cost-effective alternative to one or other form of preventive maintenance, as it is almost always more costly to *repair* a faulty system or component than to *prevent* failure occurring, when workshop staff time, workshop overheads and operational delays are taken into account. Only if the port has ample stocks of reserve equipment, readily pressed into service when a machine breaks down, is it operationally acceptable to operate-to-failure – and then it is easily demonstrated that the port is penalizing itself by unnecessary capital investment and additional maintenance demand! There is another overhead in that the Supplies Department has to hold a very wide and full stock of spare parts, as replacement parts *must* be available for any unexpected failure, whereas preventive maintenance, with its regular inspections, usually provides adequate warning of the need to purchase extra spares.

Another serious disadvantage of having a policy of operating-to-failure is that there is no possible way of planning and scheduling work entering the workshops. Inevitably, failures will not occur at convenient intervals, spreading the load on maintenance staff neatly over the working week, but will arise in unpredictable peaks. Various informal 'laws' will ensure that such peak breakdowns occur at the most inconvenient times – when all the berths are occupied by ships, the cargo storage areas are full and all but a standby team of engineers are on holiday! There is, then, little to be said for corrective maintenance being anything but an essential element of a basically preventive-maintenance-based policy; it should not be considered a reasonable option in anything but the most exceptional circumstances.

6.3.4 Designed-Out Maintenance

In contrast with the policies considered above, which attempt to minimize or prevent the effects of equipment failure on cargo-handling operations, designing-out maintenance sets out to eliminate (or, more realistically, significantly reduce) the *need* for maintenance. Engineers have, of course, always been aware of the need to improve design of machinery and plant to make it more reliable in operation (or, at least, they *should*), but it is only recently that this has reached the point where it can be considered a formal *policy*. It is certainly a highly desirable principle, particularly with respect to plant with high maintenance costs and whose failure has a significant impact on the cost of cargo-handling operations.

The need for maintenance can be reduced considerably at the specification and design stages when procuring new equipment. Structures should, for example, be so specified and designed that they suit closely the conditions in which they are to be located and used. Careful structural design, and the equally careful choice of materials and finishes, can eliminate the causes of rust and other types of corrosion, of metal fatigue and other incipient maintenance problems. For example, rust can be prevented or delayed by designing the frame of a straddle carrier or gantry crane so that the surfaces shed water and so that there are no pockets to trap pools of water. Similarly, in areas of the world where humidity is high (and inevitably, in seaports, salty!) electrical components, such as relays and switches, and electronic modules can be protected against corrosion by encapsulating them, placing them within enclosed racks, and then housing the complete system within an air-conditioned electrical 'room' built into the structure of the equipment (for example, a rubber-tyred gantry crane or quayside container crane).

These principles have been applied for some time, but more recently port engineers have begun to take an active and informed interest in more detailed aspects of equipment design, to the extent of experimenting with modifications, building rigs and changing system specifications, with the aim of reducing maintenance. The stepping-off point for much of this work is a comprehensive EMIS. Analyses of equipment and component histories pinpoint areas where faults are common and repair and preventive maintenance costly, and suggest ways in which improvements are both possible and economically worthwhile. For example, the engineers at one major port visited were particularly enthusiastic about designing-out maintenance – largely because maintenance engineers receive very high salaries and workshop services are accordingly expensive. They have modified the suspension of their straddle carriers, using a novel plastic-based material for the springs, and claim that the life of the unit has been extended indefinitely by so doing; previously, the suspension unit had to be replaced quite frequently. By changing their tractor water-cooled engines to air-cooled alternatives, and by modifying the individual greasing points to a central lubricating system, they have greatly extended maintenance intervals. Although these (and other) modifications, which are now available off-the-shelf from the manufacturers, have increased the purchase price of the units, they have greatly reduced maintenance costs.

It might be argued that the adoption of this policy is only practicable in ports whose engineers have considerable expertise – and the time necessary to undertake the necessary research and development – and that its benefits are likely to be felt only in the long term. However, it can be counter-argued that LDC ports are in a position to benefit from developments of this sort arising from work in the ports of Europe and North America, since they are (or should be) available in new models from the manufacturers. All that is needed is for port engineers to keep abreast of the developments, by reading the professional literature and trade magazines, by attending conferences and generally keeping in touch with engineers in other ports, and by cross-questioning manufacturers' representatives closely when procurement of new equipment is being planned.

There is no reason, either, why the many excellent engineers in the ports of developing countries should not take a close interest in the equipment being used in their own ports, watching it in operation and monitoring its maintenance, as well as examining closely the analyses of the EMIS data, so that they can identify systems and components that are causing particular maintenance problems under their conditions. They may not be in a position to undertake research and modification of those items, but could well be able to interest the manufacturers is doing so; it is certainly in the interests of the latter to take notice of any such possible beneficial modifications. As a long-term policy, designing-out maintenance has a great deal to commend it, and engineers must take every opportunity to support it.

6.3.5 Development of a Maintenance Plan

Evidence collected during this survey indicates that engineers in many LDC ports have not properly thought-through the options available for the maintenance of equipment and other port assets, and have not adopted appropriate and cost-effective policies. As already mentioned repeatedly, one of the causes is the lack of an effective EMIS providing reliable data on which to base the selection of a policy. As equipment increases in complexity and cost, and as delays to ships and cargo become more and more expensive, so the need for an effective maintenance plan becomes more pressing. The correct choice will allow managers to plan and control maintenance more precisely.

In practice, the choice of maintenance policy will be a compromise between what is desirable and what is attainable under given circumstances, and the port's maintenance plan will include a number of approaches, relating to the various types of equipment used and the components they contain, but with the unified aim of minimizing maintenance costs and total equipment operating costs. For example, a port's maintenance plan for its straddle carrier fleet might be for 'hours-of-work-based preventive maintenance', within which will be 500-hour, 750-hour and 1,000-hour schedules, with listed procedures for individual systems, sub-systems and components.

Among the factors to be considered when selecting an appropriate policy are the port's previous experience of particular types of equipment, component failure rates and repair times, spare parts availability, the skills of the technicians and the facilities available in the workshops, the support available from manufacturers and external contractors, and the costs of maintenance from the alternative sources. Developing a maintenance plan requires the systematic analysis of these factors and the available options (not ignoring the possibility of modifying some of the factors to suit the plan; for example, workshop resources can be upgraded, and technicians can be given further training, stores procedures and management can be improved), with the aim of making the best use of the engineering facilities and maximizing the availability and working life of the equipment.

6.3.6 Maintenance Strategies

6.3.6.1 Introduction

Strategic decisions on where equipment preventive maintenance and repair will be undertaken are of vital importance at the time of formulating a maintenance plan. Ports surveyed in this study have adopted a wide range of strategies in this respect, from, at one extreme, ports which undertake *all* maintenance of plant, craft, civil works and mobile equipment themselves, to the other extreme where all maintenance is contracted out, to one or more external organizations, and the ports' Engineering Department merely acts as a co-ordinator and supervisor of these activities. These options are briefly discussed in this section.

6.3.6.2 On-Site Maintenance

Most of the ports visited and surveyed, particularly those in developing countries, are responsible for all or most of their own maintenance work. Only a few reported that certain specialist work is carried out by external contractors or equipment suppliers, and several explained that they are obliged to maintain internally because no external contractors are available locally – or at least none of adequate quality – and because they are unable to obtain support from equipment manufacturers or their local agents (where there are any).

Adopting this strategy compels a port to provide extensive workshop facilities and equipment and to employ technicians with a wide range of skills, whatever the level of demand for individual services. Overheads can be very high under these circumstances, and maintenance can easily be more expensive – particularly in a relatively small port – than if it were to be contracted out. On the other hand, on-site maintenance gives engineers maximum flexibility and control when scheduling maintenance and planning equipment allocation; many ports will gladly pay the price to retain such control.

6.3.6.3 External Maintenance Contracts

A trend observed during this study, and detected in the literature, is for ports in both developed and developing countries to contract out more and more of their maintenance. Only a small minority of ports rely exclusively or even largely on contractors as yet, but a substantial number stated that specific categories of maintenance are now regularly contracted out. Particularly significant is the growth of maintenance contracts between ports and their equipment and system (e.g. engine) suppliers.

In developed countries, the primary objective of the increasing dependency on contract work, particularly on bulk terminals, in the past decade is to reduce departmental overhead costs, by having fewer technicians in the Engineering Department. In European ports, where this strategy is common, it is possible because of the many competent engineering companies, component suppliers, manufacturers' agents and representatives – and even equipment manufacturers themselves – operating near the ports and offering competitive and competent services. Contracts often started with such minor, specialist services as motor rewinding, but have spread to full engine overhauls, tyre replacement, fabrication and complete refurbishment of equipment.

The scope for expansion of external maintenance contracts in developing countries is rather limited. There are often no competent local engineering companies near the ports and, even if there were, they would have difficulty in purchasing and holding spares. It is rare for manufacturers to have local agents – at least with anything approaching the required competence. It is unlikely that these problems will be resolved, either, as conditions are so different from, say, Western Europe. External contractors there can offer economic prices for maintenance because they can expect a high throughput of work from a wide catchment area, keeping their overheads down. In a developing country, the port may be the only major user of cargo-handling equipment – possibly the only heavy engineering industry in the locality – and it is difficult to see how a contractor could hope to service its machines any more cheaply or more efficiently than the port itself. Only the more general services (such as motor rewinding, overhauls of standard truck and tractor engines, welding and fabrication) are likely to become available, even in the longer term.

An alternative approach is, however, discernible in LDC ports: annual or similar maintenance contracts taken out with the equipment manufacturers. For example, in one of the ports visited, the container terminal company has entered into contracts with the two suppliers of its cargo-handling equipment, at a cost of $500,000 a year. The contract requires the manufacturers to retain a small permanent staff on site, and to supply all necessary spare parts. Senior managers justify the expense by the security the arrangement provides. Similar arrangements are more usual in relation to technical assistance projects funded by aid agencies, where manufacturers of the supplied equipment place maintenance staff on site during and after the commissioning of equipment, to help to establish an adequate maintenance facility, to carry out the first few services, and to provide some training for local technicians. However, such arrangements rarely last long enough to be really effective, even when a substantial fleet of equipment is involved.

Although external contracts offer the potential for substantial cost savings and a more reliable service, they will only be effective if properly co-ordinated with port operations, and if managed closely to preserve maintenance standards. There was evidence that, in some cases, inadequate control had led to long delays in returning equipment to the port and to higher maintenance costs than would have been the case if the work had been performed in-house. Indeed, few ports seem prepared to risk contracting out *all* their maintenance, even where competent external organizations are available to do it, and the more likely pattern to develop (in Europe, at least) is for all preventive maintenance and most routine repairs to be undertaken by the port, leaving major overhauls and specialist work to be contracted out. European ports are fortunate in having a selection of very competent local suppliers and contractors, in a highly competitive market, able and eager to become contractors and offering a guarantee of keeping equipment in as-specified condition.

In developing countries, similar contracts would be very beneficial for many ports, should they become available. The most likely trend, however, is for more contracts to be taken out with manufacturers and suppliers, particularly for assisting port engineers over the transition period when new technology is introduced. Such contracts are expensive – and paid in foreign currency – but they undoubtedly can (and do) work well. They must not be short-term ventures, however, but must last until local technicians have acquired all the relevant skills, knowledge and experience – at least five years should be the norm. International agencies have not appreciated the time required to transfer technological skills from the developed to the developing world; it is important that they do so.

6.3.7 Maintenance Tactics
At the tactical level, within the Engineering Department's maintenance strategy, a major choice to be made is whether assemblies and components should be removed from a piece of equipment, on failure, and immediately replaced with a serviceable unit, or should the workshop staff repair the fault and replace the original unit before returning the equipment to service? There are subsidiary decisions, too: if a component is exchanged, should it then be refurbished (and returned to the stores for future use) or scrapped? If the item is to be refurbished, should this be done in-house or contracted out?

Several factors influence the repair/replace decision, but the major factor is the cost of equipment unavailability. Fault diagnosis and repair take time, tying up maintenance resources and valuable cargo-handling equipment in the process. If equipment is out of service for long periods while assemblies are stripped down and repaired, operations can be considerably delayed. It is largely because of this that many ports now make extensive use of the tactic of component exchange; they hold stocks of systems, subsystems and assemblies (from complete engines and electric motors to printed circuit boards), ready to exchange for faulty units; ports commonly purchase such exchange units when acquiring a fleet of equipment, e.g. for every 20 tractors they might buy two replacement diesel engines. The exchange operation is completed quickly and the equipment is returned to Operations with minimum delay, while the faulty system is repaired and reconditioned at leisure and then returned to stock for future use.

A related tactic is to exchange regularly components which are inexpensive and simple to replace – such items as spark plugs. These, too, may be cleaned, adjusted and later used as exchange items – a process hardly worth doing in developed countries, where new components are available quickly and cheaply, but possibly of great value in an LDC port, where all spares are difficult to obtain and require foreign currency. The only uncertainty about such a tactic is at what intervals to exchange the item; the intervals need to be short enough to ensure that no breakdowns or reductions in performance result from their non-exchange, and not too short to make the operation uneconomic. Opportunity Maintenance would be the appropriate strategy within which to fit this tactic.

In many ports, exchange items are not held in stock – or at least they are rarely held in sufficient quantities to ensure their constant availability – and it is the common practice to remove parts from another machine awaiting repair. The principle underlying such 'cannibalization' is that it is better to get one machine back into service than to have two sitting in the workshop awaiting (different) spare parts. There are certainly circumstances when the tactic has merit, particularly if the cannibalized unit is in a relatively poor state, has been out of service for some time and is likely to remain so because the particular spare parts needed to repair it are unlikely to be delivered soon. The danger is, however, that the practice will become endemic and customary, and that it is not controlled.

In several of the ports visited, it was obvious that cannibalization is the rule, rather than the exception, and the workshop areas are littered with semi-derelict machines from which many (sometimes most) parts have been removed; these machines are unlikely ever to see operational service again. The senior engineers *must* make strict rules in relation to cannibalization:

— no component or assembly should ever be removed without the authorization of a senior manager (at least the workshop manager);

— the removal must be recorded immediately on *both* Job Cards (that relating to the machine from which the part is removed *and* that for the machine under current active maintenance);

— at least one replacement part must be ordered immediately;

— as soon as that part is delivered, it must be installed in the cannibalized machine – and all relevant records and Job Cards annotated accordingly;

— unauthorized removal of any assemblies, sub-assemblies or components must be *strictly* forbidden.

6.3.8. Debriefing Meetings
A very productive tactic in the drive toward improvement of port maintenance is to hold regular informal 'debriefing' meetings of workshop and other engineering staff, possibly restricted to individual working units (one technician team and its foreman, or one workshop), possibly open to larger groups of engineers. At these meetings, staff could report on problems recently experienced and solved, could suggest improvements to strategies, tactics and practices, discuss performance targets set, missed or achieved and generally review the past week's or month's work.

At one European port, the entire technical staff meet for 'breakfast meetings' on Saturdays (unpaid, and out of normal working hours), and all have the opportunity to express their views, to question senior staff and to receive information on the terminal's activities. Such meetings are extremely useful for building the team spirit so valuable to a modern port, as well as motivating the workforce and promoting improvements to maintenance performance. Smaller group meetings can also form the basis for quality circles (see Section 6.6.6).

6.4 Maintenance Facilities

6.4.1 Range of Facilities
The range of maintenance facilities required by a port depends on the maintenance policies, strategies and tactics pursued – particularly the extent of the port's reliance on the services of external contractors. Those whose policy it is to provide a full range of services to its marine craft, civil works and cargo-handling operations may need the following types of facilities:

Slipways	Electrical supply workshop
Dry docks	Locomotive workshop
Lay-up berths	Carpentry workshop
Marine workshop	Workshop stores
Central workshop	Central stores
Satellite workshops	Fuel stores
Terminal workshops	Fuel tankers
Lubricating truck	Mobile crane-servicing unit

Whether it is worthwhile to provide all these facilities obviously depends on the level of use they will receive. It is unrealistic for a port to construct or to continue to maintain such expensive facilities as slipways and dry docks if it has few marine craft and their maintenance is intermittent; external contractors could be used instead (if available) or a nearby port or naval dockyard, or the port could make do with makeshift facilities, perhaps beaching the craft on the foreshore for routine hull inspection and maintenance – after all, most routine mechanical maintenance can be done afloat. Similarly, specialized workshop facilities such as foundries, fabrication sections and electrical/electronic clean-rooms are only economic if there is sufficient demand for them and there are no suitable local contractors.

So, when planning a new port, or when periodically reviewing a port's maintenance function (an exercise which should take place regularly within the port's planning sections and committees), senior managers must identify the full extent of the maintenance activities likely to be needed within the port:

— what specialist workshops will be needed?

— which activities can be combined within one central workshop?

— should satellite and/or terminal workshops be set up?

— can all marine mechanical/electrical maintenance be carried out in the central workshop?

— will there be sufficient shaft grinding/aligning and other specialized work to justify the establishment (or retention) of a large marine workshop?

Clearly, several policy and strategy options are open to the port.

If it has been decided that a series of workshops are justified, the next decision concerns where they are to be located. Satellite and terminal workshops should be as close to their related operational areas as possible, to minimize travel distances and response times – but not so close as to interfere with equipment activities and flow patterns. Workshop stores, holding spare parts and consumables in regular use and with a high turnover, should be located adjacent to or within the workshop, while strategic spares should be held in a central stores (which will probably also house the offices of the Supplies administration). Fuel and lubricant stores must be sited in a secure and safe location which is convenient for mobile equipment to visit or from which materials can easily be distributed to plant in operation. Open maintenance areas, fitted with suitable platforms and access structures, are also necessary for large mobile plant (straddle carriers, rubber-tyred gantry cranes), and equipment parks are also needed to serve as depots for the port's fleets of cargo-handling equipment.

All these facilities should be reviewed regularly, to ensure that they continue to meet the port's needs at a time of rapid change within the industry. Developments must not be allowed to happen in an *ad hoc* and unplanned way; it is almost always possible to find means of improving efficiency by careful redesign and relocation of facilities, but it is far better to get the decisions right in the first place.

6.4.2 Central Workshop Layout

A large central workshop will need to provide a wide range of mechanical, electrical and other services for the port's equipment stock, and these should be organized and laid out following good, practical principles.

1. The first of these is **segregation** of the different activities: specialist separated-off areas or 'shops' are needed to accommodate engine and transmission overhaul, machining, fabrication and welding, foundry work, and electric motor and component overhaul. These activities must be kept separate so that they do not interfere with each other.

This is best achieved by dividing the central workshop into distinct areas for mechanical maintenance, for electrical maintenance, for steel work and fabrication, for tyre replacement and repair, and for engine reconditioning. Separate working areas should be set aside for forklift trucks, for tractors, trailers and other mobile equipment, into which these vehicles can be driven easily. Clean work (overhaul of hydraulic system components, diesel engine injection systems, electronic and electrical repairs) must be kept completely separate from dirty work (battery maintenance and charging, welding, foundry work and forging), by segregating it in special rooms, with filtered air or, preferably, full air-conditioning.

A central workshop maintaining equipment used in conventional general cargo operations is

143

likely to need to provide the following facilities, services and amenities:

1. Cleaning bay
2. Mobile crane maintenance area
3. Tyre change area
4. 35t lift truck maintenance area
5. Trailer maintenance area
6. 5t lift truck/tractor/vehicle area
7. 3t forklift truck maintenance area
8. Steel and fabrication area
9. Engine reconditioning area
10. Electrical maintenance area
11. Tools store
12. Shower, WC
13. Personal lockers
14. Rest-room
15. Meeting room
16. Supervisor's office
17. Routing desk
18. Administrative office
19. Workshop manager's office
20. Fuel station

The numbers before the listed items refer to the model layout for a central workshop illustrated in Fig. 6.4.2 (taken from Jerusel, 1988), which is intended to serve a six-berth general cargo port and incorporates the general principles discussed in this section.

2. The second principle of good workshop layout is **integration**: all the equipment, tools, spare parts and supporting facilities required to carry out a particular maintenance task must be located close to the work area. Each area or 'shop' must be as self-contained as possible, to avoid delays in collecting tools, etc. for the job.

3. The third principle is good **space utilization** – making best use of the available ground floor area and vertical space. Floor space must be sufficient for equipment to manoeuvre and park, for maintenance equipment (portable workbenches, jacks, trolleys etc.) to be moved in, and to allow such activities as tyre replacement to take place. Vertical space should be exploited by installing storage racking and by locating offices (for managerial, supervisory and clerical staff) and amenities above workshop floor level wherever possible.

4. A fourth principle is **sensible location**: activities should be located so as to permit a logical flow of work during the maintenance sequence. Where possible, drive-through should be provided for, with doors on opposite walls; this makes it much easier and less dangerous to manoeuvre trailers and broken-down equipment into and out of the building. The doorways must be big enough for the tallest and widest equipment envisaged to be maintained in the workshop, and fitted with roller doors which can be opened just high enough to suit the work being done.

5. The final principle is **safe working**: the workshop must be planned to be as safe as possible to work in. Incompatible activities should be separated to avoid interference and

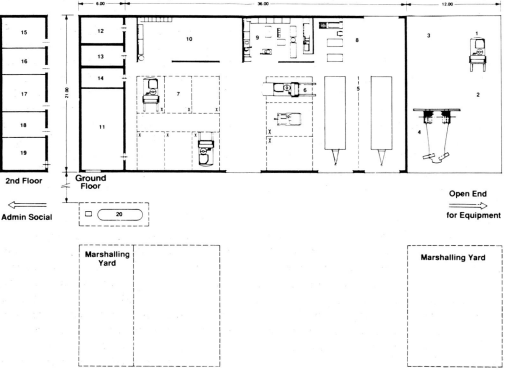

Figure 6.4.2: Layout of Central Workshop for Conventional Cargo Handling Equipment

danger – battery charging must be confined to a separate room (because of the gases discharged in the process and the corrosive nature of the materials used), and tyre inflation needs to be isolated within a safety cage. Curtains are useful for segregating dangerous activities, and walkways and safety rails need to be installed around all stairs and high working platforms. Firefighting equipment must be located wherever there are potential fire risks. Floors should be easy to clean (all oil spillages must be removed immediately) and provided with a non-slip surface.

6.4.3 Workshop Services and Facilities

Among the many services that need to be installed at the workshop is a steam or high-pressure water cleaning apparatus, so that parts or all of a piece of equipment can be thoroughly cleaned before being worked on – and, indeed, at regular intervals during its working life, to keep it in good condition. All workshop buildings also need good general lighting, as well as additional 'spot' lighting for individual work areas, benches and machine tools. A compressed air supply should be provided, with outlets at appropriate work points, and a ring-main electricity supply must be installed for portable and mounted tools and machines. Hand-tools should be powered from a low-voltage main; in the UK, for example, the system must be supplied from a centre-tapped transformer providing 110 V (plus and minus 55 V relative to earth potential).

Among other facilities needed are inspection pits and elevating ramps, to allow access to the underside of vehicles. One European port's Engineering Department has elaborated on that requirement by building the entire central workshop over a basement, with several sets of stairs leading to it from the ground floor, and with a series of bays within it, open to the main floor above and fitted with tool and spares racks. The technicians in that workshop have unparalleled access to the vehicles parked above the bays, and can work on them in complete comfort. The engineers claim that the extra expense is more than paid back in terms of speed and quality of maintenance work on its forklifts, tractors and other vehicles.

The workshop also requires to be fitted with such lifting devices as overhead cranes (remotely controlled from the workshop floor) and portable hoists for safely lifting the heaviest components and assemblies into and out of the equipment, and moving them around the workshop bays. In specialist straddle carrier workshops, movable and elevatable platforms are needed so that technicians can work safely and conveniently at all heights. Fixed platforms are also useful.

The central workshop should be supported by a mobile workshop, equipped to carry out repairs and routine maintenance in operational areas. Not only is this essential for the rapid repair of breakdowns of small mobile cargo-handling equipment on location, but also for all work on quayside cranes, rail-mounted yard gantry cranes, conveyors and other bulk handling plant and for mobile cranes and rubber-tyred yard gantry cranes which cannot be accommodated in the workshops. The van should be fitted with a workbench, vices and a range of hand tools and measuring instruments, as well as a comprehensive stock of such small spares as hoses, fuses, plugs and cables, nuts and bolts, washers, grease guns and lubricating oils. The aim is to enable general maintenance and minor repairs to be carried out where equipment is located, with the minimum of specific preparation and delay.

6.4.4 Workshop Equipment

The range of equipment and tools needed in the workshop will depend on the type of work undertaken there; in most ports, this is likely to be extensive. In many of the LDC ports visited, however, the supply of machine and hand tools falls far short of what the engineers need, in quantity, variety and quality.

Since most LDC ports carry out their own fabrication and machining, such machine tools as universal lathes, shapers, vertical and horizontal milling machines, welding facilities, pedestal drills, and reboring, honing, crankshaft grinding and line boring machines will need to be available. Machines of these types were certainly seen at many of the ports, but often their age and condition make it very unlikely that they would be capable of precise work. At some ports, on the other hand, even the oldest machine tools had clearly been well looked after and were being expertly used; there is no reason why this should not have been the case at all the ports.

Another range of equipment needed includes such test and measuring equipment as pressure gauges, electrical multimeters and oscilloscopes, test pumps, micrometers and gauges. These, too, seem to be in very short supply in many LDC ports, and there is a particular shortage of electronic measuring and test equipment.

Hand tools are, of course, of fundamental importance to maintenance engineers, and a crucial aspect of workshop management is the way these are distributed to the technicians. There appear to be three general approaches. In many LDC ports, all hand tools are held centrally in a tool store, and they are issued from there to technicians on request. This practice is followed both to safeguard the workshop stock against loss (tools seem regularly to be 'mislaid' or pilfered) and to ration those tools not available in sufficient numbers to issue them permanently to all technicians. The problem with this degree of control is that it inevitably causes delays to maintenance, as technicians collect (and sign for) tools and return them after use – there are also problems of non-return, causing further delays as tools are searched for. There is also the point that the practice does not help to create trust between workshop staff or to foster good man-management relations.

A more appropriate practice – and the one almost universally followed in European ports – is to provide each technician, on appointment, with his own tool box and personal set of hand tools. The technician signs for these and assumes full responsibility for them as long as he is in employment at the port, not only keeping them safely but also maintaining them in good condition. Special tools that are only needed occasionally are held in the workshop tool store, and issued on presentation of the appropriate Job Card. An interesting procedure adopted in one LDC vocational training college associated with a nearby port is to issue the trainee technicians with a set of individually engraved metal tokens; one of these has to be presented every time a special tool is issued from the store, and is placed in the allocated storage position of that tool, in a drawer or on a shelf. There is no confusion over who has that tool, and security is as tight as possible – no token, no tool, and if no tool, the token indicates unequivocally who is holding it. The system is simple, easily understood and highly recommended for wider use.

An alternative to personal issue of tools is to provide a number of mobile workbenches, each fitted with a solid work-top (with vices and clamps permanently attached) and with trays and racks of all the hand-tools needed for maintaining that workshop's range of equipment. Each 'work-trolley' is used by the team of technicians allocated to a job, avoiding any conflict or misunderstanding over tool ownership when several men are working on the same machine, and allowing the complete setup to be moved easily to wherever that team has to work.

Comprehensive lists of the standard workshop equipment and tools required for the maintenance of container-handling and general-cargo-handling equipment are given in Jerusel (1988) based on workshops serving a two-berth container terminal and a six-berth general cargo port respectively.

6.4.5 Spare Parts and Materials
A reliable supply of spare parts and consumable materials is essential to the successful operation of the maintenance function. If spares and materials are not immediately available when needed for preventive maintenance and for emergency repair work, when all the port's investment in workshops, facilities, tools and employees' skills counts for nothing. Yet deficiencies in the management of workshop and other supplies is among the most serious problems facing port engineers, and is one of the areas where significant improvements are urgently needed. Stock-holding policies need to be reviewed and improved, spare parts procurement procedures need to be carefully examined and revised, and stores control systems thoroughly overhauled. This topic is considered such an important aspect of this survey that Chapter 7 is devoted to it.

An interesting observation arising from the study is that, although 'waiting for spare parts' is such a common complaint of operators and engineers alike, and although spares usually have to be purchased at considerable expense from overseas suppliers, few (if any) LDC ports seem to have considered the strategy of making spare parts for themselves. In some LDC ports, at least, there is no shortage of the necessary machine tools (lathes, milling machines and drills), and labour is available in considerable quantity, so it is surprising that some, at least, of these resources are not employed usefully to machine spare parts. This would be a useful exercise for apprentices and junior technicians, as well as possibly accelerating the return to service of much-needed equipment.

6.5 Planning Maintenance

6.5.1 Scheduling
Developments in the maritime transport industry in recent years have forced ports to offer an around-the-clock cargo-handling service, seven days a week, especially at modern terminals accommodating large vessels with high operating costs. Inevitably, this has meant that cargo-handling equipment has to work longer and longer hours, leaving less time for routine maintenance, and so it has made it increasingly necessary to plan and schedule maintenance carefully. Essential preventive maintenance has to be completed as programmed, so that operators have all the machines they need to meet their cargo-handling requirements, particularly at peak demand times.

The prime objectives of maintenance scheduling are to reconcile the demand for equipment (including tugs and other marine craft) and facilities (such as lock entrances and swing-bridges) for operational purposes with the need to fulfil preventive maintenance requirements, and to plan the most effective use of workshop and staff resources. Engineering managers have to make sure that no machine or facility misses its prescribed preventive maintenance appointment, that every breakdown or accident receives prompt attention, and yet that equipment and services are available to operators when they are needed; these are not easy demands to satisfy!

The maintenance schedule must be based on the expected workload and the likely operational demands during the planning period, and this requires a general understanding of the characteristics of the workload and the nature and capacity of the maintenance resources. The workload can be divided into two categories: deterministic and probabilistic. The deterministic (or predictable) workload is that which can be reasonably accurately forecast in advance; preventive maintenance work, and long-planned major overhauls and refurbishment fall into this category. The workshop manager and his planning staff know in advance that these are due and can also forecast how long each task is likely to take. The probabilistic (or unpredictable) workload is primarily corrective maintenance – breakdowns and accidents during operations; these are impossible to forecast, except in terms of statistical probability, based on experience and the EMIS records – planning can only be in the shortest term (periods of hours, at most). A feature of the probabilistic workload is that it inevitably fluctuates widely, and the time needed to complete each job is also unpredictable.

The deterministic workload should be predictable from the EMIS records (if reliably maintained), although most ports start from manufacturers' recommended maintenance programmes when new cargo-handling facilities, berths or terminals are being established. Provided accurate data are available, the engineers can assess the time that will be needed to complete each routine service, they know when each machine is due to be serviced, and so can schedule appointment times and durations to suit both operators and technical staff. Programmes can be arranged (in outline, at least) and circulated to all relevant staff a week or even a month ahead, and the individual jobs are initiated by the EMIS; in the most efficient ports, they are now triggered by the computer issue of a Job Card (see Chapter 9), but even a 'manual' system is capable of preparing a realistic schedule sufficiently in advance to ensure that the manpower, spare parts and other resources needed for a job are available on time.

As far as possible, preventive maintenance should be scheduled for times when the equipment is least likely to be needed by operators, and arranged so that the workload on the engineering services is spread over the week. Only one or two machines should be scheduled to be in a workshop area at a time, leaving the majority of units available for operational work. As has been stressed frequently in earlier sections, this aspect of engineering management demands the closest co-operation between workshop and operations staff.

The most difficult maintenance work to manage is, of course, that which arises at random from equipment failure and accidents. It can only be 'scheduled' in the sense of fitting it into the workshop's existing programme as soon as possible. Clearly, the engineers need to follow some form of priority rule; usually, equipment which has broken down in service and which is urgently required by operators must take precedence over routine maintenance on other plant, unless a spare replacement machine of appropriate type can be brought in. Inevitably, unless spare technicians are available, and there is space in the appropriate workshop area, work in progress will have to be set aside and work due to start shortly will have to be postponed; the workplan must be treated as flexible, and the routing desk has to adjust it constantly in the light of events.

The obvious message is that a maintenance schedule is essential if the workshop is to carry out its function effectively, but it must be treated as an outline plan only. The weekly schedule must be reviewed constantly, as circumstances change, and checked against the latest estimates of equipment requirements. The daily workplan has to be amended, almost from hour to hour, to take account of breakdowns and accidents to key machines, of changes in operators' needs arising from delays in arrival of vessels, and of revised estimates of the amount of work to be performed. It may well not be possible to do a preventive maintenance job at exactly the time planned, in which case that machine must be re-scheduled for the next most convenient slot in the programme. It is absolutely essential that no machine misses a service altogether, and engineers must not succumb to the temptation of postponing a 250-hour service, say, until the next planned 250-hour slot; the danger is that the 250-hour tasks will be overlooked and a 500-hour schedule followed instead.

6.5.2 Work Planning

Work planning is the short-term component of maintenance scheduling: the planning of jobs in detail for the next workshop shift or the next day. It consists of ensuring that the relevant Job Cards have been completed and are to hand, that all facilities (work bays, staff and tools) have been reserved, and that all the required spare parts and materials have at least been requisitioned and preferably are already in the workshop. The aim is to streamline and co-ordinate all the separate activities, so that the work is performed to maximum efficiency.

The workload for each workshop section has to be carefully predicted and the work flow appropriately sequenced. Clearly, before the routing desk can finalize the workplan, it must know exactly when equipment will be available for service (see Section 6.5.4) and how long the service or repair will take. The total workload for each workshop has to be taken into account, so that it can be spread out over the various work areas, staff and shifts. Considerable planning skill is required, as well as first-hand knowledge of maintenance engineering and a reliable EMIS. The most difficult aspect is to slot in the unpredicted repair work in the least disruptive manner, while being as responsive as possible to the minute-by-minute needs of operators.

6.5.3 Long-term Maintenance Planning

Planning and scheduling of maintenance is not only performed for the next few days but must also take into account the work that is due to be done over the months ahead – perhaps up to a year. Engineering staff have to work out what major overhauls, refurbishment, structural cleaning and re-painting and similar jobs are due, and how long they will take, and then these major tasks have to be fitted into the long-term workplan of the Engineering Department. Just as for short-term work planning, the necessary resources, parts and materials must be reserved and acquired in readiness; in many cases, these major jobs will require spare parts and materials that are not normally kept in stock in the stores, so they will have to be ordered in good time (the delays and causes of delays in the procurement of spares are discussed in Chapters 5 and 7). Specialist technical skills may also have to be reserved, and often external contractors will have to be brought in; ample notice is needed for both these events.

The marine maintenance section, for example, normally schedules the dry-docking of vessels at least several months in advance. Its staff plan in detail all the different tasks that will be performed, adopting Opportunity Maintenance strategies to the full, to take advantage of having the craft available for an extended period. They also plan the skills and resources needed, including all externally contracted activities. Civil maintenance works – particularly of the port's roads and quay areas – also need to be planned well ahead and to be carefully phased to cause the minimum disruption to operations.

Major overhauls of the engines in a fleet of mobile equipment can also be phased so that sufficient units are retained for operational use and the workload on engineering staff is evened out. Plant to be refurbished should also be identified well in advance; the preparation of the equipment plan is usually the appropriate occasion for doing this. Senior engineering planners are then in an excellent position to programme these time- and resource-consuming major works for minimum disruption to operations

and minimum pressure on workshop staff and facilities.

6.5.4 Availability of Equipment for Maintenance

The key to good maintenance planning is the intelligent scheduling of work: organizing the release of equipment from operations, the balance of priorities and the allocation of resources. Ultimately, the authority for making these arrangements must rest with the engineers, but that authority has to be exercised within a sensible framework.

The central problem is that operators, naturally, want cargo-handling equipment to be available to them exactly when they need it, while engineers want access to the equipment when its planned service is due. This is more than a potential source of conflict, and it is very important to adopt a management procedure mutually acceptable to both operators and engineers. Operators must also be accurate and reasonable in their estimates of expected workload and equipment demand, and engineers must be equally precise in their predictions of how long the maintenance will take, and when the equipment will become available for operations again. The approach which has proved most acceptable, and which is practised in the majority of the successful ports, is to organize daily planning meetings, at which operators (traffic managers) and representatives of the Engineering Department (routing desk officers or their equivalent) exchange information on cargo-handling and maintenance demands for the following few shifts, consider the operators' equipment requisitions and the engineers' list of available, serviceable equipment, and agree on an equipment supply allocation mutually acceptable to the two parties. This allocation then forms the basis of the workshops' workplans for those shifts.

As already discussed, even this short-term workplan cannot be considered sacrosanct; operational circumstances may well change during a shift, the cargo workload will fluctuate, and accidents and breakdowns will upset the planned maintenance workload. So the traffic managers and workshop routing desk staff must keep in constant touch as the shift progresses; indeed, communication between all levels of operational and engineering staff is essential if their respective activities are to be smoothly co-ordinated. As far as possible, the needs of operators must be given priority, and the routing desk must be as flexible and understanding as possible. In return, operators must be realistic in their requisitioning of machines, asking only for what they really need to perform their cargo-handling efficiently. If operators retain equipment unreasonably, preventing it receiving its due maintenance, the engineers must exercise their ultimate right to insist on its being released when the extreme limit of its scheduled 'window' is reached.

The workshop routing desk has a crucial role to play in planning and scheduling. It is, in effect, a local planning unit, making full use of the OMIS and EMIS records to look as far ahead as realistically possible, to estimate workshop workloads and to draw up an achievable schedule. Machinery must be established through which they can be immediately informed of breakdowns or accidents (by drivers, traffic officers or berth supervisors, as appropriate), enabling them to adjust the maintenance workplan almost minute by minute, as necessary. It is their responsibility to ensure that the Engineering Department fully carries out its duties in keeping operators supplied with the equipment they need.

6.5.5 Maintenance Records

Again and again in this report, the value of good records to effective maintenance has been stressed. A complete history must be compiled of the maintenance and repair work carried out on each item of equipment on the port's inventory. It is on the basis of this asset history that senior managers can take decisions on the timing of equipment replacement, and on the suitability of the port's maintenance policies and strategies. From the point of view of maintenance itself, records are needed for engineers to carry out detailed analyses of component failures, so that they can recommend design changes or technical specification changes when procuring new machines. Accurate information about the cost of maintenance will lead to improved planning of work and, when assessed against the department's budget, will provide a means of management control in the workshops and of assigning greater individual employee accountability. These and other aspects of engineering management information needs are examined further in Section 6.7.

6.6 Maintenance Procedures

6.6.1 Issue of Work

As well as improving maintenance planning and scheduling, there is considerable need for LDC ports to improve their maintenance practices. A set of procedures must be established and rigorously followed, covering the complete process from first identification of the need for maintenance to quality control checks and returning the machine to service. The procedure must begin with the issue of the job, in the form of a Work Order or Job Card, by the routing desk or equivalent workshop planning unit. As will be explained in Chapter 9, the Job Card is a product of the EMIS, bearing all the details of the machine, the work to be done, the materials to be used and so on. Ultimately, it will contain a history of the work carried out, the time taken and the costs of the job.

Job Cards for preventive maintenance can be made out well in advance – perhaps a week or more – so that the routing desk has time to estimate workloads, schedule the work and prepare the necessary spares and materials. At that time, the job will be given an approximate appointment time or a 'time window' of a few days, within which it should be carried out. It is then a matter of negotiation with operators to organize release of the machine within that window, as has been described earlier. For emergency breakdown and repair work, of course, there is no opportunity to do that. Even so, a Job Card should be made out as soon as the problem is reported, and issued to the allocated maintenance team as they are dispatched to the job. At that stage, the Job Card will carry only the bare details of the problem, but further details will be added as the fault is diagnosed and the appropriate worksheet selected to guide the technicians in putting the fault right.

The Job Card is, then, the basic management tool of maintenance, and of extreme importance in the control of workshop activities and costs. Its issue and handling must be carefully planned and organized, along the lines described in more detail in Chapter 9.

6.6.2 Equipment Cleaning

The first task of workshop staff when equipment arrives for its scheduled preventive maintenance is to clean the machine thoroughly. There will be a properly equipped bay, just outside the workshop building, to steam-clean or high-pressure wash the framework and body panels of all oil, grease and dirt before the machine is moved into the workshop. The main reason for this operation is that, apart from making the technicians' work more pleasant, it prevents the possible contamination of internal parts and components when panels are removed and access gained to mechanisms and controls. It is also important to keep the workshop floor clean, for safety reasons, and removing grease and dirt outside the building makes a major contribution to that aspect of good housekeeping. The washing water must drain into a sump and not be allowed to flow untreated into the public drainage system or the sea.

For emergency maintenance, complete pre-inspection cleaning may not be practicable. After all, the equipment will probably have broken down out on the berth and first inspection, at least, will take place there, if not the entire repair. Nevertheless, the technicians must clean up the machine area being investigated as thoroughly as possible under the circumstances, to improve ease of access to inspection covers and body panels and to reduce the risk of introducing contamination into the mechanisms. Of course, if the Operations managers ensure, as they should, that the operational equipment is cleaned routinely and regularly by workshop staff, then grease and dirt should never be allowed to build up to any extent, and only minimal local cleaning will be necessary at this stage.

6.6.3 Fault Diagnosis

The first stage in corrective maintenance is inspection of the machine by senior technical staff (a foreman or supervisor, perhaps) to locate and diagnose the malfunction. This is a critical stage in the process, of course, as mistakes here could lead to unnecessary and inappropriate work, and wasteful expenditure of technician time and resources. So the most experienced and skilled of the workshop staff should be assigned to fault diagnosis, particularly in the case of breakdown in operations of key cargo-handling equipment. This is also an area where specialization is an advantage; a foreman technician who has concentrated on straddle carrier work is more likely to be able to identify the cause of a failure than one who works on those machines infrequently.

As soon as the fault has been diagnosed, or at least the suspect system, assembly or component pin-pointed, the details are entered on the Job Card and the necessary instructions for further diagnostic inspection or repair added. At the same time, the engineer or the routing desk staff will assign a priority level to the job, and it will be slotted into the workplan – possibly immediately, if the equipment is in demand by operators. The necessary resources (the maintenance team, tools and equipment, spares and materials, workshop bay or mobile facility) will be allocated and assembled, with all details filled in on the Job Card as the preparation proceeds.

6.6.4 Allocation of Work

When the Job Card is made out, either in advance of a preventive maintenance service or as the cause of an unpredicted failure is diagnosed, the workshop supervisory staff or routing desk must allocate all the resources necessary for the work. First, the appropriate section, area or bay of the workshop is identified and reserved, and then the process of requisitioning and collecting the tools, equipment, spares and materials for the job is started. The aim is to have all the required items on hand before the work starts, so Requisition Forms must be made out and issued in good time. The scheduler also needs to know what engineering skills will be needed, so that the appropriate team of technicians can be assigned to the job – mechanics, electricians, hydraulic system specialists, welders or whatever.

At the beginning of the scheduled shift, the maintenance team is assigned to the job and the Job Card is issued to them by a routing desk engineer, Shift Superintendent or the foreman responsible for the particular section or area of the workshop. It is the responsibility of that person to make sure that the team understand *exactly* what the job entails. The technicians must read the Job Card, listen to the instructions and sign the Card to accept their responsibilities and to confirm that they fully understand what is involved. Either on the Job Card or accompanying it should be a full checklist of all the steps involved in carrying out the service, and it might also be appropriate to issue the relevant maintenance manual, particularly if the service involves the complete dismantling of a system or assembly. Many routine tasks will have already been reduced to a simplified (and well-illustrated) set of operational steps on a standard job-aid or worksheet; the more detailed the checklist instructions, and the more care that is taken in describing them, the greater the likelihood of the work being done correctly. Each step must be ticked off and initialled by the team as they complete it; this is a vital element of the work control and quality control procedure, adopted commonly in many heavy engineering industries but surprisingly rare in port maintenance. It is all part of the EMIS, on which effective equipment management so much depends.

Another important task in maintenance management (essential for allowing the routing desk or planning unit to schedule the work) is the setting of performance standards: standard times for completing each routine maintenance task. These should be calculated on the basis of manufacturers' estimates, workshop records (the EMIS again) and work-study measurements, and agreed with the workshop staff. Such work values can then become the basis for performance targets set for incentive schemes. However, workshop staff performance must not be based solely on job completion times (Mean Time To Repair); quality of work is equally important. Each job must be inspected while it is being carried out, and again after completion (see Sections 6.6.5 and 6.6.6). All sub-standard work must be noted and reject rates recorded for each technician or team. These can then be used with other indicators of workshop quality (such as Mean Time Between Failures) when calculating incentives and bonuses for engineering staff; this is discussed further in Section 6.8 and Chapter 8.

6.6.5 Supervision of Work

Close and constant supervision of maintenance work is essential if its quality is to be improved and sustained. The supervisors and foremen assigned to the different sections or areas of the workshops are responsible for the immediate issue of the work instructions to the teams and for making sure that the technicians know precisely what they are to do. The same supervisory staff are then responsible for monitoring progress on the jobs, for checking each stage in their performance and for approving the work as it proceeds. All sub-standard or suspect work must be rejected immediately, and repeated under supervision or transferred to a more experienced technician.

Workshop supervisors must also ensure that good 'housekeeping' practices are observed within and around the workshops:

— Working surfaces and floors must be kept clear of oil, grease and dirt, and any obstructions.

— Hand and machine tools must be looked after properly – kept clean, sharpened and adjusted, put away safely in tool chests, lockers and storerooms.

— Portable gear and equipment should be used carefully, cleaned, and returned to the correct storage position after use.

— Cargo-handling equipment being serviced or awaiting spares must be parked in the appropriate bay, and systems, assemblies and components removed from the machines must be set aside carefully, fully protected and labelled ready for reassembly.

Supervisors have an equally important role at shift change or work hand-over times. If work is not complete at the time a maintenance team finishes its shift, so that work has to be suspended or handed over to another team, it is essential that a full record is kept of tasks completed, the current state of the equipment, the location of removed parts, of materials and tools, and so on. This information must be conveyed in some suitable form (preferably on or attached to the Job Card, as well as verbally) to the job supervisor, so that he can then inform the team resuming the work. Even if the same team intends to continue their work on their next shift, it is essential that the supervisor be informed of progress to date, as a precautionary measure. If the supervisor himself will not be on duty to instruct a take-over team, then all the information and documents must be given to routing desk staff, so that the job can be issued afresh at the appropriate time.

Clearly, supervisory staff (those designated Shift Superintendent, Foreman or the like) are extremely important in the successful management and performance of the Engineering Department, and their position and role must be well defined within the

Department's management structure. Their responsibilities must be spelt out in their job descriptions, and they must be given the necessary authority to control the day-to-day maintenance work of the maintenance teams under their direct control (two or three teams per foreman, two or three foremen and their teams to each Shift Superintendent). Where there is no routing desk or equivalent planning unit within the workshop, the supervisory staff will have an even more crucial role, in requisitioning spare parts and materials, allocating work and recording all data relevant to the EMIS. It is preferable, however, for their duties to be restricted to the direct management of the workshop teams, leaving all scheduling and planning duties to routing staff.

6.6.6 Quality Control

The Chief Engineer, through his Senior Mechanical/Electrical Engineer and the Workshop Managers, must ensure that all maintenance work is carried out to a specified standard and that equipment never leaves a workshop in sub-standard condition. Indeed, the aim must be to keep the port's equipment up to its original manufacturers' specification throughout its working life. This requires the establishment and constant observance of strict quality control procedures. As described above, supervisory staff must be held responsible for monitoring work as it is carried out, inspecting it closely after every stage and before a team is allowed to 'sign-off' after completion of the service. The supervising foreman must himself then sign the Job Card to acknowledge acceptance of the workmanship; from that moment he is held accountable for the equipment's subsequent operational performance.

Substandard work calls for prompt disciplinary action. It must, of course, be immediately remedied and note taken of the person responsible for it, but this should be followed by appropriate procedures. If the deficiency is serious, or is one of a series of instances of poor workmanship on the part of the technician, then penalties might need to be imposed: first, that person will have participation in the current incentive scheme withdrawn and bonuses stopped; for more serious offences, a letter of warning should be sent to him by the Senior Mechanical/Electrical Engineer, and ultimately a disciplinary hearing, under the Chief Engineer, might be called. These matters are discussed further in Chapter 8.

Workshop management, from the Manager himself through the Shift Superintendents to the Foremen, must be given the necessary authority and status to carry out their duties effectively. It is their responsibility to motivate workshop staff, to instil pride in the performance and appearance of the workshop, and to maintain the quality of output of their units. One way in which they can achieve these aims is to adopt the strategy of establishing Quality Control Circles. These have been shown to be remarkably effective in supplementing the technicians' engineering skills with the right attitudes, motivating them to take an enthusiastic interest in their work. Quality Circles will be discussed in Chapter 8.

6.6.7 An Independent Inspectorate

An extremely effective way of achieving quality control throughout the whole Engineering Department is to establish an independent inspectorate unit within it, covering civil, mechanical, electrical and marine maintenance, and reporting directly to the Chief Engineer (as shown in Figure 6.2.2B). To ensure complete independence, the Inspectorate must have direct access to the General Manager in the event of a dispute with the Chief Engineer, and must not be in a position where pressure can be brought to bear by either engineers or operators on matters of safety. The primary responsibility of the inspectorate is to ensure that all statutory and other official regulations with respect to equipment standards, safety, maintenance and operation are complied with, but the inspectors can be equally valuable in making spot checks on all aspects of the port's maintenance function.

The engineers in the inspectorate are charged with making regular inspections to make sure that cargo-handling and other equipment is in good, safe working condition, and that all statutory inspections and tests are carried out when they are due. Their spot checks, carried out without warning, can in addition ensure that routine maintenance work and emergency repairs are being carried out correctly and that the port's maintenance work, of all types, is of an appropriately and consistently high standard.

Their constant visits to the different areas of the port and their accumulated knowledge of the Engineering Department's practices and procedures also make the inspectors extremely valuable members of long-term planning units, and they should be brought into all meetings at which port maintenance is reviewed.

6.7 Maintenance Costs

6.7.1 Maintenance Budgets

Expenditure on engineering services is a major component of the operating budgets of ports. This is well illustrated by Table 6.7.1A, which shows the 1988 budget for the Engineering Department of a medium-sized LDC port, covering the civil, mechanical and electrical sections. The departmental budget represents 40% of the port's operating budget, and 26% of the total port budget for the year. Wages and salaries are the single biggest item (37% of the budget), with spare parts another major item (18.5%).

Although the data in Table 6.7.1A appear to be fairly comprehensive, they are not, in fact, sufficiently detailed to distinguish cost centres within the engineering department (such as civil, marine and mechanical maintenance) nor cost sub-centres (such as asset groups). In this, they are typical of budgetary control systems in many ports, particularly those of LDCs. However, it is possible to interpret some of the financial data collected during the survey to provide a rough indication of annual equipment maintenance expenditure levels. Table 6.7.1B shows such estimates for five of the ports participating in the study (port C is in a developed country, the others are LDC ports), expressed also as percentages of the ports' operating costs and operating revenues.

If the five ports featured in Table 6.7.1B are typical, therefore, about 14% of a port's operating

Table 6.7.1A Engineering budget for LDC port, 1988

Expenditure Item	Budget ($ million)	Item as % age of Engineering Budget	Item as % age of Port Operating Budget	Item as % age of Total Port Budget
Wages, Salaries etc.	4.97	37.0	14.5	9.5
Overtime payments	1.05	8.0	3.0	2.0
Fuel, Rates, Insurance	1.00	7.5	3.0	2.0
Spare parts	2.49	18.5	7.5	5.0
Depreciation	3.34	25.0	10.0	6.5
Welfare services	0.12	1.0	0.5	0.3
Supplies	0.25	2.0	1.0	0.5
Miscellaneous	0.10	1.0	0.5	0.2
Total	13.32	100	40.0	26.0

Table 6.7.1B Equipment maintenance costs at selected ports

Port	Estimated Equipment Maintenance Cost/year ($ million)	Cost as %age of Port's Operating Expenditure	Cost as %age of Port's Operating Revenue
A	8.1	18.5	10.5
B	2.5	7.5	4.5
C	45.0	15.0	12.5
D	18.0	12.0	7.0
E	3.0	11.0	7.0
Mean =	14.0		10.0

Table 6.7.1C 1988 Budget for an LDC container terminal

Expenditure Category	Budget ($)	Proportion of Total Budget
1. *Salaries and Wages*		
General	273,077	
Operations	246,154	
Engineering	241,538	
Incentive payments	141,538	
Overtime	69,615	
Total	971,922	47%
2. *Supplies*		
Stationery	12,307	
Spares (Consumables)	59,615	
,, (Mechanical)	294,230	
,, (Electrical)	91,154	
Other	13,846	
Total	471,152	23%
3. *Fuel and Power*		
Electricity	307,692	
Fuel and lubricants	169,230	
Total	476,922	23%
4. *Other*		
External maintenance contracts	88,462	
Computing services	34,615	
Miscellaneous	25,923	
Total	149,000	7%
Grand Total	2,060,000	100%

expenditure is accounted for by the cost of equipment servicing and repair, which is equivalent to about 10% of total operating revenues. The variations between the ports are primarily explained by the different numbers of employees in the engineering departments and by differences in salary levels. In one of the LDC ports visited, for example, over 7,000 people (51% of the total workforce)

are employed in engineering (which includes drivers, in that particular port). In contrast, a major European port – handling four times the volume of cargo of that LDC port, and with a much higher degree of mechanization – has only 230 engineering employees, and another (with an even higher cargo throughput) has just 200. In the LDC port just referred to, engineering staff wages and salaries account for 46% of the port's total wages expenditure, and over 50% of all supplies expenditure is for the purchase of spare parts for equipment maintenance. The total expenditure on running, servicing and repair of equipment represents about 40% of the port's total revenue budget.

The importance of equipment costs to a modern cargo-handling terminal is illustrated in Table 6.7.1C, which summarizes budget estimates for an LDC container terminal handling 100,000 TEUs a year. By careful interpretation of the data, it is possible to calculate the total equipment maintenance budget (including engineering salaries and wages, and the purchase of spare parts and consumables); it comes to about 45% of total terminal budgeted expenditure. Direct operating costs (similarly estimated, and including driver and other employee salaries, fuel and power costs, etc.) represent 43% of the total budget, leaving only about 12% for administrative and other overheads.

6.7.2 Equipment Maintenance Costs

Table 6.7.2A (taken from Jerusel, 1988) presents typical maintenance costs for different types of cargo-handling equipment in European ports and the relationships between maintenance cost and replacement value for those types of machine. The costs, at 1987 prices, are based on the operating conditions (with high utilization and availability levels), manning levels and salaries in Western European ports; as a guide to interpretation, one of the major European ports visited spends, on average, about 55% of total maintenance costs on employees' salaries, about 27% on materials and 18% on external contracts.

Comparative data for LDC ports are not easily assembled, because of their lack of good financial records, but some estimates have been prepared for two major LDC ports, and are presented in Tables 6.7.2B and 6.7.2C. It has been possible to calculate separate costs for preventive and corrective maintenance in these ports, and these demonstrate clearly contrasting maintenance strategies in the two ports: the first relies extensively on corrective maintenance (spending between 60% and 80% of total expenditure on that) while the second port obviously attaches much greater importance to preventive

Table 6.7.2A Typical maintenance costs for equipment in European ports

Equipment Category	Maintenance cost per Operating Hour ($)	Annual Maintenance Cost as Proportion of Replacement Value
Rail-mounted level-luffing quay crane	17-21	2%
35t Toploader	17-23	9-14%
12t forklift truck	9-15	7-12%
5t forklift truck	5-7	12-15%
3t forklift truck	4	16-20%
Tow tractor	2.5	8-10%
Drawbar trailer	—	0.3%
Mobile crane	21-26	2-4%

maintenance (70-90% of total expenditure). Tables 6.7.2B and C also show that average maintenance costs per unit of equipment are not greatly different in these LDC ports from those at the European ports featured in Table 6.7.2A, even though technicians' salaries in LDC ports are only 7-15% of those paid in Europe (Jerusel, 1988).

The significance of employee salaries and spare parts expenditure in the maintenance costs of equipment at two LDC ports is demonstrated in Tables 6.7.2D and E. Table 6.7.2D shows that, for conventional general cargo handling equipment,

employees' salaries and wages represent about 55% of total maintenance costs, while Table 6.7.2E data (the most comprehensive and reliable LDC data collected during the study) indicate that expenditure levels are about evenly split between labour and spare parts costs at that port. Jerusel (1988) states that spare parts costs in LDC ports are between 1.4 and 1.8 times the cost in developed countries.

This study also attempted to investigate the relationship between annual maintenance costs and asset age, but very few of the ports surveyed recorded the data needed to enable such an investigation to be carried out. Discussions with European engineers provided interesting but contradictory views: some believed that maintenance costs increased steadily with age (but had no data to confirm that) while others thought that costs remain stable for the first few years of operation and then increase, as corrective maintenance becomes more frequent and as major overhauls become necessary. However, one terminal with a reliable EMIS reported that costs rise in the first two to four years of operation (as minor manufacturing faults become apparent and are rectified) and then remain stable for several years. There are, clearly, no good generalizable data at the moment on this aspect of maintenance costs, and accurate records for each asset throughout its life would yield much valuable information to take into account when considering whether to replace or refurbish equipment.

Table 6.7.2B Annual maintenance costs for container-handling equipment in an LDC port (in $)

Equipment Type	Preventive Maintenance Cost/Unit	Corrective Maintenance Cost/Unit	Total Cost per unit
Quayside gantry crane	19,276 (28%)	48,864 (72%)	68,140
Yard transfer crane	15,500 (38%)	25,260 (62%)	40,760
Front-end loader	4,125 (19%)	17,803 (81%)	21,928
Tractor	676 (20%)	2,624 (80%)	3,300
Mean %age =	(26%)	(74%)	

Table 6.7.2C Annual maintenance costs for LDC port (in $)

Equipment Type	Preventive Maintenance Cost/Unit	Corrective Maintenance Cost/Unit	Total Cost per unit
Quayside gantry crane	53,405 (88%)	6,305 (12%)	60,963
Yard transfer crane	21,775 (80%)	5,693 (20%)	27,468
Straddle carrier	26,411 (77%)	7,844 (23%)	34,255
Front-end loader	17,060 (75%)	5,594 (25%)	22,654
Tractor	7,424 (68%)	3,466 (32%)	10,890
Forklift truck	3,590 (60%)	2,376 (40%)	5,966
Mean %age =	(75%)	(25%)	

154

Table 6.7.2D Annual direct maintenance costs for conventional cargo-handling equipment at a major LDC port, 1985-86 (in $)

Equipment Type	Labour costs	Spares costs	Total	Costs/Unit
Electric wharf cranes	784,385 (55%)	640,154 (45%)	1,424,539	35,613
Mobile cranes	220,230 (56%)	173,308 (44%)	393,538	30,272
Forklift trucks	534,154 (52%)	491,385 (48%)	1,025,539	13,494
Mean %age =	(54%)	(46%)		

Table 6.7.2E Annual direct maintenance costs for an LDC container port (in $/unit)

Equipment type	Labour costs	Spares costs	Total costs
Container crane	34,033 (56%)	26,930 (44%)	60,963
Rubber-tyred gantry	16,551 (60%)	10,917 (40%)	27,468
Straddle carrier	14,234 (42%)	20,021 (58%)	34,255
Front-end loader	10,606 (47%)	12,048 (53%)	22,654
Tractor	5,331 (49%)	5,559 (51%)	10,890
Forklift truck	2,590 (43%)	3,376 (57%)	5,966
Mean %age =	(49.5%)	(50.5%)	

Table 6.7.3A Estimated average equipment operating costs at European ports (in $/unit)

Equipment Type	Annual Running Costs	Annual Maintenance Costs	Total Annual Operating Costs	Annual Operating Hours	Hourly Operating Cost
Container crane	300,000	100,000	400,000	3,500	114
Straddle carrier	180,000	60,000	240,000	3,500	69
Rubber-tyred GC	185,000	65,000	250,000	3,500	71
Rail-mounted GC	250,000	100,000	350,000	4,000	88
Terminal tractor	110,000	20,000	130,000	4,000	33
Front-end loader	170,000	40,000	210,000	3,000	70
Reach-stacker	170,000	35,000	205,000	3,000	68

6.7.3 Total Equipment Operating Costs

The relationships between running costs, maintenance costs and total operating costs of equipment are illustrated in Table 6.7.3A. The data were collected in a survey of container-handling equipment in European ports (Thomas & Roach, 1988); salary levels are, of course, much higher than in LDC ports. The hourly operating costs have been calculated on the basis of estimated annual hours of operation as measured by hour-meters, and not by allocation records.

Table 6.7.3B summarizes the operating costs for a range of equipment types at the only participating LDC port that maintains anything like a comprehensive equipment operating and maintenance performance information system. The Table is a continuation of Table 5.5.2, and the same cautionary provisos apply: the running hours are estimates based on allocation records, and labour costs are also estimates (but based on known salary and manning

levels). The costs are strikingly lower than those estimated for European ports. The hourly operating costs, for example, are in many cases only about one-third of the European values. There are two major contributory explanations: first, the driver and technician salary levels are much lower, and secondly the European figures include departmental and administrative overhead costs, while these are excluded from the LDC port data. However, even if these additional costs were to be included, operating costs in LDC ports are still likely to be lower than in developed countries.

6.7.4 Recording Maintenance Costs

The establishment of good budgetary and cost control procedures is essential if the objective of improving the maintenance of equipment and other port assets is to be achieved. The first step is to designate each workshop as a separate cost/revenue centre, and each major section within it (e.g.

155

Table 6.7.3B Average equipment operating costs of container-handling equipment at an LDC port (in $/unit)

Equipment Type	Annual Running Costs	Annual Maintenance Costs	Total Annual Operating Costs	Annual Operating Hours	Hourly Operating Cost
Container crane	97,467	60,963	158,430	3,500	45
Straddle carrier	44,732	34,255	78,987	1,400	56
Rubber-tyred GC	54,312	27,468	81,780	2,000	41
Terminal tractor	31,482	10,890	42,372	1,800	24
Front-end loader	29,709	22,654	52,363	1,500	35
Forklift truck	18,960	5,966	24,926	1,200	21

fabrication section) as a cost/revenue sub-centre. All expenditure incurred in carrying out servicing and repair, and all revenue 'earned' by 'hiring' the equipment to operators, should then be allocated to the appropriate cost centres. In this way, managerial cost control and accountability will be tightened, and valuable information will be collected for maintenance planning purposes and for setting workshop performance targets.

The second major step is to set up a reliable means of recording all maintenance and repair costs, for each unit of equipment on the asset register, classified by the type of work (e.g. Routine Service, Breakdown Repair, Accident Repair, Overhaul, Refurbishment), and giving full details of all spares and materials used, labour salaries and a proportion of the departmental overhead costs. Procedures for recording these data are discussed in Chapter 9.

Keeping good records of this kind will provide managers with a complete history of the costs of maintaining each type and unit of equipment and, when combined with the matching operating data, will allow measures of equipment performance to be accurately calculated. The complete cost information will be of immense value when engineers are deciding whether to refurbish or replace a particular asset, will offer an effective means of monitoring maintenance costs, and will be a vital input into the process of preparing Engineering Department budgets.

6.8 Maintenance Performance

As part of the drive to improve efficiency and managerial accountability, records should be regularly collected on the performance of the workshops and other engineering units. The volume and quality of the maintenance work must be recorded, and the performance of individuals and teams of technicians monitored. Records must be kept of the frequency, causes and extent of equipment downtime resulting from breakdowns, classifying the precise reasons for the breakdowns and the hours that the equipment is out of service

under (or waiting for) repair. Performance targets should be set for each class of equipment, in an effort to improve the quality of corrective maintenance work and to reduce the time taken to complete it. A useful measure (successfully used as an engineering target in one LDC port) is the hours-out-of-service (because of breakdowns) expressed as a percentage of total possible working hours. A target percentage is set for each class of equipment, against which actual performance is assessed.

Records should also be made of the total time each unit of equipment spends under preventive maintenance in a given period. When this is combined with downtime resulting from breakdowns and accidents, a measure of total downtime is obtained which, when combined with such other important measures as machine running hours, will give an indication of the performance of the maintenance function. Other measures, such as Mean Time Between Failures and Mean Time To Repair are valuable elements of the EMIS, and should be recorded for each class of equipment (see Chapter 8). These measures can be used to set workshop performance targets and as the basis for an incentive scheme for employees.

The measures of performance can then be combined with the expenditure data to provide a full analysis of the equipment maintenance costs and to assist in the preparation of a set of financial performance measures, such as Total Maintenance Costs per Running Hour and Hourly Operating Costs per Machine. This information should be regularly distributed to key personnel in the Engineering Department so that they can monitor the performance of their section and, if that performance falls short of the set targets, take the necessary remedial action to improve the efficiency of the maintenance services.

6.9 Recommendations

1. Ports should urgently review the organization of their engineering departments, to ensure

that it is suitable (in terms of division of responsibilities, levels of authority, lines of communication, etc.) to meet present maintenance demands and is sufficiently flexible to respond to changes in the nature of the engineering services required.

2. To reflect the increasing importance of maintenance, staff functions should be created for engineers to be responsible for planning and co-ordinating the port's maintenance work.

3. The status of engineering, particularly the maintenance function, within the port organization must be upgraded to reflect the increasing dependence on mechanical equipment, and increased authority should be given to engineers directly involved in maintenance work.

4. Special attention must be given to the key appointment within the Engineering Department – the Workshop Manager; he is responsible for planning and scheduling maintenance and controlling workshop activities and workload, and must have outstanding technical competence, managerial skill and enthusiasm for workshop engineering.

5. LDC ports must change their engineering departments' management culture, to give more emphasis to customer service and performance-orientated maintenance.

6. At the terminal organization level, clear lines of reporting should be introduced between engineering and operations units, to create a partnership and promote teamwork between those staff.

7. Multi-skilled technicians and technician teams should be developed to give the workshop manager a great deal of flexibility when planning and allocating work.

8. A routing desk must be set up, staffed by engineers with appropriate qualifications, to plan and co-ordinate the maintenance workload in the workshops.

9. Within the Engineering Department, the mechanical and electrical functions should be (re-)organized as one branch, to minimize the risk of conflict and to improve staff communications and the planning and co-ordination of maintenance.

10. Management style within the Engineering Department must change, with the appointment and development of staff with a practical background in engineering and a willingness to get directly involved in workshop activities.

11. The principle of accountability must be embodied within the engineering organizational structure, establishing clear lines of authority, and making each employee fully aware of his individual responsibilities and accountable to his immediate superior for his performance.

12. Clear departmental and individual performance objectives must be set, against which targets the achievement of individual employees, workshops and the Engineering Department as a whole can be assessed.

13. If appropriate, the maintenance function should be decentralized, with terminal or sectional workshops responsible for undertaking routine maintenance and minor repairs and a central workshop for more substantial and specialist work.

14. Manning levels in the workshops must be set at realistic levels, based on work-study techniques and designed to provide a lean, efficient and well-supervised service.

15. LDC ports must upgrade the skills of existing technicians and take steps to recruit better qualified personnel in the specialized crafts and trades, such as electronics and communications.

16. The effectiveness of engineering services should be improved by revising shift and staff working times in the workshops, off-setting them from operational working hours to ensure that, when equipment is available for maintenance, technicians are on hand to service it.

17. Engineers in LDC ports must thoroughly assess the policy options for maintaining equipment and other port assets, and incorporate the most appropriate and cost-effective policies in a comprehensive maintenance plan.

18. In the maintenance plan, engineers must prescribe the most appropriate maintenance strategies, for example selecting 'on-site maintenance', 'external maintenance contracts'

or a combination of these; all strategic decisions should be taken on the basis of dependability and economy.

19. Appropriate maintenance tactics must be determined at the time of formulating the maintenance plan, and these must be vigorously applied in the workshops.

20. A set of procedures must be established, and rigorously followed, covering the complete maintenance process – from first identification of the need for maintenance to the quality control checks carried out before returning the machine to service.

21. Senior managers must periodically review the maintenance function, to assess the type of maintenance facilities currently needed to provide an efficient service.

22. Efficiently located and well designed workshops should be provided, laid out according to the principles of segregation of activities, integration of facilities, space utilization, smooth work flow and safety.

23. A full range of essential facilities (including hand, machine and specialist tools) should be provided in all workshops, and these should be regularly maintained to a high standard, so that the technicians can carry out their maintenance work efficiently and safely.

24. Each technician should, on appointment, be provided with his own toolbox and personal set of hand tools, and should assume full responsibility for keeping them safely and maintaining them in good condition. Alternatively, a number of mobile workbenches should be provided, each fitted with the hand tools necessary for maintaining that workshop's range of equipment.

25. Special tools that are only needed occasionally should be held in a workshop tool store, and issued on presentation of the appropriate Job Card.

26. A maintenance schedule must be drawn up, to enable the workshop to carry out its function efficiently, allowing the demand for equipment and facilities for operational purposes to be balanced against the need to fulfil preventive maintenance requirements, and making the most effective use of workshop and staff resources.

27. Engineering managers must ensure that no machine or facility misses its prescribed preventive maintenance appointment, that every breakdown or accident receives prompt attention, and that equipment and services are available to operators as soon as they are needed.

28. Work planning (the detailed planning of jobs for the next workshop shift or the next day) must be introduced, to streamline and co-ordinate all the separate workshop activities.

29. Major overhauls, refurbishment, structural cleaning and repairing, and similar jobs, must also be scheduled into the long-term workplan of the Engineering Department.

30. Daily planning meetings must be held between operators (traffic officers) and representatives of the Engineering Department (routing desk officers), to allow the exchange of information on cargo-handling and maintenance demands for the following few shifts, to balance the operators' equipment requisitions and the engineers' list of available, serviceable equipment. This meeting must agree an equipment allocation mutually acceptable to the two parties and forming the basis for the workshop workplans.

31. Since good records are essential to effective maintenance, a complete history must be compiled of all the maintenance and repair work carried out on each item of equipment on the port's inventory.

32. The most skilled and experienced workshop staff should be assigned to fault diagnosis, a crucial stage in the maintenance process; mistakes here can lead to unnecessary and inappropriate work, and wasteful expenditure of labour, time and resources.

33. Workshop supervisory staff (or the routing desk staff) must allocate the maintenance jobs to the appropriate section, area or bay of the workshop; they must then process the requisitioning and collection of tools, equipment, spares and materials so that these are all to hand before the job is started.

34. A full checklist of all the steps involved in carrying out a preventive maintenance service must be issued (on the Job Card or as a separate worksheet) to technicians when they are allocated to a job; each step must be ticked off

and initialled as it is completed, as a vital element of the work control and quality control procedures.

35. Standard times should be established for completing each routine maintenance task, based on manufacturers' estimates, workshop records and work-study measurements, and agreed with the workshop staff.

36. Close and constant supervision of maintenance work is essential if its quality is to be improved and sustained, and so the position and role of supervisory staff in the organization must be clearly defined and they must be given the necessary authority to control day-to-day maintenance work.

37. Strict quality control procedures must be established and constantly followed by supervisory staff, to ensure that equipment never leaves the workshop in sub-standard condition.

38. There should be an independent inspectorate, directly answerable to the Chief Engineer, to ensure that all statutory and other official regulations with respect to equipment standards, safety, maintenance and operation are complied with, as well as to reinforce quality control procedures in the workshops.

39. Budgetary and cost control procedures must be improved significantly, and the maintenance budget must be set at a level which presents a realistic financial target for engineers while allowing them to sustain the resources needed to keep plant in good condition.

40. Each workshop should be designated a separate cost/revenue centre and each section within it a cost/revenue sub-centre, so that all expenditure incurred in carrying out maintenance and repair and all the revenues earned from these activities (paid in the form of hire rates) can be allocated to the relevant cost centre.

41. Procedures must be established and rigorously applied to record all maintenance and repair costs for each piece of equipment on the asset register, classified with respect to the nature of the work carried out, and with all costs of spares and resources used detailed.

42. Financial data should be periodically analysed to prepare such indicators as Maintenance Cost per Unit and Hourly Equipment Operating Cost, for regular distribution to engineers and operations managers.

CHAPTER 7

Supplies Management

7.1 The Importance of Supplies to Maintenance

The management of the procurement, storage and supply to the Engineering Department of the spare parts and consumables needed for servicing and repair of port equipment, plant and civil works must be considered an integral element of the maintenance function. Inefficiencies and deficiencies in Supplies obviously have a direct effect on the ability of the engineers to perform their jobs; indeed, complaints about the supply of spare parts were amongst the commonest in this survey.

Some indication of the significance of the Supplies function can be gathered from the fact that three of the largest ports visited carried, respectively, 34,000, 41,500 and 60,000 items in their stores. For just one 36-tonne heavy-duty lift truck, the recommended list of spares to be stocked includes 320 different parts, a total of 1,350 items (Jerusel, 1988). One Asian port stocks eight different grades of lubricating oil alone. The value of spares stocks held in the ports surveyed varied between $900,000 (in a self-contained container terminal) and $11 million, and can amount to 25% or more of the port's cargo-handling asset value. Annual expenditure on spares ranged between about $300,000 and $6 million – on average, about 25% of total annual maintenance costs. Some representative data on spares, collected during this survey, are presented in Table 7.1.

Although it is common to think of the function of the Supplies unit of a port in terms of the provision of 'spare parts' for maintenance and repair, in reality the range of materials provided by the unit is much wider than that. In the first place, they have to procure, store and issue both engineering and non-engineering materials; the latter include such items as stationery (plain and printed, for typing, handwritten and computer-output use), other office consumables, office and related machinery, cleaning and similar materials and equipment. Engineering supplies can be divided into: replacement spare parts (components, assemblies and sub-assemblies, body panels, motors and engines, etc.); consumable spares (filters, gaskets, tyres, fanbelts, batteries and bulbs, etc.); oils and greases, gases and detergents; tools (hand and machine tools, drill bits and workshop consumables such as emery paper, cotton waste, paper wipes and welding rods); and general spares (nuts and bolts, washers, nails) and raw materials (metal rod and bar, timber etc.).

Table 7.1 Values of Spares Stocks in Representative Ports (in $)

Port	Stock Value	Annual Turnover	Maintenance Costs/Year	Spares/ M & R Ratio
A	2.7 million	6.3 million	15 million	18%
B	7.0 million	4.0 million	83 million	5%
C	N/A	2.2 million	7.5 million	29%
D	900,000	N/A	N/A	—
E	N/A	309,000	1.4 million	23%
F	N/A	500,000	2.5 million	20%
G	11 million	2.0 million	22.3 million	11%
H	5.3 million	890,000	2.36 million	38%
I	1.9 million	3.0 million	29.5 million	10%
J	N/A	295,000	600,000	50%
K	2.85 million	2.03 million	6.0 million	30%

It is because of this very wide range of materials stocked, the diversity of port units served, and the duties of the department in terms of procurement, storing, issuing and recording of those materials, that in this chapter the function will be referred to consistently as 'Supplies Management', rather than the more commonly used 'Spare Parts Management'. Indeed, it is why the function merits a chapter of its own, to reflect its importance in port maintenance.

Discussion of the function will begin with a survey of some of the more significant problems and deficiencies relating to Supplies observed and detected in this survey, will continue in Section 7.3 with a discussion of the procedures and practices to be followed in a well-managed Supplies Department, and will end, in Section 7.4, with a consideration of the alternative systems of organization of the Supplies function.

7.2 A Review of the Supplies Function

7.2.1 Introduction

Although many of the criticisms levelled at those responsible for the supply of spare parts and other materials for maintenance are probably not fully justified – the faults may well lie elsewhere – there is no doubt that deficiencies in this area do cause very significant problems for port engineers. The port visits, conversations with maintenance, operations and supplies staff, the questionnaires and other information sources revealed a wide range of weaknesses in supplies management, from insufficient or incorrect stocks, errors in inventories and records, delays, poor location and communication, to lack of skills and knowledge, and financial and other constraints. These and other failings will be discussed in turn in this section, not primarily to apportion blame but to indicate how principles and practices need to be improved in Supplies Management.

7.2.2 Insufficient Stocks

Engineers would argue, with some justification, that spare parts and consumables that are regularly needed for preventive maintenance, or commonly have to be replaced after accidents – those normally referred to as 'stock items' in the supplies inventory – should be literally available 'off-the-shelf' when they request them. That this is by no means always the case is a sign of management failure somewhere. Insufficient stocking could, in fact, be due to a variety of factors:

— lack of forward planning on the part of supplies procurement staff;

— failure of the supplier to meet his target dates;

— failure of the purchaser to discover what the lead time for supply is likely to be;

— delays in placing the order;

— book-keeping and recording errors within the stores;

— errors in estimating demand.

The latter could be at least partly the fault of the engineering department; as will be discussed later, it must be the responsibility of the engineers to establish what supplies are needed for maintenance and repair, and in what quantity they are likely to be used. At one port, at least, stock levels were determined by the stores organization itself, without reference to the engineering department – an initial quantity of spares was purchased when the equipment was delivered and the stores assessed maximum and minimum holdings for subsequent years on the basis of draw-off from that initial stock; this arrangement is a most dangerous one, and is likely to lead to insufficiency of stocks sooner or later. Indeed, in most cases the failure to procure and stock sufficient spares and other materials for the port's equipment and other maintenance must be laid at the door of the Supplies unit.

The consequences of insufficient stocks are extremely serious. 'Waiting for spare parts' was one of the commonest reasons given for equipment lying idle in or near the workshops. In one port visited, for example, on a particular day 34 workshop jobs were scheduled, of which eight were 'completed', eight others were 'in progress', three were not started and fifteen were 'waiting parts' – 45% of the machines in the workshop that day were not being worked on because spare parts were unavailable, and several of the largest and most expensive of them (heavy-duty lift trucks) had been waiting for several months for parts. The knock-on effects on operations are obvious, and the upsetting of workshop schedules must not be overlooked, either, nor the congestion likely to be caused by partly-dismantled machines in and around the workshops.

7.2.3 Incorrect Stocks

An alternative explanation for a 'stock' item being, in fact, out-of-stock could be that the spare part in the appropriate slot on the storeroom shelf is not the one needed. A mistake could have been made when requisitioning or ordering, possibly a careless mis-reading of a multi-digit reference number. Another common mistake is to misinterpret the spares manual supplied by the manufacturer, and to give the code number for an equivalent part belonging to an alternative component, sub-system or system. For example, a leading UK forklift truck manufacturer offers six different ram assemblies for one model of truck; each assembly is illustrated in the manual and has its own set of numbered spares. The illustrations of the assemblies are extremely similar, and the parts numbers are confusingly alike, so it is relatively easy to make a mistake when identifying and writing down the part number.

Again, the item of equipment might have been modified since it was supplied – perhaps several years previously – so that the original spare part (as listed in the manufacturer's manual) is no longer suitable. Frequently, manufacturers are at fault in that they do not inform their agents or customers that changes have been made. Whatever the reason, if the asset register has not been updated and the changes noted, the procurement officer may well order a part which no longer fits. The error may not, in fact, be evident until an attempt is made to fit the spare part during a maintenance or repair job.

Another frequent cause of inappropriate spares being stocked is that mistakes were made when deciding which components should be kept in stock when the equipment was purchased. All ports reported that the initial list of stock items was chosen at least partly on the basis of the manufacturer's recommendations, possibly modified in the light of engineers' experience – or guesswork. Injudicious choice of stock items easily results in the purchase of parts that are never needed during the life of the machine and the overlooking of parts that turn out to be regularly required.

Another aspect of incorrect stocking, frequently reported in LDC ports, is the presence in the stores of large quantities of spare parts that are no longer needed, because the equipment they relate to is out of service or has been scrapped. In several countries, it seems almost impossible to remove cargo-handling equipment from the asset register, even when it is totally derelict and has been abandoned by the engineers and operators, and the related spare parts are still carried by the stores. In one case, an extensive range of spares for forklift trucks no longer in use was observed, and in another some 500 solid-tyred wheels were in stock for trailers that had been written off some years previously.

All such errors of stocking are instances of failure of supplies management, in one form or another – faults in the related information systems or in communication between engineering and supplies departments. Weaknesses in these areas are, unfortunately, not uncommon in LDC ports.

7.2.4 Poor Stock Identification and Recording

Even in a relatively small port or an independent terminal, a stores will contain a very large number of different items – certainly many thousands, if not tens of thousands. Clearly, if the required part is to be found quickly and correctly, meticulous attention must be paid to the identification and marking of the spares as they are delivered to the port (or returned to the stores after repair and refurbishment). Every part needs to be clearly marked in some way with the code or reference number which identifies it in the spares inventory. A large part can have a label firmly affixed to it, while small parts should be collected into a sealed plastic bag or container, and the identifying code fixed to that. The part(s) then must be stored in a bin or similar container on a numbered shelf or rack (preferably in some logical sequence and grouping), and its storage position accurately recorded in the stores inventory or ledger, so that it can be located with ease and certainty.

Inspection of the workshop stores in several of the ports surveyed gave cause to doubt whether the location of the spares is as carefully recorded as is essential, and the labelling of individual parts left a great deal to be desired. Clearly, many spares had spent long periods of time in the stores, and had

become extremely dirty and rusty, obscuring whatever identifying mark might once have been attached. Rack numbering was also less than clear, and it is extremely doubtful whether the storekeeper and his staff would be able to locate those parts as quickly and accurately as they should.

The situation is not helped greatly by the cumbersome nature of the recording system – the stores ledger, register or inventory. Ideally, given the vast size of the spares stock in most ports, the inventory should be computerized, with terminals at every receipt and issue point, but most ports still rely on a card- or ledger-based system. While a card-index system *can* be effective, it does take a great deal of effort to keep up-to-date and accurate, and it is all too easy for cards to go missing, particularly if (as observed in some cases) they are removed from the drawer or Cardex frame to take to the shelf position when retrieving a part. Handwritten entries can also be easily misread, and are readily obscured by grimy fingers. The system is, then, extremely vulnerable in careless hands, and some of the stores systems visited appeared extremely susceptible to error. Many of them seemed to depend largely for their everyday effectiveness on the experience and memory of the storekeeper, rather than on the accuracy and ease of use of their record system.

Even in ports where the record system appeared to be very comprehensive, the recording of the information required frequently leaves much to be desired. In one case, although a system existed for allocating costs of materials (as well as of labour and other services) to individual machines, it was admitted that this had not been done for over two years; staff shortage was claimed as the reason. No stores system can ever provide an effective service unless it is itself efficient, and this it cannot be unless a comprehensive system of recording exists and is faithfully operated.

7.2.5 Delays in Issuing Spare Parts

By far the commonest complaint of engineers, in relation to supplies, is that there is frequently a very long delay between completing a requisition for materials and spares and their issue at the workshop stores. Although there are suspicions in some quarters that some, at least, of these complaints are excuses for deficiencies within the engineering department, there is good supporting evidence for the truth of most of them. 'Waiting for spare parts' is, indeed, a regular state of affairs in many ports, leading to equipment being out of service for far longer than it should be, and drivers and maintenance staff being idle for much of their time.

There are a variety of different possible (indeed, actual) causes of delays in supplying spares. Supplies staff commonly give as the major reasons administrative and bureaucratic procedures within the port and/or relevant ministries (which certainly exist, and will be considered later in this section) and delays on the part of suppliers, particularly overseas suppliers. There are, however, good grounds for doubting whether the latter complaint, in particular, is justified; a review by Jerusel (1988) revealed that, in four surveyed ports, the greater proportion of the delay occurred between placing a requisition with Supplies and issuing of the order to the supplier (Table 7.2.5), suggesting that the fault lay within the port (possibly within the Supplies Department itself) rather than with the supplier.

Table 7.2.5 Sources of delay in spares supply (after Jerusel, 1988)

Port	Delay between request and issue of order (%age lead time)	Delivery time from supplier to stores (%age lead time)	Total request-to-delivery lead time
A	81%	19%	41 days
B	85%	15%	21 days
C	86%	14%	58 days
D	95%	5%	40 days

Internal procurement procedures thus have a considerable influence on delays in supplying spare parts. Among the possible reasons for delays within the Supplies Department itself are:

— insufficient staff to cope with the workload (an unlikely cause in most LDC ports visited, where the Supplies units had total staffing levels of between 125 and 450, compared with a major UK port with a staff of under 20);

— poorly trained stores staff, who waste time searching for spares (because they do not understand the record system) or looking through the parts manuals for the correct part number;

— cumbersome procurement procedures, requiring the passage of a request to order through a series of committees, tender boards or similar bodies, and needing authorizing signatures from unnecessarily senior managers (who may be away from the port for long periods, during which time requisitions sit on their desks, awaiting approval);

— stores not open when the parts are required – many stores operate solely on a daywork basis, whereas the port may be operating on a three-shift system, and maintenance staff need access to spare parts for breakdown or accident repair at any time;

— stores located a long way from user departments (see Section 7.2.6);

— lack of sense of urgency on the part of procurement staff – they claim that engineers fail to give a realistic priority ranking to requisitions (usually demanding 'urgent' attention for all requests), and leave it to Supplies staff to order priorities. They are, in any case, remote from the pressures of the workshops and may not understand the urgency of need for parts.

In their defence, Supplies staff often claim (with justification) that the engineering staff give them far too little warning of the need for supplies. Frequently, workshop managers wait until a piece of equipment has been stripped down for maintenance before requisitioning parts from the stores. Since it appears to be impossible in many LDC ports for spares to be issued 'over the counter' from the stores (though no satisfactory explanation was ever given to the team as to why this should be), delays in delivering the parts to the workshop are inevitable. Engineers can easily forestall such delays by issuing requisitions to the stores as soon as a preventive maintenance job is scheduled and its Job Card prepared; if the maintenance planning procedure is working well, this should give the stores staff several days to locate and issue the required parts.

7.2.6 Inappropriate Location of Stores

It might appear obvious that the stores holding the engineering spares that are regularly accessed for preventive maintenance should be sited near to the workshops, but this is not always the case. In one LDC port, the main store is situated no less than 8 kilometres from the port, and even the subsidiary store is over 2 kilometres from the main workshops. When it is realized that this is a port where internal transport is often a problem, the absurdity of the arrangement is clear. Not only are delays in obtaining parts for maintenance inevitable, but workshop staff spend a great deal of their time travelling to and from the stores, waiting for transport to get there and then waiting for the part to be found and issued, before starting the journey back.

It should be possible to organize the stores in such a way that items regularly needed in the workshops are stored either in or very near the workshop buildings, with only slow-moving (perhaps 'strategic') spares kept in a central stores. Even then, there should not be significant distances between the central stores and the working areas, unless an efficient and dedicated delivery system is available. In all cases, the location of the stores must be geared to the needs of the user (the Engineering Department) rather than the convenience of the Supplies Department.

7.2.7 Deficiencies in Supplies Personnel

The survey revealed in several ports considerable inadequacies in the personnel employed in the procurement, storage and issuing of supplies, so supporting some, at least, of the complaints of engineers. As will be shown in Section 7.3, the Supplies function demands a range of skills, and is by no means a straightforward series of operations. The Supplies staff accordingly need to be carefully selected, well qualified, trained and experienced if the unit is to perform effectively. Unfortunately, there is clear evidence that little importance is attached to staffing needs, that the Supplies Department staff are given a fairly low status in the organizational structure of the port, and that the required skills are often lacking.

First, all Supplies staff need a high level of clerical skill and knowledge. It is not sufficient for them to be just adequately literate and numerate, as the job of tracing, ordering, recording and keeping track of tens of thousands of items requires a considerable facility with figures and codes. They need to be able to read accurately the engineering drawings in the maintenance and spare parts manuals, to identify complex reference codes and to understand fully the stores' stock inventory and parts record system.

Staff also need to understand the port's own internal requisitioning and ordering procedures. They have to be familiar with the committee and tender board system, governmental and central bank regulations, customs procedures and a host of other administrative and bureaucratic rules and processes.

Then some, at least, of the clerical staff need to have had an engineering background, to be in a position to track down difficult to obtain components, working through suppliers' catalogues to find alternative sources of supply, appropriate substitute parts, and so on. Storekeepers and their assistants also have to have **at least** an interest in machinery, so that they can, with experience, understand the nature of the parts they are storing and issuing. They need to know how best to look after their stock, too; care and correct storage are important if the components are to be kept in good condition. It is very rare indeed to find stores staff with adequate knowledge of conditions of storage, correct greasing of parts, and so on, and very common to find racks of rusted, corroded and unusable spare parts.

7.2.8 Poor Internal Communications

A major shortcoming in the supplies process in some ports can be traced to an unsatisfactory relationship between the Supplies and Engineering staff. The organizational and administrative relationship between the functions varies considerably (as will be discussed in Section 7.4), and it is common for the functions to be separate departments, reporting independently to top management. The aims of the departments are, of necessity, different: Supplies will wish to keep costs as low as possible, by stocking the minimum number of items, purchased as cheaply as possible, and will be happiest when the least demands are made of their staff; the engineers, on the other hand, would prefer immediate access to every part, component and assembly that they might need, each manufactured to the highest technical specification, and obtainable with the minimum of administrative procedures.

If the system is to operate effectively, there clearly has to be compromise between these extreme ambitions, and each function has to appreciate and sympathize with the needs of the other. Good communication and an easy working relationship are essential. Unfortunately, these are sadly lacking in too many ports, and the survey revealed considerable antipathy and suspicion between the parties. Engineers accused the Supplies staff of delaying orders to suit their convenience, of not appreciating the urgency of engineering (and operational) needs, of purchasing low-quality substitute parts, and of generally obstructing the work of the engineers. Supplies personnel, on their part, look on many engineers as unreasonable in their attitude to procurement and supply, of leaving requests for parts to the last minute, of being imprecise and inaccurate in their identification of components, and of being unhelpful in reducing stock-holding and the search for alternative, cheaper parts.

Whatever the truth of the accusations (and there is evidence for all of the claims being justified in some instance or another), the basic underlying problem – which *must* be remedied – is a failure of management: the failure to establish good communications between the departments, the lack of an appropriate organizational relationship. As with most management problems, the solution is not an expensive one, and rests entirely on discussion between the parties and a willingness to sort out the difficulties. Proper inter-departmental procedures must be established, and effective, fool-proof links between the engineering and supplies information systems (see Chapter 9).

7.2.9 Procurement Constraints

The procurement of spare parts and other materials is just as vulnerable to governmental and related controls and regulations as is the purchase of cargo-handling and other equipment, as was discussed in Chapters 2 and 3. Although the individual order value may be much less – so much so that it is difficult to understand the need for tight control –

many ports suffer from the same range of regulatory procedures. Strict financial limits are placed on supplies expenditure, particularly where overseas suppliers are involved, and approval may have to be obtained from the Treasury and/or the Central Bank before foreign exchange can be committed and an import licence issued.

In one case, only local suppliers are allowed to tender (with preference being given to companies actually owned by nationals) and, if they do not carry the required items or are not stockists, they in turn have to trace and purchase from an overseas supplier. On receipt of an offer, the local company submits a price to the port, which in turn has to be approved by the appropriate Tender Board before the order can be placed. When manufacturing and delivery times are added to these procedural delays, it means that a piece of equipment could be out of use for up to two years.

In some countries it appears that spare parts can be purchased easily from local agents, although the parts have to be imported in the first place, whereas importing them directly from the manufacturer raises foreign exchange and import problems.

Possibly as a reflection of these controls, the port itself often imposes a rigid series of administrative hurdles between the request for parts and authorization of an order. At the very least, each requisition has to be signed by a suitably senior engineer – usually according to a strict hierarchical sequence related to order value. There may then be a necessity to go out to tender, for even modestly priced spares, and then for bids to have to be filtered through one of a series of Tender Boards, again dealing with specific order value ranges.

Some governments insist that, even after an order has been approved and placed with an overseas supplier, the spares must be inspected at the factory (usually by an approved, independent specialist) before import is permitted. Then follow a series of customs procedures, the imposition of import taxes or duties, and ultimately the supplies are delivered to the stores – perhaps many months after the initial request from the engineers.

The actual procedure to be followed when ordering supplies may vary according to whether the item is a 'stock item' (i.e. normally kept in stock, and reordered when the stock level has fallen to a predetermined value) or a 'non-stock item' – one which is needed only occasionally, or which was not expected to be needed at all during the working life of the equipment. Procedures also differ according to whether the item can be obtained from a national manufacturer or through a national or local agent or distributor. Supplies procurement procedures are, in many cases, just as complex and difficult to comply with as those involved in the procurement of capital equipment; often, in fact, they are the same procedures and regulations. There is no doubt that such controls and regulations are a severe hindrance to the effective functioning of the Supplies Department and the efficient working of the Engineering Department. In many of the ports visited and surveyed, these constraints were regularly identified as a most serious obstacle to the proper performance of the maintenance function.

7.3 Supplies Procedures and Practices

7.3.1 Introduction
In many ways, the Supplies Department resembles a retail business purchasing products in bulk from suppliers and 'retailing' them in units or small quantities to its customers. Like any business, it must establish and follow strict procedures that allow its activities to run in a smooth and fully controlled manner, day by day. These procedures include systems for accepting orders (requisitions) from its 'customers', for purchasing requisitioned items from its suppliers, receiving and checking the goods on delivery, controlling and caring for the stock, and issuing the items to the customers. It also needs an appropriate array of stores facilities, an effective stores records system and its own budget. These supplies procedures and practices will be considered, system by system, in this section.

7.3.2 Requisitions
Every supplies transaction must start with a requisition from the user department; in the present context, this will be the Engineering Department. As soon as the Engineering Management Information System triggers off a Job Card for a particular maintenance task, the responsible engineering manager should issue an internal Requisition Form (see Section 7.3.7), listing all the parts and consumable items that will be needed to carry out the job. If the job in question is a preventive maintenance task, the items needed will be known in detail in advance of the planned date, giving Supplies (initially, the appropriate store-keeper) time to check the stock position and to collect the items ready for issue. Little or no time will be available for corrective maintenance jobs, in general, as these will arise unexpectedly from breakdowns or accidents during operations; indeed, exactly which parts will be needed may not be known until the equipment has been stripped down and inspected, so that the requisition cannot be issued until the work is actually in progress.

The Requisition Form will have to be signed by an appropriate member of the engineering staff, and it is usual to set upper limits to the value of requisitioned parts authorizable by each category of staff. Indeed, in some LDC ports, even modestly priced items have to be authorized by senior engineering staff. It is much more reasonable to allow the routing desk engineer, a supervisor or workshop manager to authorize requests for small-value items, and only require requisitions of higher-value parts to be approved by more senior staff, possibly the Chief Engineer or his Deputy. However, if parts requisitioning by workshop staff is to be allowed, it is advisable to make and adhere to the general rule that *all* requisitions must be countersigned by the person immediately superior to the one making out the requisition. This is, after all, the simplest of management control measures to follow, and offers a greater measure of security and control than the practice followed in a few ports of allowing technicians to *authorize* the requisition of spare parts.

On receipt of the requisition form, the storekeeper must check first that the form has been properly completed, with authorization by the relevant engineering staff member. If the appropriate signature is in place, the storekeeper must next check that the requisition carries all necessary details of the items required: their descriptions, stores reference numbers, the quantity required, and the equipment for which they are needed. The code numbers and descriptions are checked immediately against the stock inventory, to check that the part exists and that the code and description match. If all is well, the stock position can be verified and the part collected from its store position. After issue, the storekeeper will retain a copy of the requisition, for entering cost details and for charging the spares against the job number, equipment code number and cost centre. Further details of the requisition procedure will be discussed in Chapter 9.

The procedure should be as simple as that for stock items, as a well-managed stores will have the required part in stock at all times (through the stock control procedures). For non-stock items, of course, the next step in the process will be the ordering procedure.

7.3.3 Procurement

Supplies are purchased under two circumstances. Stock items are ordered (either automatically or by request of the Engineering Department) when the stock level has fallen to a predetermined value, while non-stock items are ordered when the engineers specifically requisition them – either for a planned major maintenance or refurbishment job or for an unplanned repair following a breakdown or accident. The former case gives the procurement staff time to carry out the process at leisure, with the opportunity to source the parts for maximum quality and minimum cost, and following all the required documentary procedures and regulations to the letter. Non-stock items may pose particular problems, as they are often needed very urgently indeed.

Whatever the urgency of the order, a good Supplies Management Information System (SMIS – see Section 7.3.7) will contain sufficient data for the procurement staff to make sensible and rapid decisions about their course of action. Against the part number and description in the SMIS will be found details about the source – or alternative sources – of the part (manufacturer, supplier, distributor or agent), whether local, national or overseas, the normal delivery time, its cost, whether special import licence, tax or customs duty are imposed on it, whether it may be imported freely or is under government control for some reason, and any other special factor relating to its purchase. Only for very unusual and unexpected items should the procurement officer have to search suppliers' and manufacturers' catalogues and price lists for the parts.

In a relatively unregulated port and country, the next step may be to establish the most appropriate source of supply, if alternatives are available. At its simplest, this may merely involve a series of telephone calls, for quotations and delivery times. At the other extreme, and where port and government restrictions are severe, it might be necessary to invite three or more tenders in writing, or even to go to open tender. It is extremely desirable for the procurement of spare parts to be kept as free of such controls as possible, as they usually need to be purchased without significant delay, and often are needed urgently; this is one of the areas where LDC ports should be considerably freed of unnecessary controls as a matter of priority.

Assuming that all port and other formalities have been complied with, and the way has been cleared to place the order, the procurement officer can write out (or arrange for the computer to print out) the order, making sure that all the details are correct: part number (as identified on the supplier's list), decription, quantity, delivery address, terms of purchase, and so on. If there are any deviations from the details as supplied by the engineer on the original requisition, the procurement officer *must* check with the engineer before dispatching the order, in case some confusion or error has crept in.

Finally, the order must receive the appropriate authorization signature. This is often, as in the case of the requisition, a matter of order value; the more costly the item, the more senior is the person authorized to sign the order. For modestly priced items, one of the Supplies Department staff may be authorized to sign, while more expensive parts may require the head of the department to sign. Large orders may well have to pass to one of the Directors (perhaps of Finance) or the General Manager or his Deputy. Again, while some means of control over expenditure is essential in the port, it is important to keep such formalities to a minimum, and to delegate authority to as low a level within the Supplies Department as practicable. Otherwise, delay is almost inevitable – and that could be very costly indeed, if an important piece of cargo-handling equipment is unusable in the meantime. In the most successful ports, authority to order urgently needed items is delegated to the supervisor on duty, without the necessity to seek higher authority; this is a very desirable situation.

Purchasing limits or ceilings seem to be a fact of life in many LDC ports, and it is striking that many of the most successful ports in Europe have almost abandoned such limits for the purchase of engineering spares. The principle adopted in those ports is that the equipment *must* be returned to service as quickly as possible, so that it can earn its keep and perform its job of moving cargo. A delay of even a day or two, while bureaucratic procedures are gone through and successive signatures obtained from more and more senior staff, can cost the port dearly in terms of cargo and ships delayed and possibly customers lost. The contrast between that philosophy and the tight controls of some LDC ports, where senior management – or even Board – authority might be needed for expenditure of a few hundred dollars, is very marked. Those ports, it must be said, are among the most problem-hit as far as maintenance is concerned; the rigid spares procurement controls and rules do not make a positive contribution to the problems.

After an order has been sent off to the supplier, the procurement officer should inform the engineer who requested the item that it has been ordered. Then, over the days or weeks that follow, the officer must chase progress on the order, keeping the requisitioning engineer fully informed on progress and, if delivery is delayed, of the action being taken. Only when the item has been delivered should that file be closed and the order and associated documents passed on to the next stage in the procedure.

7.3.4 Receipt
Engineering supplies are normally delivered to one of the stores – either the main or central stores or one specifically designated for receipt of supplies. There the items are unpacked and checked carefully against the delivery note, order and requisition form. It might be necessary to check further, perhaps against the manufacturer's manual and specification sheets, to ensure that exactly the right part has been supplied and that it matches the specifications exactly.

When the part has been checked, the purchasing section of the department should be advised that the delivery can be accepted, and the invoice (when it arrives) can be processed. The date of delivery, a note of acceptance and definitive cost details can then be added to the initiating Requisition Form and to the SMIS, while the requisitioning engineer or workshop can be informed that the item has arrived. In the case of a stock item, it will be the storekeeper of the relevant store who is informed of the delivery, and the stock inventory will be updated accordingly.

7.3.5 Stock Control
A major activity of Supplies staff must be the strict control of the stores stock, an activity encompassing the recording of all transactions, the tracking of stock levels, ordering of stock items, adjustment of the inventory and so on. In practice, stock control appears poor. At one port visited some years ago, several cases of spares had been received and placed in the stores, still packed in their boxes and their contents unchecked. By the time the stores staff got around to unpacking and labelling the parts and placing them in bins at their designated storage positions, some items had already been removed; no records existed of their removal or distribution.

When a new stock item is agreed with the engineers, the first task of the Supplies staff is to give that item a reference code within the appropriate sequences. Codes of nine or ten digits are commonly used, one group indicating item type, another group designating equipment type (and possibly system and subsystem type), another its stores location, and so on. The number is unique to that particular item, but also allows the item to be related to the machine type in which it is used and even the system or assembly within that machine. Many components and assemblies (e.g. engines, transmissions, bearings, filters, capacitors and other electrical items) may be common to several pieces of equipment and thus interchangeable; the unique number allows such interchangeability to be established more easily. It is through its code number that the part is identified within the stores system, cross-referenced to all the other data used by Supplies staff – cost, source, delivery time, and so on.

The item is then entered in the stores inventory or ledger, with a Minimum Reorder Level (MRL) as agreed with the engineers. The level chosen will be a compromise between the engineers' desire for constant accessibility of the part, in case it is needed for maintenance or unexpected repair, and the Supplies staff's wish to keep stock to a minimum and reduce overheads. The MRL figure will be arrived at by working out the expected usage of the part for, say, a year and the delay between ordering the part from its suppliers and its delivery. If the related piece of equipment is new to the port, the resulting MRL will only be a best estimate, and usage will have to be monitored carefully and the MRL adjusted in the light of experience. In fact, this principle should be followed rigorously for *all* stock items, as demand can vary considerably with time, especially as the equipment inventory is added to or trimmed. It is not unknown for spare parts to be re-ordered for equipment which is being phased out, so that when the last piece of that equipment is written off, a considerable value of unwanted spares may have to be disposed of from stock, at great financial loss to the port.

Although all stock items will have a notional MRL, automatic reordering should not be applied blindly to slower-moving items, such as motors and gearboxes. These may well be stocked as strategic spares (those that are not likely to be needed frequently but are vital to the operation of a piece of equipment and would, if not immediately available in an emergency, cause considerable difficulties to Operations) rather than as routine items, in which case re-ordering should only be initiated after discussion with the engineers and authorization by them. For normal stock items, on the other hand, assuming that financial constraints allow, re-ordering should be carried out automatically by Supplies staff when the MRL is reached (but subject to regular review, as pointed out above).

As soon as a stores transaction has occurred – whether receipt of new stock or issue of items from stock – the stock inventory must be adjusted to show the current level for those items. The inventory is only of use to Supplies and Engineering staff if it is absolutely up-to-date at all times; an inaccurate inventory is misleading and dangerous. Keeping the inventory current and accurate is a primary task for the Supplies staff. They must also ensure that the stock inventory is made available to workshop and other engineering staff, both for giving information about spares (reference numbers, source, etc.) and for advising on current stock position. Ideally, each appropriate engineer should have desk access to the inventory (as a weekly printout, perhaps, or through online terminal access), though this survey has demonstrated how rare that facility is provided; in most LDC ports, the engineers have no access to the inventory at all, apart from visiting or telephoning the stores and asking staff there to consult their own copies. This is a very unsatisfactory substitute for a regularly distributed and updated inventory.

Updating the inventory must, of course, also be done every time obsolete stock is disposed of, a procedure which should be done regularly and with as little bureaucratic hindrance as possible. In several LDC ports, procedures for disposal of old stock (or, indeed, old equipment) are so complex that the process can take years to achieve, while in the meantime stocks clutter the storeroom shelves and the port's workshop areas.

Another aspect of stock control is the monitoring of the condition of the stock items. On arrival, they need to be checked for condition and then prepared for storage, either as advised by the supplier or as instructed by an engineer. They may need coating with preservative, packing in plastic bags or containers, and storing in controlled conditions of temperature and humidity, if they are not to deteriorate so as to be unusable when called for. All advice on storage conditions must be followed to the letter to prevent expensive spares deteriorating to an unusable state (a not unusual event in LDC ports).

7.3.6 Stock Issue

Issue of stores items, whether stock or non-stock, should be a straightforward process, but certain documentary and security procedures need to be followed if stock control and accounting are to be maintained. First, the Requisition Form should be checked for accuracy, completeness and authorization. Then, when the stores item has been located, it can be handed over directly to the workshop representative against his signature of receipt. There is no reason why issue should not be an over-the-counter affair of this type, though the evidence collected in this survey suggested that it may not be; in some ports, apparently, there is always a delay between receipt of a request and issue of the item, even if there is urgency to obtain the part for a maintenance job in progress – it seems almost to be a matter of principle on the part of stores staff to introduce a delay!

Provided there are no security or other reasons to delay the process, it seems a prime duty of the storekeeper and his staff to make stock issue as rapid and smooth as possible, to expedite maintenance. It is clearly an advantage, then, for the stores to be as near to the workshop as possible – preferably adjacent to it or in it. There is much to be said, from the functional point of view, for having satellite stores or sub-stores located in or next to the workshops, for the immediate issue of consumables and regularly used stock items, leaving only strategic stocks and slow-moving items to be kept in a central stores. Indeed, several European ports and terminals allow the workshop to maintain its own stock of rapidly-moving consumable and similar items – already 'issued' by the main stores, and documented and controlled by workshop staff. An alternative arrangement is to have a member of the Supplies staff attached to the workshop, to ensure that stock control is efficiently maintained; these arrangements will be discussed further in Section 7.4.

If it is not possible for an item to be issued from a workshop stores, or for the stores to be located near to the workshop, then it is essential to ensure that an efficient transport system is maintained, to deliver the requisitioned spares to the workshop without delay – this is all part of the 'issue' process, and must be achieved rapidly and smoothly if the maintenance function is to work unhindered and efficiently. Similarly, the documentaion related to requisition and issue must be kept as simple as possible, without endangering security and record-keeping.

7.3.7 Stores Records

References have already been made several times to the various components of the Stores record system. It is so important in the procurement, control and issuing of spares and consumables that it merits the establishment of a full Supplies Management Information System (SMIS), comparable to and linked with the other MISs of the port, particularly the Engineering Management Information System (EMIS). At its least elaborate, the SMIS should consist of a series of uniformly designed and printed forms, of which the Requisition Form is the prime mover. It should be developed by and distributed by Supplies, though it will, of course, be held and used at the workshops and engineering offices. It will contain space for indicating the issuing source (workshop, planning unit, routing desk, etc.), the item(s) requested (code number and description), related Job Card number, cost centre to be debited, signature of authorizing engineer and signature of the receiver of the item. It should also allow insertion of cost information (possibly added later, in the Supplies office) and have code numbers indicating the piece of equipment for which the part is needed – this will be on the Job Card as well, of course.

Other SMIS forms include order forms, tender documents and other items relating to the procurement function. These should be designed and used in accordance with Finance or Accounts Department formats and procedures, since they are very much part of the responsibility of that department. They still need to be fully cross-referable to the Requisition Form and other documents of the SMIS, however, and ideally should have the same general layout and terminology, to avoid possible confusion. (Indeed, there is a very strong argument for developing a uniform style and format for *all* documentation used by the port.) Copies of these procurement-related documents will be held by the Supplies Department, as part of its own record system, though the Finance/Accounts Department may well have overall responsibility for them.

Another major component of the SMIS – indeed, its central document – is its Stock Register or Inventory. This holds complete details of every component, spare and consumable item held in stock, including its description, its unique reference number, its manufacturer's and/or supplier's part number, its source, its stock level, the delivery lead time and its cost at last order. The Inventory must be as up-to-date as possible; certainly, the master copy must be updated at least daily. Copies must be circulated to all workshops and engineering offices and, of course, to all store positions. Within the stores, it will have its counterpart in the card-index or similar system recording every item kept in that storeroom, with its current stock level and shelf storage position. This system, too, must be absolutely up-to-date, and it is the responsibility of the storekeeper to ensure that every new stock delivery or issue is immediately recorded on the appropriate card or ledger entry, adjusting the current stock level record accordingly. It is essential that the history of a component should be traceable, from the time it is ordered, through the time it is incorporated into the piece of plant, and right up to the time it is finally scrapped.

The final element of the SMIS should be a directory of suppliers. This could take many forms, and may well be a shelf-full or filing cabinet of catalogues, price lists and reference books, but its function is to give the procurement staff immediate access to current information on suppliers and spares, so that new stock or non-stock items can be traced quickly when a requisition is received from the engineers or when a new piece of equipment is delivered to the port. The directory needs to be cross-referenced, whenever appropriate, to the Stock Inventory sourcing records, and such cross-references need to be updated regularly. In many European ports, such a directory (as well as related information provided by professional associations and similar bodies) is regularly searched by procurement staff for new sources of components and common items, as alternatives to supply by the equipment manufacturers. It is well recognized that manufacturers (who frequently, in fact, assemble their equipment from parts and systems supplied by other manufacturers) tend to charge more for spares than do the original makers of those items, and it is quite usual for Supplies staff to purchase from the component makers, rather than the equipment suppliers. Indeed, many European ports, and some of the more successful LDC ones, insist when purchasing new equipment that the suppliers provide full parts lists, giving direct sources of all items (as discussed in Chapter 4, Section 4.3.3.6). Not only does this strategy often produce dramatic cost savings over the life of the equipment but also can reduce supply lead times considerably, by eliminating one stage in the supply process.

Although reference to SMIS documentation has been made consistently throughout this section as if it was, indeed, paper-based (and in the majority of ports this is still the case – as books, files and Kalamazoo-type cardex systems), the complexity of the system obviously calls out for computerization. In many European ports, computerization of their MISs began with the stores inventory, for this very reason, and has only recently spread into the engineering and operational areas. Only by placing the Inventory, the Register of Suppliers and other data onto a computer database can the full benefits of direct sourcing, immediate stock update and inventory access be realized. Computer files also permit extensive cross-referencing of records, so that errors show up clearly and incorrect information can be rejected; in manual systems this is not necessarily so, and the survey demonstrated repeatedly that much information is recorded and then forgotten! The question of the benefits of computerization will be considered again, in relation to the EMIS, in Chapter 9.

7.3.8 The Supplies Budget

A repeated message throughout this report has been the need for all units of the port to be continually cost-conscious, to maximize efficiency and minimize waste. This applies to the Supplies Department no less than to anywhere else, and the Department should have budget targets and controls just like other departments. After all, Supplies is a major spending unit of the port; Table 7.1 demonstrated the extent of its expenditure, and Jerusel (1988) quotes figures indicating that in Western European ports materials account for about 20% of the expenditure of a quayside gantry crane workshop, 43% of that of a mechanical handling equipment workshop, with perhaps an average of 27% overall. In an LDC workshop, where labour costs are likely to be lower but spare parts costs much higher, Jerusel estimates that about 75% of total maintenance costs are likely to be accounted for by materials.

In the light of such figures, it is perhaps surprising that in some ports (especially in Europe) the cost of spare parts is rarely a matter of concern; the philosophy is that the engineer *must* maintain the piece of equipment. Some form of cost control is normally deemed necessary, but certainly not to the degree imposed in some LDCs, where competitive prices and even tenders have to be obtained for such small and low-cost items as spark plugs. However, if the cost/revenue centre approach is to be applied (as it should) to the Supplies Department, a budget needs to be established for the year ahead, based on past records and the maintenance budget for the year, if only as a performance target for Supplies staff to aim at.

Cost control then becomes a routine part of the Supplies management process, and procurement of spares will be approached in the same spirit as that of high-cost equipment – but with a realistic balance between effort and possible return. The procurement staff will need to know, for example, what the price of an item is before purchase. Prices can be obtained in a number of ways:

— For low-value items, and for more costly items for which a competitive price cannot be obtained in the time available (for example), the current price can be obtained from the appropriate catalogue(s), kept in the SMIS, or directly from the supplier.

— A number of suppliers can be invited, by either selected or open tender, to quote against a specified number or range of items.

— One or more suppliers can be invited to quote for the supply of items for a term period (e.g. a year), based on a bill of quantities and schedules of prices. All the items which a supplier can offer are listed, with a quoted price for each item. Normally, the numbers expected to be purchased over the term are stated and the tenderer is asked to state what discount will be offered on a volume or order-value basis. Such a term contract allows a large range of everyday items (often the low-value ones which are administratively relatively expensive to buy in small quantities) to be purchased quickly and economically, without the necessity of seeking quotations and tenders on every occasion.

— A contract can be negotiated with a supplier for a single item or for the term supply of groups of named items.

— Where local agents hold a wide range of spare parts, an agent can be contracted (either by tender or by negotiation) to hold a specified range of spare parts, from which the port can draw or 'call-off' as required. The agent is responsible for ensuring that minimum agreed stock levels are maintained and for storage, relieving the Supplies and stores staff of these chores – and the port, of course, of the expense of storing the parts.

Clearly, because of the expense involved in providing storage facilities and the staff to look after the stock, it is desirable from Supplies' point of view to limit the range and quantity of materials stocked, and considerable thought and discussion has to be given to the question of what spares to stock. As discussed in Chapter 4, when a new type of equipment is being purchased, the almost universal procedure is to purchase with the equipment the spares recommended by the manufacturer as sufficient for the first year or so. If the port has some experience of that type of equipment, or one similar to it, the general approach is to modify the manufacturer's list in some way, to take into account local conditions and circumstances; sometimes, the list is shortened but often it is added to, if engineers know from their EMIS records that some components or assemblies are particularly prone to wear or damage under the port's particular operating, climatic or other conditions.

In complete contrast to this cautious approach, many European ports take the view that, during the warranty period, there should be no need to stock parts at all, apart from consumable items, such as oil and air filters, which have to be replaced regularly. These ports rely on the rapid supply of any parts unexpectedly needed, either direct from the nearby factory or from a local depot or regional store. Only rarely is it possible for an LDC port to enjoy the luxury of such warranty service, however desirable it is from the points of view of engineer and Supplies officer alike. By the end of the warranty period, the engineers will have gained a good idea of what parts should need to be stocked, and can discuss with Supplies the appropriate stock level and MRL for those parts.

Understandably, of course, Supplies (and Finance) staff wish to keep the volume of stock as small as possible. Spare parts are often very expensive, particularly in LDCs. Manufacturers' and agents' mark-up on spares is high – one port quoted a figure of 350% – and customs duties of 100% and more are common. So there is a very large capital investment tied up in materials that may lie on the shelf for long periods of time. Not unnaturally, ports in countries where agents or suppliers are able to import freely keep stock holdings to a minimum, but in countries where foreign exchange controls and the need to raise Letters of Credit are obstacles to rapid delivery,

and where local agents (where, indeed, they exist) do not hold stocks, ports feel bound to hold a large range and volume of stock items.

Some Supplies departments try to get around the problem of spares capital by finding cheaper substitutes for the makers' own parts, often manufactured locally. This strategy at least allows sufficient stocks to be held to permit rapid return of equipment to service, but engineers frequently complained to the team that such substitute parts are often inferior in quality and wear out quickly. They often cause accelerated wear of other components, too, and can lead to partial or complete failure or collapse of the piece of plant. Bearings, for example, may have physical dimensions identical to those of a maker's 'official' part, but their load-bearing and speed ratings may not be equivalent. Such purchasing economy is, then, often a false one; price should not necessarily be the prime criterion when sourcing, and the engineers' approval must be sought for any alternative source of supply or 'equivalent' part.

It is also worth bearing in mind, when choosing spares for newly procured equipment, that parts and systems do not necessarily change significantly from one generation of equipment to the next. On a quayside gantry crane, for example, the electric motors, structural components and other parts may well remain constant for five years or more, despite changes in model number. Many of the stockable spares for a new crane may well be already stocked for an existing crane. Indeed, it is only electronic control gear and similar 'high technology' systems that are almost *certain* to be different from an older model. It is, therefore, very important for the engineers and supplies officers to check very carefully the manufacturers' list of recommended spares, reviewing what is really different from the existing stock before placing a spares order.

Another strategy for reducing expenditure on supplies stocks is to consider refurbishment of replaced components, either within the port's workshops or at a local specialist contractor's. Even when spare parts are readily available, ports often find it possible to renovate more cheaply (and perfectly effectively) than to buy new, and the case for refurbishment is even stronger in LDCs, where supply lines are extended, spares costs are high and delivery much delayed. It is surprising, then, to find that few of the ports visited undertake refurbishment work, apart from the rewinding of electric motors and the overhauling of engines in a few of them. Where refurbishment is practicable, it should be the responsibility of the Supplies Department to issue the order, to take the item back into stock after completion (giving it a new Inventory number) and to cost it separately from the job which removed it from its original equipment location. The part can then be re-issued as required, through the normal requisition procedure.

Following the cost-consciousness approach through, the next responsibility of the Supplies staff is to monitor the use of the stock regularly, to increase the stock level of items that are being used more rapidly than expected, perhaps to transfer to the 'stock item' list such 'non-stock' items as have been purchased, unexpectedly, several times, and to reduce the stock levels of (or eliminate from the inventory altogether) stock items which have not moved in a significant time period. The aim is to pare down the quantity of stock held (and so to reduce to a minimum the capital tied up in stock and storage space) while continuing to maintain the level of materials supply required by the engineers. Clearly, any changes in stock level or range must be fully discussed with senior engineers before decisions are taken; only the engineers will be fully aware of the consequences of any proposed changes.

A final step in the cost-control process would be to adopt a thorough cost/revenue centre philosophy, treating the user department (the workshops and other engineering units) as sources of income, and the spares and consumable purchases, as well as staff costs, heating, lighting and other overheads, as expenditure items. The aim would then be to balance income and expenditure, setting targets for reducing the latter year by year. Labour, accommodation and overhead costs could be averaged over a year's transactions (remembering that every item passing through the stores is handled at least three times – receipt, storage and issue) and a per-transaction charge added to the item purchase price when costing it out to the recipient unit or Job Card code. Where multiple sets of the item are stocked, perhaps purchased at different times and at varying prices, it is usual for an averaged price to be used as the item cost; the inventory data on cost must then be re-calculated every time a new purchase is made. Slow-moving items and those stocked singly can be charged out at replacement purchase price.

By adopting a cost/revenue strategy for the Supplies Department, the general principle of accountability can be extended to this section of the port, too. Management can be made accountable for the running cost and efficiency of the Department, can be rewarded for meeting or exceeding budget and other performance targets (perhaps Mean Time to Satisfy a Request), and can be made to balance the books in terms of income and expenditure.

7.3.9 Stores Facilities

The stores and procurement aspects of the Supplies Department are essentially service units to the engineering maintenance function, and this must be borne in mind when organizing or reorganizing the stores. The storerooms, store buildings, yards and/or compounds should be designed and sited so that the items stocked are stored correctly and can be made readily available to the appropriate engineering section. In practice, port development is generally piecemeal, over a long period, and little coherent thought has generally been given to the siting, design and equipping of the stores. This is evident in a visit to an old port, where spare parts are often stored in buildings which have been pressed into service when no longer suitable for other port activities, or have been erected as a 'temporary' expedient many years ago. The stores buildings are generally old, frequently in need of repair, they lack adequate natural or artificial light, are not sealed against entry of dust and have no special provisions for storing components or materials requiring special storage conditions.

At a few ports visited – generally those where specialist berths and terminals have been constructed recently – stores facilities appropriate to the stock to be stored there have been provided next to the workshops. Such stores indicate what can and should be done, and throw into sharper relief the shortcomings of most stores facilities, which are inadequate and usually badly sited; in one case, as mentioned earlier, the two principal stores are located 2 km and 8 km distant from the port workshops.

Only in a small port or an independent terminal is a single stores likely to be sufficient. In most cases, cargo-handling and other facilities are spread out over a relatively large area, and it is usually more convenient to provide a number of stores. Slow-moving spare parts and materials, as well as strategic or security spares held for emergencies, can well be housed in a central or main store, not necessarily sited near to any particular operational or maintenance section. The items held in a central store (which will include civil engineering and non-engineering supplies as well as mechanical and electrical materials) are generally large, and adequate notice can normally be given to the stores staff when they are required, so that they can be delivered to the appropriate location in good time. On the other hand, consumables and fast-moving spares are generally small and are often required quickly (e.g. to repair a broken-down or accident-damaged machine), so they should be readily available to workshop staff, and the buildings in which they are stored should be at least near to the appropriate workshop.

So in a reasonably sized port, the stores complex

172

may well comprise a main stores and a number of satellite stores located near the individual workshops. In addition, each workshop should have its own small store, in which small items (nuts and bolts, cleaning materials, fuses, fan-belts etc.) can be held for immediate access at times when the main and satellite stores are not open. Technicians should have easy access to those workshop stores, with the minimum of formal procedures necessary before removing the material. However, the stock still needs to be controlled and monitored, and it is important to have a responsible person in charge of it, keeping records and maintaining stock security. A novel approach recently adopted in one port is to issue each workshop technician with a bar-code reading device and to attach a unique bar-code to each stock item, Job Card and other document. When a spare part is needed, the technician takes it from the shelf, 'wipes' his reader over the bar-code, then over his own bar-coded badge and the Job Card, so that the SMIS and EMIS are immediately updated with the information that the designated technician has removed that part and that it is to be debited against that particular job in his name. In one operation, then, all the requirements for access, security, stock monitoring and updating, etc. are simultaneously taken care of.

Security is normally a significant feature of stores management. Stores buildings and compounds should be secure against unauthorized entry, and access to points where stock items are delivered or issued must be clearly defined. No unauthorized person should be permitted to pass the counter or other serving point, and only the storekeeper and his assistants should be allowed within the storage area. No item should be allowed to pass over the counter without a properly authorized requisition and without a signature of receipt from the engineering representative collecting it. The stores inventory must also be updated immediately, either by keyboard entry at the time of issue or by entry in the stores card-index, with central register updating at the end of the day.

Conditions of storage must be carefully planned, supervised and controlled. Manufacturers' recommendations must be observed as closely as possible. For example, items which are affected by temperature or humidity changes should be stored in air-conditioned cabinets or rooms; some types of paint are among materials that have a very short life if exposed to high temperatures but can be kept for long periods at low temperatures. Tyres can be stored for longer periods without deterioration if kept in subdued light. Special facilities should be provided for the storage of hazardous materials, such as oils, volatile and inflammable materials, and corrosive liquids.

Generally, storekeeping in LDC ports leaves much to be desired. Little or no attempt is made to segregate items adequately or to store them correctly. Steel components are often stored on concrete floors, unprotected against corrosion. Hydraulic components are not protected against dust. Ferrous components are frequently not protected against atmospheric moisture and are allowed to rust to the extent that they are no longer of any use. It is not uncommon to see delicate items placed in a heap in a bin, unprotected from each other. Items such as gears, sharp-edged tools and electrical components should be individually wrapped or sealed in polythene, and stored in bins or separately on shelves. Larger items can be stored on racks or pallets, but in every case care must be taken to ensure that components cannot be damaged when adjacent items are handled. It is vital that all racks, bins and other receptacles are clearly labelled to indicate the items stored there, and that care is taken to ensure that newly delivered items are stored in their correct places.

It is very important that stock is stored in such a way that access to them by stores staff is easy and unobstructed. Too often, large and unwieldy items are stacked in front of racks and in aisleways, making access to smaller, shelved items unnecessarily difficult; damage is likely when staff have to stretch to reach a storage position. Lifting devices such as small cranes or forklift trucks should be available to handle large components; such items are frequently damaged when being handled without special lifting gear.

General 'housekeeping' is just as important in a stores as in a workshop or operational area. It is absolutely essential for floors to be kept clear and clean, shelves to be kept free of dirt and dust, and, as far as the stock itself is concerned, 'a place for everything and everything in its place'. Observation in ports around the world reveals that housekeeping is not always what it should be, and many stores fall far short of the ideal. The most efficient ones appear to be those that specialize in a relatively narrow field, such as marine stores. Here the types of spares held are limited in range and of a specific nature, and more often than not the stores are orderly and components well looked after. It is suggested that these stores benefit by having staff with a seafaring background (in the country's navy or merchant marine), during which they received good training and worked in a disciplined environment. Certainly, stores staff need to be trained specifically for their jobs, just as for any other port activity; experience suggests that many ports, particularly in the Third

World, fail to provide that training or to select staff with the appropriate background, experience and skills for their jobs.

7.4 Stores Organization

7.4.1 Introduction

The status and position of the Supplies function within the port are among the most variable of all the activities surveyed in this project, and responsibility for the procurement, storage and issue of spare parts and consumables varies widely from port to port. Often, Supplies staff are accused of being 'remote' from the daily needs of cargo-handling and maintenance, and give less than appropriate urgency to those needs. On the other hand, Supplies is frequently not accorded a status reflecting the actual importance of the function in the port organization. In too many ports, the purchasing and stores function is not considered to be part of the maintenance team, whereas in reality it is a very significant contributor to (or inhibitor of) engineering effectiveness.

The quality of Supplies managers and their attitude to the task of providing a service to engineering (and other) departments varied considerably. While Supplies managers claim that they clearly understand that their unit exists to provide such a service, inspection of their procedures and the evident lack of urgency in performing them indicate that they do not do so in some cases, particularly in LDC ports. These are often the ports which experience greatest difficulty in obtaining supplies (because of governmental, financial and geographical constraints) – just those where it is of greatest importance to have a dedicated and forceful procurement organization.

The Supplies unit must have a clearly defined structure and be staffed by personnel skilled in the duties they have to perform. Those involved in procurement must be tenacious, have an enquiring disposition and the will and ability to maintain pressure on suppliers when necessary. Stores management must be responsible and responsive to demands, and staff need knowledge (either first-hand or acquired in post) of a wide range of mechanical, electrical and other specialized spares.

Clearly, if the Supplies unit is to function effectively and to contribute to the smooth running of the Engineering Department, it must be accorded appropriate status, be placed suitably within the port's organizational structure, and itself be provided with sufficient trained staff within a suitable organizational hierarchy. These are the topics to be considered in this section, under the headings Management Responsibility, Organizational Structure and Establishment.

7.4.2 Management Responsibility

The organizational structure, and the officers to whom stores and procurement personnel reported, varied widely in the ports visited and contacted during this survey. In a sample of ten ports, there were two cases in which an independent Supplies or Stores Division reported directly to the General Manager, on an equal status with Engineering, Operations and other Divisions. In three cases, the function was the responsibility of the Head of Finance, either as a separate Department/Section or as two units – Procurement and Stores. In another three ports, Supplies was a Department within the Administration Division, while in two cases the Chief Engineer (or one of his managers) was completely responsible for the Supplies Section.

In only two of the ten ports, therefore, was Supplies directly related to the engineering function, although it was reported that several ports had formerly organized the stores within the Engineering Department and had recently changed to an alternative arrangement. The obvious first question, therefore, is: which is the most appropriate arrangement and position for the Supplies function? There are arguments in favour of both approaches.

A strong case can be made for control to be exercised by the Engineer. Responsibility then lies wholly within one department (reducing the temptation to blame others for inadequacies) – and in this case the one with the specialist technical knowledge to ensure that the correct components are purchased, or suitable substitutes where appropriate. The Engineer should be aware of the priority to be placed on ordering and chasing orders for spare parts, and will thus be able to eliminate delays which can and do occur when responsibility is divided. In ports where Supplies is an independent Division, or a Department of Finance or Administration, the engineers tended to complain of inefficiency, lack of technical knowledge, bureaucratic delays and tardiness, failure to chase orders, and lack of communication within stores and procurement. Where Supplies is part of the Finance or Administration divisions, the argument goes, there is a tendency to understock the stores, and to go for the cheapest source of components and materials, ignoring questions of quality and lead time.

The arguments *against* Supplies being an Engineering responsibility may be just as strong. The one most frequently quoted is that engineers, when in charge of purchasing supplies, tend to overstock with engineering components and consumables, giving priority to ready availability of spares at the

Within the administrative and procurement functions of the unit, the staffing will again be fixed relative to workload, though with the minimum of one of each of the specialists as indicated in Figure 7.4.3. It must also be recognized by senior management that these posts *are* specialized ones, requiring training, specialist knowledge and the experience that can only be acquired with time. Managerial staff should have graduate qualifications – degrees or diplomas – and should become members of appropriate professional bodies, such as Institutes of Purchasing and Supply. In too many ports, Supplies (especially procurement) posts are considered as just general clerical posts, requiring no professional qualifications, and staff are moved between departments without considering the effect on the skills and abilities of the unit. The organizational structure and job categories within Supplies must allow a reasonable career structure for all its staff, without their having to move to other disciplines for career advancement (this general principle is addressed further in Chapter 8).

7.5 Recommendations

1. Policy makers and senior port managers must establish supplies management procedures that effectively control the purchase, storage and issue of spare parts and other supplies for maintaining plant, equipment and other port facilities.

2. Requisition procedures must be set down which enable the Engineering Management Information System to initiate action on the spare parts needed for preventive and corrective maintenance, and allow the stores to prepare these well in advance of the work.

3. Authority for authorizing the requisition of all routine and inexpensive spare parts must be given to workshop supervisory staff, with senior engineers' sanction only required for expensive items.

4. All Requisition Forms should be counter-signed by an immediate superior, to improve security and control of the issue of spare parts.

5. Simple procurement procedures must be laid down, free from rigid controls and regulations, to allow parts to be purchased quickly and at minimum cost.

6. Authorization to order spare parts should be delegated to as low a level as possible within the Supplies department.

7. Efficient stock control procedures must be established, covering the recording of all transactions, the tracking of stock levels, ordering of stock items and adjustment of the inventory.

8. All stock items must be given an appropriate and unique reference code number, for use in the stock control procedures.

9. A minimum re-order level (MRL) must be set for each stock item, as agreed with the engineers and based on the expected usage and ordering-delivery lead times.

10. Re-ordering of stock items should normally be carried out by Supplies staff, and financial and other constraints should be removed or eased to allow this to be performed smoothly and quickly.

11. On delivery to the port, all stock items should be appropriately prepared for storage (e.g. coating them with preservative, packing them in plastic bags or containers) and they should where necessary be stored in conditions of controlled temperature and humidity, to prevent deterioration.

12. Appropriate central, satellite and workshop stores should be established, to ensure quick supply of spares when needed and to guarantee good conditions of care and security in storage.

13. Slow-moving spares, 'strategic' spares and items common to several types of equipment should be kept in a central stores, while regularly used spare parts and consumables, with a quick turnover, should be held in satellite or workshop stores, to permit immediate issue.

14. A comprehensive manual or computerized Supplies Management Information System (SMIS) must be established to regulate requisition and stock control procedures, and to maintain a directory of suppliers and other information necessary for procurement.

15. Strict budgetary control procedures should be introduced to cover the management of supplies, treating this function as a cost/revenue centre.

16. Cost-consciousness must be fostered in Supplies staff, by establishing measures to minimize purchasing, stock holding and issuing costs.

17. The importance of the Supplies function within the port organization must be recognized, and its contribution to maintenance effectiveness and corporate objectives acknowledged, by giving it full departmental status.

18. The responsibilities and authority of the Supplies Department should be clearly delineated, and procedures must be set up to ensure full co-operation with the Engineering Department, with the engineers retaining authority to determine the range of spares maintained, to approve stock levels and to authorize the purchase of alternatives.

19. The Supplies Department must recognize that its primary function is to provide a *service* to the Engineering Department, keeping it supplied with all the spares and consumable materials it needs to perform its maintenance duties without delay or hindrance.

20. An appropriate organizational structure must be devised for the Supplies Department, preferably with separate Stores and Procurement sections.

21. Appropriate manning levels must be set for the Department, with all staff professionally qualified and trained in the specialist skills of procurement and stores management.

CHAPTER 8

Management and Manpower Development

8.1 The Role of Manpower Development

Although ports are of necessity becoming increasingly dependent on machinery for carrying out their primary function, of handling ships and cargo, and on automation and computers for much of their planning, control and administrative work, there can be no argument but that, as in any other business, success ultimately rests on the skills, attitudes and efforts of their management and workforce. In this chapter, the human resources of port maintenance departments will be surveyed, in terms of the recruitment, training, career development, motivation and performance of their managers and manpower.

It is, regrettably, true that many (if not most) of the worst features of ports, particularly in LDCs, can be ascribed not to lack of equipment (although there may well be a shortage from Operations' point of view) or of financial resources (however real that lack may be) but to the poor performance of labour and management; this applies in Engineering no less than in other departments. Conversely, it is salutary to see what can be achieved in terms of performance in a poorly-resourced port which is fortunate in having innovative and inspiring managers and an enthusiastic workforce who are wholeheartedly supportive of them. In itself, this should encourage ports to devote more attention to management and manpower development; for a relatively small financial investment, but with substantial effort to reorganize career structures, training and incentive schemes, enormous improvements can be made to port efficiency and performance – without dependence on massive international aid or technical assistance projects. Much can be achieved from within the port, using the port's own resources, if a new attitude is taken to manpower – the port's most important asset – and its development. Too many managers look on manpower development as a regrettably necessary *cost*, rather than as an *investment*, whereas investment in manpower development is really the least-risk solution to many port problems, with a very high rate of return.

In the next section, some of the particular problem areas observed and discussed during this survey will be described, preparatory to considering, in Section 8.3, the major factors contributing to a successful manpower development strategy. One of these factors – training – is considered at greater length in Section 8.4, and the other fundamental factor, employee attitude, is discussed in Section 8.5.

8.2 A Review of Manpower Problems

8.2.1 Introduction

Although the ports visited and contacted in this survey displayed a very wide range of management and manpower structures, as well as considerable variation in their commercial success and efficiency, certain deficiencies in human resource factors seem to be regularly associated with poor performance, no less in their engineering function than in their cargo-handling, administrative, financial and other activities. These deficiencies include: a lack of management and supervisory skills; problems of technical and craft skills; the attitude of maintenance staff; poor salaries and promotion prospects, and a lack of incentives; the absence of accountability; inadequate training facilities, opportunities and systems; poor internal communications; and excessive or unbalanced manning.

In this section, these broad problem areas will be considered in turn, as a means of highlighting the influence of manpower and management deficiencies on port performance, with respect to the maintenance function, and to draw attention to how those aspects of engineering management can be improved.

8.2.2 Management Skills

Managers in the Engineering Departments of ports visited and contacted during this survey seem universally to have received an appropriate professional training for their jobs. They are, by and large, graduates of university engineering faculties; a university engineering degree is generally the first qualification specified at recruitment. The more junior managers may have a polytechnic degree or equivalent qualification, but the general feeling is that there is no shortage of university graduates applying for posts in port maintenance in most countries (though some reservations are expressed about the *quality* and the relevance of the professional training these graduates have received).

The professional skills are, then, apparently not in short supply. There was some discussion as to the relative merits of a civil engineering degree (on the one hand) and a mechanical or electrical engineering degree (on the other) as qualifications for senior staff in ports; traditionally, it seems, civil engineers have tended to be appointed to the most senior posts – Director of Engineering, Chief Engineer, or equivalent – with the mechanical and/or electrical graduates attaining only positions below them in the Engineering Department hierarchy. There is clear evidence, however, that this situation is changing, as was discussed in Chapter 6. As the operational dependence on complex cargo-handling equipment has increased, so have the role and status of the mechanical/electrical engineer improved, and there are now many managers with mechanical and electrical engineering degrees directing port engineering departments.

So, although some doubts may be justifiably expressed about engineers' practical skills (Chapter 6), maintenance problems are not likely to be the result of a lack of professional ('theoretical') engineering qualifications. However, it is all too obvious in many ports that managers lack the necessary skills in the equally important area of *management*. In no port was it stated that qualifications in management and supervisory skills are prerequisites for appointment to even the highest posts in the Engineering Department, nor is it obligatory for managers to receive regular (indeed, any) training in those skills. There is little doubt that, if one factor can be identified as being responsible for the poor performance of the maintenance function in ports, particularly (though by no means exclusively) in the LDCs, that factor would be the profound lack of management skills.

Many of the individual deficiencies to be identified in this section can, ultimately, be traced back to the inability of engineering managers to *manage* effectively – to plan, organize and supervise the work of their departments, and to motivate and lead their workforce, from supervisors, foremen and technicians down to artisans and assistants. To take just one example, 'housekeeping' in the workshops is much neglected in many ports: equipment, tools and rubbish are not cleared away after work; oil, grease and dirt are allowed to accumulate;

consumables are carelessly left around the benches and floors; hand and machine tools are neglected – not cleaned or greased, nor sharpened and adjusted; there is a general air of unkempt disorderliness and mess. None of these are reflections of lack of finance, manpower or professional skill; they are all products of a management that fails to manage and just does not care about the ethos of the department. Indeed, even if the port has adequate finance for equipment, has a pool of technically qualified people from which to recruit, and has good workshop buildings and maintenance facilities, the engineering function can still fail miserably to meet the needs of its customers in Operations if it is not well managed.

This lack of management skills, a prime factor in poor engineering performance (and, consequently, of inadequate satisfaction of operational demand), can fairly easily be put right by an effective training programme. And this can be provided at relatively little expense to the port – certainly when compared with the budgets handled by the Engineering Department and the revenue at stake if equipment and civil works deteriorate through poor maintenance.

8.2.3 Technician Skills

In some parts of the world, as this survey has revealed, there is a significant shortage of suitable recruits for the craft-level posts in maintenance, particularly in the mechanical and electrical (especially electronic) disciplines. Engineering workshops in ports of those countries report that the artisans and technicians lack the skills to perform routine mechanical servicing and repair, let alone the more complex tasks of maintaining hydraulic and electronic systems and components. The difficulties caused by the poor quality of recruits are aggravated by the inadequacy of the training provided by those ports – if, indeed, any is offered at all; it is often the case that the ports (frequently quite small and uncompetitive) have no suitable resources or facilities for offering training, and maintenance staff receive only the most rudimentary of 'sit beside Nellie' on-job training after recruitment. Full-blown apprenticeship schemes are the only realistic solution to the recruitment problem in countries where the school system is not capable of producing technically-trained school-leavers, but it is just those ports and countries where such schemes are no longer provided – if, indeed, they ever were.

In other countries where maintanence problems were evident, there seemed not to be a shortage of suitable recruits to engineering, and the team was assured that the required skills were there. The ports even provided technical training (of variable quality and extent), both formal and on-job. School-leavers often have technical or trade qualifications – at least of basic level – and technical/vocational colleges exist or are being established nationally and regionally to provide a pool of potential recruits already trained to use hand and machine tools, familiar with internal combustion and diesel engines, hydraulic systems and basic electrical circuits. Yet the state of the workshops and of the ports' equipment, infrastructure and building provides ample evidence that all is far from well with the engineering workforce. Either the claimed skills and abilities are illusory or other factors are involved; the latter seems to be the case in several of the ports visited.

Among those factors is probably the lack of craft skills among the junior, middle and senior managers. They have had no experience in using the day-to-day *practical skills* that are the essence of port maintenance, and would be totally incapable of carrying out the repairs and services in the workshops and on the berths that they expect their technical staff to do. It can, of course, be argued that engineering managers (particularly the more senior ones) should not be expected to possess and be capable of applying those skills – the actual maintenance and repair tasks are for technicians and artisans, not those in authority over them. Such an attitude is particularly prevalent in LDC ports, where the title 'manager' is firmly associated with desk and white collar, and even a 'workshop manager' is content to remain in his office all day, rather than venture onto the workshop floor to supervise, advise on and assist in the actual work of maintenance. This is a very dangerous attitude, and is to a large extent responsible for the poor performance of the maintenance function in those ports.

At the very least, engineering managers need to know, from practical hands-on experience, what the problems, processes and procedures of maintenance are if they are effectively and knowledgeably to manage the unit and their staff. At least, they should be prepared to join in the work as necessary, becoming part of the team when circumstances demand it. It is surely significant that the ports with a good maintenance record, contributing to commercial success and a high reputation, had practically orientated and experienced engineers, in even the highest posts within the Department, who were quite ready to roll up their sleeves and take part in the workshop's activities when problems and emergencies arise, and when the maintenance function is being audited and reorganised. Once again, training is a vital factor in this aspect of management and manpower, as will be considered later.

Of probable equal significance is the lack, in many Engineering Department hierarchies, of a tier of lower management between the workshop foreman and a desk-based manager. This level is seen as a very important one in European ports and the best of the LDC ports, and is given a variety of names, including Superintending Engineer, Supervisor, Workshop Manager, and Meestergastr. The key feature of this position is that it links the technicians in their daily work with the engineers who are responsible for forward planning, strategy and the broad principles of maintenance. The occupant of the post is essentially a practical engineer, with years of experience in heavy industry – in Europe he may well have spent his earlier years as an engineer with a crane or truck manufacturer, or as a sea-going engineer – and with a strong enthusiasm for machinery and its maintenance. In addition, he has an aptitude for, and has been trained for, man-management and for organizing engineering facilities. His particular combination of technical, organizational and managerial skills is regarded highly in the most successful ports, and the absence of this tier of management in the less successful ports (or the lack of the right persons to fill those posts) is a matter of some concern.

Another factor which is almost certainly significant is that, although the maintenance staff probably possess (or at least were taught) the necessary craft skills to perform their jobs, they do not, for one reason or another, make use of their skills. The lack of good supervision and management are certainly contributory factors, but a major problem appears to be a lack of motivation on the part of the technicians and artisans; this will be considered next.

8.2.4 Maintenance Staff Attitudes

There was clear evidence of entirely inappropriate attitudes in several of the engineering departments visited, displayed at all levels within the hierarchy. At the more senior levels, the attitude was manifested by the desk-bound lack of involvement with workshop activity already referred to, while at technician and artisan level it was evident in the grim conditions that existed in the workshops and the derelict equipment littering the sites. Technicians often seemed to have no work to do, springing to spurious action when the visitors entered the workshops, even though no convincing job seemed to be in progress. Where equipment had been dismantled for maintenance, the components were scattered in disarray, often on the dirty floor, and some machines seemed destined never to be reassembled.

Clearly, effective port maintenance cannot be practised in such conditions; the staff just do not seem to care about their work, and it is very unlikely that preventive maintenance is paid more than lip-service under those circumstances. The problem seems to be a combination of lack of motivation and absence of discipline – at least partly attributable to bad management, no doubt, but also very much to do with the wage/salary structure and lack of incentives, as will be shown shortly.

In complete contrast to the black picture painted above, there were other ports where, in spite of many resource difficulties, there was a tangible feeling of enthusiasm within the workshops. Staff were eager to show the visitors around, to talk about their work and to demonstrate their active involvement in the organization of their own units and activities. Housekeeping in these ports was exemplary, with floors and working surfaces clean and well organized, equipment being worked on kept clean and its dismantled parts laid out neatly. Tools and machinery were well looked after, put away after use and used with at least reasonable skill. Again, it is worth emphasizing that this was not the result of lavish spending on the engineering facilities – nor, indeed, of notably high wages – but of skilful motivation of the workforce; they really seemed to care about their work and the success of the port. It is difficult to propose any *a priori* reasons why this state of affairs should not be imported into those ports so conspicuously lacking it at the moment, and staff motivation is clearly a priority area for management attention.

8.2.5 Salaries and Incentives

Successful ports are generally distinguishable from unsuccessful ones by their wages and salary levels and by their use of incentive schemes. Ports that are competing successfully and, on any measure, can be said to be efficiently operated and maintained, by and large have salary levels for their management staff at least comparable to the equivalent posts in other industries in the country. Indeed, wages and conditions of work for technical and related staff are often rather better than those that they could attain outside the port, and hard work is generally encouraged by effective – and fair – incentive schemes.

The same can usually not be claimed for the least successful ports and those expressing the least satisfaction with their performance. While managerial salaries are often not markedly inferior to related scales outside the port (indeed, in many cases they are identical, as national civil service and parastatal scales are imposed by the government), there are usually no incentives for management and

supervisory staff, and the 'job-for-life' principle leaves them with no urge to succeed or improve. At lower levels within engineering, the situation is often much worse. Wages are set at a below-subsistence level, and port managers admitted openly that it was literally impossible for those employees to support a family on their port earnings; two or even three jobs were essential to provide for the basics of life. Under such circumstances, it is hardly surprising that absenteeism is rife, that little effort is (or can be) put into their maintenance activities and that every opportunity is taken to leave before the end of shift, to take up their secondary work.

In other ports, the low basic pay is made up by a very high proportion of overtime or bonus work. In one case, the total pay for artisan-driver grades was some three times the basic pay. This was, undoubtedly, the port's way around imposed pay scales set at absurdly low levels, but the result is to debase the whole concept of bonuses and incentives. They become the norm, not reward for effort, and lose their function in providing staff motivation.

Low incomes are no contribution to worker loyalty, motivation or discipline. They are major factors in poor performance, in all aspects of port work. In several cases, they undoubtedly provoked malpractice and corruption among portworkers, particularly among those directly involved in cargo-handling. These were in a position to demand 'informal' payments from agents before goods would be handled from ship to shore or between inland transport and the storage areas. It seems inevitable that similar (if rather less obvious) means of extortion are practised in engineering departments, too; such practices undermine the good name of a port and make it very difficult to improve management and port performance.

Clearly, without adequate financial reward for their labour, the workforce cannot be expected to carry out their responsibilities wholeheartedly and honestly. There seems little prospect for improvement in engineering or operational efficiency until salary scales are made at least comparable with competing employment outside the port, provide a reasonable standard of living and, through realistic and fair incentive schemes, give employees a reason for working to the best of their abilities.

One source of motivation that is sadly lacking in many ports is the prospect of promotion to a higher grade, with greater job satisfaction and better pay. In some of the ports investigated, the career structure is extremely rigid, often nationally imposed, and the opportunities for promotion, e.g. from artisan grades to technician, and from senior technician to junior manager, are either absent or only notionally available, by gaining extra qualifications through training for which no provision is made in the port. At managerial level, it is often impossible for engineers to attain senior administrative levels, as they are imprisoned within 'technical' schemes of employment. In other ports, promotion is automatic, based on years of service and seniority; while such a strategy might engender loyalty, it does nothing to advance the exceptional talent or reward extra effort. To maximize its usefulness as an incentive, promotion must be a reward for excellence, and a flexible and extended career development pattern must be provided for all employees; this will be considered further in Sections 8.3 and 8.5.

8.2.6 Accountability

A particularly significant aspect of the poor management structure and strategy of many ports is the lack of accountability within the system. Responsibility and authority are confined to the topmost tiers of management – often to the General Manager and his Deputy only – and all decisions have to be referred upward. Middle and junior managers are deprived of any ability to manage, to control events and to take immediate decisions on matters which come within their province. Not unnaturally, this tends to induce a responsibility-avoiding attitude and tempts engineers (for example) to avoid the necessity for making decisions, introducing changes and generally improving the performance of their units.

This lack of authority is most marked in financial matters, as discussed in previous chapters. Requisitions in many ports have to be passed well up the organizational hierarchy for authorization, even for relatively trivial sums. There is often an elaborate and rigid machinery for approving expenditure; junior staff (such as workshop managers and superintending engineers) may have authority to spend only a few hundred dollars on spares, while purchase of parts to the value of a few thousand dollars might have to be authorized by no less than the General Manager. At the very least, this rigidity introduces unnecessary delays into the urgent business of serving the port's revenue-earning equipment, and betrays a fundamental lack of trust in the lower ranks of the port's staff – hardly likely to engender that spirit of involvement and loyalty which should be part of the port's environmental atmosphere.

Responsibility without authority is the worst aspect of a poor management structure. It is a symptom of that lack of accountability which is such a feature of the port industry – and not just in developing countries. Individuals at various levels of management and supervision are not in a position to control their own affairs or to take decisions unhindered by rigid regulations, and cannot realistically be held accountable for their actions (or lack of them). In a well-structured management, every individual, whatever level he occupies, has defined areas of responsibility, within which he is allowed to exercise his authority but for which he is inescapably accountable. If top management insists on retaining the right to take all decisions, it cannot make middle and junior managers responsible for errors of omission or commission, and cannot expect them to exercise initiative, to improve or to innovate.

A particularly damaging instance of the lack of accountability generally existing in ports is in the sphere of costs. It is almost universally the case that engineering departments and sections are not treated as cost/revenue centres. At best, the cost of running the maintenance function is calculated somewhere within the Finance Department, but rarely is the Head of Engineering made aware of those costs, or given any financial targets to aim for. Further down the management structure of the Department, the question of costs is never raised, and the workshop manager, for example, has absolutely no idea what his unit costs to run, nor what his operation *should* cost if properly run. Without a clear idea of the cost of maintenance, it is impossible for the Engineering Department and its individual sections and managers to evaluate the efficiency of its service, and difficult to set up realistic and useful targets for performance, month by month and year by year. The managers cannot be made *accountable* for their actions.

As is discussed at greater length elsewhere (particularly in Chapter 6), it is strongly recommended that each independent unit within Engineering (and all other port departments) be made a cost/revenue centre, being accountable for all expenses involved in its operation and being credited with an appropriate 'income' for all its services to Operations (for providing equipment in good order for each shift) and other departments (e.g. for repairing and decorating housing stock, supplying mains electricity and water). Each unit can be set targets, and the head of each unit (from the Chief Engineer down to the foreman in charge of a gang of fitters) is responsible for achieving or surpassing those targets. Even within a maintenance gang, an individual technician can be made accountable for his work: every time he signs a Job Card to indicate completion of a particular maintenance task, he accepts responsibility for and is made accountable for his work. In no port visited or contacted is this principle taken to its logical conclusion, though one extremely successful European port is advancing rapidly in that direction.

8.2.7 Training

The centrality of training in manpower development has been touched on several times already in this chapter (and, indeed, earlier ones). It is an essential element of any reasonable career structure and could be expected to be built-in to the Personnel function of all ports, especially at a time when technology is advancing so rapidly in shipping, cargo-handling equipment, cargo-tracking, administration, invoicing and almost all other aspects of port activity. Promotion should be through training and individual development, recruitment should be followed immediately by several strata of training, and changes in job function as circumstances alter should automatically be accompanied by retraining.

Sadly, this has proved not to be the case. As a generality, the ports surveyed were less than wholehearted about training, in spite of claims to attach great importance to it. Almost all ports offer some form of driver/operator training, for example, but this varied enormously from a few hours of working alongside an experienced driver (but one untrained in the skills of instruction) to a fully organized two-week or longer course, with formal, classroom instruction (on the machine, its operation, safety, working practices, etc.) and well-planned practical instruction on a purposely laid-out driving area. Ports offering little or no training for drivers excuse themselves by insisting that all recruits for driving posts must have public driving licences first. However, accident records in those ports and complaints from engineers about damage and excessive wear-and-tear to the machines are surely evidence that those ports that do offer extensive training are not wasting their time.

For machines new to a port, the common practice is to rely on manufacturers to provide the initial training, either for selected, experienced drivers who then become instructors for their fellows, in classical 'cascade training' fashion, or for all the drivers on the berth or terminal (almost always a container terminal, in practice). Again, there were many complaints, from both operations and engineering managers, that the training provided is inadequate, either in quality (the foreign instructors frequently had language difficulties and had not themselves been trained as instructors) or quantity (the courses were too brief and ended before all the potential drivers had been through them) or both. Once the terminal is in full operation, it is not easy to release machines for training purposes, nor is it safe to train drivers in operational areas; quayside and rubber-tyred gantry cranes and straddle carriers cause particular problems in those respects. Careless and unskilled operation of cargo-handling equipment is a frequent cause of complaint in most ports, both in Europe and elsewhere.

As discussed in Section 8.2.2, little or no management training is offered in ports, apart from occasional opportunities to take short courses in local or national management training colleges or institutes. Rarely is such training provided on a regular, formalized basis, nor is it seen as part of a staff development programme. This is a serious omission and must be accepted as a major cause of the poor management evident in many areas of the port organization, not least in engineering. Most of the deficiencies already referred to (wrong attitudes to work, lack of motivation and accountability, poor delegation and so on) are symptoms of the lack of management training.

Most ports provide some form of safety training, often imposed by government regulation and law. However, there is evidence that this is often not of particularly high quality and that it is of inappropriate, conventional lecture form. Indeed, this is a general criticism of the port training observed during the survey: it is heavily classroom-based and instructor-centred, with little opportunity for individual or group work, practical exercises, work with simulators, audiovisual materials etc. In general, the only courses offered which deviated from the highly conventional seem to be the TRAINMAR and *Improving Port Performance* (IPP) courses developed and provided by UNCTAD, and it is probably significant that these are very highly appreciated by both instructional staff and the trainees.

Training facilities are extremely variable in quality. At one extreme are ports with no reserved accommodation for training at all, or with none that is in regular use. At one port, the 'training centre' demonstrated was a single, filthy classroom with a few rows of chairs, a blackboard and a torn screen. The projection room seemed unequipped. There was no indication that the room had been used within recent history, and equipment and materials for training were non-existent. At the other extreme there are ports, particularly in Asia, which have extremely well equipped, staffed and resourced training centres, offering facilities for all levels and varieties of training, with formal, timetabled courses and a regular training schedule. Some have the latest video and other audiovisual equipment, and staff skilled in writing, producing and editing training materials. Examples of materials shown to the team were very impressive; clearly, the employees of these ports were given the training opportunities and facilities that should be the accepted norm in a modern, competitive industry. Computer laboratories had been recently installed in two ports, and a programme of computer familiarization training was in full swing for all categories of staff, from the most senior of managers to clerks and technicians.

It is both sad and significant that this standard of training facility, backed up by well-trained and enthusiastic staff and with an adequate, fixed budget for its activities, is a rarity in ports. In some countries, where both a rudimentary port training centre and a national or regional maritime training institute exist side-by-side, and where it might be expected that an excellent, integrated programme of courses would be available for all port staff, there is strong evidence of unnecessary and unproductive rivalry, resulting in overlap of responsibilities and inadequate course provision. Even where facilities are available, then, there is no guarantee of adequate course provision. As in all areas of port performance, much depends on the quality of management within the training function, and ports with management and organizational inadequacies in other areas seem also to be those where the training function fails to meet its obligations.

One extremely disappointing aspect of the training survey is the total lack of resource-based learning, even in the best-provided ports; the instructor-centred approach seems endemic in the port industry. No example was found of the use of open- and distance-learning techniques to provide specialist courses, as a substitute for sending senior staff away from their jobs to overseas institutes for extended periods, or to enable older employees to upgrade their technical skills (e.g. in electronics). No port seems to use resource-based open learning techniques to make training available to individuals, in their own time and without needing to delay training until a large group is assembled. These are, of course, just a few of the benefits of self-paced, individualized courses and materials. In Europe and, particularly, North America, industry has rapidly realized the value of providing a learning resources centre on site, well equipped with purchased and purpose-produced training materials, not just for improving job-related skills at relatively little expense and with the minimum disruption to the routine, but also for inspiring individual responsibility for staff development and increasing motivation in the workforce.

A major deficiency in most ports nowadays is the lack of an apprenticeship scheme. Those ports that still operate such a scheme proclaim its benefits, in terms of a ready supply of skilled young recruits, already familiar with the port and its work, and imbued with the port's ethos, before being employed. The dropping of apprenticeship schemes is, perhaps, understandable where recruiting has almost stopped as employee numbers have been trimmed to improve efficiency, and also where the state has taken over craft training in a well-organized way. However, in too many cases it was apparent that the port has merely shrugged off the responsibility for basic training, without making the necessary links with the new public training institutions to ensure that the craft training being provided in them is sufficiently orientated to the sort of skills needed in modern port engineering. There were complaints that the right sort of training was not being given, but little or no attempt was made to establish the port as a partner in those vocational/industrial training centres, a partnership that would clearly have been welcomed by the teaching staff of those centres, perhaps including port visits, gifts of redundant lift trucks and other equipment, secondment of port engineering staff, and so on. It is certainly significant that the complaints of a poor choice of recruits and a lack of engineering craft skills were loudest in those ports which have no apprenticeship schemes and little contact with technical schools, colleges and institutes in their locality.

Another aspect of the inadequacies of the training function in many ports is the uncertain status of the activity within the port organization. In some ports, the Training Unit exists as a section of the Personnel Department, while in others it reports directly – but rather informally – to the General Manager while being administratively within the Secretary's Department. In others the Training Centre is a Division or Department in its own right, with a budget approved by the Board. In too many, however, the 'Unit' is in practice just one manager, with responsibility for what little training exists and few resources (and no staff) to fulfil that responsibility. Physically, the unit could be anything from a purpose-built and lavishly equipped college, in its own grounds some distance from the port and with a staff structure and staffing level that would be the envy of many state colleges, to a small room in the headquarters building or a corner of a workshop. If training really is as important to the success of a port as all senior managers claim (and this report confirms), then one would expect a reasonably uniform level of provision (related, of course, to port size); this is clearly not the case at present.

In addition to resource provision, there should also be well-established and regular opportunities for training; it should be built into the career pattern, provided as a right to all employees so that they can prepare for promotion, upgrade and refresh their skills, and retrain as the nature of their jobs changes. In no port contacted could training be considered as attaining this ideal. Nowhere are training opportunities provided so regularly as to deserve the

tion of manpower development, and in no [an] a recruit expect to be given training [ely] as a means of personal development and in [ration] for promotion. At best, promotion is followed by whatever training might be considered relevant by a superior, as and when it is available from the training unit or a suitable external agency. At worst, no training is provided other than on-job experience under the tutelage of an experienced employee.

The situation can be summarized as the lack of a proper manpower development plan; this will be discussed further in Section 8.3. The range of training courses that should ideally be available to port employees is discussed in detail in Section 8.4.

8.2.8 Communications

The essence of successful operation of a complex industrial enterprise, consisting of a number of semi-independent units, each with its own duties, responsibilities and activities, is the complete integration of those activities into a smooth-running entity. In the context of this survey, the Operations, Engineering and Supplies Departments need to work closely together, interleaving their work completely so that the primary activity of handling ships and their cargoes can proceed without let or hindrance, while still allowing maintenance to be carried out as planned, with all spares and consumables on hand as needed. That is much more simply described than achieved, as the activities involve a great deal of machinery and hundreds, if not thousands, of employees. The integration of work within and between departments can only be achieved if there is good communication between managers and workforce.

The port visits were particularly revealing in this context. At first sight, the necessary communication routes had, in most (but by no means all) cases, been set up, and managers claimed that communication between individuals and departments was good. Indeed, one port relies on this to an unusual extent, as the engineering function is split over several sub-departments, each autonomous, and equipment operation and servicing are curious processes involving several sub-departments at a time; the system would, indeed, collapse if the managers involved did not constantly keep each other informed and discuss every planned activity in detail beforehand. Closer examination of the situation, in many ports, revealed that the communication process was not working as well as claimed. Individual complaints, in both Operations and Engineering, demonstrated that there was suspicion and resentment between those departments;

operators felt that the engineers were holding on to equipment unnecessarily, and that there were delays in completing services and repairs, while engineers complained that operations managers would not release equipment for servicing, were requisitioning more units than they needed, and so on.

Part of the problem seems to be a lack of regular consultation. In the best ports, operations, engineering and planning staff meet regularly to plan their activities in harmony. Daily, weekly and monthly meetings are routinely held, covering different levels of planning and review of activities. Deployment of equipment is decided to the matual satisfaction (or at least accepted compromise) of Engineering and Operations, and release of equipment for maintenance is agreed as near to the ideal time as possible. Outside these routine meetings, the managers at those ports are in constant touch with each other and with their staff, informing each other on changes of plan, emergencies and unexpected developments. Documents are passed to and fro in accordance with laid-down procedures, and appropriate records and summaries are circulated following an agreed scheme (the details will be discussed in Chapter 9).

In many ports, however, the managers seem not to communicate with each other. Operations staff are told by the engineers what equipment they will receive, without the opportunity of discussing needs, and engineering managers are told by operators that they cannot have the equipment they want for maintenance. There is little communication over problems, and the barest minimum of detail is revealed of accidents and breakdowns, of delays in obtaining spares and completing maintenance jobs. At worst, the lack of information is aggravated by *mis*information, concealing the true state of affairs, the real condition of equipment, the actual operating performance.

Although much of the problem arises from bad management practices and inter-personal difficulties (hardly surprising when so little attention is paid to the need for training on supervisory and inter-personal skills), these are undoubtedly contributory factors. In many ports in Africa and Asia, for example, the communication infrastructure is in a very poor state. Telephone systems do not work, radio systems have completely broken down, and the paper-based information system is unwieldy and unused. At the very least, as much attention should be given to the maintenance, repair and refurbishment (or replacement) of these communication systems as to the cargo-handling and marine equipment and the civil infrastructure, as without good communications a modern port cannot function efficiently. It is an astonishing contrast to see a new container terminal in action, with computer tracking of boxes and automated planning and recording of operations, while in the same port it is impossible for a workshop manager to telephone his superior in the Engineering Department office.

8.2.9 Manning
It is generally true to say that the engineering departments in the ports surveyed are not under-manned. Indeed, in many cases their staffing level is, to say the least, generous. In one port, engineering services accounted for about half the total workforce of some 15,000 people, and in another about one-third of the 22,000 employees were in engineering-related posts. By European standards, these are examples of massive over-manning, but there are good reasons for this, apart from the less good reasons of historical labour-intensity, union strength and government reluctance to reduce the number in employment.

One reason why these LDC ports have large engineering departments is that they undertake (and, because of local circumstances, need to undertake) such a variety of engineering duties. Whereas, in Europe, a port can happily contract out specialist work, such as casting, forging, bodywork repair, milling, grinding, fabrication and engine overhaul to reliable local engineering companies, this is impossible in many African and Asian ports; they have to be able to carry out those tasks in-house. Some of them are, accordingly, equipped with an array of very large workshops, in which everything from a diesel locomotive to a domestic refrigerator can be serviced, and their workforce is large and diverse to suit. The Civil Engineering section may have the responsibility of repairing and decorating houses, supplying the port with electricity and water, as well as maintaining the quays, breakwaters, dock buildings, roads and railway system. The Marine Engineering section looks after tugs, pilot vessels and other craft, as well as the surveying and dredging work and maintenance of navigational aids.

Even so, it is evident that the engineering workforce is often larger than it need be, and there is often an inappropriate distribution of skills among the various units. As the complexity and sophistication of the cargo-handling machinery has increased, there has in many ports not been a corresponding shift from the more traditional skills (welding, fitting, casting, milling) to the newer ones (servo-system maintenance, electronic and inst-rument engineering, automation, diesel-electric servicing). While some sections of engineering are overmanned, therefore, others have difficulty in recruiting (or being allowed to recruit) the technicians they need. One port is currently facing the difficulty of absorbing into equipment main-tenance staff displaced from the ferry service, which is contracting.

It is encouraging that some ports are in the process of rationalizing their engineering workforce, either 'freezing' posts and slimming down by natural wastage, or re-training suitable staff for transfer to new posts. In one port, where an extensive computerization programme is about to begin, large numbers of clerks and secretarial staff are being retrained as keyboard operators. Problems will still remain with unskilled labour, formerly employed in heavy-engineering workshops and lacking the ability (often late in their working lives) to learn the new trades, possibly even lacking such basic skills as literacy and numeracy, which are now essential in all branches of engineering.

Another problem area is the imbalance between desk-bound and practically-skilled engineers. Reference has already been made to the noticeable gap in the range of posts in engineering, between the administrative and technical grades. Ports lacking this Superintending Engineer grade seem to be making little or no effort to introduce it, and their maintenance service is suffering as a result. That gap must be filled if there is to be a substantial improvement in engineering effectiveness.

Current attempts (often encouraged by forward-looking governments) to increase productivity and efficiency by reducing the size of the workforce are frequently hampered by another aspect of the manpower imbalance – the lack of a clear career structure. Junior managers and technicians see no possibility of advancement and promotion, because of the log-jam of more senior staff above them, and the absence of a defined manpower development plan. This will be considered at length in the next section.

8.3 Manpower Development

8.3.1 A Manpower Development Plan
There were several references in Section 8.2 to deficiencies in port performance arising from the lack of a career structure (specifically in the Engineering Department but often applying also to other areas of the port). Categories of engineering staff are often constrained in their career prospects by regulations limiting the posts available to them, by reason of initial education, technical qualification or employment scheme. The training and further education which would, theoretically, allow them to move from one category or stream to another are unavailable to them, and the port has no clear plan

for the development of its employees.

A Manpower Development Plan is essential in a modern port, which is now the employer of a wide range of transport and engineering specialists, rather than of a large force of unskilled dock labourers. The plan must encompass:

— a formal policy on the ideal staffing level and a strategy for achieving it;

— a clear policy on recruitment and the required qualifications of new entrants to the various departments;

— an open and attractive career structure for all categories of employees, with training-for-promotion provided at all stages;

— a salary, wages and benefits structure attractive to recruits and experienced staff with the skills required;

— a system of welfare and other amenities, incentives and bonus schemes to attract and retain staff;

— a corporate ethos within which effective, enthusiastic teams of specialists can be built up.

These are the topics to be discussed in this section.

8.3.2 Recruitment

The common approach to recruitment is to wait until a vacancy or group of vacancies occurs, to seek approval for filling the post through the internal bureaucratic procedure, and then to advertise in the local press. This process often takes time and does not guarantee that suitable applicants will come forward, particularly for specialist technical posts within the Engineering Department. It relies on there being a suitable pool of qualified applicants locally, who would be attracted by the pay, conditions and prospects offered by the port. In many ports, these circumstances do not exist, and recruitment is often a problem. Few ports seem to have developed a policy of forecasting staffing needs and planning ahead to meet those needs.

A recognized method of approaching that problem, for posts above the basic levels, is to plan for succession, developing and training junior staff to take over higher posts as they become vacant. For new-entry posts in engineering, the best approach is undoubtedly to recruit from the port's own apprenticeship scheme. Where there is no scheme, the good ports maintain contact with local schools and colleges, inviting groups of students to look around the port, and even encouraging students to work in the port in the holiday periods, to gain experience and the wish to be employed there after graduation. Where the port is expanding one of its

specialist sections, a similar low-key recruitment drive could be pursued in universities and polytechnics, and better students could be encouraged to come to the port through scholarships and similar awards. In a competitive market (e.g. electronics, computer science, automation and communications) it is no longer sensible merely to wait for a vacancy and then to try to fill it.

The recruitment process itself needs to be clearly thought-out. Too many ports still rely on the formal interview, often involving the General Manager and departmental heads even for very junior posts. Aptitude tests and technical tests should be employed wherever possible, to ensure that the recruit is entirely suitable for the post. Where appropriate, medical tests should be carried out; physical fitness, perfect vision and colour vision, ability to climb and work at heights, etc. are all requirements for some engineering jobs.

Although the administrative procedures relating to recruitment must be strictly controlled, to ensure fairness, with the appropriate regulations on employment followed carefully, the bureaucratic element must be kept in firm check. In many ports, the ability to fill the post appropriately is restricted by unnecessary controls, with too many committees and boards involved in the process. There are often port and union restrictions on appointment, for example, limiting the appointment to current employees only, or to sons and daughters of employees. While there is much to be said for encouraging employees' children to apply for posts in the port (the family connection tends to promote loyalty and provide motivation to succeed), appointment must be made purely on the basis of suitability for the job, without favour.

A very important aspect of recruitment, with considerable benefits during the later working life of the recruit, is the writing and issuing of a detailed job description. In many ports, job descriptions seem not to exist, or at best exist as outline descriptions only, filed away in the Personnel office, and are not issued to staff. The appointee must know from the first day of his employment exactly what the duties of his job are, to whom he reports and who reports to him, what lines of communication he must maintain, and so on. It is not enough merely to give him a statement of the terms and conditions of employment (though these, too, must be unambiguously stated); he must be told exactly what is expected of him. Any alterations to the nature and scope of his job thereafter must be made through negotiation, with appropriate training or re-training provided. He must also be told clearly what the career structure associated with his appointment is, what extra qualifications he is expected to obtain, what professional associations he will be encouraged to join, and what opportunities for personal development will be presented to him. After all, every individual appointed is – or should be – a component of the port's Manpower Development Plan, and should be treated as such from the moment of appointment.

8.3.3 Career Structure

A good engineer, like any other port employee, needs to know that an attractive career lies ahead of him within the port. If he realizes that promotion is unlikely, or that moving up the organizational structure is dependent on the promotion or retirement of the person superior to him, he may well be tempted to leave the port for more promising employment elsewhere. At the very least, he is unlikely to put his full effort and initiative into the job.

It is essential, therefore, for the Manpower Development Plan to include clear, realistic career structures for all streams within the Engineering Department. In addition to annual salary increments and merit awards, which will probably be the subject of union or staff representative negotiations, promotion potential must be built-in to every post. Any regulations restricting employees to particular grades or promotion streams must be linked to training schemes and qualification-linked provisions. The most promising staff must be allowed to transfer from one category or stream to another as a reward for particular effort and as a way of retaining the services of the brightest employees.

Promotion through training and qualification requires the implementation of regular staff appraisal, of course, as well as the provision of a wide range of internal or external training programmes. Every manager should be made responsible for – and trained to apply – formal appraisal of his subordinate staff, on specified and detailed bases appropriate to the job specification. He must then propose the employee for regular and relevant training courses, either to remedy deficiencies in skills or performance or to provide extra knowledge and skill in preparation for promotion and increased responsibility. Such courses would include not only technical training but also courses on interpersonal skills and supervisory techniques. Where further educational qualifications are required, e.g. to allow a technician with a trade qualification to advance into junior management through an advanced technical qualification or a degree, then provision must be made for that employee to take time off (perhaps on a part-time basis) to pursue the relevant courses at a local university or polytechnic, or through a distance education agency.

8.3.4 Training

Clearly, the keystone of a successful Manpower Development Plan is an effective and comprehensive training facility. All but the smallest of ports should have an adequate training unit or centre, adequately staffed and resourced, to provide – or at least manage the provision of – a range of courses sufficient to support the career patterns of all the port's employees. The devising and regular revision of the port's Manpower Development Plan, which must be kept appropriate to the overall management objectives of the port and its Corporate Plan, must involve the Head of Training or Training Manager, and adequate resources must be given him – in terms of staff, materials, accommodation and budget – to allow him to meet his obligations.

Most ports fall far short of this ideal at the moment, evidently lacking a Manpower Development Plan. Without such a plan, it is not surprising that the training programme lacks direction, is disorganized and haphazard, with a miscellaneous collection of courses on offer. Only when the exact numbers requiring training in every topic are known, and when they will be available for courses, can a course timetable be drawn up, courses developed and instructors and materials prepared. Training must be seen and acknowledged to be an integral part of manpower development, and a full programme of training must be provided by some appropriate means. The course range is discussed at length in Section 8.4.

8.3.5 Salaries and Conditions of Service

It should be self-evident that, if ports are to attract and retain the quality of workforce, at all levels, that they need in the present highly technology-dependent and competitive environment, the financial rewards and conditions of service must be made appealing. Staff salaries and wages need to be more than sufficient to provide a reasonable quality of life, and must be competitive with those offered by similar industries nearby for employees with the same qualifications and experience. Conditions of work must also be comparable – preferably better – so that good recruits can be attracted and subsequently retained. In the case of engineering managers, the salaries must also be comparable with those of equivalent managers in other port departments.

It is consequently surprising to find that those conditions are certainly not met in many ports. There are ports where the bulk of the labour force cannot earn a subsistence wage from a standard week's work (Section 8.2.4), and where overtime and bonus payments have to be provided to overcome that deficiency. This is clearly an impossible situation, and should not be permitted to continue. There are also several ports where engineering management posts are not paid as much as similar posts in industry, so that good engineers are tempted away from the port, just when their experience and skills are reaching their peak. In a competitive world, the port, too, must compete in the technical labour market.

Terms and conditions of work need to be attractive, also. Even where a port's wages and salaries are comparable with those outside (frequently they are controlled, in any case, as part of the civil service and parastatal employment scheme), staff loyalty and motivation will only be retained if their working environment – in terms of comfort, hours of work and involvement – are attractive. This is not always easy to ensure in the Engineering Department, as workshops tend to be difficult to make comfortable working environments (though it is clear that they *can* be made so, as proved by the workshops of at least two of the ports visited). Another problem is that hours of work have to be fitted in with demand for maintenance; in the best-run ports, peak demand for maintenance corresponds to lowest operational activity – usually the afternoon and night shifts. Clearly, working unsocial hours must be fully compensated for by benefits (in income or kind) to maintain the loyalty and enthusiasm of engineering staff. The various possible forms of incentives and benefits will be discussed in Section 8.5.

8.3.6 Motivation

The aim of training, good salaries and conditions, and the Manpower Development Plan in its entirety, is to motivate the port's employees to give of their best. It is not enough that they carry out their jobs to the bare letter of the job descriptions, doing just the minimum to get by. To be commercially successful, a port needs its employees to put maximum effort into every aspect of its work. Every employee must be encouraged to increase performance and efficiency constantly, to suggest and put into practice improvements in strategies and practices and to be constantly cost-conscious. This survey has demonstrated repeatedly that the most successful ports are those in which the enthusiasm of their employees and their commitment to the port's objectives are unmistakable.

Motivation is not a simple matter, and many elements may have to be introduced to provide motivation in the body of the workforce. Obviously, incomes have to be sufficient to maintain a reasonable standard of living, but additional bonus

and incentive schemes are, realistically, necessary to inspire that extra degree of effort and loyalty. Targets need to be set in all areas of port activity, so that particular performance effort and excellence can be suitably rewarded.

Not all motivational devices are financial, however. A good manager can inspire his staff to work well through his own skilled management techniques, which reinforces the message already presented several times, that regular management training is an essential for improving port performance. Another strategy that has proved extremely effective in promoting a motivated workforce is the introduction of Quality Control Circles (commonly referred to just as Quality Circles). In several Asian ports, Quality Circles have been established (by the workforce themselves, with merely support and encouragement by managers) in operational, engineering and administrative units throughout the port, and remarkable results have been achieved, not just in improving the quality of work at those units, but in enhancing the working environment and motivating the employees. These and other motivational strategies will be discussed further in Section 8.5.

8.3.7 Welfare and Amenities

Among the conditions of service that are often very effective at both attracting recruits to a port and motivating the workforce are the various welfare and amenity benefits that are provided. The port workforce is usually large enough to justify the provision of a full medical service on-site, and in the largest port this might include a hospital. Some of this service is, generally, mandatory, as part of a 'health and safety at work' legislative regulation, but most of the successful ports have taken the provision beyond that level, offering regular health check-ups and even a free medical service for the families of employees. A healthy workforce is, of course, better able to give a good day's work, but the motivating effect of a medical service must not be overlooked.

Several LDC ports have found it necessary or beneficial to provide housing for their employees, either free or at subsidized rents. In some cases, house prices and rents near the port (often located in or near a city or major town) are far too high for the lower-paid staff to consider paying, and accommodation is in very scarce supply. In such ports, the provision of housing is almost obligatory, and there are housing 'colonies' within the port estate or nearby. Schools, shops and other facilities for the employees' families may also be provided on those estates, and collectively such amenities offer extremely valuable incentives to employees. Port housing is only attractive to potential employees, of course, if there is no tax penalty involved; in at least one LDC, such housing benefit is taxed at an absurdly high – almost penal – rate, which negates its provision almost entirely.

Among other amenities usually offered are sports and games facilities, and a recreational and leisure centre. These are relatively inexpensive ways of providing incentives; they are, like the medical service, obvious ways of getting around national wage scales and government-imposed limits to wages. They are also excellent ways of motivating the workforce and engendering a good team spirit, which will be considered in the next section.

8.3.8 Teamwork

If it is be as effective as it should be, the port workforce needs to be organized into teams. At some levels, the teams have to be formal and overt; this is certainly the case in the engineering workshops, where multidisciplinary teams of technicians are needed, in which mechanical, hydraulic, electrical and electronic skills need to be combined. At higher levels, it is a matter of encouraging managers in the various sections to adopt a co-operative, team approach to their work, communicating with each other regularly, taking decisions in concert and with full consideration of the consequences of those decisions on the functioning of each other's units.

The team idea needs also to be extended to the wider context of the port itself, in the sense that every member of the workforce needs to feel part of that larger team, sharing the corporate objectives and upholding the company ethos. It is within this larger team that company loyalty is engendered and discipline can be maintained, and it deserves much closer attention from senior management than it appears to receive at present. Among the strategies that can be used to engender and maintain that team spirit are:

— regular communication from the Board and General Manager on the activities and plans of the port – newsletters, posters and even 'corporate video' presentations are used effectively for such communication in many industries;

— publication of a company newspaper or magazine – this is an extremely effective vehicle for communication, for promoting safety, for announcing training courses and inviting applications, for publicizing sports and other leisure activities and so on, and should be introduced in every port;

— regular meetings of staff within a unit or department – as a means of communicating policy and management decisions, as well as 'de-briefing' on recent activities, problems and successes;

— suggestion schemes and quality circles – the latter in particular seem to be the most effective way of building team spirit and promoting enthusiasm and loyalty yet devised;

— (in theory at least, though perhaps not in current practice) worker councils which offer staff at all levels the opportunity to make suggestions and contribute to decision-making.

Several of these rather unquantifiable aspects of manpower development will be considered again, in the context of employee attitudes, in Section 8.5, and the principles involved must also be incorporated into all training schemes provided by the port, which is the subject to be covered in the next section.

8.4 Training Systems

8.4.1 Introduction

Again and again in this chapter, the central role of training in management and manpower development has been demonstrated. The training function is an inescapable constituent of the manpower development plan, and comes into play in all stages and at all levels – immediately after the recruitment, for remedial and refresher training, for promotional upgrading, for retraining and for instilling the corporate ethos and motivating the workforce. In this section, the whole range of training categories and applications will be discussed, as well as sources of training, materials and methods, facilities, resources and budgets.

8.4.2 Induction Training

Immediately after recruitment to the port staff, all new employees need a brief period of induction training before being allocated fully to the department and section to which they have been appointed. This period is essentially a time of orientation and familiarization, in which the port, its structure and organization, its objectives and range of activities are introduced. It is more correct, however, to consider induction as having two distinct elements: *company induction*, in which the newcomers are introduced to the port, and *job induction*, in which they are introduced to their own roles and duties within the department and section to which they have been appointed.

Company or port induction is generally a brief – often skimped – introductory session, presented by a relatively senior manager, possibly with a member of the Personnel or Training staff in attendance. A film or videotape may be shown, followed by one or two overhead transparencies or slides depicting the port's layout and organization. Induction is almost universally disliked by management and training staff, as a routine and uninteresting chore. Yet it is, in many ways, a crucial point in the working life of the new employee. In those few hours of initial contact with the port, if sufficient care is not taken, a negative attitude to the new job can be created which may be prejudicial to the individual's success in and satisfaction with the job. The opportunity is there to depict the port, its operations, responsibilities, role in the country's economy, objectives and future developments in an exciting and motivating way. The newcomers' roles in the organization can be explained and made to sound important. The facilities, amenities, promotional opportunities and other incentives can be described in an attractive way, and the recruits made to feel welcome with a purposeful team.

At least as important, the port induction session is the occasion for instructing the new employees on the safety and security rules and regulations of the port. This is a duty not to be taken lightly; it needs to be performed seriously, with full audiovisual support and active participation. Tours of various port areas are needed, to emphasize the dangers and demonstrate the 'go' and 'no-go' areas; the first exposure to straddle carriers, yard gantry and container cranes should be sufficient to make the point that a port is an extremely hazardous industrial environment. Finally, there is a need and an opportunity to explain to the new employees their terms and conditions of work, their rights and duties as employees, the availability of welfare, medical and union facilities, and so on.

Depending on the nature of the job, and on the recruits' previous experience and qualifications, *job induction* could be more or less extensive. At the minimum, it will take the form of an informal on-job familiarization course, during which an experienced engineer or technician (ideally one who has received specific training in how to deliver on-job instruction) will demonstrate the practicalities of the job. At the other extreme, it is likely to involve substantial, formal classroom-based instruction integrated with practical training under controlled conditions, before the necessary – possibly extended – period of supervised on-job training.

Clearly, if it is to be done properly (as its importance demands), induction training needs to be given at least as much attention by senior management and the training staff as any other branch of training. One of the main problems about it is that staff are generally appointed in very small numbers at a time – often singly – and so induction training is either presented perfunctorily (because it has to be done so frequently by the same unfortunate staff) or is delayed until sufficient newcomers have accumulated to make it worthwhile (in which case some 'inductees' may well have been in post for many weeks before being welcomed to the port!) A good solution is to prepare port induction as an audiovisual 'package', constantly available in the training resource area, so that one or a few new recruits can view it in pleasant surroundings on their first morning in the port. A member of the training staff can then take the group around the port, informally conveying the other information and answering queries in the process. The job induction element is, in any case, largely the responsibility of the head of the particular department or unit in which the recruit is to work, and must of necessity be presented to one or two individuals at a time. Even so, preparation of an introductory package for the specific unit and post would be a valuable contribution to the first few days in the port.

Induction does, therefore, need to be taken very seriously and prepared in exactly the same way, with just as much care, as the most advanced of technical courses. It will, in any case, be presented more frequently than any other course prepared by the training unit!

8.4.3 Apprenticeship Schemes

At one time, apprenticeships were the norm in engineering industries worldwide. It was the accepted route into a lifetime's occupation – an extended period of basic craft instruction, followed by attachment to a skilled craftsman to learn the practicalities and finer points of the trade. A well-planned and executed apprenticeship scheme was (and remains) an excellent basis for a technical career. In some of the ports visited, it remains so, and some splendid apprenticeship schemes were demonstrated to the team, consisting of one or two years of classroom- and workshop-based basic craft training (usually covering all the specialisms likely to be encountered in later life), followed by one or two more years of specialized training, covering one or more craft areas only, and usually including a period of experiential training on secondment to an engineering workshop within the port.

The best of the apprenticeship schemes are fully integrated with nationally regulated programmes, and the syllabus, standards and examinations are subject to inspection and approval from the Ministry of Education. Such schemes are well-structured, fully programmed and closely supervised, and there is little doubt that the graduating apprentices are ideal recruits to the Engineering Department. Even where the port is autonomous in the design of the apprenticeship porgramme, it is usually such a well-established entity, with many years of successful presentation behind it, that its quality is largely assured. Its syllabus is traditional, its skills inventory accepted without question.

The traditional apprenticeship is, however, disappearing fast from the ports industry. For a variety of reasons (including the drastically reduced need for engineering recruitment, the improved craft training available in schools and colleges, and the increased reliance by the port on externally contracted maintenance) ports have decided that it is no longer necessary to provide the staff, resources and accommodation required to run extensive, four- or five-year courses. In many cases, this decision is justified, and little harm seems to have been done to the port's supply of technicians and craftsmen, but in some countries it has resulted in a strongly perceived shortage of skills. Abandoning the apprenticeship is really only safe where a country has established a network of well-endowed and reliable industrial and vocational training institutes, which present, in effect, a national apprenticeship scheme. Some of these were demonstrated to the team, and seemed (on brief acquaintance) to be excellent. Provided the port maintains close contact with its local institute, assisting where possible and guiding course content where feasible, it may well not miss having its own apprenticeships. There is one proviso, however: the port cannot assume that a graduate from one of these institutes will have that familiarity with the port and its particular brand of engineering that is the hallmark of the port apprentice. The new recruit will need a much more extensive period of closely supervised on-job training, probably including formal technical training, before being allowed to become established in post.

8.4.4 Management Trainee Programmes

The equivalent to an apprenticeship scheme for managerial recruits is a management trainee programme. Although such programmes are relatively common in large commercial and industrial companies in Western countries, they seem not to be found on any scale in ports, particularly in LDCs. Where they do exist, they contribute significantly to management style and skill, and should be adopted much more widely.

The essence of a management trainee programme is that a recent graduate of a university or polytechnic, before taking up his appointed post in a port department, is given an extended period of experiential training in a wide, but relevant, variety of departments and sections. The intention is to expose the new employee to as broad an experience as possible of the workings of the port before specializing on just one aspect of its activities. In the process, the recruit gathers a clear idea of the inter-relationships of the various operational and other units and is more likely to be able to participate fully in the team approach thereafter.

In the case of appointees to the Engineering Department, the ideal management training pro-gramme will be more ambitious than the conventional 'executive-style' scheme, in that the first year of the recruit's port career will take place in the workshops. There, the recruit will take full part in the maintenance programme, practising (or perhaps learning for the first time) the fundamental, hands-on skills of an engineer alongside the technical staff who he will eventually be supervising and managing. Only after this practical experience will the trainee manager start touring and working in the various office-based sections of the Engineering Department, learning the planning and other skills associated with the work of the department. Ideally, he should also be exposed to at least a few weeks of working in the Operations Department, learning how the port's primary activity is carried out. This will give him a much more thorough understanding of the needs of traffic managers and their staff than he could ever gain from sitting in his office. Experience in the Finance and Commercial Departments would also be invaluable.

A management training scheme of this type, giving recruits first-hand experience of all aspects of the work of the department and of the port as a whole, would go a long way to overcoming the common deficiency observed in engineering managers: their lack of understanding of, and apparent non-interest in, the activities of the workshop staff. It should help to weld the department into a unified team, removing the currently common gulf between office and workshop staff.

8.4.5 On-job and Inservice Training

Although the designations 'on-job training' and 'inservice training' suggest that they are different, basically the process is the same; the former refers to the practical training of a new employee, the latter to the training of an existing, experienced employee on some new task or variant of his job, e.g. when a technician is transferred to the maintenance of a new type of equipment. Even in ports lacking a full training facility, some form of on-job and inservice training is always provided for operational and engineering employees. Indeed, it is difficult to think of any engineering task which does not need explaining and demonstrating at least once to a new recruit – and that is what 'on-job training' amounts to, in many ports. Basically, the process is simply an occasion when the learner sits or stands alongside an expert technician and is shown how to perform a particular task. He then attempts the task for himself, is corrected or re-instructed, and repeats the performance until he has acquired a level of competence that satisfies the expert.

There are several major deficiencies in this training strategy.

1. Its success depends on the ability of the expert to transfer his skills to the trainee. In the majority of cases encountered, however, the 'instructor' has not received any training, or even advice, on how to carry out his instructional duties; the quality of instruction must, therefore, be extremely variable, and little or no mechanism exists for establishing and maintaining standards.

2. There is no formal system for evaluating the success of the training and assessing the competence of the trainee; the training ends either when the time allocated to it ends or the instructor decides that the trainee has acquired sufficient skill.

3. No attempt is made to list and quantify all the separate skills required by the trainee to perform his duties, and there is no mechanism by which the acquisition of those skills can be checked and the trainee certificated as having attained full competence to carry out his job.

These are, indeed, severe limitations on the effectiveness of informal on-job training. In spite of the critical importance of the correct and skilful performance of maintenance and repair jobs, not only to the efficiency of cargo-handling but also to the safety of drivers and other personnel in the operational areas, on-job training is being treated by ports in an extremely perfunctory manner; a great deal more organizational, supervisory and instructional effort needs to be invested in it in the majority of ports.

The first essential of this form of training is that its curriculum needs to be planned with just as much care and in at least as much detail as that of any classroom based course. Objectives need to be spelt out precisely – exactly what the technician should be able to do after training, in terms of actions, conditions and degrees of accuracy. The complete list of defined objectives then becomes the basis for scheduling his instruction and also the checklist against which his achievement of the objectives, and acquisition of the required skills, is subsequently indicated (by the signature of a competent assessor). The on-job instructor – who must be both a skilled and experienced practitioner of the required skills *and* a trained instructor – then uses the checklist as the basis of his training sessions. When all the required skills have been checked off, the trainee should not be allowed to practise those skills in the workshop unsupervised until his competence has been independently tested by a senior technician (the superintending engineer or workshop manager) and he has been authorized or certificated accordingly.

Only by formalizing on-job and inservice training in this way can the engineering function be assured of the full competence of its workforce, and its ability to carry out the very complex and demanding jobs it is expected to perform in the modern, machine-dependent port.

An aspect of inservice training that causes considerable concern in many ports is that provided by the manufacturers of equipment, when new machines (particularly if of radically new design as far as that port is concerned) are being delivered. Problems arise particularly over language difficulties between the manufacturers' instructors and the trainees; often, instruction has to take place in a common, third language, with which neither side is particularly familiar. Another complaint is that the instructors are primarily engineers, and have had no training in the skills of instruction. Finally, it is claimed that insufficient time is allowed for the full transfer of skills.

As discussed in Chapter 4 (Section 4.3.6), these deficiencies can best be overcome if, when the contract for supply of the new equipment is being drawn up, the technical (and, indeed, operational) training desired is specifically included in it, with full details of the content of training, the training methods and materials to be used, the qualifications of the instructors and the duration of the training. The behavioural objectives should be stated, so that the success of the training can be accurately assessed at the end of instruction; only if this is done can it be established that the manufacturer has fulfilled the terms of the contract. This element of the contract is as important as any referring to the engineering and performance specifications, but it is extremely rare for this degree of attention to be given to it.

A useful variant of the manufacturers' inservice training, and one that can avoid the danger of insufficient time being allowed, involves the application of 'cascade training'. Instead of relying on the time immediately after delivery, when the supplier's engineers are on-site, for the training, a small number of very experienced engineers (and drivers, possibly) are sent in advance to the manufacturer's factory, to study the equipment as it is being assembled, to learn about its construction and functioning, and to practise maintenance procedures on completed and stripped-down machines. When they are fully trained, these experts then return to their port and, on delivery of the machines, can train their colleagues at leisure, taking as much time as is necessary. This strategy is certainly a successful one in many industries, and should be employed whenever a major development involving new equipment types is undertaken. It still requires the careful specification of the required training within the procurement contract, of course.

It must not be forgotten that on-job and inservice training within the Engineering Department includes training for managers. Even after completing a management trainee programme, the manager-to-be needs to be given specific instruction on carrying out his particular job within the department, and also courses on interpersonal and managerial skills. The former is likely to be an informal on-job sequence, under the direct supervision of the section head; it needs just as much care in specifying objectives, by task analysis, and checking attainment of the required knowledge and skills, as does the technical training for workshop staff. The management skills component is more likely to involve an external agency – a national or regional management or business college, perhaps, or a maritime training institute of adequate size and resources to justify the employment of specialist management training staff – unless the port is a very large one with a fully established training centre. It is essential for management skills training to be of the highest possible quality, if port management is to be improved to the extent needed.

8.4.6 Refresher and Remedial Training

If on-job and inservice education are inadequately provided in many ports, refresher and remedial training are almost non-existent, yet they form the backbone of industrial and management training in most large companies in Europe and North America. It is, after all, just common sense to provide extra training if experience shows that a particular employee has failed to acquire a necessary skill or has, through sheer familiarity and carelessness, developed bad habits in performing a routine task. However skilled an employee, it is inevitable that he or she will, over the years, forget many of the details of the professional or technical knowledge initially learnt as a student or trainee, and will need refresher courses at intervals, both to revise previously learnt

knowledge and to learn about developments in his/her specialism that have occurred since the period of initial education and training. Regular staff appraisal by every head of a unit is a prerequisite for effective and appropriate refresher/remedial training.

So regular refresher courses, or short sessions of controlled on-job refresher training, must be included in the training unit's curriculum, and all employees must accept that they will, in due course, be placed on those courses – they are a routine part of their employment, not just an imposed punishment for poor performance. Indeed, if the management development plan is properly implemented and presented to the workforce, regular periods of refresher training will be considered one of the benefits of and incentives for good performance. The range of courses should be as wide as possible, ideally covering all aspects of the port's work (though some of the more specialist topics may have to be covered by inviting experts in from outside or sending staff on external courses), and every employee should expect to attend one or more courses at intervals of one or two years. In computer maintenance companies in the UK, for example, each employee now receives on average 7.5 weeks of training every year. Every manager in the most successful European industries attends a management skills, leadership or innovation course at least every two years throughout his period with the company. Those companies insist that, without such refresher training, it is impossible to maintain their competitive position.

A particular form of refresher/remedial training is re-training, in which employees are given instruction in a new technique being introduced into their work, or for a new job within the department, when reorganization or rationalization involves a change of duties, or when new equipment has been purchased. In the engineering field, retraining is needed when new cargo-handling equipment has been purchased, or when new diagnostic aids (such as condition monitoring) are being introduced. All staff need retraining when computers are introduced into the port's management information system (see Chapter 9), when new safety and security regulations are implemented and when new operational or administrative practices are brought in. Retraining puts particular pressure on the training unit, as it often involves the instruction of very large numbers of staff over a very short period. Clearly, the training staff need to be parties to all the planning that takes place before the changes are implemented, and must be given the resources necessary to provide the training to the required standard. Audiovisual materials and 'packaged' courses (particularly computer-assisted) are extremely useful for retraining tasks.

8.4.7 Training for Promotion

As discussed in Section 8.3.3, the Manpower Development Plan and the employee's career structure are heavily dependent on the provision of carefully planned sequences of training in preparation for promotion. At regular intervals (at the least annually), all employees should have their performance appraised by their superiors, and their potential for promotion assessed. Those recommended as suitable for promotion should then be considered by an appropriate committee of managers and, if approved, will be placed on the list of candidates for appropriate management or technical training courses.

The staff appraisal process is itself a skill which has to be acquired – and trained for – in all managers, and an appropriate procedure for appraisal, with appropriate forms and checklists, has to be established carefully through discussion at senior management level and supervised very closely, to ensure fairness. One of the LDC ports visited has developed an extremely comprehensive system, with separate, printed appraisal forms for senior and junior officers. Each form contains twenty questions on the knowledge, competence, problem-solving ability, supervisory skills, commitment and attitudes of the employee. Each question is answered by ticking a Likert-type scale, and each is provided with suitable 'prompts' and notes to assist the manager in choosing the appropriate response. At the end of the form are spaces for an overall grading, for comments (a checklist of suitable words to use is included) and for recommendations – confirmation in post, clearing of an increment, or stopping of payment of the increment. These are excellent appraisal tools, and systems of this sort should be used in all ports.

If staff development is to be effective, each career structure needs to be specified within the manpower development plan, and the respective job descriptions used to list the skills required to be achieved at each stage. The necessary courses must then be devised and timetabled, so that the process of promotion through training can become a routine and established element of the staff development process. There is little evidence that this formal approach to staff development exists in ports at the moment. Promotion seems to be a far less organized process than it should be, and too often rests on years of service and seniority rather than potential and specific training. Not only is this alarming and disappointing, but it is also surprising, as several of the ports visited have adopted formal staff appraisal schemes and have well-founded training centres, yet they are still not routinely practising 'promotion-through-training'. There are signs, however, that staff development is beginning to be treated more seriously in those ports, and the basis for the process is at least in existence.

8.4.8 Sources of Training Assistance

In many LDC ports, the training unit is small and under-resourced, and is quite incapable of providing the range and quality of training so desperately needed to improve the performance of engineering and other functions. In the long run, in all but the smallest ports, the necessary resources need to be found to establish the training unit in a form adequate to meet the port's needs, but in the meantime alternative sources of training are required (and, indeed, are already used) from outside the port. Even in the largest ports, of course, external assistance is often required for the more specialized training that small numbers of their employees need.

The most convenient sources of training assistance would be educational and industrial training establishments located near to the port, either national or regional institutions, or local colleges and schools. For more advanced training, universities or polytechnics have to be considered. Most LDC ports do, indeed, have fairly convenient access to some such provider of training, and some are very well served. In African countries, for example, there is a growing provision of technical schools and industrial/vocational institutes, running nationally controlled and defined courses for technicians. Asian schools and colleges, too, are producing technical graduates to an acceptable standard. As was remarked in Section 8.4.3, it is for this reason that apprenticeship courses are less common in ports now than formerly.

At levels above the basic craft skills, however, it is not so easy to locate suitable external courses. The main problem is that colleges and similar institutions are unlikely to have sufficient demand for port-orientated training to develop courses designed specifically to match the needs of ports. Management courses will be generalized, for example, with little content directly applicable to ports. The same will be true for advanced engineering skills courses, operators' and planners' training, and so on. The only satisfactory solution is for training managers, jointly with the relevant heads of departments, to investigate the syllabuses of all likely sources of training very carefully, selecting the most relevant courses and liaising with the teaching staff of the institutions to try to make the training match the port's needs as closely as possible. The closer the relationship between the port and the institution, whether it be a school, college, vocational training institute, polytechnic or university, the greater the likelihood of relevant courses being available. The relationship could extend, with considerable benefit, to direct contribution from the port, in the form of financial assistance, gifts of equipment and machinery, scholarships or even seconded staff or co-opted instructors. What is certain is that, unless some such direct effort is made to involve the port in the provision of external training, it will not be exactly what the port needs.

If appropriate courses are not available locally, nationally or regionally, it might be necessary for the port to consider overseas training. The major drawbacks are that overseas courses are likely to be expensive and that attendance means that staff (usually the more senior and least dispensible staff) have to leave their jobs for extended periods. Financial assistance, in the form of bursaries and scholarships, is sometimes available from international sources to enable senior staff to attend courses and conferences, and to visit or tour overseas ports. These should be taken advantage of whenever possible, as experience (particularly working experience) overseas is a valuable contributor to staff development. However, it is very important to establish the precise relevance of the course or visit to the staff in question, to ensure that it fits fully within the career structure and training needs of the individual, that it is properly organized, structured and assessed – and that it is not a holiday!

Manufacturer's training has already been referred to in Section 8.4.6, and its benefits and deficiencies assessed. Less formal contact with manufacturers is also of benefit to engineering staff, when they are considering procurement of new equipment or changes in engineering and maintenance procedures. Certainly, contact needs to be maintained with as many manufacturers of port-related equipment as possible, to keep up to date with developments in technology and servicing, and overseas visits could well form a significant element of such contact.

8.4.9 Direct Training Assistance

Another approach to the satisfying of training needs where training resources are lacking is to make use of direct training assistance, probably as part of a technical assistance project. Overseas technical and training experts can be brought in, either to organize a course of instruction or to provide it directly. The experts could be part of a project organized by one of the United Nations agencies, e.g. the ILO or UNCTAD, or independent consultants, contracted under the terms of the main development project, or perhaps experts from the country or countries funding the project through a bilateral or similar aid scheme.

Whatever the source of the assistance, experience has proved that it can be extremely effective, particularly where it is orientated towards making the port, through its existing training staff, self-sufficient after the project is ended. However, success is by no means assured, and many technical assistance projects have failed to meet expectations.

One of the principal reasons for this is that insufficient care has been taken, in the early stages of the project, to determine exactly what training assistance is needed. What has been almost universally lacking from such projects in the past has been a preparatory training audit, in which the knowledge and skills of the existing port staff (specifically, in the present context, its engineering personnel) are carefully assessed, a task analysis of required maintenance procedures carried out, and a training 'budget' drawn up, representing the disparity between present and required skills. This should then form the basis of the training curriculum, from which the course materials and resources can be developed. The audit also needs to evaluate the existing training facilities, and a plan agreed as to how they can be brought up to the level required to accommodate the desired training. Only when the courses, materials, staff and facilities have all been prepared should the training project begin.

Even when the courses have been presented, the project is not complete; there still remains the vital task of evaluating the training, checking that the defined objectives have been met and the required skills have been transferred to the workforce. If necessary, the contracted technical assistance team should remain on site until they, and senior port management, are satisfied that the project aims have been met.

Although numerous port development schemes have included technical assistance in the training field, the present survey has not identified any scheme in which the procedure just outlined has been followed. The training element is, all too often, almost an afterthought, and has never been developed in the structured way outlined. The fact that such training has often been successful (as seems to be the case in a current multilateral project in Africa) is almost certainly due more to the skill, enthusiasm and flexibility of individual engineer-instructors, who have the ability and motivation to adjust their instruction to meet unexpected problems and demands, than to the systematic and analytic approach which should be applied.

Indeed, one particularly striking aspect of training need that has emerged from this survey has been the urgent necessity to introduce a training audit as a routine part of all technical assistance projects. A separately contracted, independent consultant should be employed to carry out the audit, to monitor the preparation and presentation of the courses, and to evaluate them when they are completed. Any payment for the training component of the project should be withheld until the consultant is satisfied that the objectives have been fully achieved.

8.4.10 In-house Training

Wherever it is feasible, it is most desirable to provide all forms of training in-house, in or through the port's own training unit. Only in this way can the port have complete control over the content, quality and time of delivery of the training it needs. It is, however, an expensive facility to provide, and a careful cost-benefit analysis has to be undertaken before a decision is made to establish or expand a training unit. In practice, however, that analysis will almost certainly support the need for a training unit, except where the port is extremely small, and its workforce too few to merit even a modest training facility. The size and resourcing of the unit will, of course, depend on the size of the workforce, and a greater or lesser proportion of the training may still have to be provided through the sorts of external sources discussed in Section 8.4.9.

At the very least, in even the smallest of ports, a Training Manager is needed. He should be located administratively within an appropriate department – preferably Personnel – and be responsible for evaluating the need for training and the appropriateness of the various external sources. The manager will also organize the various types of on-job and inservice training that will still have to take place within the port, advising the instructor-drivers and instructor-engineers on how to set about their training tasks, bringing in outside experts when necessary, and helping managers with their staff appraisal. The training manager will also have the duty of arranging overseas courses and visits for staff, of organizing and helping to present induction training (which must take place within the port) and of assisting with recruitment and appointment procedures.

Ideally, however, the Training Manager will have a staff and a training facility in-house, equipped with classroom, workshop and outside training areas, resourced with teaching equipment and materials, and with a budget adequate to support a full range of courses and activities. Even so, it is very unlikely that the training unit will be able to deliver *every* course called for, and it will still be necessary for the training manager to arrange for some training to be 'bought-in' from the types of external institution described in Section 8.4.8. For example, in one Asian port, 1,102 employees were trained in 1986, 68% of them at the Training Centre, 29% at external institutions within the country and 3% overseas.

There is, of course, one other approach, which is a half-way house between those described above: the establishment, in collaboration with other ports in the country or region, of a Port Training Institute. This would have the staff, facilities and resources of a major port Training Centre but would exist to serve the needs of a number of smaller ports, none of which would be able to justify the investment in and upkeep of its own Centre. Such institutes can offer excellent training at an economical level, and have the potential, at least, of fully satisfying the training requirements of those ports which are urgently in need of assistance at present. However, the quality of these institutions and their courses is variable, and the port Training Manager must check that the courses offered are suitable and of acceptable standard.

It is very disappointing to find that a detectable animosity exists between some institutes and the ports that they should be serving, often engendered by overlapping responsibilities and ambitions between them and the ports' own training staff, and by unclear definitions of objectives and boundaries. Clearly, if the benefits of having a centralized training facility are to be realized, there must be full collaboration and the closest of relationships between the ports' training staff (who still have their own internal needs to satisfy, in terms of the organization of training and the delivery of induction and inservice training) and that of the Institute. The relationship needs to be solidified by such strategies as having port management represented on the Board and/or Faculties of the Institute, arranging secondment and co-option of port staff to the Institute for appropriate sections of the courses, and encouraging Institute staff to make regular visits to the port.

8.4.11 Training Facilities and Resources

Where it has been decided that the majority of the training is to be provided in the port's own training centre, there are a number of facilities and resources which have to be established. First, the centre needs accommodation including at least one classroom, large enough to take a group of 15 to 20 trainees (more in a large port), and offices for the training staff and their secretarial help. A training workshop is needed, and an open area for driver training and for technicians to work on large cargo-handling equipment. A library and open learning/resource centre are extremely desirable, as are rooms for audiovisual technicians to prepare materials, edit videotapes, maintain teaching equipment, and so on.

The various rooms then need to be appropriately equipped. The classroom needs to be fitted with whiteboard and screen, overhead and slide projector, videotape player and monitor. The workshop has to be provided with workbenches, hand and machine tools, demonstration and practice machines, a materials and tool store, and so on. Also needed are wallcharts, display exhibits, materials for making audiovisual aids, a photocopier and office equipment (preferably now a word-processing computer or, even better, a desktop publishing setup). A requirement that is becoming more and more urgent in ports is a computer laboratory, in which all categories of port staff can become familiar with this new office, management and workshop tool, and where they can be taught how it can be applied in their particular posts.

As has been demonstrated in several ports, including some in Asia, the training centre can make excellent use of simulators. These need not necessarily be vastly expensive and complex, but can even be built within the port, using the skills and materials available within the engineering sections. Among simulators demonstrated during this survey were crane-drive simulators (on which electrical technicians learn to diagnose and cure switch, relay and motor faults), marine diesel engine control simulators, and hydraulic system simulators – all built in-house at modest expense. Some ports, both in Europe and Asia, are considering the purchase of much more elaborate gantry crane driver simulators, possibly as a collaborative venture, and there is general acceptance of the great value of such devices in operator training. As far as engineer training is concerned, however, a great deal can be achieved with less sophisticated simulators, and with simulations running on microcomputers.

The open learning resource centre, where provided, needs to be equipped with self-access audiovisual and computer-driven training devices, on which training packages can be used by trainees individually (or in small groups) and independently. Although such centres are becoming increasingly common in Europe and North America, providing filmstrip, videotape, videodisc and computer-based training courses on a wide variety of job-related and general educational subjects, no example of such an application of educational technology in ports was found during this survey. Since self-access training is such an effective method, and one that contributes greatly to job-satisfaction, individual development and career enhancement, it is disappointing that it has not yet been taken up in ports.

Training resources on the sort of scale described here require substantial funding, of course, and few ports currently support their training units to that extent. Most ports provide at least a notional budget (in one case, a very generous one – on paper, at least) but few in practice actually fulfil their responsibilities. There must be some agreed formula for funding training preferably in terms of a percentage of turnover or some other measure of the port's activity. In the most successful industrial organizations, a figure of between 1% and 3% of annual turnover is often quoted, and one very successful Asian port (which currently presents some 700 courses a year) has recently agreed to set aside a budget equivalent to 3.5% of the wages and salaries bill for the Training Department. Such a budget allows the Department to be fully staffed, with administrative and secretarial staff, Chief Instructors for technical (civil, mechanical, electrical and electronic), management and supervisory, operational and clerical training, supported by full-time and part-time Instructors and audiovisual technicians. In another large Asian port, the staffing complement will be over 60 when the Training Institute is fully operational, but this is an exceptional case. Usually, the training unit has between 5 and 10 full-time staff, with another 10 to 20 available part-time as needed.

The training staff themselves need to be trained, though there is much variation in the seriousness with which ports take this rather obvious obligation. Some centres and 'colleges' are staffed with experienced operational and engineering staff with little or no training in instructional techniques, though the shortcomings of this situation are now being appreciated, and short courses and seminars are being provided in most of these cases. In other centres, all instructional staff are given full training (often the TRAINMAR training-of-trainers and course development courses), with regular refresher courses to update their skills and knowledge; this should be the case for all port training centres – indeed, they should ideally adopt the philosophy of some of the industrial/vocational training institutes currently being set up in Africa and Asia, in which all potential instructors are given a three-year full-time course in instructional techniques. As pointed out in Section 8.4.5, the need to train instructors applies equally to the part-time instructor-operators and instructor-engineers who are responsible for on-job and inservice education.

8.4.12 Training Methods

It was mentioned in Section 8.2.7 that the tendency in ports is for training to be extremely conventional in nature – classroom-based lectures, instructor-centred demonstrations and sit-by-Nellie on-job training. The now generally accepted truth that little is learnt in a lecture, while most is understood by doing, seems to have had little impact on port training staff. It is probably indicative of the generally inadequate training given to the instructional staff that they appear to be unaware of (or at least indifferent to) alternative methods.

Among these preferred approaches are group-learning methods, in which discussion, problem-solving and team-building techniques are used, and individualized and self-instructional methods, where the onus is on the individual trainee to work through prepared material, at his own pace and even (where practicable) in his own time. Where technical skills are being acquired, the key factor is learning for mastery – the skills have to be acquired in total, and all elements of the course must be mastered. In these cases, group instruction by lecturing is entirely inappropriate, as it takes no account of individual differences in learning rate and preferences in learning style. Similarly, where the aim is to acquire new knowledge, the training must involve individual effort and self-assessment of achievement – such as, for example, in the *Management of General Cargo Operations* materials in the *Improving Port Performance* series.

Management and supervisory skills courses should rely heavily on group exercises, role-playing and video-recorded feedback. Interviewing and questioning skills, counselling techniques and decision-making are other aspects of management training that are far better treated through role-play and simulation techniques than by lectures. Computer-based materials and interactive video are ideal resources for this type of course, particularly where individuals and very small groups require training.

For technical training, of course, much depends on practical work in a training workshop, under close supervision by a skilled technician. Even so, a great deal of 'theory' is involved, and this can well be conveyed by the same sort of self-instructional and individualized approach as suits other topics. Working from manuals and worksheets will be a common element of the jobs of maintenance technicians, and so it should also form a prominent part of their training, which reinforces the value of the individualized approach. Such aspects of engineering as fault-finding and diagnosing are ideally taught through computer-assisted and interactive video techniques, as has been proved conclusively in European and North American industrial training. It is a small step from there to full simulator training, and (as mentioned in Section 8.4.11) this is an extremely effective training medium for maintenance staff.

The broad message is, then, to use training techniques that actively involve the trainee in the learning process, in contrast to lecture-based teaching which places the trainee in a passive role. Such methods have another benefit: they often allow trainee assessment to be built-in, usually as both self-assessment and objective-testing components.

Where the aim is to provide trainees with specific skills and knowledge, it is clearly important to check that those have been fully acquired at the end of the course. It may often be necessary (or at least desirable) to issue certification or authorization at the end of a course, in which case it is absolutely essential to measure achievement of the course objectives and to incorporate reliable trainee assessment; the training method adopted must provide for this. It also needs to incorporate evaluation of the course itself, to check that it is achieving its own objectives; the evaluation must be detailed enough to allow the course to be revised and improved ready for its next presentation.

8.4.13 Resource Materials

A major impediment to the wholesale adoption of the resource-based, individualized and self-instructional training techniques advocated in this chapter is the lack of ready-prepared instructional materials. Such materials take a great deal of time and skill to prepare – instructional designers accept development time to course length ratios of as much as 100:1 – and port training centres rarely have a sufficient supply of either. TRAINMAR is one source of advice, support and training programmes to help training staff to acquire the necessary skills, while the ILO and UNCTAD have at least made a start on preparing some port-orientated and craft-orientated materials centrally for use in ports worldwide. They also provide training courses to furnish instructors with the abilities to present and maintain those materials.

It would be extremely valuable if these agencies, and others, could continue to develop materials centrally, to offer port training centres the support they need in improving the quality of their courses and to encourage the adoption of more learner-centred techniques. The materials should include videotape and videodisc recordings, instructional texts for trainee use, group exercises and audiovisual materials for instructor-led problem-solving and other sessions, and computer software, for computer-assisted learning, interactive video and simulation training. Never before have trainers had so many effective training media available to them, many of them suitable for open learning, resource-based approaches. It is to be hoped that their use will spread, encouraged and supported by international agencies. They do much to promote individual responsibility for learning and development, to motivate staff and instil a positive attitude to their jobs. It is this aspect of manpower development that will be considered next.

8.5 Changing Attitudes

8.5.1 Attitudes and Port Maintenance

In Section 8.2.4 the relationship was pointed out between employee attitudes and the effectiveness of the maintenance function; in many ports, there seems little likelihood of any improvement in the way equipment and infrastructure are maintained unless and until significant changes are induced in the way staff respond to the challenges of their work, and in the way managers carry out their responsibilities. Some of the obstacles in the way of such changes, and possible methods of overcoming them, were outlined in Section 8.3.6, and in this section these, and other aspects of the problem, will be looked at in more detail. They are considered in terms of: accountability, responsibility and authority; setting group and individual targets; providing incentives and rewards for achieving the targets; other ways of motivating staff; and quality circles and suggestion schemes.

8.5.2 Accountability

A striking feature of many of the ports that are evidently experiencing difficulties with port maintenance, and in which engineering (and other) performance falls short of an acceptable norm, is that the organizational structure allows little or no delegation of responsibility or authority, and individuals accept (and are given) no accountability for their performance. Almost all power of decision is retained within top management; middle and junior managers are not expected, or allowed, to contribute to planning and decision-making, and are given no authority to make changes, order spare parts and so on. Technical staff take no part at all in the organization of their work, and consequently tend to exert the minimum of effort, taking no interest in the work of the engineering sections; they do, at best, what they are directly told to do, and no more.

In this sort of atmosphere, it is not in the least surprising that maintenance is badly done, that equipment sits around the workshops for many weeks awaiting repair, that the workshops are allowed to sink below a sea of grime, rubbish, grease and oil, and that employee discipline is lax. No amount of overseas aid or technical assistance will improve the situation more than temporarily, unless a major effort is made to shake up the management structure and management-labour relations. Modern management techniques must be adopted, starting with a positive effort to delegate responsibility *and* authority as far down the hierarchy as possible. Every manager should be given full responsibility for running his section, subsection or unit, every

workshop manager or superintending engineer made entirely responsible for the operation of his workshop (including realistic authority for ordering tools, consumables and spare parts), every foreman given full control over his gangs and the work they do, and each individual allowed (under appropriate supervision) to perform his tasks to the best of his ability, with full support and encouragement from above.

Along with responsibility, of course, goes accountability – and this is the principle that seems sadly lacking in the majority of LDC ports. When every individual within the hierarchy knows exactly what his duties are, and is given all the resources, support and authority to perform them, then he is appropriately *accountable* for his actions, and must be aware of and accept that fact. Acceptance of this management principle has several important consequences and qualifications:

1. In order for every port employee to know what his duties, responsibilities and lines of authority are, he must be given a full, detailed and clear job description from the moment of his appointment or promotion (Section 8.3.2). In too many ports, this is not done effectively at the moment. The job descriptions must also be reviewed regularly, to ensure that they continue to reflect the realities of the posts and their functions.

2. A crucial factor in ensuring that each employee is permitted to perform his duties effectively is a clear line of communication between the individual, his superiors and his subordinates. He must be continually aware of all the surrounding parameters that affect his performance, be told of all potential problems, all changes in circumstances and the current status of all activities within his sphere of influence. In return, he must be able effectively to perform his own duty of communicating as appropriate in the other directions. A good Management Information System is essential to allow this to happen (Chapter 9).

3. Then, in order to assess how well each department, section, unit or individual is performing, targets need to be set and 'output' measured against those targets. Furthermore, groups and individual employees must be provided with incentives and rewards, and motivated to achieve the objectives set for themselves, their units and the port as a whole.

These contributors to the concept of accountability, and its success, are discussed in the following sections.

8.5.3 Setting Targets

If every department, section, unit and individual is to be made accountable for achieving its prescribed objectives, performance targets must be set and achievement of those targets evaluated regularly. The setting of appropriate targets is, of course, an integral part of corporate planning, equipment planning, operational planning and manpower development; the process has been referred to many times in this survey. In each case, the principle is straightforward: the value of some appropriate indicator, or group of indicators, is agreed between the various concerned parties as a target to aim for over a fixed period of time. The indicator value is chosen on the basis of past performance, observed performance in comparable ports and departments elsewhere, and on theoretical calculations of what is possible. The value must be set at a realistic level; too low and it does not induce the desired improvement in performance, too high and it inhibits the group or individual from even attempting to reach it. At the end of the period, the target is reviewed, and is either reset or adjusted downward or upward in the light of experience – again, with agreement between the parties.

For some port functions, the target parameters are easily chosen. In Operations, for example (as discussed in Chapter 5), convenient measures for gangs or individual drivers would be the volume of cargo handled per hour, per shift or per ship's time in port, or the number of moves achieved per hour (in the case of a container operation). For the berth or terminal, total throughput or, better, the cost per tonne or cost per box move might be used. In Engineering, however, it is perhaps not so easy to define targets. One possibility is to use a monthly availability figure for the equipment maintained by a workshop, while maintenance gangs could be assessed on the basis of Mean Time To Repair (MTTR) measures for the jobs they undertake, or Mean Time Between Failures (MTBF) for the equipment that they look after (see Chapter 6). Some such measure *can* be devised and agreed, as proved by experience in several ports visited, both in Europe and Asia, and they can have a dramatic effect on performance and efficiency. Cost-based measures are also very important, to make every individual cost-conscious; if the workshop or other engineering unit is made a cost-revenue centre, with every staff member aware of the unit's budget and its accumulating costs, then repair cost indicators would be extremely effective.

If these targets are to be applied to individuals, then clearly there has to be a formal means of measuring and recording their performance. This is one of the functions of the Management Information

System, as will be shown in Chapter 9. It is also a responsibility of each manager, as far as the employees reporting to him are concerned. Each employee must have a personnel record – part of the staff appraisal mechanism – and performance indicators must be regularly recorded in that file. For workshop staff, much of the data will be available from the Job Cards (see Sections 6.6 and 9.3.2), but the workshop manager will also need to award merit points for other aspects of the employee's work: attendance, diligence, initiative, discipline, and so on. De-merit points may also be recorded, for carelessness, accidents, indiscipline etc. Points will then be added for the achievements of the group of which that individual is a member (in terms of MTTR, MTBF, etc.).

The same principle applies to managers, but in their case many of the targets set will be for performance of the unit that they head, and of the staff that they manage. Every manager will have his own set of targets, right up to the Chief Engineer, whose targets are in essence those of the entire Department. His accountability is, after all, for the performance of the Engineering Department as a whole, for which he must accept full responsibility.

8.5.4 Rewards and Incentives

Achievement of set targets can often be a reward in itself. This has been strikingly demonstrated in computer-based and interactive video training programmes, where students and trainees have been seen to work long and hard just to get answers right and 'beat the machine' – affective behaviour which is not commonly observed in lecture-based courses! Realistically, however, the motivation for achieving and surpassing targets has to be some more tangible reward, primarily in the form of bonus or incentive payments (other motivating means will be discussed in the next section).

Several ports surveyed already operate bonus schemes for Operations staff, in the form of percentage payments, or fixed additional payments, for achieving set cargo-handling outputs. In one or two ports, these are awarded on a complex sliding scale: a minimum performance level below which only the basic salary is earned, with a graduated series of levels above that, triggering off increasing bonus awards for that week or month. Often, the scales are linked to qualifying targets, such as total hours worked, and are conditional on discipline, attendance, safety and similar behavioural performance – perhaps in the form of de-merit awards. The end result is that the drivers and other staff are highly motivated to work hard, without endangering safety to cargo, life or limb (accidents trigger de-merit points or even total disqualification). Individual performance is often the unit of measure on container terminals, though group or gang performance is more usual on general cargo and bulk berths.

For engineering staff, a similar incentive scheme can be operated (though only one port of those surveyed seems to be operating such a scheme at the moment), using values of MTTR, MTBF, availability or repair cost as the targets. The reward mechanism has to be a little more complex than for Operations, however, and a computerized Management Information System is almost essential to work out the rewards. They have to be based on a careful analysis of maintenance records over a rolling past period (perhaps a month or even three months), and the target levels triggering off the rewards may have to be adjusted regularly. Where such a scheme is in operation, it works on the basis of graphical printouts of workshop performance over time, with target levels overlaid so that managers can assess eligibility for payment.

Whatever scheme is adopted, it must be fair – and be *seen* to be fair. Management must be prepared to adjust and negotiate in the light of experience, setting targets and bonus levels to maximize effort without endangering efficiency or safety. Well-organized incentive schemes work extremely well – far better than the almost automatic bonuses awarded in some ports, either not based on stated targets or else triggered off at absurdly low output levels, so that every employee always receives the bonus payments, whatever effort was put into the job. Such schemes make a mockery of incentive payments, and have no place in a modern port.

8.5.5 Motivation

Employee motivation can be effectively provided by means other than financial ones – indeed, in some countries and political systems, only non-financial rewards may be permitted. Provided the basic wages and salaries are at least sufficient to allow a reasonable standard of living, other incentives can be remarkably effective in motivating staff to perform to the best of their ability.

Perhaps the most obvious motivating strategy is to offer the employee an attractive career structure, with opportunities for performance-led promotion throughout his working life. If the manpower development plan is properly implemented, such a career pattern will be firmly in place, and appropriate training will be available at all stages, in preparation for promotion. Regular staff appraisal, properly carried out and monitored by senior Personnel Department managers, will be essential if such an approach is to be successful, and the port must abandon any remnants of traditional, automatic promotion-by-seniority or by favour.

The promise of training can itself provide good motivation, particularly if the achievement of extra qualifications (for example, membership of a professional association, or acquisition of extra craft skills) brings with it accelerated salary increments or opens up a new route to promotion. For example, a craft-certificated technician could be offered time off to obtain a part-time degree or similar higher qualification, which then allows him to move into a management stream, or an artisan could be rewarded for extra effort by being allowed to take a craft course, opening up the technician posts to him. Alternatively, the educational inducement could be in the form of scholarships for the children of employees; in some countries, this might even be more attractive than a salary bonus.

The various welfare facilities and amenities provided by the port are other motivating factors, particularly in LDCs where health services, recreational and sporting facilities are in short supply. Such amenities cannot be treated as incentives to improve performance, of course, but they undoubtedly cement relationships between management and labour and promote loyalty to the port. Sporting activities are also excellent contributors to team building, which is a vital factor in improving group performance and intra- and inter-departmental communication.

Perhaps the most powerful motivating strategy in many LDC ports is the provision of housing for employees, particularly those in the lower grades whose income is often well below that needed to purchase (or even rent) accommodation near the port. At the very least, being housed by the port strengthens the link between employee and employer; the employee will work hard to hold onto his job and his home. Under some circumstances, it could provide even more motivation, and can become a positive incentive; it has been suggested that, particularly in countries whose political system rules out financial bonuses and incentives, the employee could be allowed to 'buy' his port-built home through the gaining of merit points. These would be linked to the sort of target performance measures discussed in 8.5.3, with 'points' being awarded for attaining or passing targets, for particular effort, for initiative, and so on. Each group of merit points would count as a 'mortgage payment' on the house, with point values being set so that it would be realistically possible for the employee to 'pay' for the house within, say, ten to fifteen years. When the required number of merit points had been acquired, the house would be effectively owned by the employee. To ensure that the port's available stock of houses did not diminish, as employees retired they could be encouraged to sell their houses back to the port, at current market values, allowing them to purchase retirement homes outside the port, in an area of their own choosing.

To make this scheme even more attractive, and to motivate the employee's family to add their encouragement to spur him on, the housing estate should be provided with all the necessary amenities, in the form of shops, medical centre, school and transport services. It is difficult to see how the scheme could succeed for long if the estate is a bleak collection of garden-less houses, miles from the nearest town and devoid of the facilities that wives and children need to make their lives pleasant. On the other hand, a well-planned housing incentive scheme could be the best possible way of motivating port employees to work hard and to stay in their posts until retirement.

A final form of motivation is, in a way, a very negative one – but no less effective for that. The possibility of de-merit awards has been mentioned several times; this could be extended to cover a wide range of disciplinary strategies. In somes LDC ports particularly (though not exclusively), employee discipline is a major problem, particularly in driver-operator and technician-artisan grades. Offences range from idleness, lateness and absenteeism, through accident-inducing carelessness and insolence to criminal acts, such as theft and violence. While some ports seem unable to combat such problems – a job in the port is a job for life, whatever the employee does – and suffer the consequences in constant labour problems, poor performance and a bad reputation among shippers and shipowners, others have a battery of remedies for them and have overcome the problems completely.

There must be a formal system for maintaining discipline, incorporating a set sequence of procedures for dealing with any instance of breaking the rules. Minor or first offences would be dealt with by the employee's direct superior, more serious or repeated offences by the Head of Department, and so on, until a formal enquiry procedure is imposed, for the most serious offences. For each level of proven rule-breaking, a suitable penalty must be imposed, ranging from loss of merit points or bonus payments for the least serious up to fines and suspensions for more serious ones. The port *must* reserve the right to dismiss an employee (after going through a formal enquiry and any subsequent permitted appeals) where this is justified, whatever the political philosophy of the country.

Some ports have such a thorough disciplinary procedure, and use it whenever necessary. Every accident is fully investigated, and any contributory carelessness or rule-breaking on the part of the driver or other employee concerned is penalized severely; fines of a week's salary or more can be imposed, and

for damage to cargo-handling equipment a cash fine representing a proportion or all of the cost of repair can be exacted. As mentioned in Chapter 5, annual salary increments can be witheld, promotion deferred and other penalties in kind applied. Provided such disciplinary measures are fairly applied (they need to be monitored very carefully by top management), are clearly included in the terms and conditions of employment, and have been agreed formally with unions and other representative bodies, then they must be an extremely valuable management tool for those occasions when the more attractive forms of motivation prove insufficient.

8.5.6 Quality Circles
One of the most encouraging and, in many ways, surprising observations to emerge from this survey is the success of quality circles in several LDC ports. Often from very modest beginnings, through the initiative and enthusiasm of one manager but with the full support of top management, the concept has spread to all areas of those ports, with results that must have well surpassed initial expectations. This is not the place to describe and explain the concept, except in the briefest outline. Basically, groups of employees organize themselves into working parties to investigate selected problems, analyse the causes, suggest solutions and, in many cases, carry through the solution to its concrete conclusion. Although the quality circles are self-initiated and independent, they have the formal support of facilitators and co-ordinators appointed from more senior staff, and their members are given initial training in problem-solving and group work techniques.

Quality circles were demonstrated to the survey team in many port sections, but among the most dramatic presentations were those made in engineering workshops, where striking improvements have been made in housekeeping and maintenance procedures, saving significant sums of money and improving the quality of services. Perhaps more important, the quality circles have often improved the working conditions of their members significantly and increased their job satisfaction. This is, in fact, the only reward that the circles offer; in no port are there cash incentives associated with the quality circle movement, nor is the achievement of cost benefits among the foremost aims of senior management in encouraging and supporting the circles. Always, the prime objectives are to increase the participation of port staff in the planning and organizing of their work, to involve them more in the structuring and activity of their own sections, and to increase their motivation to put effort and initiative into the job.

These objectives seem to have been achieved to a remarkable degree. The difference in appearance, organization and efficiency between workshops in which quality circles are active and those where the philosophy has not been adopted is striking, and is matched by the difference in attitude of the workshop (and, indeed, other) staff, too. The increase in confidence and readiness to talk to visitors is just one aspect of this difference; even where education levels are fairly basic, and language difficulties existed, workshop staff were eager to 'present' their quality circles and to demonstrate on the ground what they had achieved. The development of well-knit teams of techicians and of extremely positive attitudes to work is striking.

It is difficult to think of any one innovation that has a greater chance, at the least possible financial and administrative cost, of improving the performance of engineering and other port departments than the introduction of the quality circle philosophy. If, as this survey suggests, human factors lie close to the root of current LDC port inefficiencies, and a fundamental change of attitude on the part of management and labour is the key to tackling that problem, then the introduction of quality circles must rank amongst the highest priorities for port management.

8.6 Recommendations

1. A Manpower Development Plan is essential if the current deficiencies in port performance arising from human resource factors are to be overcome, particular in the Engineering, Operations and Supplies Departments.

2. A clearly thought-out and appropriate recruitment procedure needs to be introduced for each category of technical staff, relying more on aptitude and technical tests than on formal interviewing techniques at the time of selection.

3. For posts above the basic level, the recommended recruitment method is to plan for succession, developing and training junior staff to take over higher posts as they become vacant.

4. Detailed job descriptions should be written for each post and issued to recruits on appointment, care being taken to ensure that all recruits clearly understand what is expected of them.

5. The Manpower Development Plan must include clear, realistic career structures for all streams within the Engineering Department,

with promotional potential built-in to every post, and with the most promising staff able to transfer from one category or stream to another as reward for particular effort and as a way of retaining the services of the ablest employees.

6. A policy of promotion-through-training must be introduced in LDC ports, supported by regular staff appraisal and the provision of a wide range of internal and external training programmes.

7. An effective and comprehensive training facility should be established, adequately staffed and resourced to provide a sufficient range of courses to support the career patterns of all the port's employees.

8. The salaries and wages, and the terms and conditions of employment, of all port staff must be more than sufficient to provide a reasonable quality of life, and must be competitive with those offered for the same qualifications and experience by similar industries nearby.

9. Motivational devices must be adopted to encourage every employee to increase performance and efficiency, to suggest and apply improvements in strategies and practices, to be constantly cost-conscious, and to be committed to the port's objectives.

10. Ports must promote teamwork at all levels in the organization, to engender loyalty, maintain discipline and motivate staff.

11. Immediately after recruitment to the port, all new employees should be given company and job induction training, prepared and presented to a high professional standard, to mould their attitude to their work and the port organization.

12. A well-planned and implemented apprenticeship scheme should be provided, either in-house or at approved technical schools or colleges.

13. All new staff must be given extensive, well structured and closely supervised on-job training.

14. Management trainee programmes should be provided for newly recruited engineers, giving instruction in practical workshop skills, general management training in all sections of the Engineering Department, and experience in a wide range of port departments.

15. Engineers must be trained in inter-personal and managerial skills, either at the Port Training Centre or (more probably) at an external training organization, such as a maritime institute or business college.

16. Present on-job and in-service training schemes need to be improved, and a great deal more organizational, supervisory and institutional effort needs to be invested in them.

17. If personnel training is to be part of the contract of supply of new equipment, the technical specification must include full details of the duration of training, the training methods and materials to be used, and the qualifications and experience of the instructors.

18. The practice of 'cascade training' for operating and maintaining new types of equipment is supported, provided that it is well designed and organized.

19. Refresher, remedial and re-training schemes should be included in the port's training curriculum, and all employees must understand that they will be given such courses at regular intervals during their career.

20. LDC ports should maintain a register of approved sources of training assistance, both national and international, and the Training Department should keep in close contact with external agencies providing direct training assistance.

21. All technical assistance projects involving direct training assistance should be preceded by a training audit, carried out by a separately contracted, independent consultant, who should monitor the preparation and presentation of courses and evaluate them on completion.

22. In all but the smallest of ports, an in-house Training Department, headed by a Training Manager, is needed to plan, design and present a range of courses and training activities.

23. The port Training Centre must be well supplied with classrooms, office accommodation, a training workshop for technicians, and an open area for driver training; a library and open learning/resources centre are also desirable, supported by audiovisual technicians.

24. The Training Centre must be equipped with a variety of teaching aids and audiovisual equipment, and the training workshop must be provided with workbenches, hand and machine tools; also needed are wall-charts, display exhibits, computer laboratories, and simulators for technician and driver training.

25. The Training Department must be given an adequate budget, preferably specified as a percentage of turnover or of some other measure of the port's activities; funding equivalent to between 1% and 3% of annual turnover should allow the Department to be adequately staffed and resourced.

26. Training staff must be given training in modern instructional techniques, including group learning activities, individualized and self-instructional methods.

27. Training techniques that actively involve the trainee in the learning process should be used for all training, with self-assessment and objective-testing built-in; testing and certification should be part of all courses.

28. Additional resources must be directed to developing good quality instructional materials, particularly for engineers and technical staff engaged in port maintenance, to improve the quality of LDC port training and to encourage the adoption of learner-centred techniques.

29. Modern management techniques must be applied to change employee attitudes, starting with a positive effort to delegate responsibility and authority as far down the organizational hierarchy as possible.

30. Every manager must be given full responsibility for running his section, sub-section or unit, every foreman given control over his team, and each individual allowed (under appropriate supervision) to perform his tasks to the best of his ability, with full support and encouragement from above.

31. Every employee must accept the management principle of Accountability and must be made responsible for his actions, provided that he is given all the resources, support and authority to perform them.

32. To ensure that each employee is permitted to perform his duties effectively, there must be a clear line of communication between the individual, his superiors and his subordinates.

33. Performance targets must be set for each department, section, unit and individual, and achievement of those targets must be evaluated regularly, so that all can be made accountable for achieving the prescribed objectives.

34. Management should investigate the scope for, and introduce, effective incentive schemes as means of providing motivation for achieving and surpassing performance targets.

35. The incentive scheme adopted must be fair and be *seen* to be fair, and must be adjusted in the light of experience to maintain maximum effort without endangering efficiency or safety.

36. LDC ports should investigate the possibility of introducing such incentive rewards as career development and training opportunities, welfare and recreation activities, and provision of housing as additional forms of employee motivation.

37. The Quality Circle philosophy should be adopted, as a great opportunity to motivate staff and improve the performance of engineering and other port departments at the least possible financial and administrative cost.

CHAPTER 9

Engineering Management Information Systems

9.1 Existing Systems

9.1.1 Introduction

It has been demonstrated repeatedly in earlier chapters that almost every port maintenance and operational activity depends for its effectiveness and efficiency on the availability of relevant, accurate and comprehensive information. Equipment planning (Chapter 3) is virtually impossible without traffic forecasts, operational indicators, asset register data, maintenance records and cost information. In procurement (Chapter 4), technical specification (both performance- and engineering-based) has to be based on analysis of past and current data on operating performance and maintenance history, as well as on suppliers and *their* past performance – not to mention the process of Life Cycle Costing, which is utterly reliant on comprehensive information. In operations (Chapter 5) the vital business of cost control revolves around operating records (Section 5.4), and effective maintenance management (Chapter 6) requires a wide range of record types for all aspects of planning (Section 6.5) and costing (6.7). Supplies management (Chapter 7) can only be performed efficiently and organized appropriately if it is based on a good record system for stock control and procurement. In other sections of the port, personnel records, salaries and bonuses, as well as appraisal, training and manpower development (Chapter 8) all depend on information.

The collection, compilation, analysis and presentation of all this mass of information needs to be carried out within the framework of a formalized *system* – in general terms, a Management Information System. Historically, this would in practice be a motley collection of separate systems: one in Personnel (salaries and wages), one in Accounts (billing and costing), one in Operations, one in Planning, one in Engineering, and so on. One of the secrets of a successful *modern* port is the integration of these separate elements within one, unified system. This is, indeed, a major conclusion of this survey: the engineering records system – the Engineering Management Information System (EMIS) – must be an intergal component of the port's overall Management Information System. It is misleading to consider the EMIS as a physically separate system, as it should not be possible to disentangle it from the Port MIS, but in the account that follows, it will be necessary to use the term EMIS to describe and discuss those parts of the MIS that apply specifically to, and are the responsibility of, the Engineering Department.

9.1.2 The Variety of Existing Systems

The survey has revealed a surprising diversity of information systems, from at one extreme a meagre file of flimsy paper sheets to, at the other extreme, mainframe computer installations of extreme complexity and with a larger attendant staff than some other divisions of the port. It has also demonstrated a widespread misunderstanding of the value, purpose and benefits of an MIS, and a surprising lack of appreciation of the importance of such a system in the modern port.

It may be as well, then, to start this chapter with the clear statement that an MIS is not necessarily a complex and expensive mainframe computer installation – even though many of the largest and most successful ports have gone down that route. It could equally be a system of paper-based reports and records, provided that these contain all the information needed, that they are well kept, carefully analysed and circulated regularly to those needing to use the information.

The essential elements of an MIS (whether the component EMIS or the entire Port MIS) are, then, that:

1. It is a **system** – a formalized sequence of activities and records, available to all who need it *when* they need it, and in a convenient, easily managed and maintained form;

2. It contains all the required **information**, accurately recorded and updated, analysed and presented in usable and easily comprehended form;

3. It is a **management** tool – an indispensable instrument in the decision-making process.

One of the most surprising outcomes of this investigation has been the realization that the ideal MIS is an extremely rare phenomenon; in only one or two ports does the installed MIS satisfy its requirements to the full (or nearly so) while, in the vast majority of the ports visited, investigated or responding, the MIS is either practically non-existent or is inadequate in one or many crucial respects. In the following section, the major deficiencies of current information systems are surveyed, as a preliminary to discussing, in Section 9.3, the components and totality of an idealized EMIS. In Section 9.4, the uses and benefits of the EMIS are described, and Section 9.5 discusses the physical nature of an EMIS and how it should be designed. Finally, Section 9.6 surveys the ways in which an EMIS can be (and should be) used by various departments, units and individuals within the port organization.

9.2 Deficiencies of Engineering Management Information Systems

9.2.1 Introduction

The survey has demonstrated very widespread deficiencies in ports' engineering information systems – probably more than in any other aspect of maintenance management. Few, if any, of the systems investigated appear to meet all the needs of their users; in even the best-run ports, complaints were received about the EMIS by the survey team. In most cases, managers appeared so unfamiliar with the requirements for and benefits of a good EMIS that they did not know what to complain about!

Just about every possible deficiency was observed by or described to the team. In an attempt to discuss the major categories of deficiencies, as a prelude to defining a good (if not 'ideal') EMIS they will be outlined under the descriptive headings of: incompleteness, unreliability, lack of system maintenance, poor design and non-use. The symptoms tend to spread across these artificial boundaries, of course, but the headings will provide a useful framework for discussion.

9.2.2 Incompleteness of the System

Many systems fall at the first fence by not covering an appropriate range of engineering information and not going into sufficient depth – they are conspicuously incomplete. Even the poorest Port MIS does at least record what items of equipment are owned (or were purchased by) the port – it contains at least a rudimentary Asset Register. Commonly, systems include files containing the issued daily

equipment Requisition Forms and the Job Cards issued by maintenance staff. However, these components are often not linked together as an Asset History, so that is is not possible to summarize the working life of the individual items of plant and equipment in the port's inventory, nor to pool data by manufacturer, type, age or other category. Without this sort of information, managers are not in a position to base their decisions on procurement, asset disposal and other aspects of planning on solid facts.

It is very common for the EMIS to contain only outline records of what maintenance jobs have been done, with no information on the operational performance of the machine – cargo handled, hours worked, hours idle, fuel consumed, and so on. To give a full picture of the merits and deficiencies of each machine, all these data (and others) need to be linked together.

A particularly notable omission from the majority of systems studied is information on costs. Almost all managers agree with the thesis that ports have to be competitive and that all employees have to be cost-conscious, yet few existing systems include thorough and complete data on the costs of operating and maintaining the port's equipment and other assets. In a few ports, cost data are added after the records have reached the Accounts Department, just before they are filed away in the archives, but the information is not made available to the engineers and operators, and they seem almost universally to be unaware of what it costs the port to run their departments. Without cost information, it is not possible for financial targets to be set in the workshops and on the berths, nor for life cycle costing and similar approaches to be used in making decisions on procurement, scrapping and replacing of equipment. Even in ports where cost data are recorded in the EMIS, it is uncommon for them to be allocated to individual items of plant or equipment (machines tend to be grouped for costing, at best) and very rare for the detail to go down as far as functional systems, sub-systems or components – yet engineers can make extremely valuable use of such data when they are available to them.

The hours of work performed by port equipment are often not reported within the MIS, and only in the case of container cranes is it even fairly common for ports to record the hours of use of component systems (e.g. of the hoist motor, the trolley and spreader) in addition to that for the entire machine. Yet component use data are very important when assessing the performance and reliability of equipment, in considering replacement, and when modifying and improving design features to increase efficiency.

Fuel consumption is often not entered into the MIS, even though it may be recorded at the workshop or the fuelling point. Availability, utilization and downtime are not regularly recorded, even in the most successful ports; often availability has to be estimated roughly when needed, by subtracting from the total inventory the number of machines in the workshop for maintenance at a particular time.

Another major omission in many systems is information on civil maintenance. Although this is generally considered not a major problem area in ports, it still needs records for budgetary purposes and for calculating overhead costs for other port activities. Direct links between the quality of civil engineering, the efficiency of operations and demand for equipment maintenance (through wear-and-tear and accidents) have been demonstrated in earlier chapters; there need to be corresponding links in the port's MIS too. The marine maintenance sector is also not well represented in current information systems, probably again reflecting the lesser importance attached to it (unjustifiably and dangerously) by management. It is true that much marine maintenance is carried out on board the vessel by its crew, in isolation from the rest of the maintenance system, but these data, too, should be input to the EMIS; this will be of increasing necessity as condition monitoring becomes more common in the marine equipment sector.

The labour element is often missing from records – the hours worked by drivers and maintenance technicians, whether they were in normal shift time or paid at overtime rates (and, if so, what rates), what salary grade applies to those staff, and so on. Such information is absolutely essential for any proper calculation of the costs involved in operating and maintaining the port's assets.

9.2.3 System Unreliability

A frequent complaint of managers is that they cannot rely on the data recorded within the EMIS. This is too often taken as a reason (or excuse) for not extending an existing system, making it more comprehensive and, particularly for not computerizing it.

The possible causes of unreliability can be grouped under two headings:

1. **Carelessness** in recording information. For example, a driver cannot be bothered to note the time of starting work, stopping work temporarily, and so on, so that the recorded values for working hours are inaccurate. He may not record the full reasons for stoppage of work (delay to cargo? congestion? accident?

breakdown?). He forgets to record a fuel fill-up, an oil or water top-up. Indeed, in some ports, drivers even refuse totally to fill in equipment logbooks. A maintenance technician writes down a vague, incomplete description of work done, forgets to fill in the times of starting and completing the job, the lubricants used, the parts replaced. Mistakes are made over the equipment asset register number or the stores code for the replacement parts. Schedules are not updated, open files are not closed, changes to procedures and routines are not recorded. The stores inventory is not updated when an item is issued or a refurbished item is returned, and the spare parts reorder level is not adjusted when equipment is disposed of. Mistakes are made when summarizing the daily and weekly data for the monthly reports to managers. There is often a general lack of caring about accuracy of records, usually because those recording the data do not understand or appreciate the value of the MIS to the port's efficiency and profitability, and supervisors, foremen and managers do not exercise their quality control responsibilities when signing the various data forms.

2. **Falsification of data.** Often, it is not to the advantage of staff to be honest and accurate when recording data in logbooks and report sheets. A driver is hardly furthering his career in recording a complete and accurate account of an accident caused by his carelessness, or the total idle time spent while on quay transfer duty. A technician may be excused, perhaps, for glossing over the reason why a job scheduled for two hours takes four, or that the wrong replacement part was requisitioned from the stores. On a wider and more damaging scale, the engineering department managers in some ports are less than honest when entering demand and availability figures; operator's demands are scaled down to cover up a shortfall between demand and supply, and to make low availability of machines (because of poor servicing or a desire to reduce pressure on maintenance) look less damaging in the eyes of senior port management. Operators, too, are often guilty of falsification, requisitioning equipment for an entire shift or day when only needing it for part of a shift, and then entering an inflated figure for hours of use to justify their requisition. Either ports must somehow improve the degree of honesty, through better supervision and spot-checking, or they must rely more on automatic recording of data – for

example, through the use of hour-meters and electronic data recorders.

A particularly strange instance of falsification of MIS data occurs where assets are not removed from the asset register when they are no longer used or serviceable. Some ports are reluctant to dispose of their assets, by scrapping and/or selling them, and items are kept on the asset register long after they cease to be usable (Chapter 3). This gives a false impression of the port's stock, and makes equipment planning very unreliable, as well as making it difficult to make out a case for a quite justifiable replacement by new equipment. The EMIS *must* be kept up to date, reflecting a true picture of the current state of affairs.

9.2.4 Unmaintained Systems
Leading on from the last point made, it is clearly essential for the EMIS to be kept up to date by all its users. However, operators frequently claim that they are under extreme pressure and have neither the time nor the staff to enter and revise data promptly – daily or hour by hour, as conditions change. Engineers become so familiar with their routine tasks that they no longer issue full job details to their staff, and so details of exactly what tasks were completed are not recorded. Workshop schedules are left for days on end without updating, and records of the current status of jobs are not maintained.

In several ports visited, a fully implemented EMIS was described and demonstrated during workshop visits, but it was obvious to the observer that the system was not being kept up to date: wall-board schedules of work in progress, work due, work awaiting spares and work completed were sometimes days old. Files of records (including, in one case, the card-based Asset History records) were covered in dust and out of order. Books of specially prepared forms were clearly not being used. It was clear that much of the day-to-day work was being carried out on a word-of-mouth basis, both in operations and in engineering (and in work crossing department boundaries), so that the need for reporting was forgotten and no written records existed of what had been done.

In many cases, records are not passed regularly between departments, so that Finance staff do not receive records of maintenance work for calculating costs. Supplies clerks do not receive information about depleted stores in time to reorder them, and the Stores Inventory does not get updated; in one port it was said that the Spares Catalogue had not been revised for two years! Engineers cannot know what spares are available in such cases and which need reordering, and Accounts managers can have no firm basis for estimating budgets. In one extreme case, the Engineering Department planning staff had lost track of where mobile cargo-handling equipment was in the port, so that they could not reclaim it for planned maintenance. They had, until a year or so previously, allocated to one member of staff the job of cycling around the port each day, noting the location of all mobile plant; this task had been dropped on the grounds of economy, to be replaced by a system of painting on the chassis of each serviced unit the date of its next due visit to the workshop – when that unit was subsequently brought to the workshop for repair, that date could be checked for imminence.

9.2.5 Poor System Design
Even in ports where the need for and benefits of an EMIS are clearly appreciated, managers had occasion to complain about the existing system to the team, because it was badly designed and is difficult to use. In several ports, very elaborate systems of forms have been designed and introduced (often by Technical Assistance consultants), which have proved to be difficult to use, time-consuming and non-uniform. Each form was designed independently (sometimes by successive teams of consultants), using different terminology and layout, so that mistakes are made in data entry and staff are tempted to ignore or skip over items (or to leave the forms in their tear-off books, which seemed often to be the case). It is quite clear that in several ports only lip-service is being paid to their very thorough and comprehensive systems of forms. Even where they are faithfully filled in by maintenance staff, the resulting data are frequently difficult to collate, interpret and analyse.

Even the most expensive computerized system can fall down on the question of design. In one or two cases, there is a strong suspicion that the EMIS is over-elaborate, churning out so much information – often irrelevant to the recipients – that it is ignored. Vast quantities of printout paper arrive on a manager's desk, when all that is required is a brief summary (preferably in graphical, easily understood form) of those data immediately relevant to the job of that individual.

In computerized systems, screen display design is often poor – a conventional spreadsheet layout on a 'green screen', familiar to and easily understood by the data-processing experts who designed it, but obscure and confusing to non-computer experts. Data need to be simply and clearly displayed, preferably colour-coded, and with revealing charts and graphs available at the press of a key, every item clearly labelled and self-explanatory. Printouts, too, need to be designed for engineers and workshop managers, not for accountants used to dealing with serried ranks of figures; this is emphatically not the case, even in the two or three most successful and innovative ports visited.

Commonly, the system imposes on busy managers too many forms to fill in and a succession of daily, weekly, monthly and annual summaries to be calculated and filled in by hand, with insufficient staff to carry out the tasks. At the other extreme, insufficient data are requested and insufficient instructions are provided; this is common in maintenance job-sheets, which give no details of the steps to be carried out in performing a job, and provide no spaces for technicians to indicate (by their initials or signature) exactly what steps have been carried out (Chapter 6).

A common failure of systems design relates to the circulation and communication aspects of the system. Data have to take an appropriate route through the organization, being communicated to all who need it, analysed at every stage of aggregation and compilation, fed back as appropriate after analysis, and so on. The mechanism of this circulation system is often very badly thought out, so that managers complain of not getting access to the information they need, *when* they need it. Too often, the team observed boxes and files of raw data piled up, not being processed through the system into useful and usable form.

The stores inventory is often the first part of an EMIS to be implemented, and is also usually the first to be computerized, but rarely is it designed for easy and instant access by engineers – they are given no copy of the spares catalogue, no online access to the database. To the engineer, the extent of the stores stock is a mystery. The result of such poor design of the system means that it often takes several days for an engineer to discover whether a part is available. When spares are ordered, the system rarely allows the engineer to chase progress on the order, as no current status reporting is built-in.

Systems designers must remember that keyboard entry is difficult to many non-computer staff. Certainly, managers and technical staff need computer familiarization and systems training, but there seems no good reason why data input should not be simplified, with mouse- and menu-based interrogation and calculator-style keypad entry, nor why touch-screen alternatives should not be considered where data access, rather than input, is needed. For workshop use, sealed and protected keypads are needed, to withstand greasy hands, and voice-recognition systems should now be exploited whenever possible; these are also useful in stores applications, where they significantly accelerate access by non-computer-literate staff.

Often, the system is not designed for the input of relevant information and for output of relevant analyses. EDP staff or Planning Department staff may set up the MIS without consulting the operations and engineering staff on exactly what they want out of the system; this is the worst kind of design fault, as it is inexcusable and easily avoidable. It encourages the strongest opposition to the system by engineers and other users, and does nothing to break down attitude barriers which are almost inevitably erected on the introduction of any novel system to the port. Attitude changing is frequently the major difficulty faced by innovators, in EMIS and other systems implementation.

9.2.6 Unused Systems

The consequence of the various deficiencies described in the previous paragraphs, particularly those of unreliability and poor design, is that in many ports the EMIS is not used when it should be, for assessment of performance, for costing and for planning.

Many ports have piles of unopened files gathering dust, their Asset History cards filed away unreferred to, piles of computer printout unread. If a system fails to do its job, it will not be used. This applies not just in LDC ports or unsuccessful ports but also in European and relatively successful ones. It is, in contrast, noticeable that in the best-run ports, with the highest performance records and the keenest will to compete, the EMIS (indeed, the entire MIS) is used to the full, data are analysed exhaustively and regularly, with immediate access to all relevant data for every operator, engineer and administrator.

Clearly, if a Stores Inventory is out of date or inaccurate, it will not be used. If operating performance records are unreliable, they will not be referred to. If records of workshop activities are incomplete, the planners will have little reason to analyse them and use them. If data input and access to information are difficult, because of poor systems design, then managers will not bother to consult the system. If operational and maintenance cost data are incomplete, then Finance and Planning staff will have no incentive to use the system.

Probably, lack of analysis is the main deficiency in most systems. Frequently, a great quantity of data is collected, but no staff or resources are available for analysing it. Even in the better European ports, it is often left to the initiative of individual engineers and workshop managers to carry out analysis of performance data from operations and maintenance, to detect trends and identify problems; if such individual motivation were not there, the system would not be used. Several apparently efficient ports admitted to a poor linkage between data interpretation and its use in decision-making – self-identified as a management communication failure. In a major European port, with an elaborate computerized EMIS, managers admit that the system is not used for decision-making, even though it produces large quantities of data. They say that no-one is responsible for collecting and analysing data, issuing summaries and acting on them, and the engineers complain that the EMIS does not generate the sort of information that they need. The workshop managers, in particular, claim to receive very little information from the system.

Professional education and management training could well be at the root of such failures of the information system. Many managers seem not to have grasped the value of the MIS in their daily work; they have not been told about it during their professional education, and have not been trained in its use within the port. It is not surprising that only the enthusiastic individual will be motivated enough to look for new ways of using the EMIS and to suggest improvements in its design and operation.

In many cases, the lack of use of the EMIS reflects (indeed, stems from) the absence of the cost/revenue centre philosophy. There is no motivation for managers to use the system, and they are allowed to go on doing their jobs the way they have always done, with no incentive to improve, to change, or to benefit through experience.

9.3 The Components of an Engineering Management Information System

9.3.1 Introduction

Although existing information systems vary widely in nature and physical embodiment, it is possible to build up a model of the elements of an effective system from first principles, as it were. Some components can be considered essential and central elements of the EMIS, while others are auxiliary elements, constituents of other sub-systems accessed by (or requiring access from) the EMIS itself in the course of its activities. In this Section, these elements will be considered in turn, without being concerned, for the moment, about the physical nature of the (E)MIS; this will be discussed in Section 9.4.

9.3.2 The Job Card

The basic element – the foundation stone – of any EMIS is the Job Card – alternatively referred to as a Work Card, Work Order Card, Job Sheet or similar name. Although this might vary considerably in form and detail, it is essentially an acceptance and

authorization by the engineers of a maintenance or repair job, and a statement of its issue to named workshop staff. It contains a description (in greater or lesser detail) of the tasks to be performed in carrying out the assigned job, and ultimately records the completion of work.

In its simplest form, the Job Card is, literally, a printed card on which a responsible member of the Engineering Department (usually a planner or someone with a planning/scheduling function as part of his job specification) has written or typed the required information:

— the asset number and description of the machine or plant to be serviced;

— the date of receipt of the request for service (which might be a scheduled preventive maintenance appointment, 'requested' by the planning unit or automatically issued by the EMIS itself, or else an unscheduled repair, asked for by the operator to whom the machine was allocated and in whose jurisdiction a fault or accident occurred);

— the date of issue of the Job Card;

— the names of the issuing officer and designated workshop staff (the foreman of a maintenance gang or a responsible individual in the gang – a 'nominated competent person');

— a statement of the nature of the job to be done (e.g. 'Monthly service B'; 'Repair to a damaged headlamp'; 'Replace front nearside tyre');

— spaces for the nominated technician to acknowledge receipt of the job and to claim completion;

— space for a foreman or supervisor to sign approval of the completed job;

— spaces for noting the spares and other materials to be used on the job.

Those are, however, just the bare minimum of details that should be provided for on the Job Card. A strong case can be made for making it much more informative than that – it is, after all, the initial entry point for data into the EMIS, and needs to be as comprehensive as reasonably possible. It should, for example, record:

— the time of starting the job;

— the time of completion;

— details of the number of staff employed on the job, their grades and their individual signing-on and signing-off times.

These data will provide the basis for calculating labour costs when the job is completed; clearly, some way of denoting whether payment will be at standard shift rate or overtime rate is also needed.

Somewhere, too, detailed instructions about the job to be done need to be set out. In some systems, such details are included on the Job Card itself, but this was not seen in any of the ports visited, though several issued worksheets or job-sheets as addenda to the Job Card – a reasonable substitute. The instructions should set out all the steps in the job, in sufficient detail to allow the technical staff to know precisely what they need to do. Each step should be unambiguously described, not just in terms of 'Check that the . . .', but 'Check that . . . and if . . . then . . .'; there must be no misunderstanding over what the technician must actually *do*, nor any temptation to skip detail on the basis that 'he knows what that job is about'. Spaces should be provided alongside each instructional step, for the technician to tick off or initial each step as he completes it; this is a particularly useful strategy where the skills of workshop staff are not well developed, but is in all circumstances a valuable contribution to quality control and individual accountability.

It is, admittedly, not so easy to provide this depth of detail for unscheduled maintenance and repair jobs, where the precise actions needed will not be known until the equipment has been inspected and the fault has been diagnosed. Even then, however, standard worksheets should always be available for detailing the steps necessary for dismantling, inspecting and reassembling every system, subsystem and component, and these can be issued as soon as the nature of the job has been assessed on-site or at the workshop. At the very least, the relevant maintenance manuals and engineering drawings must be available in the workshop, either in the form provided by the manufacturer (if these are clear and comprehensive enough to be understood by the workshop staff) or (which seems, in the light of comments from nearly all the ports surveyed, more likely) revised and improved versions of them, rewritten by experienced engineers to suit local circumstances – the technicians' skill level, language and ability to interpret diagrams. The manual must then be issued, entire or in part, with the Job Card or as soon as the likely source of the fault has been indicated. The maintenance manuals will also, of course, be the source of the procedural steps included *on* the Job Card, where that desirable strategy is adopted.

A vital element of the Job Card is space for recording the spare parts and consumables used in the job. For a scheduled preventive maintenance job,

these details will be largely or completely known in advance, in which case the items should already have been listed on the card before issue and, indeed, should already have been requisitioned from the stores, to avoid wasting technicians' time obtaining spares from the stores once the job has been issued. There will be, in any case, an associated Supplies Requisition Form to be completed at an early stage in the process, and this will need to be cross-referenced to the Job Card, by writing on it the Job Card number and the equipment's Asset Number.

Finally, it is extremely desirable for the Job Card to accommodate entries for costing purposes, though these may well be added at a later stage in the process. They should include the cost of all materials, both consumables and spares, and the cost data relating to the labour element of the job. These items will be considered at greater length in Section 9.3.7.

The Job Card is, clearly, the initializing phase of the Information System, the basic data entry component of the system. From it, information flows in several directions: first to the workshop staff who are to carry out the maintenance, secondly to the Stores, thirdly to the Finance Department, and fourthly to Personnel (for working out salaries, overtime and bonus payments). Later, it will be used as the basis for analysing the reliability, maintainability and future of that item of machinery.

9.3.3 Maintenance Schedules

Another essential component of the EMIS is the scheduling system. This could take the form of a wallchart, a handwritten register or a set of loose-leaf, pre-printed forms; more likely, two or more of these formats will be used, to cover the various applications of the schedule. Whatever its form, it sets out the maintenance plan for the next week or month (or, indeed, longer periods), timetabling when each machine needs to be taken out of operational service for routine maintenance and what form that maintenance will take. Such a schedule is considered essential by all the major, successful ports, which have adopted preventive maintenance as their primary maintenance strategy. The planned service intervals that form the basis for the programme are initially derived from manufacturers' maintenance manuals, but are modified with time and experience to reflect the needs and circumstances of the port.

In its simplest form, the maintenance schedule is chalked up on a blackboard or written onto a pre-formatted timetable. A more elaborate and very effective system was seen in one Asian port, taking the form of a large white-board, inscribed with week and day columns and with rows for the equipment being serviced. The shift slots are provided with hooks onto which labelled tokens are hung as technical staff are allocated to a job. The tokens are colour-coded by trade, so that the system displays at a glance information on what jobs are in progress, which staff are allocated to them, which staff are in reserve, which jobs are in abeyance or waiting to be started, and which jobs have been completed.

The scheduling board is located in the planning section of the Engineering Department or workshop, and duplicate versions should be placed in the individual workshops, so that the workshop manager has immediate access to the current status of all jobs, can allocate further jobs as they arise and can check progress. The wall-mounted timetable is backed up by a more permanent version, either written up in register form or as loose-leaf pages in a file. This is the only permanent and long-term record of the maintenance schedule, accumulating over successive shifts and showing how it is modified as the hours and days pass and circumstances change.

The maintenance schedule, and the process of scheduling, are frequently the province of a routing desk within the engineering or workshop organization. The routing desk (or its equivalent function) plans the work of an individual workshop or a group of workshops in broad outline for the following week or more, generating Job Cards and requisitioning the necessary supplies (in conjunction with the supervisor responsible for the particular category of equipment) well before the day of the service. Nearer the time – probably the day before – the planners finalize the schedule, adjusting the preliminary plan in the light of which machines can most conveniently be spared from operations duties and what emergency jobs have arisen. Then, at the begining of the shift, the desk issues the Job Cards and associated worksheets or manuals to individual technicians or gangs.

The routing desk (or its equivalent) is thus the allocator of engineering resources, ensuring that work is tackled in order of priority, to suit operators' needs, and that emergency work – repairing equipment damaged by accidents or that have broken down while in use – can be slotted-in without delay. The Maintenance Schedule is the planners' basic tool, and a vital component of the Engineering Management Information System.

9.3.4 The Maintenance Database
In addition to the individual Job Cards and schedules which relate to specific maintenance jobs and how they are timetabled, the EMIS needs a set of more comprehensive and permanent records which collect together information relating to individual and groups of machines and their constituent systems and components. Collectively, these records constitute the database for the EMIS, upon which plans and decisions are based.

The first of these record systems is the Asset Register, the inventory of the port's plant, equipment, buildings and other assets. It lists every owned item and identifies it by code number and full description (e.g. equipment type, capacity, manufacturer, date of acquisition, location or storage position within the port). Linked to the Register (at least through the individual asset code number but possibly through a more formal linkage) should be the set of Asset History records. These provide a cumulative account of the working life of each asset, e.g. the hours of work of a cargo-handling machine, its preventive maintenance sessions, its breakdown and damage repairs, etc. Every maintenance job performed on that asset should be entered on its Asset History card or file, detailing all the spare parts used, consumable items exchanged, fuel used and so on. The Asset Register and the Asset Histories form the foundation on which equipment planning (Chapter 3) can be soundly based.

The Job Cards and maintenance schedules will also, of course, form part of the database when they are filed away after completion; they are the permanent records of the workshops' activity and will be used periodically for assessing engineering performance and for other purposes.

9.3.5 Analysis
The final essential element of the EMIS is an activity or function rather than a physical entity – the process of analysis of the collected data and assembling them into forms suitable for the various decision-making activities that (should) follow. The central activity is the collation of related data and their aggregation into suitable groups, followed by interpretation of the assembled facts and figures, and circulation of that interpretation to appropriate managers.

It is at the stage of analysis that the EMIS becomes most valuable. When data on an individual machine are assembled over time, the engineers can gather a view of its performance, reliability and suitability for refurbishing or replacing. Individual systems, e.g. suspension of a particular model of straddle carrier, can be analysed and recurrent faults identified. Usage of spares can be analysed, to check unanticipated levels of use or unexpected wear.

Whereas most ports have established at least a rudimentary system of data gathering on maintenance jobs, very few have adopted a thoroughgoing analytical procedure, and analysis is the weakest link in the information chain in the majority of ports. Yet it is clearly of utmost importance; the database can only reveal its important secrets if related facts and records are assembled into monthly or annual summaries, are investigated for trends and are linked to data collected in other segments of the MIS.

The analytic function has to be established, in terms of location, process and staff, and adequate resources must be provided to allow it to operate effectively. It is a component not just of the EMIS but of the port's total internal communication system, since its outputs (the periodic summaries, audits and evaluations) must be circulated to all managers for whom that information is relevant – and *only* to those, of course.

The information is communicated not just for information's sake, of course; the (E)MIS is only of value if its analysed data are acted upon. The analyses are fed back into the system so that the system itself can be modified in some way; the system needs to respond to, or adapt in response to, the analyses. As will be discussed in Section 9.4, the analysed data are used to control maintenance work, to modify schedules and practices, to identify problems, control costs, and so on. In their raw form, the data cannot readily be used for these purposes. They need to be aggregated, compared, plotted, summarized and averaged to provide the basis for informed action.

Clearly, presentation style is important. If managers are to understand what the analyses have demonstrated, the data and trends must be presented in unambiguous and readily grasped form. Graphical or pictorial representation, showing trends, is very effective, especially if different colours are used to represent different aspects of the information presented. Bar charts and line graphs are ideal, particularly if backed up by neatly tabulated and annotated figures. The graphs should be clearly marked with norm or target values, with off-target and out-of-norm segments highlighted to draw managers' attention quickly to them.

9.3.6 The Basic EMIS
Although several other important components can – indeed, should – be added to complete the system, in essence a basic EMIS can be assembled from just the components described so far: Job Cards (the data entry stage), Maintenance Schedules (the organizational framework for the work), the Records (providing the continuously updated database of facts and figures) and the Analytic function (to interpret and organize the data and

feedback information on which to base relevant response).

It is, perhaps, surprising and disappointing that even this very basic form of EMIS is not present in complete form in many of the ports surveyed in this project. In a few, the Job Card and Scheduling components are poorly developed, in several the Records component is incomplete or otherwise inadequate (see Section 9.2), and in many an Analytic component is missing altogether. Without a complete Basic EMIS, it is difficult to see how effective, responsive and appropriate decisions can be taken on maintenance management.

9.3.7 Resource Costs
It has been pointed out previously (in Chapters 5 and 6, and in Section 9.2.2) that information on costs is conspicuously lacking in many ports – or at least in their engineering and operations departments – and not just in the developing world. This report strongly supports the cost/revenue centre philosophy for providing motivation and accountability in all port departments, and the accurate, reliable and comprehensive collection of cost data is a prerequisite for adopting that philosophy. The EMIS plays a prominent part in that costing process, beginning with the Job Card component, as mentioned in Section 9.3.2.

The Job Card should have spaces for recording not just the materials used in the job in question (consumables – such as lubricants, oil and air filters, antifreeze – and replacement parts: sparking plugs, batteries, gaskets etc.) but also their costs. These might have to be filled in after the job is completed, either when cost data are conveyed to the workshop from Supplies or Accounts or when the Job Card (or its duplicate copy) is forwarded to the Accounts Department as part of the MIS procedure. At that stage, too, Job Card details of hours worked by maintenance personnel will be costed, at standard or overtime rates, as appropriate, and these costs will be entered into the system. Finally, appropriate overhead charges will be added, expressing at least the notional costs of providing the workshop, tools, electricity and administrative facilities which made the servicing possible.

The total cost figure finally arrived at is an important management tool, as will be discussed in Section 9.5.

9.3.8 The Supplies Management Information System
Although the Supplies Department will be responsible for, and heavily dependent for its success-

ful management on, its own Information System, it is so firmly bound up with the EMIS as to be considered almost a constituent part of it. Almost every maintenance job will involve the requisition of consumables (oils, greases, cleaning materials, etc.) and spare parts (bearings, filters, engine components, exhausts, body panels, chains etc.) from the stores. Indeed, in all the ports surveyed, the Engineering Department is by far the largest customer of the stores section, consuming over 75% of the stores' turnover. The EMIS and the Supplies Management Information System (SMIS) are clearly interlinked.

The primary means of communication between the systems is normally the Requisition Form, completed in the workshop (or its planning office) and signed by a foreman or other responsible officer; in many LDC ports, a frequent complaint is that the requisition has to be signed by too senior a manager, and there is often a strictly observed set of rules on the authorization hierarchy, related to the cost of the item – a common cause of delays in completing maintenance jobs. The Requisition Form identifies the supplies needed by name, description and code number – usually the Supplies Department's own stock code number. If the item required is a 'non-stock item' (see Chapter 8) it may not have a port code, in which case the manufacturer's reference number should be used and a different Requisition Form may have to be used, too. Whatever the nature of the item required, there must be no ambiguity over its identity.

On issuing the requisitioned item, the storekeeper requests a signature of receipt from the maintenance section representative, and he in return has his copy of the Requisition Form annotated to confirm the issue. The stores' copy goes into Supplies' own MIS as a record of the issue, and the item is deleted from the stores inventory; this might trigger off a re-order, if the minimum stock level is reached. When the requisitioned item is delivered to the workshop, the Job Card is updated to record the receipt of the material or spares, so that it can in due course be costed to the job.

The EMIS and SMIS also interlink through the Stores Inventory. It is extremely useful for the Engineering Department to have copies of the inventory (either as a printed catalogue or via computer terminal access), so that the workshop manager or routing desk can check quickly on the name and code number of the required item and discover its stock position. For preventive maintenance jobs, this will be done as the Job Card is prepared, ideally well in advance of the performance of the service, so that the workshop can be assured of the arrival of the supplies before the

machine is stripped down. The survey has revealed, in too many LDC ports, quite inexcusable and damaging delays in issuing of spares from stock, and even more alarming delays in procuring non-stock items. This reinforces the need for close – and early – collaboration over this phase of every engineering task, and firm interlinking of the EMIS and SMIS.

Deficiencies in system interlinking are all too common in ports. Frequently, for example, the Engineering Department has no direct access to the Stores Inventory, and so has no knowledge of the current stock position nor ready information on spare parts designation and code numbers. At best an unnecessary telephone call has to be made, during which the stores staff have to look up their own records; at worst one or more visits to the stores have to be made, and there is considerable delay before the spares Requisition Form can even be filled in. Improvement in this area is one of the simplest that could be made to maintenance management, and there seems no reasonable excuse for delaying that improvement.

9.3.9 The Operations Management Information System

Just as the EMIS and SMIS are (or should be) closely linked, so also does the Operations MIS (Chapter 5, Section 5.6) need to be firmly connected into the EMIS.

The engineers need to know, when analysing their equipment records and when scheduling their maintenance, the hours of work performed by the units, their fuel consumption, any defects noted by their drivers and many other aspects of their performance on their berths, quays and terminals. This information has to be entered into the EMIS from the Operations Department or the Engineering Department in some way. Normally, the source of the information is the vehicle logbook, in which the driver will have recorded times of starting work and finishing, with delays and idle times. He will also have noted any unusual noises, exhaust emissions, instrument warnings, etc., that he has observed and, if the defect is a serious one, will have described in the logbook or accompanying report sheet the exact nature of the defect, breakdown or accident before returning the vehicle for workshop attention or calling out the mobile workshop to the work location. At the end of the shift, the details will have been transferred to the workshop's Daily Equipment Record.

All these observations and records should be transferred to the EMIS in some appropriate fashion, to form part of the database for subsequent analysis and feedback. If the equipment is normally stored at or near the related workshop, the data will normally be transferred at the end of the shift or day, but if machines are parked at or near the work location between periods of use, some means has to be established of transferring data – preferably daily – between the Operations and Engineering Departments. The departments also need to pool data on utilization, downtime and availability for planning purposes; some of this will be collected by one department, the rest by the other, but they must be exchanged and analysed for the mutual benefit of both when deciding to replace equipment, add to the port's stock or scrap machines.

The two systems must also be linked for maintenance scheduling purposes. On the basis of planned intervals between services or of hours worked, the maintenance staff will know when they require access to a machine for preventive maintenance, but its availability for maintenance can only be agreed with Operations shortly before the planned (or adjusted) date and time, depending on pressure of cargo-handling work. So the EMIS must somehow issue to the Operations Department or Terminal Manager a request for access to a machine on a particular day, and then operational and maintenance planners will need to negotiate release as near to that day as is convenient for both departments. It helps considerably to avoid conflict if the process is built into the respective Information Systems, with automatic issuing of requests to initiate negotiation for access.

9.3.10 The Status of the EMIS

The Engineering Management Information System can, clearly, become a very elaborate management tool within the Engineering Department, with well established links to other departments and systems. Indeed, as will be seen in Section 9.5, it could well be integrated with Personnel and Finance Department systems, and with the Planning and Development Department as well. Its central position within the management of a modern port is now self-evident. That very elaboration and pivotal position inevitably cause problems for managing the system itself and turn the spotlight on the physical nature of the system and how best it can be organized, which will be considered in the next section.

9.4 The Nature of the EMIS

9.4.1 Conventional Systems

Traditionally (in those ports with an honourable history of incorporating maintenance data in their Management Information Systems) the EMIS has consisted of an array of specially designed forms, on paper or card, bound or loose-leaf registers, and card indexes of varying degrees of elaboration. Such systems are still to be found in many African and Asian ports (and a not inconsiderable proportion of European ones, too). Often, the variety of printed forms amounts to hundreds, each designed for one specific activity within the sequence of documentation procedures. In some ports visited, the EMIS forms were designed as part of a Technical Assistance (TA) project by a foreign expert (or, in one unhappy case, by a succession of consultants as part of a sequence of TA programmes; the resulting assemblage of incompatible and confusingly dissimilar forms has done little to encourage accurate and consistent recording and analysis of equipment data).

There is no doubt that a paper-based system can work satisfactorily; indeed, until recently it was the only way in which management could effectively monitor, control, modify and plan the maintenance function. Even today, several successful European ports still rely largely on card and paper systems for issuing, monitoring, costing and evaluating maintenance, though usually that system is in the process of being replaced. The main problems with such a conventional EMIS are that it is bulky and unwieldy (paper accumulates at an alarming rate) and that it is time-consuming to operate effectively, particularly its analytic component.

The first problem is the sheer bulk of the resulting paperwork. In a large port, the files of collected Job Cards and schedules, Asset History cards, Requisition Forms, etc. accumulate in vast quantities, and storage in readily accessible form becomes very difficult. In several ports, records occupy rows of shelves in workshop and administrative offices – usually gathering dust, because the second problem is that bulky files are difficult to access for analysis; indeed they discourage managers from attempting to analyse the data on a regular basis.

The more succesful ports *do* analyse their paper-based data, however. The survey revealed several instances of dedicated engineers painstakingly extracting comparative data from the workshop and other records, producing monthly summaries, graphs of trends in usage and reliability of their equipment, and even data comparing machine types and manufacturers. All admitted, however, that it took up large amounts of their valuable time – time better spent on improving equipment management than on desk-work with pencil and calculator. In most ports, managers admitted that they cannot spare the time or the staff for such summarizing and analytical tasks, although they recognized the need and value of doing so.

One or two improvements on the conventional system were noted in the survey. In one port, the bulk terminal had adopted a loose-leaf file record system (the 'Visualizer', by the Swiss firm Syscon) which allows a month's daily records to be compared at a glance, by offsetting them in such a way that related columns and rows overlapped, revealing the totals columns in register alongside each other. In other ports, the Job Cards are designed for a 'T-Card' system, also allowing at-a-glance inspection of schedules of jobs due, jobs in hand, jobs suspended and jobs completed, while colour-coding can identify machine type, berth/terminal location, designated workshop etc. These and other modifications to the basic system can help to simplify management of the EMIS, but ultimately the problems of manager-intensive searching, collating, analysis, summarizing and circulating of data remain a major obstacle and disincentive to full use of the information.

For this reason, and because of the increased flexibility and versatility brought with it, many ports have computerized their EMIS or are in the process of doing so.

9.4.2 Computerized Systems

Transferring the engineering (and other) management information to a computer system does not merely overcome the problems of the sheer volume of data, its storage, access and interpretation, but also opens up possibilities of greater control, increased detail and deeper analysis. Ports that have gone the furthest with computerized systems are among the most efficient, cost conscious, competitive and successful in the world, and the computer terminal has become the most-used tool on the engineer's desk and workbench.

There are several very significant benefits of computerizing:

1. Data can be quickly and easily stored, in as great detail as desired. Asset histories need not stop at the level of category of machine (e.g. tractor) or, at best, individual unit (tractor No. 32), but can include details of repairs to and performance of systems (e.g. drive system), subsystems (e.g. engine) and even components (e.g. crank case). Ports using this approach to maintenance management give their engineers immediate online access to comparative data on every aspect of their work, which has led to remarkable improvements in routine maintenance, in designing-out defects, in making

better-informed procurement decisions and so on.

2. It is easy to link computer systems together. The EMIS can become an integral part of the port's master MIS, with access to (and contributing its own data to) operational, financial and personnel databases. Information can flow freely in all directions, and responsibility, cost-consciousness and accountability can be firmly based on sound, up-to-date knowledge. Managers can constantly monitor progress in other departments, chase the spare parts orders, etc. from their own desks. However, the system still allows sensitive information to be protected, by limiting access (by identity code) to those with a right to know.

3. The computer relieves engineers (and their counterparts in other departments) of the time-consuming burden of analysing, summarizing and circulating maintenance-derived data. The system performs those activities rapidly and effortlessly, displaying the results immediately and simply, as tables and graphs. Decisions can be taken on the basis of current factual evidence rather than guesswork, and the weekly and monthly summaries are always on hand when the need for a decision arises.

4. Whereas one component of a paper-based MIS is confined to a small area (one or two offices or even desks within an office), a computer-based system is distributed and generally available – everyone can have access to it. Paradoxically, it combines openness with tighter control.

5. One computer data entry can be used in a variety of contexts, serving several systems and functions, whereas in a paper system each data record has to be repeated several times if it is needed in different contexts. For example, a mechanic's hours of work on a particular repair need only be entered once in a computerized EMIS to be immediately available to the Personnel MIS (for calculating his wages and bonuses) and the Accounts MIS (for costing the job) as well as to the engineers when reviewing work values and workshop performance; with a paper-based system, the data would have to be recorded on several forms and ledgers.

Computer systems are, of course, expensive to instal and maintain, and ports are still reluctant to make that investment. Managers (particularly senior managers) frequently voiced objections to computerizing, when the issue was discussed during this survey, and there is evident lack of enthusiasm in many quarters. The objections can generally be accounted for in terms of (undeclared) fear of the unfamiliar, and perhaps also anxiety that younger subordinates might acquire or demonstrate skills that the senior managers do not possess. There is also the undeniable fact that many managers just do not comprehend the benefits that a computerized MIS can bring, in terms of time-saving, quality of records and analyses, and increased competitiveness. For example, several of the most successful ports reported savings of tens of thousands of dollars a year in terms of better spare parts control alone, through computerizing, while others have demonstrated increased operational efficiency and reduced maintenance costs as a result of modifications initiated by analyses of the aggregated asset sub-system data.

The question of cost is also becoming less of an obstacle as hardware prices fall, in both absolute and relative terms. A desktop microcomputer is now more powerful than a minicomputer of just four or five years ago and a mainframe of 15-20 years back. Storage capacities of 300 Mbytes or more are now available in a microcomputer, with operating speeds far greater than could have been contemplated for mainframes not so long ago. It is, then, quite realistic to propose a microcomputer (or networked group of several micros) as the basis for a complete EMIS for a modest-sized port, and even very large ports can be fully served by a current 'superminicomputer' to which terminals are attached for data input (in Finance, Personnel, Supplies, etc.) and with micros serving as terminals in Engineering and Operations, allowing local analysis of data drawn from the central database and immediate online access to Berth Scheduling, Ship Planning, Stores Inventory and other information sources. In fact, the majority of applications and benefits to be discussed in Section 9.5 can only be fully realized in a computerized system. As one participant in the survey observed, ports cannot afford *not* to have a fully-fledged EMIS, because without it the port's competitive position is dangerously undermined.

9.4.3 Designing the System
Whatever the physical nature of the (E)MIS, it must be designed to meet fully the needs of the managers using it. Common faults of current systems (Section 9.2.5) are that they are poorly designed, are 'unfriendly' to non-expert users and do not do the job they should.

It might seem so obvious as not to need discussing that users should be involved in the design process, but experience in many ports demonstrates that too often this is not done. When the Engineering Management Information System is being developed, working groups of Operations and Engineering staff must be set up, together with the planners, administrative and EDP staff who will be responsible for establishing the system. This is obviously important with computerized systems (where the 'experts' too easily take over the design process, unchallenged by the users who have no clear idea of what the system can do) but collaboration is just as necessary for a paper-based system, if the effort of setting it up (or modifying it) is to be rewarded by its regular use.

Indeed, a persuasive suggestion made at one or two European ports with a well-established computer-based MIS, and actually being followed currently in at least one Asian port, is that user-EDP working groups should first perform a thorough needs analysis and then set up a model paper-based version of the system. They can then validate and modify the system before committing the port to computer hardware and (often just as expensive) software. Certainly, a very close collaboration between all parties involved is essential from the very earliest design stages right through to implementation. Fully computerized ports have also found it necessary to continue the working group approach after implementation, to review use of the system and to suggest and follow-through revisions and improvements in the light of experience and changed circumstances.

In the case of form-based systems, no less than for computer-based ones, it is well to remember the cost disadvantages of attempting to reinvent the wheel. Management Information Systems have been established for many years in many ports, and systems have been refined and improved to a considerable degree. Wherever possible, it seems sensible to 'borrow' and modify systems in use elsewhere rather than to design from scratch. Technical Assistance projects should include surveys of existing form-based systems, for example, taking their best features and modifying them (minimally) for local use. United Nations agencies could help by developing model forms and providing them on request. This will be considered again in Chapter 10.

As far as computer software is concerned, two opposing schools of thought exist. Several of the largest ports insist that programming has to be carried out within the port, to tailor-make a system exactly matching the port's needs. These ports express considerable distrust of commercially available software and that developed in other ports – they provide splendid illustrations of the 'not invented here' syndrome. Other ports have happily purchased (and recommend) software packages from commercial sources – often designed for fleet vehicle owners, hire companies and public transport companies – and have adapted them for use in their Engineering and Supplies Departments.

To the visiting observer, there seems little difference in quality or usefulness between the systems installed in these two types of port, despite the enormous differences in the costs and time invested in systems implementation. One port adopting the 'do-it-yourself' approach has an EDP section 250 strong, while another is still developing its EMIS software some two years after installing the first phase and several years after introducing computers to the port; that system still cannot be used fully for management decisions. There is little indication that a specially designed system engenders more satisfaction and fewer complaints from users than the off-the-shelf package – indeed, engineers complained frequently to the team about delays in getting things changed, about lack of usability and about unnecessary data output in those tailor-made systems.

The considered recommendation is that off-the-shelf software should be very seriously examined before a port embarks on the very expensive exercise of developing its own. Several commercial software packages are available, e.g. one developed by Future Technologies Ltd. (Kingston-upon-Hull, UK) for vehicle fleet maintenance, while the EMIS 'shell' developed for IBM-compatible PCs by the Arab Maritime Transport Academy, Alexandria, is worth serious consideration. It is further suggested that international agencies, such as the World Bank and UNCTAD, could commission the development of a generalized port EMIS software package, easily modifiable for local use and made available as part of TA programmes or separately. It seems a great pity that so many ports are spending time and money on repeating software design exercises unnecessarily. The provision of inexpensive software would make the prospect of embarking on computerization of its (E)MIS much less daunting for LDC ports.

9.5 Uses and Benefits of the EMIS

9.5.1 Introduction
Sections 9.3 and 9.4 have identified several areas in which an effective EMIS can improve management of the port maintenance function. In this section, these and other applications will be considered more thoroughly in turn: in maintenance planning, work control, control of spares and consumables, control of maintenance costs, equipment planning, technical and design applications, internal communications and training.

9.5.2 Maintenance Planning
The EMIS forms the basis for the planning and scheduling of maintenance. Its records should signal when equipment is due for preventive maintenance and what tasks need to be carried out during that maintenance. A fully computerized system will issue the Job Cards automatically, and even a paper-based system should include a set of equipment maintenance procedures, from which the appropriate sheet or sheets can be extracted for issuing to the technicians.

The request for access to the machine for maintenance (where Operations has 'possession' of it) is subject to convenience; it is useful to have online access to the same set of information as the Operations Department, to time the request appropriately. One port visited allows engineers direct online access to the Berthing Schedules, so that they can plan preventive maintenance for times of minimum operational demand.

Where condition monitoring is practised, the routinely gathered data can be input directly to the EMIS, allowing preventive maintenance to be 'flagged' by indications and advance warning of component or system deterioration or failure. When fully implemented, this approach allows maintenance intervals to be extended to their practicable limits, reducing unnecessary servicing.

Even where formal condition monitoring is not practised, a good EMIS allows, over time, the adjustment of maintenance intervals and schedules. As records of system and component condition accumulate, and as information on breakdowns, failures and performance levels are gathered, better judgements can be made on suitable maintenance intervals. Perhaps they will be shortened to prevent breakdowns or (more likely) extended to reduce demands on maintenance resources without endangering equipment life and reliability. In one European port, as described in Chapter 6, a closely controlled programme to extend intervals between preventive maintenance sessions has resulted in their being increased steadily from 250 hours to 350, 500, 750 and finally to 1000 hours without harm (though the latter, current schedule needs very careful monitoring, to check that faults are not being missed). Another port has gone through a similar exercise, but has come back from 500 hours to 350 hours for safety – the EMIS allows engineers to make such changes with confidence.

The EMIS also highlights, in retrospect, which particular systems or components needed attention at a particular service. In time, the schedule of jobs to be carried out during each maintenance session might well be modified in the light of analysis of the maintenance records. All the data relating to service intervals and maintenance tasks are within the system, assigned as appropriate to the Asset History Register, and the system flags up each unit as it approaches its planned service time. A computerized system is particularly good for this, as it can flash up on the screen every day those items not yet in for their planned service, the colour coding changing as the planned date approaches and then passes, increasing the indication of urgency as the days pass.

9.5.3 Control of Work

The issued Job Cards and worksheets form the basis for each planned maintenance job, and allow firm control of the job by supervisors and workshop managers. They can check against the sheet that all tasks have been correctly performed, so that quality control is given a formal framework. However, breakdown and accident repair jobs cannot have their details issued in advance, and Job Cards for them have to use general descriptions, such as "inspect and diagnose. . .", but as soon as the cause of a fault has been diagnosed, an appropriate worksheet relating to the suspect system can be issued, detailing the steps in disassembly, repair and reassembly. Again, these instructions should be set out in simple steps, so that each can be checked and approved.

As mentioned in Section 9.4, a comprehensive computerized system could embody within itself details of maintenance procedures, adapted from the manufacturers' manuals, so that technicians could call up on their own terminals diagrams of assemblies and subassemblies, instructions on disassembly and reassembly, diagnostic aids and prompts, and engineering data. No such system was found in the ports contacted, but they are in use in other industries, particularly in automobile and aircraft construction and maintenance, and there is no reason why a similar system should not be implemented in ports. As port cargo-handling equipment increases in complexity, the need for improved maintenance aids for technicians becomes more acute.

The EMIS does, then, allow close quality control, as all steps in the maintenance process are monitored. Maintenance quality should improve, and constant adjustment of scheduling and planning also makes maintenance more relevant to needs, as information is fed back from the system to the engineers. It also allows monitoring of labour effectiveness; time on task can be checked and controlled, and compared with maintenance performance targets. Not only are the records of man-hours spent on a job used in calculating costs, but they also provide a basis for

making out salary and overtime payments for workshop staff. They can also be used for working out incentive payments, if fair and realistic standards can be set for time on task and quality of work. More likely, however, is that the EMIS will provide regularly data on Mean Time Between Failures and Mean Time to Repair, from which gang performance or workshop performance values can be calculated (see Chapters 6 and 8).

9.5.4 Control of Spares and Consumables

An important benefit of a good EMIS is the advance warning it can give for requisitioning spare parts and materials for a planned maintenance job. As the Job Card is issued, so is (or can be) the stores Requisition Form for the relevant materials. Even if a particular spare is out of stock, it should give the Supplies Department an opportunity of procuring it before the job is started – or at least the chance to warn the maintenance planning unit or routing desk that the maintenance should be postponed until the spares are available.

Regular analysis of maintenance records also permits the Stores staff to monitor their stock and reordering levels, and to adjust them as appropriate to likely demand. This is particularly important as equipment ages and more of its systems and components near the ends of their working lives. Prompt adjustment of the Asset Register as equipment is disposed of also prevents re-stocking of spares for equipment no longer in service; better still, regular analysis by Supplies of the Asset Register gives advance warning of ageing equipment, so that staff can discuss with engineers the likelihood of disposal and the desirability of winding down stock levels of spares for those machines.

This sort of exploitation of the data and facilities of the EMIS can lead to substantial savings within the stores. In one Asian port, better and more responsive control of spares stocks through EMIS analysis has led to reduction of stock-holding from about $2.5 million to $1.9 million – a saving of nearly 25%.

A further potential application, already in use in one North American port, is a contribution to stores security. A perennial problem is to make spare parts available at all times that engineers are at work; this is not easy where workshops work three continous shifts, to match operational working, while stores work one or, at best, two shifts. One solution is to mark every stores item with a unique bar-code and to issue each member of the stores staff *and* the technical staff with electronic devices which 'read' the code, debiting the appropriate cost-centre and identifying the drawer of the supplies simultaneously. There is then no need for constant storekeeper attendance, and no item can be removed from the stores unaccountably. (At the very least, if such a sophisticated system cannot be contemplated, a shift supervisor or someone of similar seniority should be given a key to the stores for emergency use.)

9.5.5 Control of Maintenance Costs

A surprising and disturbing feature of this survey has been the revelation that the majority of engineering (and, indeed, other) departments are completely unaware of their own costs. They cannot, therefore, have effective budgets nor any form of costed performance targets. The EMIS corrects that failing, providing all the data needed to make an accurate costing of all maintenance jobs, including the costs of materials and spares used, labour costs and overheads (in terms of job type and hours of use of facilities; some form of 'averaging' of engineering costs has to be adopted, to produce 'standard costs'). The primary use of these cost data is to allocate costs to the 'consumer' department – Operations. This is the basis for the treatment of the Engineering Department (or an individual workshop) as a cost/revenue centre. A secondary, but equally important, use is to aggregate costs over the year, by equipment type, for calculating a maintenance budget for the following year and, in combination with related data from Operations and other cost/revenue centres, to provide the port's financial planning team with data for estimating the total port budget.

A further use for maintenance cost data is to set targets for the engineering sections; the aim should be so to improve maintenance quality (by better condition monitoring, prolonging equipment, system and component life, etc.) as to reduce maintenance costs. The cost targets need to be set below the present year's (or quarter's) actual costs, but not unrealistically so – clearly, allowance has to be made for inflation and for increases in labour and spare parts costs. Subsequently, the EMIS will allow engineers to monitor how well the workshops are meeting their cost and performance targets.

Equally importantly, the EMIS provides constantly updated information on the cost of maintaining each unit of equipment, allowing engineers to keep a check on particularly expensive machines (which could then be considered for replacement or refurbishment), components and systems (which could be considered for upgrading, modification or substitution). It also allows workshop managers to spot expensive maintenance gangs – perhaps careless about changing oil or other consumables, or slow in completing their jobs – and to take appropriate action to improve their performance.

9.5.6 Equipment Planning

A vitally important function of the EMIS is to provide much of the factual information on which the equipment plan is based (Chapter 3). It is the location of the Asset Register and of the individual Asset Histories, and the Engineering Department is responsible for updating these databases. The information on equipment efficiency, running costs, reliability and maintainability provides the basis for the planning group's recommendations on replacement of machines, in association with performance data (cost per tonne of cargo handled, cost per move, etc.) from the Operational MIS.

Furthermore, more detailed analyses of aggregated engineering data on equipment categories, manufacturers, systems and components provide the engineers with a far better basis for selecting new machines than do the 'feelings' resulting from their unquantified 'experience'. They allow the process of drawing up the engineering specification for a new piece of equipment to be firmly based on facts and comparative information on different makes and types of equipment and components.

9.5.7 Technical and Design Applications

The constant analysis of maintenance data gives engineers early warning of persistent equipment problems related to unsatisfactory and unreliable design, components and systems. At the very least, such items can be monitored closely in all the machines in which they occur, and can be replaced *before* failure, saving valuable operational time. More importantly in the long term, the engineers can investigate that component or system, to see whether it can be modified or redesigned, to improve its performance and/or extend its working life. One European port has adopted this strategy for completely redesigning the suspension on its straddle carrier fleet, with great benefit to maintenance and machine longevity. It has also greatly improved fuel economy in one model of tractor (prime mover) in its fleet, by alterations to its air-conditioning and by changing from a water-cooled to air-cooled engine. The engineers report that the manufacturers co-operated wholeheartedly in this redesign exercise (though not all are so co-operative), and that the resulting modifications have been incorporated in that model at the factory thereafter.

In the longer term, the EMIS records form the basis for collaboration between the engineers and the manufacturers to improve the technical specification and design of the next generation of equipment. Suspect systems can be redesigned and components changed, and the small gradual improvements that have taken place over the years in the port's workshops can be designed in, with the aim of improving performance and operational economy. The changes will also be taken into account by the engineers when developing the technical specifications for planned acquisitions.

9.5.8 Internal Communications

The EMIS provides the framework for regular communication between departments and units, e.g. for timetabling preventive maintenance, for reporting equipment defects while in operation, for monitoring performance and for general feedback of information. In the case of a computer-based system, it provides an electronic mail route for rapid communication between managers and other staff – with the advantages over a telephone system that numerical data can be accurately and unambiguously conveyed as or within the message, and that the information can be sent to the recipient's terminal in his absence. Technical, operational or labour problems can be sorted out at an early stage, before they become serious, and decisions can be taken jointly and amicably, to the great benefit of the management process. One Asian port has reported a rapidly accelerating usage of its MIS electronic mail facility since it was introduced last year, and a greatly improved level of communication between its engineering, operations and other staff.

A computerized EMIS is also good for progress chasing; the workshop staff have the constant ability to check the current status of a spares requisition, operators can check progress on an important equipment repair job, and so on. A major benefit is the direct communication with the spares inventory provided for engineering staff. Senior management can also take advantage of an electronic MIS to circulate information of general interest, to maintain the port's ethos and corporate objectives.

9.5.9 Training

A less obvious series of applications of the EMIS, though one which could prove extremely valuable if developed, is training. For example, the Job Card, worksheet or extract from the maintenance manual, issued with a job, could, if properly designed, be a useful adjunct to on-job training, helping a recently recruited technician in the early stages of learning the job, or an established technician when faced with a new type of machine. It is purely a question of appropriate design of the material: good use of carefully produced diagrams and carefully worded instructions can turn a conventional set of outline instructions into a valuable training aid.

A similar approach can convert job sheets into skills checklists, against which the young technician's ability to perform a pre-defined list of jobs as part of his on-job training (see Chapter 8) can be assessed.

As mentioned in Section 9.5.3, a computer-based EMIS could be used (though apparently has not yet been in the ports industry) to provide online help and data for practical training, allowing a technician to consult an engineering database from the workshop floor, to call up procedural steps, working diagrams, data on performance under test or load, etc. The system could also be developed to record information on the technician's understanding, performance and mastery. Current on-job training within the industry has not begun to come to grips with such a need; most on-job training is very *ad hoc,* and should be much more closely controlled and supervised.

Finally, the computerized EMIS could have training programs 'embedded' within its own system for training engineers to use the system. Computer familiarization courses will have to be given to all potential users of the system but, after such an introductory course, the most cost-effective way of learning to use the system is actually to *use* it under guidance. Training programs within the EMIS can perform this task of explanation, guidance and practice far better than any conventional lecture or demonstration.

9.6 Using the EMIS

9.6.1 Introduction

In this final section, the responsibilities of various staff with respect to the EMIS will be summarized briefly, to point up the widespread applicability of the system, both within Engineering and outside it, in other port departments, and to emphasize the central position of the EMIS within the port maintenance management function.

9.6.2 Maintenance Managers

Managers at various levels within the Engineering Department have crucial roles in the organization of the EMIS. First, senior managers are responsible for the initial design and establishment of the EMIS, for preventive and corrective maintenance. They work with Operations managers, Supplies personnel, Finance and (when appropriate) EDP staff, and Personnel managers to define the requirements of the system and to design its format. They supervise the implementation of the system – the design of the forms and the communication system within which they operate – and are responsible for training their staff in the operation of the system. They work closely with EDP systems analysts and programmers as they develop the software, if the EMIS is to be computerized.

After implementation, it is senior managers' job to ensure that the system is maintained – that subordinates responsible for entering data do so accurately and promptly, that forms and cards are issued and retrieved correctly, appropriately checked, approved and signed, and that analyses and summaries are carried out on schedule. If revisions are needed, senior managers must supervise the process, keeping the system in effective working order.

Within the system, it is managers' responsibility to set up and maintain the cost control system, liaising with Accounts and Operations staff as necessary to obtain the relevant cost data, and communicating engineering cost data, as appropriate, in the opposite direction. Finally, maintenance managers have the duty of maintaining the port's Asset Register and keeping up to date the individual asset histories, as each item of equipment comes within the reach of the department.

9.6.3 Supervisory Staff

Staff in the workshop planning section and/or routing desk, the workshop manager or superintending engineer (as appropriate to the particular workshop organization) are responsible for the issuing of Job Cards, for allocating labour to the jobs and for providing the relevant worksheets, check-lists and/or maintenance manuals detailing the work to be done. If spares or consumables are needed, they will requisition them in advance and ensure that they are available to the workshop technicians at the time of service.

While work is in progress, it is the responsibility of supervisory staff to ensure that the work is being done as instructed, and to a satisfactory standard. They inspect the finished job, checking it for accuracy, completeness and quality before 'signing-off' the labour and confirming by their own signatures that the work is complete.

At various set stages of the job, supervisory staff have the duty of ensuring that all relevant records are updated, by completing or issuing forms, transferring details to summary tables or keyboarding the data into the EMIS. Where appropriate, they transmit the records, or summaries

of them, to their seniors and/or to other departments.

9.6.4 Technicians

The fitters, mechanics and electricians are responsible for carrying out the work as instructed by the supervisory staff, first signing acceptance of the job and understanding of its nature and scope, and indicating the precise time of starting it. In performing the work, they follow the instructions given them on the Job Cards and worksheets, or follow the manual provided, and check off each step in the process as it is completed, waiting for inspection by a supervisor and his countersignature where necessary. The technicians may also have to collect spares and consumables requisitioned for the job, taking the Requisition Form to the stores, signing receipt for the issued supplies, and making sure they are costed to the right job number.

While work is in progress, maintenance technicians may have direct access to the EMIS, if it is computerized, to interrogate its engineering database for details on the servicing procedure, of part specifications, for engineering drawings, etc.

When they have completed the job, they obtain approval for it from their supervisor and sign-off the Job Card, once again indicating the time. If they have to leave the job uncompleted (e.g. at the end of their shift or because a required replacement part is not available), they must indicate which sections of the job they *have* completed, obtain the supervisor's signature to that and return the Job Card and associated documents to the supervisor or workshop office ready for the next team to take it over. The routing desk or equivalent function is responsible for holding the card (and holding that job 'open') until it is resumed.

On completion of the job, the supervisor returns the Job Card and other documents to the workshop manager's office for completion of remaining details (notably costs) and entry into the EMIS central records.

9.6.5 Stores Personnel

The storekeeper (or his assistant) makes contact with the EMIS when spares Requisition Forms are presented to him. He checks the form for accuracy, selects and issues the supplies requested, and obtains signature of receipt. He keeps one copy of the Requisition Form and returns the other, with the supplies, to the workshop. He then updates his own Stores MIS, deducting the issued item from the remaining stock level, and checks whether the minimum stock level has been reached, in which case he triggers the reordering process. He may also mark the Requisition Form with the cost of the issued supplies, though this is more likely to be done within the Supplies Office subsequently.

9.6.6 Personnel Department Staff

The Personnel Department may gain access to the EMIS in order to calculate salaries and wages of the workshop staff, perhaps using it to work out hours of overtime work or to calculate what incentive bonuses are due to be paid. The latter may depend on hours worked, performance targets achieved, Mean Time Between Failures and Mean Time To Repair targets exceeded, and so on. The data for these calculations will probably be entered into the system by senior Engineering Department staff at the end of each week or month; they are more likely to be based on pooled data than on individual staff records.

9.6.7 The Central Role of the EMIS

This chapter has demonstrated how the EMIS impinges on every group of activities within the port maintenance management function. It generates data for other departments and systems, and itself absorbs data from external sources, so that every section of engineering management comes within its influence.

It is hardly surprising that ports lacking an effective EMIS are those whose deficiencies are patent in other regards – they are the least efficient ports, those with the poorest record on maintenance and operations, the lowest cargo-handling performance and the lowest reputation with customers. No port of any size, if it wishes to remain competitive and to provide an efficient service to its customers, can afford *not* to establish and maintain a comprehensive EMIS. No port development project should be allowed to go ahead if an EMIS is absent and is not to be established as part of that plan; this will be considered again in Chapter 10.

However small the port, there is no reason why its EMIS should not now be computerized, for maximum efficiency, effectiveness and responsiveness. It is remarkable that, at a time when mechanization and containerization are in progress worldwide, and tens of millions of dollars are being spent on cargo-handling innovation and improvement, port information systems so woefully fall short of the ideal. Managers would do well to consider the educationist's plea (in the context of the need for precise statement of objectives): "If we don't know where we're going, how will we know when we get there?". Information on where the port's maintenance management function is going,

and its progress on the way, is essential to attainment of the port's management objectives.

9.7 Recommendations

1. LDC ports must establish an Engineering Management Information System (EMIS), as an indispensible management tool, which must be an integral component of the port's overall and unified Management Information System.

2. The basic element and data entry component of the EMIS must be a Job Card, which is essentially an acceptance and authorization by the engineers of a maintenance or repair job, and a statement of its issue to named workshop staff as the initializing phase of the EMIS.

3. The Job Card must record details of the machine to be worked on, a statement of the job to be done (with full instructions on the steps to be carried out) and records of the resources (labour, tools, workshop bay), spare parts and consumables used in the job.

4. A scheduling system must be established, setting out the maintenance plan for the next week or month, timetabling when each unit of equipment needs to be taken out of operational service for routine maintenance, and stating what form the maintenance will take.

5. A maintenance database must be set up as part of the EMIS, consisting of an Asset Register (listing all the items currently owned by the port) and an Asset History (providing a cumulative account of the working life of each asset, updated regularly from information contained in the Job Cards and maintenance schedules).

6. The data recorded and assembled in the EMIS must be regularly collated and aggregated into appropriate sets, and then analysed and interpreted for distribution in clearly presented, simple form to all relevant managers.

7. The analytic function must be established, in terms of location, process and staff, and given adequate resources to allow it to operate effectively.

8. The EMIS must record all the resource costs involved in each maintenance job – the cost of materials used (spare parts, lubricants and other

consumables), maintenance personnel hours worked (at standard and overtime rates) and overheads (as standard charges) – so that the job can be fully costed.

9. The EMIS and the Supplies MIS must interlink to give engineers immediate access to the stores inventory, for checking the current stock position and for gaining information on spare parts codes and designations.

10. The EMIS and SMIS must also be linked with the Operations MIS, so that information on equipment operation can be added to the maintenance database for planning purposes and for subsequent analysis and feedback.

11. Although a conventional, paper-based EMIS can work satisfactorily, it is strongly recommended that the EMIS, OMIS and SMIS be computerized and integrated, to allow the easy handling, storing, analysis and distribution of large volumes of data, providing greater management control, increased detail and deeper analysis of maintenance and other information.

12. Users must be closely involved in the design and development of the EMIS, starting with a thorough information needs analysis, followed by the development of a paper-based model system for validation, before committing the port to the purchase of computer hardware and software.

13. LDC ports should seriously consider the purchase of commercially produced computer software and modifying it for local circumstances, rather than developing EMIS software themselves.

14. The EMIS should form the basis for planning and scheduling maintenance, signalling when equipment is due for preventive maintenance and what tasks need to be carried out during that service, and giving advance warning of the need for requisitioning spare parts and materials.

15. The EMIS should be used by supervisors and workshop managers to control maintenance work and to provide a framework for quality-control checks on all the prescribed tasks.

16. Stores staff should use the EMIS and SMIS regularly to analyse maintenance records, to monitor their own stock and recording levels and to adjust levels to current and likely demand.

17. The EMIS must be used to aggregate costs over the year, by equipment type, for calculating a maintenance budget for the following year, for determining equipment operating costs and for setting performance targets for the engineering sections.

18. The EMIS must provide continually updated information on the cost of maintaining each unit of equipment, to allow engineers to check on particularly expensive machines (which could then be considered for replacement or overhaul, as part of inventory planning), components and systems (which could be considered for upgrading, modification or substitution).

19. The EMIS should be used to monitor closely all equipment components and systems and to allow engineers to take steps to modify or redesign items that present maintenance problems.

20. The EMIS records should form the basis for collaboration between the port's engineers and equipment manufacturers, to improve the technical specification and design of the next generation of equipment.

21. The EMIS should be used for regular communication between departments and units – in the case of a computer-based system, via 'electronic mail'.

22. A computer-based EMIS should be considered as a source of online help and data for practical training, allowing a technician to consult an engineering database from the workship floor, to call up procedural steps, working diagrams, data on performance and tests under load, etc.

23. Engineering managers must be responsible for ensuring that the EMIS is maintained, that subordinates enter data accurately and promptly, that forms and cards are issued and retrieved correctly, and that analyses and summaries are carried out and distributed on schedule.

24. All management and supervisory staff must ensure that all relevant EMIS records are updated, by issuing and/or completing forms correctly, transferring details to registers and summary sheets promptly, or by accurately keyboarding the data into the EMIS.

CHAPTER 10

Improving the Management of Maintenance

10.1 The Port Maintenance Problem

10.1.1 The Magnitude of the Problem

If there were any doubts as to the seriousness of the maintenance problems facing very many LDC ports, they will have been dispelled as a result of this survey. Maintenance deficiencies have been found to exist in all branches of port engineering – civil, marine and mechanical/electrical – but there is ample evidence that they are particularly severe in relation to cargo-handling plant and equipment. Poor maintenance practices are having a direct and damaging effect on the availability of equipment and other assets, and on the operational performance and profitability of LDC ports. Without immediate and determined efforts, the situation seems certain to deteriorate still further, as technologically more advanced equipment is purchased and as competition for maritime trade becomes stronger. It is very unlikely that the benefits of the mechanization which is now under way will be fully (or even largely) realized by the economies of those countries unless significant improvements in port maintenance are achieved soon.

The extent of the current problem must, however, be put into proper perspective. It needs to be acknowledged that there are several LDC ports (including some that participated in this survey) where the maintenance of port assets is well managed and carried out, and where operational and engineering standards are among the most efficient in the world. There are other ports where selective – and even relatively minor – improvements would yield significant benefits in terms of improved maintenance quality, better control and lower costs. In a rather larger number of ports, perhaps more profound changes are called for in a relatively restricted area of maintenance management and/or performance, but the alarming reality is that there are *many* LDC ports where maintenance deficiencies are widespread and deeply entrenched, and where a crisis point has been reached. Although the ports in the latter category can be found in all regions of the world, they are particularly concentrated in Africa, Latin America and Western Asia. It is in these ports, where the problems are endemic and acutely serious,

that the major challenge presents itself to those seeking to improve the management of port maintenance.

10.1.2 The Nature of the Problem

At first sight, it might have been expected that the maintenance problems so apparent in many LDC ports, and described in detail in earlier chapters, would be traceable to technical inadequacies and shortcomings in the engineering departments of those ports, and that improving the staffing and resourcing of their workshops would be sufficient to solve – or at least significantly alleviate – the difficulties. It is particularly striking, therefore, that a major conclusion of this survey is that the root of the problem does not lie there but in institutional, administrative and managerial areas. For example, several problems have been highlighted in connection with government-port relationships: unwisely formulated government policies and objectives (or, indeed, the lack of them); excessively burdensome Ministry regulations; restrictive controls by central planning agencies. Other difficulties relate to inappropriate port organizational structures, and to inadequate planning mechanisms within the port. Poor managerial control and a lack of effective supervision were other common causes of poor maintenance. Rarely was the technical competence of the engineers the most evident explanation of the maintenance problems observed by, and described to, the project team.

Underlying many of the institutional and organizational deficiencies is an almost universally detectable lack of employee motivation. Individuals at all levels in engineering (and, indeed, other departments) seem to have a negative attitude to their jobs and the port. It is surely no coincidence that the ports experiencing the most serious maintenance difficulties have a human resource crisis; this *must* sit at the centre of the problem in many, if not most, of those ports. This, of course, poses a major difficulty: while it is not too difficult to solve a technical problem by providing new machines or procedures, reversing employee attitudes and motivating staff to take a positive approach to their work is not a simple mattter.

10.1.3 The Spread of the Problem

Although the ports participating in this survey do not all, by any means, suffer from the entire range of deficiencies identified and described in this report, not to the same extent, there is nevertheless a high degree of commonality in both the nature of the problems and their root causes. Many of the same management and technical deficiencies were observed in all those ports experiencing serious maintenance problems. For example, most of the ports have inadequate, unreliable and fragmentary Engineering Management Information Systems, impairing the quality of decision making. Again, there are widespread shortages of the same range of managerial and practical skills among engineers in many of those ports, resulting in maintenance work of poor quality.

The fact that the nature of the maintenance problems and their causes are basically similar across a very wide spread of LDC ports does, of course, mean that the scale of assistance needed to solve those problems is very large, but it has the slight advantage that international agencies might be able to develop solutions that will have global applications.

10.2 The Nature of the Task

10.2.1 Attacking the Broad Front

There is no concealing the certainty that reducing and, ultimately, eliminating the present maintenance deficiencies in LDC ports represents a formidable task. Improving the management of maintenance, particularly in those ports where the problems are most severe, will take a great deal of effort and can only be viewed as a long-term objective. The task would be less daunting if it were possible to identify just one root cause of the problems, allowing effort to be concentrated in one area. The reality is that there is a diverse range of contributory but interrelated causes, and action is needed – and urgently – across a very wide front, from removing or simplifying government regulations and controls, and improving port administrative processes, to establishing manpower development and training programmes, and creating and installing effective management information systems.

Because the various contributory causes are so interdependent, the project team has (reluctantly) concluded that tackling just one or two of the issues is unlikely to produce more than limited success. For example, there is little benefit to be gained by a port improving its spare parts stock control if government regulations and the port's own administrative procedures cause lengthy and unpredictable delays in procuring spares; under these circumstances, it might be more sensible to follow present practices of over-stocking. Then again, it could be argued that there is no point in a port (or, indeed, a government) establishing high-quality technician training schemes, in new workshops fully equipped with expensive and elaborate German and Italian machine tools, if the young graduates then have to struggle with inadequate hand tools, in semi-derelict workshops, when they start work in the port itself. What chance is there of the recommended principle of total workforce accountability taking root if the port's organizational structure and ethos, and present management procedures, prohibit the delegation of authority to all but the very top tier of engineering (and other) management?

The conclusion has to be, therefore, that action is necessary across a very broad front indeed. All the related issues, in all the constituents of the maintenance management function, have to be identified, diagnosed and resolved if substantial improvements are to be made. In this section, the most significant of these issues are briefly picked out, from the full coverage of the previous chapters, and in Section 10.3 the implications for international agencies are assessed.

10.2.2 Government Controls and Regulations

There is no doubt among the members of the project team that the central issue in the achievement of efficient port maintenance management is the need to change existing public sector administrative procedures in many (if not most) LDCs; current institutional arrangements require radical reform. They present a series of almost impenetrable barriers to the establishment of effective maintenance policies and strategies, so that the full benefits of any attempted improvements in the day-to-day management and practice of port maintenance will only be realized if the working relationship between central government and the ports is drastically reshaped. Almost all government-port regulatory and administrative procedures *must* be streamlined, but particularly those relating to capital and revenue budgeting and planning, protocols, and procurement (especially foreign exchange) regulations.

Paradoxically, most port authorities have been given enabling legislation which sets out their responsibilities and duties, often in great detail, and which *appears* to provide them with the autonomy they need to manage their own affairs, with the minimum of government interference. In practice, of course, the public administrative systems in those LDCs have evolved in such a way that all aspects of port management come under microscopically close government scrutiny. Almost no move of any consequence can be made, no development or change can be contemplated (for example, in tariffs, incentive schemes or working hours) without governmental approval – which is often extraordinarily delayed, even when it is forthcoming at all. Efforts *must* be made to reverse this trend, and to encourage governments to allow ports far greater automomy in the management of their own affairs. Only if this is achieved can port management be expected to project the initiative, innovation and enterprise that are so desperately needed in this age of interport competition and technological challenge.

10.2.3 Management Practices

The second area that the project team would single out for particular attention is the issue of management practices, and the need for the introduction and consolidation of modern management techniques. First, the port must be set challenging (but realistic) objectives and these must then be translated into targets for port departments, units and individuals. The objectives and targets must be set in performance terms, and particularly financial ones. Procedures must then be introduced for monitoring the achievement of those targets, particularly in the areas of operations, maintenance, supplies and finance. One of the extraordinary revelations of this survey (at least as far as the project team is concerned) has been the total lack of any corporate, Board or port objectives in several ports – not to say the obvious surprise in those ministry and port officials at being questioned about such objectives. The port – and its working units – *must* know where it is going!

The government (or the relevant controlling authority) having set its objectives, the port must then be allowed to get on with the job of achieving them. Executive managers *have* to be free to take what action they see as necessary, with no government interference whatsoever *unless and until* it becomes clear that the targets are not being met. Clearly, a priority development in nearly all ports, if they are to face and achieve targets, is a comprehensive, reliable and easily accessible management information system. Only when such a system is in place can managers receive the information they constantly need to assess performance, achieve control of port activities – and particularly *costs* – and to monitor progress towards their goals. Fully developed EMIS, OMIS and SMIS systems are absolutely essential weapons in the battle to improve port maintenance.

Another area for management action is that of planning and control procedures, which are woefully inadequate in many ports. New procedures need to

be developed and rigorously followed, particularly those promoting co-operation and collaboration between engineering, supplies and operations staff. Improved communication systems are desperately needed in many ports, to reduce delays and to eliminate misunderstandings, suspicion and conflict between those that handle the cargoes and those that provide and maintain the machinery and infrastructure for them to do so.

Finally – and most essentially in this context – authority must be delegated within the port organization. In too many LDC ports, all the reins are held at the very highest levels, and managers 'on the ground' (and in the workshops) are unable to move without authorization and approval from that top tier, in even the most insignificant matters. Much greater responsibility must be placed on employees at lower levels, and the necessary authority to take action (for example, to order spare parts and to spend foreign exchange) must be awarded – with all the necessary safeguards, of course – to those who are in the best position to decide what action is necessary, and who have shown by their performance that they can be trusted with those decisions.

These fundamental changes in management practices are essential if the management of port maintenance is to be improved. They call for a bold change of direction on port policy by governments, and radical reform of management style in the ports of many LDCs.

10.2.4 Management and Technical Skills

If all the proposed institutional and management changes are to succeed, managers in the engineering departments of ports will have to acquire (and be given) a range of new skills. New posts may have to be created within engineering for recruits with new technical abilities. As this survey has indicated, there seems no shortage of graduates with the traditional engineering qualifications – on paper, at least – but there are considerable doubts about the abilities of the present generation of senior and middle managers in relation to the practical matters of port maintenance; they seem to be desk-orientated and 'theoretical' engineers, rather than the hands-on, practical men that the discipline really requires. So practical engineering skills must be imported somehow – either through retraining or recruitment – to strengthen the workshop side of engineering practices in many LDC ports.

Similarly, the technical skills of the workshop staff themselves need to be given much greater attention, from recruitment right through to refresher and remedial training. The demands for maintenance, in terms both of the quantity of work passing through the workshops and of the range of very different machines needing attention, have soared in recent years, as cargo-handling technology has developed, and there is considerable evidence of a growing gap in engineering capability related to those changes. Among the areas in which new skills are urgently needed are electronics, control engineering, communications, automation and information science. These are core skills for the new generations of cargo-handling equipment and the communication systems which lie at the heart of a successful modern port.

Almost more important than those practical and technical skills, however, are the managerial and supervisory skills needed to run, control and improve port maintenance. The team is utterly convinced of the need for urgent training of all levels of management in the fields of man-management, supervision, planning and financial control. Almost never have engineers been given training in those subjects during their university or polytechnic education, and very few ports (almost none in LDCs) offer post-appointment training in them. This is in sharp contrast to successful major companies in other industrial, commercial and service fields, where management training and retraining are routine elements of employees' lives.

10.2.5 Employee Attitudes

A key factor in achieving improved maintenance performance in ports (indeed, in any aspect of port activity) is the creation of a positive attitude in the minds of individual employees, at all levels in the department. All staff (but, in the present context, particularly in the Engineering, Supplies and Operations Departments) must have greater motivation to perform their tasks to the best of their abilities. Only if staff can be thoroughly motivated will it be possible to achieve that professionalism that is so essential to improved performance, and to adopt the management principle of *accountability* that has been pinpointed as a major agent of attitude and performance change.

Creating this new organizational ethos or environment within LDC ports presents perhaps the most formidable challenge. In spite of the attention and resources that have been given to manpower development and training in LDC ports over the past 30 years, the problems of lack of motivation and indiscipline persist. A fundamental re-think of manpower development and training strategies is called for, and much more effective means of tackling those areas must be evolved. Many

institutional changes will be necessary, too, if change is to be brought about: salaries and wages must provide at least for the basic necessities of life, and welfare and social benefits added to make port employment attractive to the best of the country's talents. Incentive schemes must allow effort to be suitably rewarded, and promotion prospects, with training-for-promotion an accepted fact of port life, must be seen to be good.

The necessary change of attitude must be introduced throughout the port's organizational structure. Senior civil servants and port managers must, by their own example, set the standards that they should expect in their staff – the change must spread from the very top downwards. The political will has to be there to overcome the many social, traditional and ethnic barriers that will conspire to make the change difficult to achieve.

10.2.6 Vested Interests

Clearly, it will not be easy to introduce all the institutional, organizational and managerial changes identified as essential to the improvement of port maintenance – the project team has no illusions about that. There will be considerable resistance to change from many quarters, from government and port officials down to the truck driver who is used to receiving 'unofficial' inducements for moving a customer's cargo quickly. There will be a distinct reluctance to 'rock the boat'. The resistance to change will be particularly strong where the 'job-for-life' mentality is firmly rooted; this is a common and major cause of the present lack of interest in improvement – or, indeed, in their jobs – that is observable in many LDC port staff. Vested interest and self-interest are usually more in evidence than job interest!

Sweeping away these restrictive and counter-productive attitudes is, nevertheless, absolutely essential if a climate for change is to be created. The necessary attitude change is not, however, going to be achievable by the LDC ports on their own; they will need major and sustained assistance from the international community. International agencies and other bodies providing loans or technical assistance must be aware of the difficulties when negotiating agreements – that is the time when they have the greatest leverage over the governments and port authorities of recipient countries, and can apply greatest pressure. The root causes of these (and the other) problems need to be identified and tackled before pumping in new resources. It is to such implications for international aid and loan organizations that attention is turned next.

10.3 Implications for International Agencies

10.3.1 Awareness of the Problems

The nature and scale of the assistance needed by LDC ports in overcoming their present maintenance problems have major implications for future projects undertaken by the international agencies. The prospects are not brightened by the received impression that strategies and techniques adopted by the agencies in the past have been less than totally successful. Indeed, it is probably not unfair to suggest that, in some instances, the projects have actually contributed to the present unsatisfactory state of port maintenance. Maintenance deficiencies are likely to remain the single most critical management problem facing LDC ports in the next decade, increasingly exacerbated by advancing technological change. Unless immediate action is taken, many of those ports will be unable to maintain their assets to anything approaching a satisfactory standard – a situation already reached in some of them, in fact. This is bound to put at severe risk the financial and practical viability of port development projects.

However, the fact that this study has been commissioned is itself testimony to the awareness by international agencies of these risks and of the potential benefits of improving maintenance performance. The World Bank *Guidelines* for effective maintenance (that are the ultimate aim of the overall project of which this study is a component) will focus attention on the current problems and will certainly make a substantial contribution to reducing their severity. Even so, the *Guidelines* will need solid and practical support from funding and aid agencies if that potential improvement is to be achieved. Some of the major implications for the agencies are considered briefly in this section.

10.3.2 Technical Assistance

The first implication of the recommended areas for specific attention is that international agencies will have to devote a larger share of port project finance to technical assistance in the future. In the past, the major emphasis in port development projects has been (perhaps understandably) on the construction of civil works and the installation of cargo-handling and other equipment. The provision of assistance and advice on management and human resource development has been relatively neglected. For example, only about 10% of current loans and grants for port projects is earmarked for technical assistance, and there have been many examples of

foreign governments and international agencies providing equipment and other assets to LDC ports without *any* technical support or advice at all. In those circumstances, it is hardly surprising that the equipment provided is subsequently poorly maintained and has to be scrapped prematurely. If a port is currently incapable of looking after the cargo-handling equipment and civil works that it already possesses, it is not realistic to expect it to be able to operate and maintain newly provided (and often technologically advanced) assets without a substantial proportion of project funding being earmarked for technical assistance.

That technical assistance then has to be properly researched, structured and implemented. The limited budgets for technical assistance in the past have meant that it has often been poorly planned and of much too short a duration. This is particularly true of aid-financed projects. Typically, expert advice is provided only during the commissioning period of equipment, and seldom has it extended over even the first year or so of operations. For many countries (particularly those in the high priority category – in Africa, Latin America and Western Asia) this is totally inadequate to allow the successful transfer of new technological skills and the introduction and establishment of improved management systems. The technical assistance component of port projects *must* be extended substantially – certainly to five years and possibly, in some cases, longer – to ensure realistically the required technology transfer.

The traditional objection to extended technical assistance, well rehearsed by international agencies, is that recipient ports become too dependent on imported expert advice. While there is more than an element of truth in this, the answer is not to curtail the assistance but to organize it more effectively. Schemes must be carefully and appropriately designed and supervised, and sufficient time allowed for technical and managerial skills to be developed before the support is withdrawn. And that withdrawal must be a gradual and controlled operation, allowing the local counterpart to take over more and more responsibility for running his operation until he has acquired all the necessary skills for self-sufficiency. Only then should the expert withdraw completely, leaving behind a skilled and capable workforce, from management down to mechanic level.

10.3.3 Management Development and Training

If the proportion of funds allocated for technical assistance is small, that devoted specifically for training and manpower development is usually pitiful. One major LDC port project currently nearing completion, which involves the introduction of new and very advanced cargo-handling technology, has assigned less than 1% of the total project cost to training and manpower development, and even this is now being cut back by the government concerned – on cost-saving grounds! This is not an isolated case. The World Bank is currently financing $91 million of project-related training in 49 African transport projects, out of a total funding of nearly $4,000 million – a proportion of 2.4%. This is quite high by normal funding standards, but an allocation of at least 5% would be much more realistic and effective.

International agencies must devote more attention and resources to manpower development and training in future port projects, particularly those with a maintenance component (which must be the majority). The new technical and managerial skills identified in this report as central to the improvement of maintenance *must* be introduced as a matter of urgency. There is a severe shortage of practical engineers, with hands-on skills and experience, and a desperate shortfall in managerial and supervisory skills. In the workshops, the skills of technicians need urgent upgrading, particularly in the electrical, electronics and communications fields. Staff at all levels in supplies and procurement need to be given professional specialist skills, as do those in maintenance planning and scheduling units and staff responsible for quality control and inspection. There is an urgent need for *all* port employees to be trained in the new computing and information technology skills, to take advantage of the management information systems that need to be installed without delay.

If all these skills are to be developed, and if management is to be strengthened through a formal policy of promotion-through-training, far greater efforts need to be expended on manpower development, and the upgrading of training staff and facilities must be a matter of priority. Career patterns also need to be clarified and improved, promotional prospects made more attractive, job descriptions revised and formalized, and considerable improvements made to salary levels, and terms and conditions of employment. These can all make major contributions to the attitude change so desperately needed in LDC ports. Workforce motivation is another key weapon in the attack on maintenance (and other) inefficiencies, and this survey recommended several promising ways in which that problem can be tackled. Possibly the most interesting and appealing of these is the introduction of quality circles, which is most strongly recommended as part of the port's manpower development plan.

10.3.4 Training Methods

This study recommends a change of direction and a new approach to management and technical training. Traditional teaching methods need to be replaced by more appropriate techniques. Traditionally, international agencies have relied on direct training assistance, with classroom-based or at least instructor-based formal teaching and conventional (generally poor quality) on-job instruction. For performance-based and skills-based tasks, such instruction is largely unsuccessful, and there is little doubt that any performance gain achieved by a technician or driver while training is in progress is not sustained after the 'expert' leaves. Such teaching methods need to be replaced by trainee-centred methods, which are much more appropriate for the acquisition of performance-based skills – particularly those exploiting the newer computer- and videodisc-based interactive systems.

The development of centrally produced, 'packaged' distance-learning materials offers the most cost-effective and realistic opportunity for the international maritime community to assist LDC ports to improve their training capability. International agencies should devote greater resources to the development and distribution of such materials, and should be encouraged to co-operate with each other to ensure that standard specifications and uniform teaching principles are applied, and that needless duplication of effort is avoided. Materials produced by different agencies, as part of a variety of technical assistance projects, can follow a standard format and apply the same, sound educational principles, ultimately building up a full, integrated range of training packages for worldwide use, covering all aspects of port activities. Among the advantages of this approach are the rapid expansion of the range of training materials available to LDC ports, the systematic and cost-effective way they can be produced, and the uniformity of presentation quality, independent of local instructor skills.

10.3.5 Institution Building

A particularly important recommendation of the study is that international agencies should pay far greater attention to institutional building and to improvements in administrative and management procedures when planning port projects. A criticism frequently received from LDC ports was that the agencies have been too concerned with the provision of physical assets, particularly civil works, and have paid insufficient attention to the institutional framework within which the new development had to function. There is no doubt whatsoever that present institutional problems contribute very seriously to the present maintenance deficiencies of LDC ports.

Of particular importance is the need to develop improved financial management procedures and controls, in engineering, supplies and operations, and to set up effective management information systems, on which all the recommended administrative improvements are so dependent. Maintenance planning, scheduling and control procedures need to be radically improved, and technical advice is needed on preparing appropriate policies, strategies and tactics for maintenance. Overshadowing all these internal, port institutional factors are, of course, the governmental ones; it is vitally important that governments be persuaded to allow ports the autonomy and freedom from unnecessary regulations and constraints that they need to improve their performance.

To allow all these institutional and other changes to be formulated and implemented, it is essential that any port development project be preceded by a maintenance audit. A team of experts should be contracted to survey the port's ability to run and maintain the proposed system, and to identify the shortcomings and the steps needed to remedy them. Several man-months of consultancy should be allocated for this crucial preliminary stage in any project, and the detailed planning of the development should await the findings of the audit. If the audit reveals particularly serious institutional, administrative or managerial deficiencies, threatening the viability of the project, then the agency should make the funding of the project conditional on the port (or government, as appropriate) putting those deficiencies right. Only when the necessary changes are in place, or there is assurance that they will be made, should the project go ahead.

10.3.6 Agency Skills

Clearly, a major consequence of agencies' taking on the added responsibilities inherent in tackling the daunting maintenance problems outlined in this report is that they will need to diversify and strengthen the skills of their permanent staff. Traditionally, international agencies in the ports field have employed civil engineers, economists and financial analysts; those were the skills most needed when providing funds and supervising port construction projects. The practice has been for those permanent staff to be supported by consultants engaged as appropriate for specific projects. However, if the problems discussed in this report are to be resolved in full, the agencies will need to engage staff with a very different range of skills, possibly on a permanent basis.

Among the fields in which expertise is now urgently required by agency staff are public administration, mechanical and electrical engineering, information technology, manpower development and supplies management. Those staff will have to have considerable practical management and technical experience and be prepared to work at workshop-floor level within the Engineering Department. They should have had line management experience in the port transport industry and, preferably, have worked in LDC ports. Only by engaging staff with these skills (and with enthusiasm for solving the problems of LDC port engineering) will the agencies be able to reinforce their reservoir of capabilities and be able to respond to the changing nature of the needs of LDC ports.

10.4 Conclusion

This study was initiated to investigate the maintenance problems and practices of LDC ports, prompted by the crisis currently facing many of the engineering departments of those ports and motivated by the strong desire to improve the situation. It is, of course, just the first phase of an extensive project being carried out by the World Bank on port maintenance, and has accordingly set out to provide a broad overview of present problems. It has proposed improvements in a range of policies, strategies and practices which it is considered will lead to better maintenance performance.

Much more work, in greater detail, will clearly be needed before the appropriate policies, practices and procedures can be precisely formulated and subsequently implemented in LDC ports. The present report is intended to set that process in motion and to provide a basis for discussion. It is hoped that it will generate interest, dialogue and (ultimately) action, as a contribution to the alleviation of ports' present maintenance difficulties.

APPENDIX 1

Joint World Bank/UNCTAD Project on Port Equipment Management

Questionnaire

Respondent: ....

Port: ....

Notes:

— Please try to answer all the questions.

— Please keep your answers brief and concise.

— Where you feel additional comment or related information would be useful, please insert it (or return on an extra, attached sheet of paper).

— Please read completely through the questionnaire before beginning to answer the questions.

Thank you very much for sparing the time to respond to this survey. When you have completed it, please return the questionnaire (by 15th April, 1988) to: Dr B. J. Thomas, Department of Maritime Studies, Aberconway Building, University of Wales Institute of Science & Technology, Colum Drive, Cardiff CF1 3EU, U.K.

---

1. Institutional and Organizational Issues

A. Equipment Management Function

— What importance is given by the Port (i.e. the Board, Managing Director, Heads of Departments) to the equipment management function?

— How does this compare with the importance attached to operational, financial and other activities?

B. Equipment Ownership

— Who is responsible for the purchase and operation of port equipment in the country's ports?

— Are public/private companies involved in the supply/rental of equipment?

— What difficulties are created by these arrangements?

C. Data on Port Equipment

— How many units of mechanical handling equipment does the port have in its dry bulk, container and conventional general cargo facilities (if available, please supply an equipment inventory)?

— What is the approximate replacement cost of this plant at current prices?

— What are the annual capital (for equipment purchase) and revenue (for equipment operation and maintenance) budget allocations, and how are these derived?

— What proportion of the port's annual operating expenditure is accounted for by maintenance?

D. Role of Central Government

— What is the role of central government in equipment purchase, and what form do controls take?

— How autonomous is the port with respect to equipment procurement?

— Are there regulations (e.g. investment limits) which might affect the port's ability to maintain its infrastructure and equipment?

E. Financial Issues

— Does the port have access to foreign exchange? If so, what are the limits on annual expenditure?

— What are the port's financial and other objectives, and do they affect equipment management?

— Are port salary levels and rates of pay nationally controlled?

— What role do unions or similar bodies play in the control of personnel engaged in equipment operation and maintenance?

2. Equipment Planning and Replacement Strategies

A. Equipment Plan

— Is there a formalized plan for the purchase of equipment?

— How are future equipment needs forecast and how are these projections incorporated within an equipment plan?

B. Capital Budgets

— How are capital budgets prepared for the purchase of new equipment and what constraints are imposed on this?

— What is the port's replacement strategy (if possible, provide examples for different types of equipment)?

C. Equipment Depreciation

— How is the useful life of the equipment determined?

— How is equipment depreciated (if available, please enclose a Depreciation Schedule)?

— How is outdated or time-expired equipment disposed of?

3. Procurement Policy and Strategies

A. Procurement Policy

— What is the port's procurement policy (e.g. international tender, local preference)?

— What problems are there in relation to that policy (e.g. Government regulations or controls)?

— What problems are caused by sources of finance (e.g. internal funds, loans from international agencies, bilateral aid and grants)?

B. Procurement Strategies

— What are the port's procurement strategies (e.g. standardization on manufacturer(s) or models)?

— Does the port rent or lease equipment?

— Does the port rely on local agents or overseas manufacturers?

4. Equipment Maintenance

A. Equipment Maintenance Strategies

— How important is maintenance viewed by the port management?

— What are the maintenance strategies (daily inspections, scheduled maintenance, crisis and accident repair, overhaul/rebuilding)?

— How is maintenance planned?

B. Maintenance Organization

— How is maintenance managed within the organizational structure of the port (organizational charts of the port and the engineering department(s) would be very useful)?

— How are the workshops organized (e.g. central workshop/terminal workshops/combination)?

— Are any maintenance activities contracted out?

C. Maintenance Facilities

— What are the present maintenance facilities (workshops, machines, etc.)?

— Are there any deficiencies?

D. Equipment Maintenance Management Information System (M.I.S.)

— What M.I.S. is associated with maintenance activities?

— What information is collected daily, weekly, monthly on equipment maintenance (sample documentation would be useful)?

— How is it analysed and in what form is it presented to senior management?

— How effective is the maintenance programme in terms of equipment availability or some other form of indicator?

E. Maintenance Costs

— How is the maintenance budget prepared, and who sets it?

— What are the annual costs of maintenance (salaries, spare parts and materials, overheads)?

— What is the relationship between annual maintenance cost, equipment value and port revenue?

— How is costing information collected and processed in relation to engineering manpower use, spare parts and materials used, tools and machines used, power and fuels, and workshop facilities?

— Is the information collected for the M.I.S. linked to the budgetary control system?

5. **Maintenance Staff**

A. Staff Recruitment

— What is the current organization and staffing of the mechanical maintenance section, and what personnel problems are there?

— How are maintenance staff recruited and trained?

— What qualifications are required?

B. Conditions of Employment

— What are the conditions of employment (hours/shifts/overtime; clothing allowances; fringe benefits; promotion opportunities; union constraints; training facilities and opportunities; terms of employment)?

— How do salary levels and rates of pay compare with those of similar industries in the region or country?

C. Training and Development

— Is there a pool of suitably educated and trained technicians and managers in the region or country?

— What manpower development and training policies are pursued (e.g. apprentice schemes, promotion through training)?

— What is the annual rate of turnover of maintenance staff (numbers and %age)?

6. Spare Parts Management

A. Spare Parts Policy

— What is the port's spare parts policy (e.g. minimum supplies at time of procurement, spares contracts)?

— Are there problems related to budgetary allocation for spare parts (e.g. a requirement for government approval; limits on foreign exchange for spares)?

B. Spares Procurement

— How is the need for spare parts determined?

— How are spare parts and materials procured?

— Are there any problems relating to spares procurement (e.g. delays in delivery of spares)?

C. Spares Management

— How is the spare stock managed?

— What minimum stock levels are kept (e.g. three months' supply)?

7. Operating Procedures and Practices

A. Equipment Allocation

— Is the equipment stock adequate to meet operational demands?

— How is equipment allocated to operations on a daily basis?

— What principles or rules are followed when allocating equipment?

B. Driver Recruitment and Conditions of Employment

— How are operations staff recruited and trained?

— What are the conditions of employment (hours/shifts/overtime; allowances for clothing/uniforms; fringe benefits; promotion opportunities; union/association constraints; training facilities and opportunities; terms of employment)? (Copies of training programmes, safety procedure documents and other records would be useful.)

— Do drivers play any part in maintenance?

239

C. Manpower Development and Training

— What manpower development and training policies are pursued?

— Are drivers given adequate training?

— What training facilities and opportunities are there for drivers?

D. Operational Management Information System (M.I.S)

— What operational M.I.S. exists in the port (sample data collection forms would be very useful)?

— What information is collected daily, weekly, monthly etc. on equipment performance (e.g. hours of work, work location, breakdowns)?

— How is it analysed and in what form is it presented to senior management?

— Does the port prepare regular data on Utilization, Availability and Downtime?

— How is costing information collected and processed in relation to manpower use and equipment operation?

8. Key Conditions

— Based on *your* experience, what do you see as the key conditions for successful equipment management and efficient equipment maintenance (if you can rank your factors in order of importance, it would be very helpful)?

9. Additional Comments

— If you have any other comments or observations of relevance to this study, please insert them here:

APPENDIX 2

Bibliography

Anon (1986) The 36 deadly sins, *Port Development International,* January, pp.14-17.

E. M. Brown & H. Benford (1977) *Ship Replacement and Prediction of Economic Life.* Ann Arbor, MI, University of Michigan, 40 pp.

E. S. Buffa (1969) *Modern Production Management.* Chichester, Wiley, 795 pp.

A. H. Christer & W. M. Waller (1987) A descriptive model of capital plant replacement, *Journal of Operational Research Society,* 38 (6), pp. 473-477.

V. Champion (1987) Maintaining the straddle image, *Cargo Systems,* January, pp. 28-31.

J. Connor & J. B. Evans (1972) *Replacement Investment: A guide to management decisions on plant renewal.* London, Gower Press, 82 pp.

R. Davies, B. J. Thomas & D. K. Roach (1987) *The Management of Equipment Procurement.* Geneva, UNCTAD (Unpublished).

Department of Industry (1977) *Life-Cycle Costing in the Management of Assets: a practical guide.* London, HMSO, 57 pp.

ESCAP (1985) *Port Management Information System.* Bangkok, Economic & Social Commission for Asia & the Pacific, 170 pp.

P. Gonon (1987) Port equipment maintenance: Agadir Seminar, 9-12 June 1987, *PIANC Bulletin,* 56, pp. 100-109.

G. Hadley & T. W. Whitin (1963) *Analysis of Inventory Systems.* Englewood Cliffs, NJ, Prentice-Hall, 452 pp.

C. M. Hunter (1981) *Equipment Operating (Port Operations Seminar for Senior Management, Istanbul, Turkey).* Geneva, UNCTAD (Unpublished).

ILO (1980) *Modular Programmes for Supervisory Development (MES).* Geneva, International Labour Office.

W. Jerusel (1988) *Maintenance of Cargo Handling Equipment.* Geneva, UNCTAD, 57 pp. + appendices (Unpublished).

A. Kelly & M. J. Harris (1987) *Management of Industrial Maintenance.* London, Butterworth, 262 pp.

J. Lethbridge (1986) The challenge of port maintenance in developing countries, in: *Maritime and Offshore Structure Maintenance.* London, Thomas Telford, pp. 1-11.

A. J. Merret & A. Sykes (1966) *Capital Budgeting and Company Finance.* London, Longman, 184 pp.

P. M. Morse (1958) *Queues, Inventories and Maintenance (Operations Research Society of America, Publications in Operations Research No. 1).* New York, Wiley, 202 pp.

E. D. Munday (1983) *Steps to Effective Equipment Maintenance: UNCTAD Monographs on Port Management, No. 3.* Geneva, UNCTAD, 45 pp.

National Institute of Port Management (1987) *Report on the Survey of Cargo Handling Equipment at Ports.* Madras, NIPM, Vol. 1 86 pp. + appendices, Vol. 2, 68 pp. + appendices.

D. Naumann (1983) Managing for successful maintenance, *Proceedings of the Third Terminal Operations Conference,* pp. 5/1-5/6.

PIANC (1985) *Port Maintenance Handbook.* Brussels, Permanent International Association of Navigation Congresses.

Port Operations Consultants (1982) *Port Maintenance Referred to Civil Works and Cargo Handling Equipment.* Washington, World Bank, Vol. 1 37 pp., Vol. 2 120 pp.

Production Engineering Research Association (1985) *Condition Monitoring and Reliability of Mobile Plant in British Ports.* London, British Ports Association (Unpublished).

M. R. Seldon (1979) *Life Cycle Costing: A better method of government procurement.* Boulder, CO, Westview Press, 283 pp.

E. V. Sonderstrup & O. Oestergaard (1986) Computerized organisation of preventive maintenance, *Proceedings of the Institution of Mechanical Engineers Conference on Port Engineering,* pp. 251-256.

B. J. Thomas & D. K. Roach (1987) *Operating and Maintenance Features of Container Handling Systems.* Geneva, UNCTAD, 90 pp.

G. Thues (1988) *Port Maintenance Personnel.* Geneva, UNCTAD, 6 pp. (Unpublished).

H. Velsink (1987) Principles of integrated port planning: Agadir Seminar, 9-12 June 1987, *PIANC Bulletin,* 56, pp. 5-24.

G. Westring (1985) *International Procurement. A Training Manual.* Geneva, International Trade Centre, UNCTAD/GATT, 316 pp.

The following journals were also referenced:

Cargo Systems

Containerisation International

Dock & Harbour Authority

Journal of the Operational Research Society

APPENDIX 3

Operations Department Objectives

The Operations Department's objectives are as follows:

(1) To provide an efficient service with adequate facilities to port users at minimum cost by attaining:

(a) *Faster turnround of vessels in port with targets as follows:*

Container vessels with average load of 150 movements — 8.5 hours gross

Conventional vessels with average load of 1,000 tonnes — 30 hours

Dry bulk vessels with average load of 5,000 tonnes — 60 hours

Liquid bulk vessels:

Fuel oil vessels with average load of 16,000 tonnes — 19 hours

Chemical vessels with average loads of 1,800 tonnes — 15 hours

Vegetable oil vessels with average load of 1,800 tonnes — 8 hours

Turnround targets will vary with tonnage being handled.

Action

(i) Better supervision of work at vessel by officers and wharf operation clerks to increase productivity and minimise delays. This includes ensuring that adequate cargo handling facilities such as pallets, forklifts and storage space are readily available. Where cargo is for direct delivery or direct loading, the officer and wharf operations clerk are to ensure that the availability of lorries and cargo flow are co-ordinated.

(ii) The officers are to ensure that export cargo is consolidated for smooth loading by vessels. Cargo in godowns must be properly stacked to maximise utilisation of space.

(b) *Shorter waiting time for berth with targets set as follows:*

Container vessels — 8 hours

Conventional vessels — 16 hours

Dry bulk vessels — 24 hours

Liquid bulk vessels — 7 hours

Action

Waiting time for vessels will be reduced if work at vessels is expedited through higher productivity brought about by action taken in a (i).

(c) *Higher productivity in handling containers and cargo to and from vessels, at CY and CFS with targets set as follows:*

Vessel/Cargo Handled	Handling at Vessels per Hour	Stuffing and Unstuffing per Shift
1st Generation and Coastal Container Vessels	20 TEUs/gross	—
2nd Generation Container Vessels	25 TEUs/Gross	—
General Cargo	16 dwt tonnes	5 TEUs
Palletised Cargo	17 dwt tonnes	12 TEUs
Rubber Bales	14 dwt tonnes	2 TEUs
Palletised Rubber	38 dwt tonnes	12 TEUs
Timber	17 dwt tonnes	—
Drums Cargo	17 dwt tonnes	4 TEUs

Action

Productivity can be increased by action identified in a (i).

(d) *Better utilsation of godown facilities with faster delivery targeted at 80% deliveries of import cargo within 7 days of discharge or within 5 days of unstuffing.*

Action

  (i) Supervisory staff will ensure proper stacking of cargo to maximise space utilisation.

  (ii) Import cargo received into godowns from lighters, vessels and containers to be palletised mark by mark and adequately identified to facilitate delivery.

  (iii) Importers to be contacted by phone after free storage period to expedite delivery. Written notice to Importers to be issued after 2 weeks of discharge.

  (iv) Export cargo received from lorries to be palletised evenly and in the same quantity to facilitate stacking and handling.

(e) *Lower percentage of LCL traffic through the port with a target of only 12%.*

Action

  (i) Encourage more container users to import or ship FCL through their own or private CFS by handling only genuine LCL cargo.

  (ii) Review tariff for LCL containers.

(f) *Better utilisation of container yard space with shorter stay of MT containers targeted at 10 days.*

Action

  (i) Plan for delivery and receiving containers at appointed days. This will expedite delivery and restrict the unnecessary early receiving of export containers.

  (ii) Encouragement of more FCL traffic will result in shift of storage of empties to the ICDs.

  (iii) Better storage and tracking of containers will enable the Commission and vessel's agents to be kept aware of the inventory of containers in the yard and to take remedial action where appropriate.

  (iv) Containers will be delivered on a first in first out basis.

(g) *Prompt delivery of FCL containers to Road and Rail Hauliers with target of 95% deliveries within 24 hours of request.*

Action

  (i) To encourage the importers of large consignments of container cargo to accept deliveries during the second shift up till 2330 hours. This will increase container deliveries which are now restricted between 0800 and 1700 hours.

  (ii) Request the two container hauliers to transfer import containers of large clients to their ICDs initially for storage and delivery as and when required by the importer. Such movements to be conducted during the 3rd shift only. The Customs Department is to be requested to extend their working period from 2330 hours to cover the 3rd shift up till 0730 hours.

  (iii) Discourage slow deliveries by importers by increasing the store-rental charges on import containers. Also to collect such charges direct from importers instead of the Shipping Agents as at present.

  (iv) To maintain a supply of a minimum of one transtainer at all times solely to service the two hauliers.

  (v) To encourage the two hauliers to increase their fleet of Prime Movers and Trailers to meet the demands of the trade.

  (iv) To introduce delivery by appointment during the 1st and 2nd shifts.

(2) To ensure that other Service Departments provide satisfactory service in maintaining Traffic Department's assets.

Action

Supervisors and gear clerks to liaise with workshop personnel on problems associated with equipment and follow up on action taken by them.

244

(3) To ensure that the Department's mechanical handling equipment are handled in the correct manner to minimise breakdown and care is taken to upkeep their cleanliness. To maintain downtime of equipment of less than 10%.

Action

    (i) All staff to ensure that cargo handling equipment is properly used by the operators. Where it is seen to have been wrongly used, corrective measures to be taken immediately.

    (ii) All operators to be given regular refresher courses on equipment care and handling.

    (iii) Supervisors and gear clerks to conduct checks that equipment operators are carrying out handing over checks and maintaining cleanliness of their equipment.

(4) To enrich Traffic Department staff's supervisory ability and knowledge of traffic operations for better control of the operations and overall understanding of the Department's objectives.

Action

    (i) Staff to be rotated in their posting to widen their knowledge of various sections.

    (ii) Procedures of operations in all sections of the Traffic Department will be available for staff who wish to know about other operations in detail.

    (iii) Better organised and planned staff training eg Inservice attachment training, supervisory and leadership courses and basic port operations courses.

(5) To foster better working relationship among staff in the Department

Action

    (i) Regular meetings and discussions with staff.

    (ii) Quality Control Circles in the department.

    (iii) Incentive schemes for the department's staff.

    (iv) Annual best transit shed competition.

(6) To foster better working relationship with Port users.

(7) To maintain safe working conditions and high level of cleanliness in the port area.

Action

    (i) Educate staff to be more safety conscious.

    (ii) Ensure staff are made aware of procedures for handling and storage of dangerous cargo.

    (iii) Ensure that equipment used is kept in safe working condition.

APPENDIX 4

Engineering Department Objectives

A. **Civil Engineering Section**

(i) To provide an efficient maintenance work by ensuring 95% serviceability of buildings, structures, roads, compounds.

(ii) To insure cost-effectiveness in maintenance of buildings, structures, roads, compounds. Maintenance cost to Current Capital Cost will not exceed the figures as shown in the attached documents.

(iii) To ensure cost-effectiveness in design and supervision costs compared to the actual cost of the works which should not exceed the following:—

	Design Cost	Supervision Cost
Below $50,000	9%	10%
$50,001 to $100,000	7½%	9%
$100,001 to $250,000	6½%	8½%
$250,001 to $1,000,000	6%	8%
$1,000,001 and above	5%	7%

(iv) To ensure that each contract is completed within the approved contract schedule.

(v) To ensure that all projects planned for a particular year are 100% implemented.

(vi) To select the most optimum and economical design for execution for major development projects.

(vii) To ensure payments for contract works are processed within 2 weeks of submission for payment.

(viii) To ensure that the final payment for contract works does not exceed the original tender amount.

(ix) To upgrade the knowledge of the civil engineers in the specialised fields of marine structure design and maintenance, port engineering planning and project management through a proper training programme.

(x) To provide training opportunities for technical assistants, technicians and draughtsmen in their respective fields and promotional prospects for all levels of staff.

(xi) To implement all port expansion projects with due consideration to the social and environmental impact.

B. **Mechanical/Electrical Section**

(i) To provide efficient maintenance work by ensuring 85% availability of port handling equipment.

(ii) To upgrade the knowledge and specialised skill of the workshop personnel through training in maintenance skill and acquisition of modern cargo handling equipment from time to time.

(iii) To ensure cost-effectiveness in maintenance of equipment. Maintenance costs will be as follows:

(1) Minor equipment such as forklift, prime movers, trailers, etc.

    (a) 1st year < 5% of capital cost of equipment.

    (b) 2nd year < 6% of capital cost of equipment.

    (c) 3rd year < 7% of capital cost of equipment.

    (d) 4th year < 6% of capital cost of equipment.

    (e) 5th year < 8% of capital cost of equipment.

    (f) 6th year < 10% of capital cost of equipment.

    (g) 7th year < 15% of capital cost of equipment.

    (h) Major overhaul in the 4th year of service < 20% of capital cost of equipment.

In the eighth year, the equipment should be considered for writing-off.

(2) Major Container Handling Equipment such as Gantry Cranes and Transtainers.

    (a) 1st to 4th year   — 6% yearly of the capital cost of equipment.

    (b) 5th to 10th year   — 8% to 10% yearly.

    (c) 10th to 15th year — 10% to 15% yearly.

    (d) Major overhaul and inspection service on every 5 years — 8% to 10% of capital cost.

After 15th year of service, the equipment should be considered for writing-off.

Maintenance Targets for Civil Works

(A) Buildings and Offices (timber/reinforced concrete)

Normal R & M	—	1st to 5th year	0.3% yearly
		6th to 10th year	0.6% yearly
		11th year and onwards	1.2% yearly
Major renovation	—	every 5 years	10%

(B) Transit sheds (steel structure)

Normal R & M	—	1st to 5th year	0.5% yearly
		6th to 10th year	0.75% yearly
		11th year and onwards	1.0% yearly
Major renovation	—	every 5 years	10%
Re-roofing	—	every 15 years	20%

(C) Structures (wharf)

Normal R & M	—	1st to 5th year	0.1% yearly
		6th to 10th year	0.2% yearly
		11th year and onwards	0.3% yearly
Major renovation	—	every 5 years	3%

(D) Roads, Compounds

Normal R & M	—	1st to 5th year	4% yearly
		6th to 10th year	4% yearly
		11th year and onwards	4% yearly
Major renovation (resurfacing)	—	every 5 years	50%

(E) Water Installation

Normal R & M (Wharf)		1st to 5th year	0.6% yearly
		6th to 10th year	1% yearly
		11th year and onwards	2% yearly
Major renovation and renewal of pipes etc.	—	every 15 years	100%
Normal R & M (Land)		1st to 5th year	0.5% yearly
		6th to 10th year	0.75% yearly
		11th year and onwards	1.0% yearly
Major renovation and renewal of pipes	—	every 25 years	100%

OVERSEAS AGENTS

If there is no agent in your country and you have difficulty placing an order, write to HMSO, PO Box 276, London SW8 5DT, England

Argentina

Carlos Hirsch, Florida 165, Buenos Aires

Australia & Papua New Guinea

Cambridge University Press, PO Box 85, Oakleigh, Victoria 3166

(stockist only)
Hunter Publications, 58a Gipps Street, Collingwood, Victoria 3066

Belgium

La Librairie Europeene, Rue de Loi 244, 1040 Brussels

Bermuda

All enquiries to
Caffrey, Saunders & Co, Shipshape, PO Box 1697, Hamilton

Denmark

Arnold Busck, Købmagergade 49, Copenhagan

Far East

Information Publications Pte Ltd, PEI-FU Industrial Building, 24 New Industrial Road, 02-06 Off Upper Paya Lebar Road, Singapore 1953

Finland

Akateeminen Kirjakauppa, Keskuskaru 2, Helsinki 10

Germany

Lange & Springer, Follerstrasse 2, Cologne 1

Elwert & Meurer, Hauptstrasse 101, 1 Berlin 62

Gibraltar

Gibraltar Bookshop, 300 Main Street

Greece

(stockist only)
G C Eleftheroudakis SA, 4 Nikis Street, Athens 126

Hong Kong

(stockist only)
Swindon Book Co, 13 Lock Road, Kowloon

Iceland

Snabjorn Jonsson & Co, Hafnarstraeti 9, Reykjavik, (PO Box 1131)

India

Arnold-Heinemann Publishers (India) Pvt Ltd, AB/9, First Floor, Safdarjang Enclave, New Delhi 110029 Branches at Bombay, Bangalore, Calcutta & Madras

Allied Publishers Private Ltd (Stockists), 13/14 Asaf Ali Road, (PO Box 7203), New Delhi 110002

Israel

Steimatzky, Steimatzky House, 11 Hakishon Street, PO Box 1444, BN E1 BRAK 5114

Jamaica

Sanster's Book Store, 91 Harbour Street, Kingston, (PO Box 366)

Japan

Maruzen Co Ltd, 3-10 Nihonbashi 2-Chome, Chuoku, Tokyo 103 (PO Box 5050 Tokyo International 100-31)

Netherlands

Boekhandel Kookyer, PO Box 24, 2300AA Leiden

Norway

Narvesen Info Center, PO Box 6125, Ettersad, N-0602 Oslo 6

Pakistan

Mirza Book Agency, 65 Shahrah Quaid-E-Azam, Lahore 3, (PO Box 729)

South Africa

Literary Services (PTY) Ltd, PO Box 31361, Braamfontein 2017, Transvaal

and
University Bookshop Pty Ltd, 622 Umbilo Road, Durban 4001

Sri Lanka

H W Cave & Co Ltd, (PO Box 25), Colombo

Sweden

C E Fritzes Kungl Hovbokhandel, PO Box 16356, S103 27 Stockholm

Switzerland

Librairie Payot, 6 rue Grenus, 1211 Geneva

Trinidad

Stephens, Frederick Street, Port of Spain, (PO Box 497)

USA & Canada

UNIPUB, 4611/F Assembly Drive, Lanham, MD 20706-4391

Yugoslavia

Jugoslovenska Knjiga, Terazije 27, Belgrade

Printed in the United Kingdom for Her Majesty's Stationery Office
Dd 289961 C20 3/89 16268